March 2013
OK.

LONG SHOT

MIKE PIAZZA

WITH LONNIE WHEELER

SIMON & SCHUSTER

New York   London   Toronto   Sydney   New Delhi

 Simon & Schuster
1230 Avenue of the Americas
New York, NY 10020

First Simon & Schuster hardcover edition February 2013

SIMON & SCHUSTER and colophon are registered trademarks of Simon & Schuster, Inc.

For information about special discounts for bulk purchases, please contact Simon & Schuster Special Sales at 1-866-506-1949 or business@simonandschuster.com.

The Simon & Schuster Speakers Bureau can bring authors to your live event. For more information or to book an event, contact the Simon & Schuster Speakers Bureau at 1-866-248-3049 or visit our website at www.simonspeakers.com.

Designed by Nancy Singer

Manufactured in the United States of America

10 9 8 7 6 5 4 3 2 1

Library of Congress Cataloging-in-Publication Data
Piazza, Mike, 1968–
    Long shot/Mike Piazza with Lonnie Wheeler.
        p.   cm.
1. Piazza, Mike, 1968– 2. Baseball players—United States—Biography. I. Wheeler, Lonnie. II. Title.
    GV865.P52A3 2013
    796.357092—dc23   2012017246
    [B]

ISBN 978-1-4391-5022-1
ISBN 978-1-4391-6303-0 (ebook)

In the story concerning "my first big-league crush," the name and details have been altered in deference to the party involved.

All photographs are courtesy of the Piazza family collection unless otherwise noted.

This book is dedicated to my incredible family.

To my mom, who gave me a firm foundation and the gift of faith; my dad, who believed in me even more than I believed in myself; and my brothers, Vince, Danny, Tony, and Tommy, whose support was unfailing and unconditional.

To my wife, Alicia, the most beautiful and generous person I ever met.

And to our daughters, Nicoletta and Paulina, to whom I say: words cannot describe the love I feel for you. I pray that you will find peace and love in your lives always. God bless you.

LONG SHOT

PROLOGUE

Including Pudge Rodriguez, who was dressed for work in his Detroit Tigers uniform, the greatest living catchers were all gathered around, unmasked, on the grass of Shea Stadium. From the podium, where my stomach tumbled inside the Mets jersey that I had now worn longer than any other, the Cooperstown collection was lined up on my right. Yogi Berra. Gary Carter. Johnny Bench, the greatest of them all. And Carlton Fisk, whose home run record for catchers I had broken the month before, which was the official reason that these illustrious ballplayers—these idols of mine, these *legends*—were doing Queens on a Friday night in 2004.

I preferred, however, to think of the occasion as a celebration of catching. Frankly, that was the only way I *could* think of it without being embarrassed; without giving off an unseemly vibe that basically said, hey, thanks so much to all you guys for showing up at my party even though I just left your asses in the dust. I couldn't stand the thought of coming across that way to those four. Especially Johnny Bench. As far as I was concerned, and still am, Johnny Bench was the perfect catcher, custom-made for the position. I, on the other hand, had become a catcher only because the scouts had seen me play first base.

Sixteen years after I'd gladly, though not so smoothly or easily, made the switch, the cycle was doubling back on itself. Having seen enough of me as a catcher, the Mets were in the process of moving me to first. It was a difficult time for me, because, for one, I could sense that it signaled the start of my slow fade from the game. What's more, I had come to embrace the catcher's role in a way that, at least in the minds of my persistent doubters and critics, was never returned with the same level of fervor. As a position-less prospect who scarcely interested even the team that finally drafted me, catching had been my lifeline to professional baseball—to this very evening, which I never could have imagined—and I was reluctant to let it go. To tell the truth, I was afraid of making a fool of myself.

It was a moment in my career on which a swarm of emotions had roosted, and it made me wish that Roy Campanella were alive and with us. Early on, when my path to Los Angeles was potholed with confusion, politics, and petty conflict, Campy, from his wheelchair in Vero Beach, Florida, was the one who got my head right. Back then, I hadn't realized what he meant to me. By the time I did, I was an all-star and he was gone. I surely could have used his benevolent counsel in the months leading up to my 352nd home run as a catcher, when detractors who included even a former teammate or two charged me with overextending my stay behind the plate in order to break the record (which I ultimately left at 396).

That, I think, was the main reason I wanted to understate the special night. If it appeared in any fashion that I was making a big thing out of passing Fisk, it would, for those who saw it that way, convict me of a selfish preoccupation with a personal accomplishment. Jeff Wilpon, the Mets' chief operating officer, had gone beyond the call of duty to put the event together, and had assured me that it would stay small. At one point, as the crowd buzzed and the dignitaries settled in and my brow beaded up, I muttered to Jeff, "So much for a small ceremony." General Motors, the sponsor, gave me a Chevy truck. (Maybe *that's* why my dad, a Honda and Acura dealer, was wiping away tears up in our private box.) Todd Zeile and Braden Looper had graciously mobilized my teammates, and, on their behalf, John Franco presented me with a Cartier watch and a six-liter bottle of Chateau d'Yquem, 1989, which will remain unopened until there's a proper occasion that I can share with a hundred or so wine-loving friends. Maybe when the first of our daughters gets married.

Meanwhile, the irony of the evening—and, to me, its greatest gratification—was that, in this starry tribute to catching (as I persisted in classifying it), the center of attention was the guy who, for the longest time, only my father believed in. The guy whose minor-league managers practically refused to put behind the plate. The guy being moved to first base in his thirteenth big-league season. The guy whose defensive work the cabdriver had been bitching about on Bench's ride to the ballpark.

But Bench understood. So did Fisk. "This is a special occasion for us catchers," he explained to the media. "Only we as catchers can fully appreciate what it takes to go behind the plate every day and also put some offensive numbers on the board."

Fisk had kindly called me on the night I broke his record, then issued a statement saying that he'd hoped I'd be the one to do it. That had made my week; my *year*. "I'm blessed," I told reporters. "I've lived a dream."

I also mentioned that I might write a book someday.

CHAPTER ONE

I celebrated my first National League pennant in 1977, in the clutches of Dusty Baker, who played left field for the Dodgers and had just been named MVP of the League Championship Series against the Phillies. Wearing a grin and a Dodgers cap, I was hoisted up in Dusty's left arm, and my brother Vince was wrapped in his right. My parents have a picture of it at their house in Valley Forge, Pennsylvania.

It was through the graces of my father and his hometown pal, Tommy Lasorda—who was in his first full year as a big-league manager—that we were permitted inside the Dodgers' clubhouse at Veterans Stadium in Philadelphia. I had just turned nine and was well along in my fascination with baseball. The season before was the first for which we'd had season tickets to Phillies games, box seats situated a few rows off third base—a strategic location that offered a couple of key advantages. One, I had a close-up look at every move and mannerism of my favorite player, Mike Schmidt. And two, Lasorda, that first year, was coaching third for Los Angeles.

He was already something of an icon around Norristown, Pennsylvania, where he had been a star left-handed pitcher, idolized especially by Italian kids like my dad, who was quite a bit younger. But I knew almost nothing about Tommy until we settled into our seats one night, the Dodgers came to bat in the top of the first inning, and my father suddenly bellowed out, "Hey, Mungo!" (When they were kids, Tommy and his buddies took on the names of their favorite big-leaguers. Lasorda's choice was Van Lingle Mungo, a fireballer for the Brooklyn Dodgers whom he mistakenly thought was left-handed.) Tommy shouted back, and it went on like that, between innings, for most of the night. I'm sure it wasn't the first time I was impressed by my dad, but it was the first time that I distinctly recall.

Even more pronounced is my memory of that clubhouse celebration in 1977. In addition to Dusty Baker's uncle-ish pickup, I remember the trash can full of ice and the players pouring it over the head of my dad's friend. I remember my first whiffs of champagne. I remember all these grown men in their underwear and shower shoes. (This, of course, was an old-school clubhouse, prior to the infiltration of female reporters and camera phones.) I remember being startled by the sight of Steve Yeager, the Dodgers' catcher, naked. And the last thing I remember from that night is my dad driving us home to Phoenixville—it was before his dealerships had taken off and we moved to Valley Forge—and then heading back out to party some more with the Dodgers' manager.

In those years, my mom would hardly see him when Lasorda was in town.

When he was sixteen, having dropped out of school by that time, my father took a job grinding welded seams at the Judson Brothers farm equipment factory in Collegeville, where *his* father was a steelworker. At the end of each week, he'd shuffle into line, just behind his old man, to collect his twenty-five dollars in cash. Then, on the spot, he'd hand over twenty-four of them to my grandfather.

That was the culture he grew up with. As a younger kid, he had a paper route and various other little jobs, and turned over most of *that* money to his father. Maybe he'd get a nickel back for some ice cream. At twenty, on the way to the train station, headed off to basic training after being drafted for the Korean War, my father, having nothing left of what he'd earned, asked my grandpa, "Hey, Dad, I don't really know if I'm gonna come back . . . but if I do, what will I have to come home to?"

His father told him, "You were put on this earth to take care of me."

My grandfather's first name was Rosario, but he became known as Russell when he immigrated to the United States from the southern coast of Sicily at the age of eleven. I should probably start with him.

I associated my grandfather with Sundays. Every week, my mom would take the five of us—all boys—to St. Ann Church in Phoenixville, and afterward my dad would say, "Let's go visit Grandma and Grandpa." Vince, in particular, looked forward to those afternoons, and made them better for the rest of us. He had a way of bringing people, and the family, together. We nicknamed him "United Nations."

Their house was in Norristown and one of the main attractions was the basement, where my grandfather kept a big wooden barrel to make wine out of grapes he crushed. Technically, it was fortified wine, a form of brandy, but we called it Dago Red. Grandpa was a handy, homey kind of guy—he kept a neat little garden out back—and on Sunday afternoons, we saw only his domestic side. There was a certain sweetness to it. But he was Sicilian to the bone, and with that came a stern, macho, controlling dimension, under which my father was brought up. You could call it a mean streak, although my dad wouldn't. In the tradition, he considered it tough love.

My father beat me pretty good. Maybe I was bad at the time. He had one of those cat-o'-nine-tails, with a razor strap that he used to cut in strips, and he'd have that hanging up on the wall. That's the way he was. But I think that gave me the toughness. He put some balls on me. He used to hit my mother, and when I got to be about seventeen I said, "Hey, Pop, don't you ever do that again. You've got to deal with me now." He stopped.

My father had his own little welding shop and used to make wrought iron railing. He even invented a thing to twist the bars. He was grinding one day with the grinder and the blade broke and hit him in the eye. He got in his car, holding whatever was left of his eye, and drove himself all the way to Philadelphia; went to the eye hospital there. Nobody knew about it until he came home. He lost the eye. My father was a tough son of a gun.

—Vince Piazza, father

The way the story goes in our family, the Piazzas had a pretty big farm in the Sciacca region of Sicily until a couple of workers on the farm were killed when a cart turned over. Their families sued, and my great-grandparents lost everything. That's when they came to America, pretty much broke. My grandmother's family was from central Italy, but she was born over here. She met my grandpa at Holy Saviour Church in Norristown. They eloped when she was seventeen.

A few years ago I visited Sicily with my mom and dad, my brother Danny, and a friend of my dad's named Gene Messina, who speaks fluent Italian. We were searching for ancestors, and a few miles east of the town of Sciacca we came upon a church tucked into a mountainside. As we approached, a priest suddenly appeared on the steps, dressed all in white. Gene walked up to talk to him and, after a minute or two, waved us over, at which point the priest informed my father, in Italian, that he, too, was a Piazza; they were cousins. Then he led us into the church, which was gorgeous, and down some steps to a cave where, in the sixth century, a hermit named Calogero had taken refuge to pray and meditate after a long journey from

Constantinople. Calogero looked after native animals in that cave, and for his good deeds ultimately became known as the patron saint of Sciacca. My dad asked how Calogero heated the place, and the priest told him to put his hand over a little hole in the wall of the cave. The air there was warm from water—holy water, the priest said—that sprang from a volcano in the top of Mount Calogero (also known as Mount Kronio). The next time my parents were at Holy Saviour, they noticed, for the first time, a statue of a priest holding a deer. It all connected.

My grandfather actually foresaw his own death, about a year ahead of the fact. Late in the summer of 1994, during my second full season in the big leagues, he was buttoning up his garden one day while Vince was visiting. Vince asked him if he was getting it ready for next year, and Grandpa said, "Nah, I'm not going to be here next year. I'm done."

On the day of his funeral, I was scheduled to film a commercial for Topps at Dodger Stadium. The company was renting out the ballpark for something like forty thousand dollars, so I told my dad that I had to stay in Los Angeles—that if I didn't, they'd get somebody else to do the spot. My father respected the dollar more than anybody I knew, and I thought for sure he'd understand. He didn't. He became very upset with me. It was a major point of contention.

Looking back, obviously I made the wrong decision. I was unforgivably selfish. But at the time, the business end of baseball was still new to me and I was uncomfortable with the idea of walking out on a good deal. I said to my dad, "Why are you so upset? You told me he used to beat the shit out of you."

I think he might have been on the verge of tears when he answered. In a voice so emotional it startled me, he said, "He made me the man that I am!"

I was born in Norristown, and yes, I lived there, on the sixth floor of an apartment building called Hamilton Hall, for two years, until Danny was born. But I grew up and went to high school in the Philadelphia suburb and my mother's hometown of Phoenixville, about ten miles away on the other side of the Schuylkill (pronounced SKOO-kul) River. I consider myself a product of Phoenixville. Nonetheless, a lot of people and articles have said over the years that I'm from Norristown, which has seemed to tick off just about everybody in Phoenixville but my dad. Actually, my dad and Tommy Lasorda were the ones who more or less perpetuated that misconception. I guess the way my father saw it, he was from Norristown and I was from *him*, so what's the difference?

The other myth is that my dad and Tommy were inseparable growing up. That couldn't have been, because they weren't in the same age group or neighborhood. They *were*, however, in the general company of each other quite a bit, only because my dad hung around the ball fields at Woodland Park, where Tommy ruled.

My father played some ball himself, and as I understand it was about as good as a left-handed shortstop could be. He hit right-handed. Not the best combination. Didn't have a lot of size, either. In fact, I'm the biggest person in my immediate family, by a long shot. That was the main reason why my dad singled me out, early on, as the son to make a ballplayer out of.

The last organized baseball he played was at Stewart Junior High, not long before he grabbed a teacher and threatened to throw the guy out the window for telling him he'd never amount to anything. That hastened the end of my father's formal education. But the fact was, he needed to get to work, anyway.

His family was so poor that, at school, he would volunteer to collect all the milk bottles after lunch, hoping that some would have a splash or two remaining in the bottom for him to drink. For coal to heat the house, he'd scavenge the city dump, two blocks away, then comb the railroad tracks for pieces that had fallen from the hopper cars. He'd fight anybody who had their eyes on the same pieces.

To my dad, fighting was a fundamental, necessary part of growing up. Day after day, on his walk home from school, he'd be met along the way by an older kid who had brought along somebody to finally take him down. "I've got a kid who'll knock the shit out of you," the older boy would tell him.

"Yeah, okay," my dad would say, before tearing into the latest foil and leaving him in tears. He claims he never lost a fight. He did, however—repeatedly—get his ass kicked by his father when he got home, for being scuffed up.

Still, in spite of the rough stuff, the family was in it together, which meant that everybody brought home whatever they could, starting as soon as possible. Long before his job at Judson Brothers, my dad caddied at the golf course where his father did maintenance. He pumped gas at night. He got up at six in the morning for his paper route, delivering the *Philadelphia Inquirer*. The route took him past a neighborhood grocery where his mother was always behind on her charge account. Most mornings, the milk had just been dropped off outside the store and my father would help himself to a quart or two. Now and then, he'd see the light inside come on for just a few seconds and then go out again, so he was pretty sure that the owners, the Schmidts, knew what he was up to; but they never said anything. Later, it ate at him that he'd taken advantage of their benevolence. When he got out of the army, he planned to face them and make restitution, but they'd passed away.

During his last couple of weeks of basic training for Korea, my dad picked up a bad infection in his foot. While he was in the infirmary, his company was shipped out. The upshot was that he had to go through training a second time, after which his orders sent him to Germany, where he served in artillery and drove a heavy piece of equipment that pulled a twenty-ton howitzer. He says his ears still ring from when they would fire that monster off. His superiors wanted him to go to Officer Candidate School, but then they found out he'd only completed the ninth grade.

He was discharged in 1954 with $325 of mustering-out pay. After a year as a merchant seaman in the coast guard, he applied for a job at Superior Tube in Collegeville. The guy who interviewed him said, "Piazza? You Italian? . . . We don't hire Italians." Then he heard they were looking for people at B. F. Goodrich, and it was true. He worked the night shift, pulling tires off the mold in about 120-degree heat, and stayed until they laid him off after seven years. He hadn't figured on sticking around for the long haul, anyway. Dad had plans, and he'd already gotten started on them.

His first used-car lot operated out of a one-car garage at his sister's house on Egypt Road in Audubon, between Norristown and Phoenixville. It was a rented house, but the owner didn't mind him being there; and neither did his sister, since he helped out a little bit with the rent. The lot was effectively a junkyard. When he left Goodrich in the morning, he'd catch a few hours of sleep, then snoop around town trying to find a junker to buy from a dealer. Some of them he could fix, paint, and sell. Others he'd park behind the garage, out of sight, and strip off the parts he could put into another vehicle or somebody's hands. He bought an old truck for hauling the scrap to the salvage yard, to be crushed for twenty-five or thirty bucks a load. Around five o'clock, he'd head home for the rest of his sleep, and by midnight he was back on the tire line, popping salt pills to keep from passing out. At eight, he'd punch out of the plant and do it all over again. To this day, there's a junkyard at my dad's first lot on Egypt Road.

He remained there for about a year after he was laid off from Goodrich, then moved to a better location in Jeffersonville and took on a partner named Bill Garber, who happened to have been a pretty good ballplayer and was a close friend of Lasorda. Tommy had reluctantly retired as a minor leaguer in 1960 and was scouting for the Dodgers, which left him plenty of time to hang out at Garber-Piazza Auto Sales. After my dad bought out Garber a couple of years later and moved across the street under the name of Gateway Motors, Tommy kept coming around when he could—by then, he had been named a manager in the Dodgers' minor-league system—for lunch and laughs.

Tommy was not, however, the most important person in my father's social life. Not after Dad went to a mixer and met Veronica (Roni) Horenci, a pretty young nurse and former high school prom queen who thought he was dapper, danced well, and looked like Tony Curtis. She might also have been impressed that he drove big, fancy cars, and she may or may not have known that they were actually inventory on consignment. Dad liked her well enough that, to spend an evening with her, he was willing to subject himself to ethnic slurs and physical challenges—which he welcomed, of course—at the Slovak Club, where her father bartended and her mother waited tables. Roni intended to become a stewardess, like several of her friends, but my dad, who was a little older, objected, at which point she said something like, "Well, then we should think about getting married." That was 1966, when, around Phoenixville and Norristown, it was still pretty scandalous for a Slovak to marry an Italian. No matter.

They were eager to start a family—Vince and I were born over the next two years—and to get ready for it, my father put everything he had into the business, including, now and then, the rent money. My mom would call him, all upset, to tell him that a sheriff's-sale sign had been posted on their apartment door. You weren't allowed to take it down. The deal was, if you didn't pay the rent, they'd carry away your furniture. Dad would end up borrowing from a friend to cover it, then pay him back the next time he sold a car. He also maintained a line of credit at the bank. The first time he failed to make a payment, a bank official told him they were going to take possession of his inventory.

With my dad sitting across the desk, the banker called a dealer in Coatesville to see if he'd put in an offer. The dealer, Jim Nelms, knew my dad and asked to talk to him, then told the bank official not to touch the cars because he'd take care of it. So my father and Nelms became partners. About a year and a half later, Dad bought out Nelms and applied for a new Datsun franchise, which was going cheap in those days, before Datsun became Nissan. Business picked up when Datsun came out with the 240Z. Then he bought a Honda dealership, which a lot of people thought was a screwy idea. It didn't seem so screwy when the energy crisis hit in the mid-seventies.

Before long he had thirty dealerships around Philadelphia. A lot of the domestics were forced to close because of the gas prices, and Dad bought up their properties. The dealership holdings led him into the real estate business, and then into dealerships in other states. He expanded into Acura—specializing mostly in the high-end line—and Acura and Honda have been his mainstays ever since. He also did well as an investor in the computer repair business. Under Piazza Management, meanwhile, he bought or built who knows how many commercial properties, including the Westover Country Club in Jeffersonville, the Bellewood Golf Club in Pottstown, and an entire historic mining town called St. Peter's Village.

All that success put my father in better cars (a Ferrari and a Lincoln Mark VI), better clothes (white shoes and leisure suits, although not the crazy guy-from-WKRP kind), and better seats for Phillies games, which he could now attend without hitchhiking to the ballpark and sneaking in (which he did as a kid, when the Phillies played at Connie Mack Stadium). As it turned out, he went big-league around the same time Tommy did.

That's when they became inseparable, as long as the Dodgers were in town. After a game at the Vet, my dad and Tommy would meet back up—along with a couple of cars full of Tommy's players and coaches—at the Marchwood Tavern, the Italian restaurant and bar that the Lasorda brothers opened up in Exton. For whatever reason, my father just couldn't get enough baseball—never could—and Tommy was his connection to it, the only guy he could truly and completely share his passion with.

Until I came along.

CHAPTER TWO

Little League was available when a kid turned eight, and to get me good and ready for it, my dad set up a mattress against the basement wall so I could fire baseballs at it from my knees. He also requisitioned a few highway cones for me to use as batting tees. I'd take a mighty rip and smack the ball into the mattress.

But that was just the opening act. The batting cage went up piece by piece, in the corner of the backyard, beginning when I was eleven.

First, it was merely a home plate underneath some netting draped around poles that my dad set in concrete. He was the pitcher. But he worked long hours and wasn't the least bit comfortable with the thought of me not hitting all that time, so he bought a JUGS machine with an automatic feeder. (Ironically, I would later do endorsements for JUGS.) Of course, the machine needed protection from the weather, so he installed a little shed over it. Then a roof over the whole shebang, like a carport. Then metal sheeting on the sides. After a while, the batting cage had morphed into a monstrosity so big and unsightly that a zoning inspector came by and asked my father what the hell that thing was. Dad said, "It's my son's ticket to the big leagues."

He even hooked up lights, and I'd be out there still hitting late at night. It's amazing that the neighbors never complained. They probably noticed that I took a lot of pride in the groundskeeping. I had a little rotor mower and tried to stripe the grass between the pitching machine and the plate, like the big leagues. I'd rake in sand around the plate. In the winter, I shoveled the snow out of there. The batting area would still be all messy and slimy, so we covered it with plywood. Other than that, the cold was not a problem. We wrapped my bat—an aluminum Bombat, made in King of Prussia, Pennsylvania—with insulation tape so it wouldn't sting my hands. (I always wore gloves, anyway, after reading that Ted Williams used to hit until his hands bled.) In the morning, I'd set the baseballs next to the stove in our rec room, and later on my mom would light the fire in time to have them all warmed up when I got home from school. Eventually we put a little portable heater out by the cage. It was crazy.

After school, I'd have some apple Fig Newtons—then they came out with strawberry—and a glass of milk, watch *Inspector Gadget* or *Gilligan's Island* reruns, then go hit for a few hours. Vince would be on his Stingray, delivering the *Evening Phoenix*, and I'd just whale away in my own little world. I rigged the feeder so that the pitches came out every six seconds. Mainly, I hit fastballs, but now and then one would act like a little bit of a knuckleball. One time I got hit in the nose. Never knew what happened. It fucking hurt.

Home plate was only a few feet from the dirt road that separated a corn-field from our lot on South Spring Lane. Invariably, an older guy named Blaine Huey would walk past on his way to Pickering Creek Reservoir ("the Res"), where everybody else hung out—there were docks, rafts, rope swings, bonfires, the whole bit—while I was whacking eighty-mile-an-hour fastballs into a net. Blaine would glance over at me, shake his head, and mutter something like "Look at this guy. Thinks he's gonna be a big baseball star."

> Thunk. Dink. Thunk. Dink. Thunk. Dink. You could hear it all the way down the street. He was out there a lot. Too much. I pretty much thought he was nuts. What I always said about Mike was, "Do you think he's gonna make it, really?" But I wasn't the only one who said that, because, who makes it, really?
>   —Blaine Huey, Phoenixville, Pennsylvania

The results of all that hitting were pretty obvious. Every spring, I'd no-tice that I was driving the ball a little harder, which only drove *me* a little harder. It became an addiction—not just hitting, but *power* hitting. From the very beginning, the major leaguers I took after were always the big, strong guys. Andre Dawson. Dave Parker. Bob Horner.

And of course, Michael Jack Schmidt, the greatest player in the history of the Philadelphia Phillies.

It happened that Schmidt hit two home runs in the first game I ever attended, sitting in the upper deck of Veterans Stadium in 1975. The next year is when my dad got season tickets on the third-base line, next to the Herr's potato chips people (who, to my delight, treated us frequently to the latest flavors, like sour cream), and I had my picture taken with number twenty himself—this was when he had his big, poofy seventies perm—on Fan Appreciation Day.

We were good Phillies fans. My dad would stomp his feet and I'd keep my eyes trained on Schmidt, checking out his mannerisms, his facial expressions—which seldom changed—and his solemn, efficient approach to the game. Years later, when I was with the Mets, one of our coaches, John Stearns, said to me, "You know, Schmidt always had the worst body language. He always looked like he just ate a lemon." There was a distinct impression that he wasn't having much fun out there. It's hard to say why that appealed to me, but it did.

For some mysterious reason, though, Schmidt had a deeply contentious relationship with the fans of Philadelphia. This was in spite of the fact that he was the best all-around third baseman the game has ever seen. To the malcontents at the Vet, it apparently didn't matter much that he won a Gold Glove just about every year, ten in all, the most of any third baseman in National League history; or that he led the league in home runs a record eight times (and from 1974 to 1986, virtually the entire period I regularly attended Phillies games, topped all of baseball *by nearly a hundred*); or that he picked up three Most Valuable Player awards; or that he carried the Phillies to the first world championship (MVP in both the regular season and World Series) in all their ninety-eight years. I couldn't begin to tell you what the people wanted from the guy. They absolutely booed the hell out of him; practically crucified him if he happened to strike out. I thought the fans were dead wrong, and their behavior provided a basis for my point of view on the player-fan relationship. For a long time—most of my career, I'd have to say—I carried a chip on Schmidt's behalf.

I tried, again and again, to get my dad to explain to me, if he could, why Philadelphians were so hard on Schmitty—much harder than they were on Larry Bowa, Greg Luzinski, or anybody else—but there was no acceptable explanation. Maybe the body language had something to do with it. Maybe the fans resented the fact that he somehow made the game look easy, as so many great players do. They called him Captain Cool, and it wasn't really meant as a compliment. Schmidt was simply the city's whipping boy, and it made me admire him all the more. I respected the fact that he wasn't another rah-rah, goody-goody kind of guy; that he'd take all the shit, convert it to energy, and shut everybody up with a three-run homer. In fact, I loved that. And I loved Michael Jack. I idolized him. I liked his game, his swagger, and especially his controlled aggression. I even liked his gold chains and open-necked shirts. They reminded me of my dad.

If you watched him as closely as I did, you could sense that there was a lot of pent-up tension inside Schmitty, a lot of pressure that he was dealing with, all of which seemed to come gushing out when he broke down at the start of his retirement speech. Later, in an interview on Tim McCarver's television show, he said, poignantly I thought, that, "[l]ooking back, I probably would have given up some of my accomplishments to have been more appreciated by the fans in Philadelphia. . . . I would have given anything to be the hero to the fans in Philadelphia, and they had no idea how hard I was working to be that guy."

Somehow, though, I think I had an idea. I felt like I understood Mike Schmidt.

In the car, on the way to a Phillies game, we'd snack on Tastykakes, and when the box was empty, my father would roll it up like a carpet, hand it to me, and say, "Here, squeeze this for a while." It was to strengthen my hands and wrists. For hitting.

When I was ready to take it up a notch, he bought me a cheap set of hand grippers at a local store. I couldn't put them down. Every night, when the light in my room went off, my mom would hear the incessant *squeak, squeak, squeak* coming from the bed. I'd squeeze those grippers literally a thousand times before I went to sleep. I squeezed them watching TV. I squeezed them in the car. I squeezed them when I was supposed to be doing homework. I was an OCD guy—obsessive-compulsive disorder—and I suppose that was a prime example.

After I wore out the store-bought grippers, I saw some advertised in a muscle magazine—probably *MuscleMag* or Joe Weider's *Muscle & Fitness* magazine, which I looked at on a regular basis—and sent off for the real McCoys from IronMind Enterprises. The "Captains of Crush," they were called. There were four levels, and only a handful of guys in the world had ever squeezed the number-one level. It was like a tire spring. I was one of the few around who could close even the number-three. On the number-twos, I'd put a coin in between the handles and hold it there as long as I could. After a while, I could move the number-one an inch or two. I was religious about those things. They don't do you much good unless you are.

Meanwhile, my dad had read in *Life* magazine about Ted Williams devising an exercise for his hands and forearms by attaching the head of a sledgehammer—or any weight, for that matter—to the end of a short rope, which was fastened to a stick, and raising and lowering it by rolling the stick in his hands. So I did that. Then, in one of my muscle magazines, I noticed an article about a guy with a handlebar mustache who did various other drills with a sledgehammer. I started out with a ten-pound sledgehammer and then moved up to a twelve-pounder. Eventually I could hold the sledgehammer straight out in front of me, then cock my wrists to raise the head and bring it down to my face in an arc. For a gag, I'd kiss it, then take it back the other way to the horizontal position. I'd do the same thing with two sledgehammers, one in each hand, dropping them slowly to the tip of my nose. And of course, a couple hundred times a day, I'd swing one like a bat.

There weren't many progressive ideas that my father was reluctant to try out. That was just his style. Dad, for instance, was into nutrition and eating healthy stuff long before it all became the fashion. He would have been the first guy in line at Whole Foods. Even now, he still eats wheatgrass—mixes it and freezes it in a plastic bag. His thing was always "If you want to be strong like a horse, you gotta eat like a horse." Oats, whole wheat, wheat kernels, grains; he's really a maniac about that sort of thing. Mom wasn't allowed to buy us Cap'n Crunch. The most sugary cereal we could have was raisin bran. And forget about candy. If we were caught with candy, it was grounds for a beating.

My brothers seemed to miss the sweets and junk food more than I did, though. They tried their best to resist the regimen that Dad imposed. None of them would eat oatmeal; but I did. Pepperidge Farm was the only whole-wheat bread back then, and I hated it because it was like chewing an oven mitt; but I ate it. I was with the program all the way.

My first team in the Phoenixville Little League was the A's, and my first official coach a local legend named Abdul Ford-Bey. He was a good baseball guy, but definitely from a different era.

I'm not sure that Abdul's drill-sergeant techniques would be politically acceptable today. There was a night game, for instance, in which we didn't play very well, and afterward he made us run six or eight laps around the whole minor-league field at Vic Marosek Park (named for one of Vince's coaches). Another time, he made us circle the bases for so long that I passed out. I can still picture the stars in my eyes before I took my leave. When they pulled me over into the shade to get me some water, Abdul was so scared he was shaking.

Abdul was sort of a guru-philosopher type, and he conferred upon us some peculiar nicknames. I was Koya, for reasons I never understood. There was another kid named Dave Jones—a pretty good player—whom he called Robot. One day, in practice, Robot's pitching, I'm playing third, and I'm daydreaming like little kids tend to do. Out of the corner of my eye, I can see Robot step off the mound and fire a rocket right at me. I turn at the last instant and am able to catch the ball, but if I hadn't seen it, it surely would have conked me in the head. I don't know whether Abdul told Robot to do that, but he got a good chuckle out of it. That scene is seared in my memory.

Not for a second, though, did I ever want to be anywhere else. I remember going up to the plate for the first time, and how excited I was to hear the PA announcer call my name, in his big, booming voice: "Now batting for the A's, number so-and-so . . . MIKE PIZ!" That's what he called me. After he realized he'd left out a few letters, it became, "Mike Pie-AY-za!"

I loved everything about Little League. I loved Opening Day, when everybody'd be in their new uniforms, looking great, and then the Tigers and Mets would play the first game—the Mets in yellow and the Tigers in maroon. I loved the free pretzels (mine with ketchup) after the games. I loved the trains that tooted their whistles as they rolled by, dramatically slow, on the tracks behind the park; all the kids would put pennies on the rails, and after the caboose had passed and we ran down to pick them up, they'd be perfectly flat. And I loved all the special days, like the time we hosted some kind of all-star game and one of the kids on the other team was Brad Kalas, a son of Harry Kalas, the great announcer for the Phillies, and Harry actually climbed up into our little PA booth and called an inning or so.

Baseball was taken very seriously in Phoenixville. In our town, at that time, nobody at the youth level was ashamed of trying to win or being the best team you could be. Because it was so competitive, people turned out to watch us play—and not just parents. Little League was embedded into the culture of the community. Starting with age twelve, most of the games were reported in the *Evening Phoenix*, complete with full box scores, including, believe it or not, pitch counts.

That year, the Cardinals were an expansion team and took me with the first pick in the draft. Playing now at the "major-league" field and installed at third base, just like Mike Schmidt, I started actually *feeling* like Schmidt—especially when I whacked a couple of home runs over the fence. That was kind of a big deal. From then on, every time I came to bat somebody would yell "Mike's up!" and about ten kids would run out beyond the fence waiting for the ball.

After our local season was over, I joined a Phoenixville all-star team that competed in the state tournament, which was hosted in a small town called Palmyra. (Because I was bigger than the other guys, I was always the only one to have my birth certificate checked.) Our players stayed in the homes of Palmyra players, and my guy lived on a dairy farm. When they grilled up the best steaks I'd ever torn into, I figured I now knew what the big leagues were going to taste like. It was a nice family, and I corresponded with them for a long time afterward.

We won the first game—I hit two homers and a triple—and kept winning all the way to the championship round against Palmyra, which came up out of the losers' bracket after being sent there by us. The title game was a circus. The Palmyra parents—who had been so hospitable to our whole team—now stood behind the backstop and heckled us from the first pitch, which was not the kind of thing that my dad was about to put up with. He tried to get a couple of our parents to walk over there with him, but he was on his own. So he joined the Palmyra people at the backstop and yelled at *their* kids, only louder. One of the officials asked him to quit, and he said he'd quit when *they* did. At least he refrained from slugging anybody. I homered to center, but we lost, 7–4.

At thirteen, we advanced to the Babe Ruth league and the games were moved to deSanno Field, where the fences were deeper and go-kart races were usually roaring on the track next to the park. I became only the second thirteen-year-old to clear the fence at deSanno, and in the district tournament hit a home run against Coatesville that the paper described as 330 feet. When I was fourteen and fifteen, the *Evening Phoenix* often described my long home runs to center field, which was where most of them went. We once had an exhibition game against a really good traveling team from Puerto Rico, and I got hold of one that, honestly, might have been four-hundred-something feet. Over the road and into a field. As far as I knew, they never found the ball. After that, they started giving kids a hot dog or something if they returned a ball hit over the fence.

> It was like a scene out of *The Natural*. The place was absolutely packed, and the clouds had started to get dark in the background. Mom was walking around with the younger kids down the right-field line, as usual—she didn't like to watch the games with me, because I could get a little loud—and I was standing behind the backstop with Butch Nattle (one of the other parents). The bases were loaded, it was a tie game or something, or maybe we were behind, and Butch says to me, "I guarantee you, Mike's gonna hit one out."
>
> Jesus Christ, he hit that ball. Against that dark background, you could see that white ball going up and over everything—the

fence, the trees, *everything*. Straightaway center field. Then the rain
and lightning started up.

—Vince Piazza

I pitched a couple of no-hitters in Babe Ruth ball, including one—a
1–0 win—in which I walked twelve batters and threw 154 pitches. Another
game, when I was sixteen, I threw 162 pitches and hit two home runs. But
that summer there was a better pitcher on our team, Joe Weber, and we went
all the way to the state championship game again, this time losing in extra
innings to Levittown. Honestly, I wouldn't remember all that—at least, not
in detail—if the newspaper clippings weren't pasted into my mother's scrapbooks.

Even though he's two years younger, my brother Danny played on our
team one year. There was an occasion in batting practice when I hit a big
fly ball out to him in right field and it plunked down right on his head, just
like Jose Canseco. We all had a good, long laugh about that—even Danny.
It might explain why he became a lawyer. Vince started out on my team, too,
then quit, came back a few years later, and quit again. His heart wasn't in
baseball. But his greatest moment is preserved in one of Mom's scrapbooks.
He once went three for three. I remembered that, but didn't remember *why*.
When I was home visiting not long ago, we came across the clipping and he
explained it to me.

He said, "The pressure was off that day, because I had already made up
my mind that I was quitting after the game. I could never do the pressure
thing. Remember the time I had to face you when you were pitching? *That*
was pressure. You threw me lobs, tried to let me get a hit, and I still struck
out. But that last game, when I knew I was quitting, I finally didn't give a
crap; and all of a sudden I'm playing good baseball. I had the game of my life."

In 1980, my man, Mike Schmidt, hit forty-eight home runs on his way to
the first of two straight Most Valuable Player awards, and my team, the Phillies, beat the Kansas City Royals in six games to win the World Series. Also,
Tommy Lasorda sent shimmering, cheesy, satiny blue Dodger jackets to me
and Vince.

Tommy was great to us, and he always kind of straddled that line between thrilling and embarrassing me. The jacket managed to do both. Of
course, we had to wear them to school—Phoenixville Junior High—and of
course, we got abused: "The *Phillies* are the world champions! Why are you
wearing a fucking *Dodgers* jacket? What's *wrong* with you guys?" I told my

dad he might as well slap a kick-me sign on my back. We were in seventh grade, and I couldn't tell you how many times I had to put up with ninth graders yelling, "Dodgers suck! Dodgers suck!" The ninth graders used to crush me. One time, when I'd had enough, this freshman rushed by me and as he did I pushed him. He punched me right in the face. The next year, the *Dodgers* won the World Series, and I'm thinking, all right, finally we get our vindication; now we can wear our Dodger jackets with pride. And as soon as we get off the bus, everybody starts in again: "Dodgers suck! Dodgers suck!" Classic Philadelphia fans. We were lucky we didn't get our asses kicked.

It was the following season that I became the batboy for the Dodgers whenever they played in Philadelphia. My first game, I showed up in a pair of really crappy Pro-Keds and desperately wanted some spikes. I put in a request to Nobe Kawano, the Dodgers' equipment manager, and he told me, no, kid, your shoes are fine. I felt like a goof but forgot about it pretty quickly. At that time, the batboy would kneel next to the on-deck circle. When I took my place, I was struck by an electrifying pulse of energy from the lights and the crowd and the game and the fastballs hitting the catcher's mitt . . . it was euphoric to me. Even better: by the second time the Dodgers came around, my dad had bought me some Mizuno spikes.

Before one of the games, I took some swings in the cage underneath the tunnel, with Manny Mota, the Dodgers' batting coach, pitching to me. Mota was throwing right over the top, like a machine, and I was just crushing the ball. My dad called Tommy to come down and take a look, and some of the coaches gathered around, and they were astounded. They were like, *What the fuck?*

(Mota was even throwing me curveballs, and I actually had a clue. For all my work with batting-cage fastballs, it wasn't as though I was completely foreign to the curve. For me, the really tough pitch, when I first saw it, was the slider. That was when I thought, what the hell was *that?* But Mota helped me hit the curveball. The first thing he told me was, "Once you recognize the curveball, wait." Most guys get out in front of an off-speed breaking pitch because their head goes down. The key is to be patient, keep your head in there, and pick up the spin. It's eyesight—locking in quickly on the ball and determining if it's going to be in the strike zone. Most good curves are out of the strike zone. When they're *in* the zone, they're probably hanging. People say that certain guys can't hit the curveball, but what's really happening, generally, is that they can't hit the off-speed pitch.)

The only problem with being a batboy was that it meant I had to occasionally miss one of my Babe Ruth games back in Phoenixville. I was down at the Vet one time when my best friend, Joe Pizzica, threw a no-hitter against my team, the Orioles. "They broke my stones about that," Joe said. "Everybody told me that was the only reason I pitched a no-hitter."

When I was fourteen, I was invited to go on the road with the Dodgers to Shea Stadium. My mom was upset with my dad for letting me do it, but Mark Cresse, the Dodgers' bullpen coach, took me under his wing and put me up in his hotel room. Tommy and most of the coaches had actually taken a limo to Atlantic City and then another limo to New York, so I rode up with Bill Russell, the Dodgers' shortstop, and his wife. Billy saw to it that I got checked into the Grand Hyatt in New York. The next day, Cresse and I went out on the number-seven train to Shea. I hit a little there, checked out Darryl Strawberry in the cage, and then ventured into the clubhouse . . . where most of the team was watching a porno film. There was one little TV in the training room, and they were all crowded around it. I have to admit that, coming from the straightlaced, deeply Catholic background that I did, it was a little unsettling. I didn't tell my mother.

Back at the Vet, I was determined to hit a ball into the seats during batting practice, and finally, that year, I popped one over the fence. It almost made me feel like I belonged there. For that matter, the players did, too, for the most part—guys like Mike Marshall, Greg Brock, Ed Amelung, and Bob Welch.

Steve Sax, however, was another story. The Dodgers used to play little games in batting practice, and occasionally I got to be on one of the teams. Mark Cresse would decide whether the ball you hit was an out or a double or what. One day, Saxie was on my team and I played like shit, made a bunch of outs. After I chalked up another one, Sax said, "That fucking kid never gets a hit!" Or something like that. He didn't mean it in a malicious way—he really didn't—but I was devastated. I mean, I was ready to cry. Jose Morales was a pinch hitter for the Dodgers, and he had this warm-up bat with the handle sawed off and a can on the end, filled with lead to make it weighted. Vince came down before the game and I was so mad that I was swinging that thing around with a vengeance, nonstop. Finally, a player named Lemmie Miller, a cup-of-coffee outfielder, walked up and consoled me. He said, "Don't let Sax get you upset." It wasn't profound advice, but it was enough.

I was sixteen, in 1985, when a Dodgers pitcher named Alejandro Pena— who had won the ERA title the year before—was rehabbing from shoulder surgery and Tommy told me to grab a bat because Pena was throwing a simulated game. Pena wasn't a hundred percent at that point, but he wasn't taking it easy on me, either. There were some breaking pitches involved. I hit a few balls hard, then banged one off the wall. Some of the coaches were exchanging glances. There was a little note about it in the local paper.

That was when Tommy started talking me up, telling everybody about this kid hitting a double off the ERA champ.

Among the baseball friends my dad accumulated over the years—most of them through Tommy—was Eddie Liberatore, a longtime scout for the Dodgers who lived in Norristown and was a consort of Joe DiMaggio and Ted Williams.

To me, Ted Williams was pretty much the head honcho of hitting. By the time I was sixteen, I'd read his famous book, *The Science of Hitting*, enough times to have it nearly memorized. I can still recite his three keys: one, proper thinking; two, get a good pitch to hit; and three, have a quick bat. As you might expect, I had tried to copy Mike Schmidt's batting style, but I gave it up when I realized how different it was from Ted Williams's—almost the antithesis. Schmitty stood deep in the box with a closed stance and his elbow up; then he'd step forward, dive into the ball, and practically hook it to left field. Williams was more about staying back, keeping your hands close to your body, your power packed in tight, and waiting. That was what worked for me. His keys to hitting were *my* keys to hitting—which, at that point, were more or less my keys to *life*.

So when he came to town for a card show at the George Washington Motor Inn in King of Prussia and Liberatore told my dad to stop by and meet Ted Williams, I felt like the luckiest kid on the continent. Then, before I know it, we're standing there, in awe, while he signs cards and bats and such—I was kind of lingering back a little bit—and Liberatore says to him, "My friend Vince here, he's got a kid who's a pretty good-looking player, and he's got his own batting cage at his house."

And Ted Williams says, "Let's go see him hit!"

It was arranged that he'd come by the next morning. Even so, I had a hard time believing that Ted Williams would actually show up at *my house* to watch *me* do what I did, all by myself, for hours and hours, day after day. But the next morning, I'll never forget, there's the car, smack dab in the driveway, and there's the Splendid Splinter himself, sure enough, headed straight this way, wearing a corduroy jacket and cussing up a storm.

Too nervous to talk, I flipped on the machine and started hitting. Fortunately, we taped it. So I can tell you exactly what Ted Williams had to say when he watched me bat in our backyard on South Spring Lane in 1985, standing a few feet to my right.

"This kid looks good. I'm gonna tell you the truth—I don't think I hit the ball as good as he does when I was sixteen, I'm not shittin' ya. . . . Try to lower the bat now. Get a little lower hand position. That's it! That's it! That's it! . . . He looks good. He really looks good. You really look great, buddy! You do!"

To my dad: "I bet you got scouts on him already, for Christ sake."

To me: "I'll be your agent, buddy!"

To Liberatore: "You know who he hits like, don't you? I'm gonna give you one guess. He's in the big leagues. You know him."

Liberatore mentions a name that can't be made out on the tape.

"No! Hell, no!"

Liberatore: "In the National League?"

"Yeah, a buddy of yours. *Mike Marshall*, for Christ sake! He looks like Marshall! He looks more like Marshall than anybody I've seen."

My dad: "Hit a couple left-handed, Mike."

"He looks good that way. Good swing. He looks good enough, he should hit *that* way, too. Yes, sir."

Dad (exaggerating): "Tommy's never seen this kid. Nobody's ever seen him."

"Cock and stride. Cock and stride. Stay back, like you did then. Stay back. Don't go out and get it. Stay back there. Do it again! Do it again! That's better! Better! Jesus Christ, I never saw anybody who could pick things up like he does. I never did."

Dad (fibbing): "He's got average, good speed, and a good glove. He can play any position."

"Well, you know, hitting's going to be his big suit."

With that, I was finished, but as I walked—or floated—out of the cage, the great man gave me his best advice of the day. "But that's only half the battle," he said. And he tapped the side of his head. "The rest is up here."

We then sat at the kitchen table for a little while, and I asked Ted if he'd sign my beat-up copy of *The Science of Hitting*. Needless to say, I still have that book. And on the first page, in Sharpie-style blue, it says:

To Mike,
Follow this book and as good as you look now I'll be looking for tickets in 1988.

　　　　　　　　　　　　　　　　　　　　　Ted Williams

CHAPTER THREE

The batting cage was not the first unusual thing to be housed in our back-yard. There was that stupid pony.

My dad always tried to do something cool for us on Christmas. One year, first thing Christmas morning, he and Mom led us through the kitchen for the big surprise, opened the door to the backyard . . . and the son of a bitch was gone! Our big surprise had escaped before we even got a glimpse of him. They jumped into their respective cars and combed the neighborhood, covering all the back roads, knocking on everybody's door. You'd think he'd have been roaming around in the big cornfield behind the house. Uh-uh. Finally, about two miles away, a lady told my mom that a pony had been strolling up her driveway and she'd put him in the barn with her horse. My dad walked it home, with Mom driving behind with her flashers on.

I mean, I give credit to my father. It was a great idea. We were plenty excited to see that pony clopping down the road. But I think we rode him one time. Whenever we'd try to get on, he'd buck us off. Tanker the pony. Shit. We supplied Tanker with a little shed and an electric fence, and there he stood.

There were plenty of things to ride, anyway, and a dopey pony could hardly compete with the likes of a snowmobile. I can still feel the exhilara-tion of firing up the Arctic Cat and racing across the open fields in ten inches of snow. Beyond our street, it was all farmland back then. And the reservoir. We built forts back there. Had some big-time snowball fights. Played hockey when the ponds froze. I'd speed-skate and pretend I was Eric Heiden. I really wanted to *be* Eric Heiden.

In the fall, we could always get up football games, neighborhood against neighborhood. Spring Lane would play Ferry Lane or Forge Manor. We'd steal tomatoes from the neighbor's garden. There's a dam nearby, and guys would dare each other to walk across the top of it. Danny did it. The area sounds rural, and to a large degree it was, back then, but the main drag, Route 23, ran by right at the top of our street. There's an old restaurant and truck stop on the other side of 23—the G Lodge, where I picked up candy bars and grape Bubble Yum. They used the G Lodge for a scene in the movie *The Happening* and called it the Filbert Restaurant. Dad still eats breakfast there.

The neighborhood had everything we needed. We could walk to the golf course. Before extreme sports had caught on, I had a BMX bike that I'd pump as fast as I could down the driveway and across the street to a ramp set up on the far curb, which would send me flying into a vacant field. Vince and his friends had their skateboards, hacky sacks, and jacked-up cars. We got cream soda from the gas station next to the G Lodge. Phoenixville, I'd say, was practically a perfect place to grow up.

It was where my mom grew up, too, except that we were raised in the suburban end of it and she came from right in the town. There was a big difference. Downtown Phoenixville, if you could call it that, had an old-school, industrial, European feel to it—mostly Italian and Slovakian—and still does. The townies tended to be the tough guys.

We experienced the town side of Phoenixville when we visited our grandmother's house. My grandfather Horenci—Mom's dad—died when I was seven, and Grandma lived alone in the left side of a narrow two-story, two-family house just across the street from the big shirt factory and around the corner from the Slovak Club. Phoenixville is primarily a steel town, and Grandpa Horenci was a welder raised in Coatesville, Pennsylvania. He was a big guy, and my grandmother was tall, too; my mother has two tall sisters. I obviously got my size from that side of the family—the Slovak side. They came from the portion of Czechoslovakia that is now Slovakia. Grandma Horenci spoke fluent Slovak. The fact is, I'm just as Slovakian as I am Italian.

Grandpa Horenci drove a '72 Monte Carlo, turquoise with a black top and black seat covers. From him I inherited my neat-freak streak when it comes to cars. He had towels on the seats, and floor mats protecting his floor mats. He'd tell us, "Don't touch the windows. Don't touch the doors." My kind of guy. I believe that, of all the relatives in our family—not counting my dad, of course—he's the one who would have gotten the biggest kick out of watching me play big-league baseball. I recall my mother being very upset when she woke us up to tell us that Grandpa had died. His funeral was my first brush with death. I remember how cold his hand felt when I touched it.

My mother has done a commendable job of respecting our family's Italian heritage—you can't beat the meatballs she makes, the size of baseballs—and, thankfully, she has also kept us in touch with our Slovakian side. Christmas Eve was always spent at Grandma's house, with our cousins and a Slovakian dinner of pierogi (kind of like dumplings, with fillings), kielbasas, and sauerkraut mushroom soup. When the family got too big for Grandma's little house, Christmas Eve was moved to ours. Vince would cut open an apple and each family member would eat a piece of the apple, a piece of a tangerine, and then a little piece of the same walnut. The philosophy is that the family that shares from the same piece of fruit will stay together. Then, on Christmas Day, it was church and turkey. Our ethnic blend was Italian, Slovakian, and all-American.

We were also down by Grandma's every Friday night, when Mom would take us into town for Nardi's Pizza. The big controversy was Nardi's versus Sal's Pizza Box on Route 23. We were Nardi's people—and I don't doubt that the location had something to do with it. Mom was partial to that neighborhood, which meant that, just before school started every year, she bought our gym shoes at Fazzini's on Main Street: Chuck Taylor high-tops—not to be confused with the wacky orange and red sneakers she picked up at Kmart, which we referred to as our bobo shoes. Downtown Phoenixville was, in effect, our shopping center. To some people, though, it might be best known as the little town that gets terrorized in the science-fiction movie *The Blob*, which was not Steve McQueen's finest hour. In one classic scene, the blob oozes into the Colonial Theatre and eats the projectionist before the moviegoers run screaming out into the street to warn everybody. That last part is now reenacted every year during Phoenixville's annual Blobfest. To my knowledge, it's the world's only annual Blobfest.

In town, everything was walking distance. My grandmother used to pin the mortgage to the inside of Mom's sweater—nineteen dollars in cash—so she could walk it safely to the bank. Grandma always worked in a factory she could walk to. However, when my mother was in high school, Grandma, who was, of course, deeply Catholic, sent her on two buses every morning to get to Bishop Kenrick (now Kennedy-Kenrick) in Norristown, where she's alleged to be the only girl ever crowned both Prom Queen and May Queen in the same year.

I have to say, my mom was very glamorous, with a Jackie O., Audrey Hepburn kind of look. Even so, while Dad could strike fear into any of the kids—me, in particular—it was Mom who was mostly responsible for the discipline in our family. She meted it out with a wooden spoon. Seemed like Danny was the one who was always catching it on the ass.

I can recall only one time when my dad got angry enough at me to work me over pretty good. I was a huge professional wrestling fan; watched the

WWF twice every Saturday. Their theme song, "Gemini Dream" by the Moody Blues, got me fired up every time. I was into all of those guys: Jimmy "Superfly" Snuka, the first one to jump off the top ropes; Bob Backlund, the people's champ; Jesse "the Body" Ventura, later the governor of Minnesota; Tony Atlas, the black guy, a big weightlifter who would raise people over his head and slam them to the mat; Ivan Putski, the Polish Hammer; Blackjack Mulligan, with the iron claw; and of course his archenemy, André the Giant. Then there were the cream-puff guys, the tin cans who would wrestle the stars. Tony and Tommy were still real young, so Danny was my tin can, the lucky recipient of all my holds and moves. I had some of those, let me tell you. When I did the iron claw, as strong as my hands were, I could really *do* it.

When I was about thirteen—which would have made Danny eleven—I put him in head scissors one day and got kind of carried away. I didn't really choke him, I don't think, but I went a little too far and he started freaking out. Then I heard my dad coming. I ran outside and tried to take cover by the woodpile, but Dad walked up and just slugged me in the face. I rolled clear over the woodpile. He yanked me up and said, "Boy, don't you *ever* fight with your brothers. You've got to fight *with* them, not against them. If there's ever a problem, you better step up and help them because you're the guy who can get it done."

Not long afterward, there was an incident on the school bus when some kid hit Vince in the stomach as we were walking down the aisle. Instinctively, I reached back and clobbered the guy. That time, Dad wasn't even upset with me. I had done as he'd said. A day or two later, the kid's father approached my dad and started to make an issue of it. My dad said, "You don't want to go there, do you?"

Dad would occasionally take me to Flyers and 76ers games. Doctor J, to me, was bigger than life. You know the famous rock-a-bye dunk he made against the Lakers? It was right in front of me.

We were sitting *on the floor*, on the same sideline where Doctor J raced Michael Cooper for the loose ball at midcourt, jabbed it in the right direction, then picked it up, took one humongous dribble, cradled it as he soared through the air, and swung it down right on top of Cooper. You can actually see me on the video of that play, right around the spot where Doctor J snatched the ball and took off. I'm wearing a red Alligator shirt, blue jeans, and Pony shoes. When I was with the Dodgers, Eric Davis was watching that video on the plane one night and I said, "Hey, that's me, right there!" It was a fun time to be a sports fan in Philly.

But I have to say, I sucked at basketball. I mean, it's almost incomprehensible how bad I was at basketball—and still am. Mom signed us up for little-kid basketball at the YMCA, along with diving lessons, and I had maybe two baskets my whole career. One time I stole the ball and I was coming up the court with it and the coach was yelling at me, "Give the ball to the point guard!" I didn't understand the concept. Naturally, I had it stolen back from me. I once fell down and cried about it, and the coach gave me a towel and said, "You get back in there and you get that fucking ball!" He actually cussed at me. My mom had a cow, as we used to say. The f-bomb wasn't heard much around our house. With my dad, it was always "Jesus Christmas!"

Golf was more up my alley. Dad would take me on Sundays to Woods Golf Center in Norristown and teach me the fundamentals. He thought I had some potential in golf, which I did. Mom and Dad became members of the Phoenixville Country Club so that I could practice there. The club had a one-armed pro, Joe Banyacskay, who was always smoking a cigar and cursing his head off. It was a hell of a walk from our house, carrying golf clubs, but for a few years I'd make that walk just about every day of the summer with my friend Marc Deye.

There was a time when I thought I might want to pursue golf, but I didn't have the mentality for it. One weekend I was playing with my dad, and playing like shit, and I had a bad attitude going on, which wasn't particularly unusual. The thing was, he was allowing me to play golf while my brothers were working. So he lit me up. "You're out here jerking off! You're done! Get out of here! Jesus Christmas!"

I made the Phoenixville High School golf team in the ninth grade, which was cool because I was able to catch rides from the older guys and no longer had to call my mom all the time to pick me up in the minivan. My golf game was long on power, but short on poise. That became obvious my junior year, when, after sixteen holes, I was leading the Ches-Mont League tournament at two over par. On the seventeenth hole, the guy I was playing with said, "Man, you're gonna win this thing." I woke up, saw where I was, and choked it away. Went from left trap to right trap to left trap to right trap. Put up an eight. I was devastated. A teammate, Mike Bland, ended up winning the tournament and went to North Carolina on a golf scholarship.

By then, golf was starting to rub me the wrong way. Literally. Needless to say, I had to do a lot of walking with the golf bag over my shoulder. The trouble was, I'd started to develop serious acne. It showed up on my face, of course—Dad accused me of eating too much sugar and called me "pimple puss"—but one day I got home after stomping around for nine holes with that strap irritating me, and when I checked to see what the problem was I found nasty pimples all over my upper back. Before long, the pimples developed into that disgusting cystic acne and became keloids, almost like boils. I still have the scars around my shoulders.

Years later, when I was playing professional baseball, I had the same sort of reaction when the strap of the chest protector rubbed against my shoulder and back. At that point, the team trainer offered to get me Accutane, but I declined because I'd read that it caused pain in the joints. I knew the ultimate solution was simply to outgrow the problem and cope with it in the meantime, which wasn't encouraging: there are people in my family who've dealt with acne into their fifties. In high school, I took tetracycline, but that didn't make it any less irritating when I carried my golf bag.

Golf was a fall sport at my high school, and with the troubles it was giving me, I'd much rather have been playing football. Truthfully, I always wanted to play football. Never could. The *coaches* even wanted me to play, because I was big and had a good arm, but my dad simply wouldn't let me. I had started pestering him about it long before high school. He told me, "The time you'd give to practicing football, you get in that goddamn cage and you hit!"

As far as he was concerned, nothing was going to interfere with me playing baseball. He wouldn't let me get my driver's license until I was seventeen, because, of course, he didn't want me straying too far from my pitching machine. Way back in grade school, he wouldn't even let me play *the trombone*.

Schuylkill Elementary had a nice little band, and I've always been interested in music. The director was a cool guy named Alan Philo, who played the guitar and rode a motorcycle, and as soon as our class became eligible for the band I talked my mom into attending Mr. Philo's parents meeting at the start of the school year. When she found out that a trombone cost two hundred dollars, she took that information straight to my dad, whose response was, "No, no, *no!*" I'm sure the two hundred dollars had something to do with it, but maybe, in his divine sort of wisdom, Dad knew I might stick with it and didn't care to watch me grow into another musician out of work. I won't say that I hold it against him; but I truly wanted to read music and learn music and *play* music, and he crushed all of that.

(Having brought up the ban on the band, however, I'd be remiss not to add that my dad, as rigid as he was on occasion, was extremely sensitive and affectionate. I don't feel like I was really deprived of anything growing up . . . other than the trombone, that is.)

Eventually my fascination with music took a different form. I distinctly remember listening to my first AC/DC record in the seventh grade—it was *T.N.T.*—and something happened; a hole inside me filled up. Right away, I drew "AC/DC" on all my schoolbooks, which at least gave them a purpose. A ninth grader noticed what I'd doodled and said, "Dude! Cool!" He was an art guy, so he grabbed my book and sketched in a few other little designs. I thought, man, look at me, I'm being accepted by a ninth grader! Baseball had never done that for me.

Shortly thereafter, I heard an AC/DC interview on the radio and taped it, along with some songs ("T.N.T.," "Highway to Hell," and a few others), on a little cassette tape recorder. There was no turning back. I must have had a hundred heavy-metal cassettes by the time I was in high school. I'd found the music that suited my personality—brought out my aggressive side. On the way to a game, I'd blast AC/DC, Iron Maiden, Metallica, Slayer, and Twisted Sister, among others, and it would send me into a frenzy.

A guy I played baseball with was one of the people who stoked my interest in heavy metal. Tony Roberts could really pick it—the baseball and guitar, both. (His sister, Kari, was on our varsity golf team and always played with a plug of Red Man in her mouth.) Tony later performed in a band with Peter Criss—the drummer for Kiss—which was ironic, because I was such a fan that I once had a friend paint my face like Peter Criss's. We used my mom's makeup.

Besides Tony, there were a few kids at school who, during lunchtime, would join me at the black-T-shirt table and discuss Black Sabbath. A hippie girl on my block had an electric guitar, and I'd go over there and fool with it. (Maybe it's just an excuse, but I think my hands were too big for the guitar.) Then there was Uncle Joe, my mom's younger brother. He lived with my grandma, had a nice stereo with big speakers, and loved his rock 'n' roll. Uncle Joe was a Led Zeppelin guy. Also Boston. The Steve Miller Band. He'd stick in "Rockin' Me," put a funky hat on my head, and I'd play along with a tennis racquet in front of the mirror.

I was all-in with the music but wouldn't describe myself as a Hessian metalhead, per se; more like a combo metalhead/jock, with a tendency toward cut-rate bling. Before rap even came along, I was throwing so many gold chains around my neck that the kids in high school called me Mr. T. There's actually a picture of me in the yearbook where I've got the poofy hair and I'm wearing a concert T-shirt and a pile of chains. And I didn't stop there. From day to day, I'd put on an Italian horn, a crucifix, my dad's dog tag, anything shiny. Strange as it sounds, I was kind of taking after my father in that respect. He was usually sporting a gold chain and a pinky ring, for starters.

I guess my mom was softened by the fact that I shared my dad's look and her brother's interest. Somewhat surprisingly, she allowed me to take the train from Devon through Philly to the Spectrum to see all those eighties groups: Judas Priest, Ratt, Dio, Kiss, Twisted Sister, Bon Jovi. That was both my release and my social life. I rejected a lot of the traditional social protocols at the time—wasn't a prom and homecoming kind of guy, and definitely wasn't into the high school hierarchy. On the other hand, I didn't push the envelope, either. We partied in the Spectrum parking lot and I drank a few beers here and there, but I honestly never felt the need to smoke pot or get involved with any experimental drugs. One time at a Kiss concert, somebody passed me a joint and I took a drag. That was it. I'd been infused with a certain code of conduct, I suppose, that kept me from going too far.

For one thing, Dad was always preaching about moderation. He was furious when I came home drunk one night. But I'd have to say that it was mostly my mom's influence that kept me from crossing the line. She was the one who carted five boys to church every Sunday and set the example by practicing her Catholicism on a daily basis.

It was something of a dichotomy for me, growing up as a dyed-in-the-wool Catholic and loving heavy metal like I did. Some of the more controversial bands, like Iron Maiden and Slayer—I'd guess that I've been to nearly a dozen Slayer concerts—were called out by Christian groups, and that wasn't lost on me. But my purpose in listening to that music was not to rebel against God and religion.

I just loved the power of it. Heavy metal was good for me.

As soon as every baseball season was over, my dad would take us down to a condo we had in Wildwood, New Jersey, on the southern tip of the state. We called it the Jersey Sho-wa.

The next town over, Cape May, is historic and picturesque, but Wildwood's style was unpretentious and very much Jerseyesque, with cheap motels and a carnival boardwalk where you could win stuffed animals and gorge yourself on cotton candy and tubs of fries. For me, it was one of the best times of the year, mostly because the pressure was off. Dad would drive us there and then head back home to work during the week. We'd spend all day at the pool or beach. Once a week, after dinner, we'd walk to a little restaurant down the street for a sundae—which, of course, we couldn't have done if Dad had been with us. Then we'd watch Yankees and Mets games, with all their great announcers: Bill White, Phil Rizzuto, Ralph Kiner, Bob Murphy, Lindsey Nelson. For some reason, I actually preferred the Mets. The Schaefer beer commercials. Joe Torre, as a player-manager, sending himself up to pinch-hit.

Dad would arrive on Friday afternoon, and the first thing he'd say to me was, "Let's go." I'd grab a bat, we'd find a field, and he'd pitch to me. There was a dumpy, sandy field up by the beach and a beautiful, manicured Little League diamond that nobody was allowed on. We were able to use the fancy field after the director saw me hitting there one day and decided he wanted some of his players to come by and watch; but we'd usually end up on the dumpy one, which I didn't mind because I could hit the ball out to the street. If I did, my dad would snarl at me to get back to the backstop so it wouldn't happen again. When it rained, we played under the walkway.

My father was a lefty, and I figure that had something to do with why I always crushed left-handers. I loved to hit off him. I just loved to *hit*, period. I couldn't get enough, and my dad was happy to take full advantage of that. If my brothers came along with us, it was mainly to shag balls. Dad would throw each of them ten pitches, then give me a hundred. Amazingly, they never rebelled. Back home, on the pretense of taking the kids to visit his mother in Jeffersonville, he'd drop off my brothers at her house, drive me over to a local field, and pitch to me until his arm wore out. When we returned to Phoenixville, my mother was always surprised that we'd had such a nice, long visit.

Another highlight of those great weeks at Wildwood was getting to see my friend Joe Pizzica. His family would vacation there, too, or he'd come down with us. I knew Joe from the all-star baseball teams in Little League, but he'd gone to the Catholic elementary, so we didn't run around together until high school. He was a lot tighter with the in-crowd than I was. Joe's buddies included Tony and John John Nattle, and we all played ball with each other, so—this is back in Phoenixville—we'd go over to one of their houses to watch Mike Tyson fights on pay-per-view, or whatever, and drink a little beer. It wasn't the Ivy League crew.

Other nights, we drove to a secluded place we knew in the nowhere farmland of Chester County, turned on the radio, and just hung out. Got drunk. We called it Ja-Blip. That lasted until Joe kind of blew me off one night. I had a crush on a girl named Kim Jeffries, who was the class president and a friend of his, and I wanted to go out with Kim and chill at Ja-Blip with Joe and those guys. But there was some kind of complication—Kim might have been seeing somebody else at the time, I don't recall—and Joe said,

"You know what, man? You don't want to hang out with us." It was sort of like that scene from *Good Will Hunting* when Ben Affleck tells Matt Damon to just get out of there and move on with his life. He was looking out for me.

I had one other heartthrob in high school—and one other strikeout. Joe was instrumental in that one, as well. Mary Lou Retton.

Actually, we both had crushes on her. This was just after she'd won the gold medal in the 1984 Olympics. I thought it was meant to be—her mother's Italian, after all. So Joe was over at my house one day and we spent the afternoon figuring out how to call Mary Lou. Somehow we found the number. I didn't have the guts to dial it, but Joe did, and I guess it threw him off when her mother answered. He was holding the phone out so I could hear, too, and he said, "Hello, is this Mary Lou Retton's mother?"

She goes, "Yes, who's calling?"

Joe just looked at me, with huge, terrified eyes, and hung up.

CHAPTER FOUR

A fellow named Joe Godri, who is now the head baseball coach at Villanova, likes to say that he was the guy who blocked me from the Phoenixville High School lineup. Godri was two grades ahead of me, and the position we both played—first base—was his until he graduated.

All the while, however, I had plenty of encouragement from the likes of my dad, my friends, Ted Williams, and—in front of the whole student body—the manager of the Los Angeles Dodgers. I don't know if my father was the one who arranged it, but Tommy Lasorda came to our high school to speak at an assembly in the auditorium, and as he was wrapping up he pointed straight at me and said, "And one day, I'm going to sign *him*."

Afterward, kids came up patting me on the back as though I'd actually *made* it. It was embarrassing, but also significant. That was when I started reading everything I could find about the baseball draft. Obsessing about it, really.

With my goal clarified and my expectations taking flight, I couldn't wait to start wreaking havoc on the Ches-Mont League. I was six foot two, uncommonly strong, and still plenty awkward—one of the youngest students in the junior class—when our coach, Doc Kennedy, turned me loose as number thirteen in purple and white, finally starting at first base for the Phoenixville Phantoms. I came out hacking.

At Phoenixville, there was no left-field fence, and with my not-blazing speed it was almost impossible to hit a home run in that direction. The situation persuaded me to drive the ball to the opposite field, which came fairly naturally. In right, however, there was a row of trees just inside the fence, and oftentimes the umpires would have to decide whether a long fly ball should be ruled a home run or not when it was cuffed around in the leaves or knocked down by a limb. I still hit twelve homers that year—and three triples, which *should* have been home runs—in eighteen games, and batted .500 with thirty-eight RBIs. My mom saw it all from her Chrysler minivan.

There has long been a misconception that I materialized out of no-where as a baseball player. The fact is, I had two exceptional high school seasons and was not unknown to the area scouts. My junior year, by some accounts, was one of the greatest high school seasons in the history of Pennsylvania. The rap was that we played in a weak league, but I don't know about that. Boyertown and Downingtown were much bigger schools than Phoenixville. They had senior classes of almost fifteen hundred stu-dents, while ours was just under two hundred.

Boyertown came in as a very heralded team my junior year—they had a couple of guys who went on to play in the minor leagues, plus *a stadium with lights*—and they won the conference, but we drubbed them when we played. Our football team took a beating on a regular basis, but there was no prob-lem in baseball. We had good ballplayers, including Mike Fuga, who later played at Temple. We kicked ass. It was disappointing that we got bumped out of the district tournament on a bad day, because I really felt like we had a team that could have gone far in state.

My senior year, those trees in right field were no longer a problem. Doc appealed to the athletic director on the basis that they were a safety issue, because an outfielder could crash into one or turn an ankle stepping on a root, and they were cut down. That opened up some airspace, and I was able to land a few shots onto the street beyond the fence and into the yards be-yond the street, even though opposing teams made it a point to move their left fielders way back and pitch me in tight so I'd pull the ball that way. One of the home runs that cleared the street (City Line Avenue) landed on the driveway of a friend, Rob Thompson, and bounced into his backyard. Rob's dad, who was watching the game from a folding chair, strolled back, picked up the ball, and gave it to me later.

But I wouldn't describe my senior year as smooth sailing. For one thing, a lot of teams wouldn't throw me strikes, so I finished with eleven home runs and a batting average that wasn't quite as glittery as the season before. The other little issue was that I totally slacked off in school—even more than usual, which was quite a feat. I mean, I was a bad, *bad* student. I think I did one hour of homework my entire high school career. I was completely un-motivated. By the time I was a senior, I had my heart so set on being drafted out of high school, and was so cocksure that I would be, that academics just didn't mean anything to me. The truth is, I'm not certain if I was genuinely eligible or not. I suspect that the principal might have pulled some strings so I could play.

Other than baseball, there was simply nothing about high school that interested me. Not even dating, such as it was. I wouldn't say that I was antisocial; just aloof, ambivalent, cynical—totally disengaged from all the structure and sis-boom-bah, as if it were a language I didn't speak. It was my rebellious stage, and I was tenacious about it, with a defiant attitude that showed even on my face: my senior year, I played ball with a goatee and Sparky Lyle chops, just to look intimidating. I was so disagreeable that I didn't even want to hang out with the family. My dad had bought a home in Boynton Beach, Florida, and we'd stay down there for a little while around Christmas. I don't know what it was that I did—just being the typical jackass, I guess—but that year my dad kept threatening me that I wasn't going. So I said, "All right, fine, I'll just stay here and party with Joe and those guys and drink beer and have fun." He said, "Oh no, you're going."

I'm not making excuses, but I suspect that my attitude was related to the pressure I placed on myself to get drafted. In my heart, I was positive that I was good enough, and felt certain—especially after what Tommy said at the assembly, although I knew better than to pin all my hopes on the Dodgers—that *somebody* would notice that and pick me. I just wasn't seeing the hard evidence of it. Eddie Liberatore would come to a game occasionally, but he never talked about drafting me out of high school. I got calls from scouts for the Giants and Blue Jays, and they'd ask me where I was playing that week, but it was never anything like "You think you'll get drafted?" or "If you get drafted, are you going to sign?" Jocko Collins, the scout who originally signed Tommy Lasorda for the Phillies, came to one of my games and watched me hit a fly ball to center, and then it rained. He left and never came back. He told somebody I looked clumsy around first base. Tim Thompson was a Cardinals scout who was in our area quite a bit and ate at the Lasordas' restaurant. My dad knew him pretty well. He told Dad that he'd give me the same advice he gave his own son: get an education.

Every time I heard from a scout, or saw one in the stands, the pressure turned up a notch. I played nervous. It started to screw ever so slightly with my confidence, which made me think about looking into college ball. So I did. It was my way of acknowledging, as a sort of formality, that, well, sure, there was always a *chance* that I wouldn't be drafted after all, as strange as it might seem.

The more I looked around, the more intrigued I became about the idea of playing for the University of Texas or the University of Miami. I read *Baseball America* religiously and imagined myself being featured in it. But Texas didn't call. Miami didn't call. I got a letter from the coach at Old Dominion University. Got another one from William & Mary. The way I had it figured, though, if I didn't get drafted I was going to be a freshman All-American, and I didn't see that happening at Old Dominion or William & Mary.

> People used to say that Mike was a machine hitter. It was obvious that he was willing to put in additional time to hit the baseball. His hand-eye coordination was good because he saw so many pitches in his drill work in the batting cage. But the scouts wondered if, when push came to shove, he would be able to translate all that to hitting a baseball off live pitching. Plus, his defensive skills didn't really show up as a first baseman. Scouts look for tools, and Mike did not run well. That contributed to the fact that a lot of people didn't notice him as a player.
>
> Probably the only position on the field where foot speed doesn't have a big impact is catcher. I remember talking to Mike his sophomore year about catching. I mentioned it to him because I knew he could flat-out hit a baseball, and I knew his dedication and love for the game. He looked like he'd have the body type for catching. So I asked him about it and I remember Mike saying, "You know, I talked to my dad about it a little bit . . ." And that was pretty much it.
>
> Another thing that people might not have realized was that Mike graduated when he was seventeen. With the numbers he put up, there should have been more scouts watching him. It was pretty evident that he had a lot of skill as a hitter. To my knowledge, there was only one scout throughout the whole process that turned in a pro report on him. That was Brad Kohler. He worked for the Major League Scouting Bureau.
>
> —John "Doc" Kennedy, coach, Phoenixville High School

The fact that I was failing to impress the right people on either front—pro or college—made no sense to me. Anyone who bothered to watch me hit on a regular basis knew what I knew, deep down, in spite of my weaker moments: that I could damn well do it. The local press was well aware of it. The *Evening Phoenix* described my home run against St. Pius X as "a mammoth two-run blast over the center-field fence." The *Daily Local News* in West Chester published a story that mentioned my relationship with Lasorda and my batting-practice privileges with the Dodgers. The Boyertown coach, Dick Ludy, told one of the papers, "Piazza's the finest hitter in the league. He's the finest hitter I've seen. He's really a prospect."

Anyway, we once again lost the league to Boyertown and fell short of our expectations. The most vivid memory of that disappointing season might have been the bus trip home from Perkiomen Valley. I was sitting in the back, right behind Tony Nattle and Joe Pizzica. They liked to dip Copenhagen tobacco, so they turned around and offered me a chaw. The next time they turned around, I was throwing up out the window. If you ask my teammates, that seems to be the thing I'm best remembered for as a high school ballplayer.

At Phoenixville High, there was a tradition by which the seniors would spend a week on the Jersey Shore after graduation. Naturally, that week fell during the American Legion season. Doc coached our Legion team, as well, and his rule was that it was okay to go to the shore as long as you made it back for the games, the drive was a little under two hours. Well, I missed a game. When I came back for the next one, Doc didn't start me.

By around the fifth inning, I was still in the dugout and my father had had enough. He stormed over to me and said, "Get your stuff! We're gettin' the hell out of here!" Doc was coaching third base at the time and sort of pretending not to notice what was going on, so there wouldn't be a scene. But it wasn't over. My dad believed that was the reason I lost out on the Andre Thornton Award at the end of the season. Andre Thornton was a power hitter for the Cleveland Indians who had played at Phoenixville High, and the Thornton Award was the big prize given annually to one of Doc's Legion players. Joe Weber won it that year, and my dad was *hot*. There were many occasions when he kept his feelings to himself, but this time he clashed with Doc. ("Come on," my mom said as we reminisced about it nearly a quarter of a century later, after a spaghetti dinner, "he clashed with everybody.") I just let Dad be Dad, and rolled with it. I didn't feel slighted. Weber was our best pitcher, and he earned it.

I was, however, selected to participate in the scouts games that were staged every year all over Pennsylvania. First came the regional events where, in addition to the games, the scouts put the players through tryouts. I think I ran a 7.2 in the sixty-yard dash, which probably got me scratched off a few scorecards right there. The scouts seemed to like my arm strength, though, which was something they hadn't seen when they watched me play first base. From the tryouts, they selected teams for the second round, and from there, guys were picked to play in the statewide east-west game in Boyertown. After my junior year, I had been invited to the first game and tryout but didn't make it any further. My senior year, I was chosen for the next round along with my teammate, Brett Smiley, the cousin of former major-league pitcher John Smiley. We drove together to the game—and couldn't find the damn thing. Got totally lost. I don't know if I'd have made the big east-west game that year, but the odds are that I would have.

I saw Mike at the Legion all-star game in Copley, Pennsylvania, right outside of Allentown. Before that, I'd seen him at the Phoenixville High School field and distinctly recall that he hit a line drive that took two seconds to hit the school building. You could see that he had the power and was not done physically maturing yet. You could see him getting bigger. He was a slow runner, but he had what we call a quick bat. He got to the ball quickly with his hands and wrists.

I typed up a report and turned in the "follow." A follow means he's a player and I or any scout would have interest in following him. I put down his worth at between four and five thousand dollars, and said that he'd be signable for that amount. Then I faxed it to our office in New York. My job was to make one report on a player and send it out, and then it's up to the teams to follow my report or not.

He was out there for anybody who wanted him. And nobody did. It surprised me, because he had power and you could see he was going to be a bigger kid. I have a copy of that report in my den, framed. The original's in Cooperstown.

           —Brad Kohler, scout, Major League Scouting Bureau

I attended a couple of other tryouts. One was at East Stroudsburg University. Another was put on by the Dodgers at some small college where I stayed in a motel with my dad. The reception was lukewarm. Teams recognized that I had some power, and also that I didn't have a true position. Most first basemen were left-handed. I was a right-handed first baseman who couldn't run and wasn't all that slick around the bag. Looking back, I might have been a better prospect as a slugging left fielder, the svelte version of Greg Luzinski.

Then the draft came, and I sat by the phone, and the draft was over.

All of a sudden, blowing off high school didn't seem like such a swell idea. I hadn't expected to go in the first round, or any such thing, but even to the end, in spite of all the signs, I'd been unable—or maybe unwilling—to actually believe that *not a single team* would find me draftable. I guess that was my first heavy dose of baseball reality. It was devastating.

For weeks, I was so depressed and distraught—pounding on my bed—that, finally, Vince and my dad bought me a brand-new Fisher stereo system, just to cheer me up. Vince said, "This is from us and the family. We love you." I still have that stereo.

A couple of buddies of mine were going into the Marines, and that sounded okay to me. I even took the test, and scored better than I had on any high school exam. Military recruiters were calling the house. It felt like my best option. If nothing else, it would give me a chance to mature, physically and socially.

My dad said, "No way in hell."

Then he made a phone call.

CHAPTER FIVE

The term is *goombah*, which is something like a godfather but not exactly. Contrary to what a lot of people thought for a long time, Tommy Lasorda is not my godfather. He's actually the godfather to my youngest brother, Tommy. With me, he had a less formal but, thankfully, very practical relationship. As an elder, advisor, and uncle figure—my goombah—Lasorda maneuvered me, step by step, from high school to professional baseball. And always in cahoots with his friend, my father.

At least some of that might not have been so necessary if I'd been more responsible about my schoolwork and realistic about my draft status. As it was, I was in dire need of an intervention. The summer of 1986 was sailing along and I was splashing around in a life jacket, just hoping to find land in the fall. And not just *anywhere*.

Even in my predicament, I was audacious enough to dream big. In spite of their apparent indifference, I still thought I could play for the Miami Hurricanes. And I had two reasons to believe it. One was my ability to hit a baseball, which I never doubted. And the other was the clout in my corner, the one-two combination of relentless father and highly placed goombah.

Not long after the draft, my dad mentioned to Tommy that I only had eyes for Miami—it seemed more accessible than Texas, since we already had a place in Boynton Beach, and much more my style—and Tommy stuck his neck out for me. He called the Miami coach, Ron Fraser, who, like just about everybody else who mattered in baseball, was a friend of his. It was a pretty big favor Tommy was requesting. He was asking Fraser to take a chance on a slow kid from a small school in a northern state who didn't actually have a position or the academic standing to qualify. Needless to say, Fraser didn't leap at the opportunity.

In the meantime, I moonlighted for an adult team called the Skippack Skippers and put my sledgehammer skills to work on the land by the house we were building in Valley Forge, overlooking the national park that preserves the location where, in the winter of 1777, George Washington camped and trained his twelve thousand men of the Continental Army. Washington himself slept in a barn on what is now our property, which covers sixty-five acres, most of which were littered with major rocks and boulders. The ones in the vicinity of the house couldn't stay there, so Dad designated Vince, Danny, and me as field labor, charged with pulling those suckers out of the lower ground and hauling them up to the high spot where an Italian stonemason would craft them into walls between the house and road. Vince ran the backhoe, Danny drove the truck, and my contribution was blowing up the boulders with my trusty sledgehammer.

It was a stroke of genius on my dad's part, because the job didn't detract from my primary occupation, which, of course, was training for baseball. Frankly, it wasn't fair. Vince and Danny put in long hours pushing the rocks into piles, where they would sit until I came by a couple of times a week on my breaks from the batting cage. But if my brothers resented the fact that I was on a separate program, they never really showed it. It was just part of the fabric of our family.

For the record, the batting cage made the move, too, more or less. Dad actually changed the design of the house to stretch the basement, so he could put the cage down there. He also painted the back wall—the hitting background—white instead of green, so it would train my eyes to pick out the ball.

That summer, through my father's arrangements with Tommy, I also spent a few charmed weeks as a junior counselor at Mark Cresse's baseball camp in California. Cresse was kind enough to put me up at his house, and to take me with him to the stadium every day around one thirty so I could work out on the field before serving as the Dodgers' batboy that night. As usual, I don't think I impressed anybody with my footwork around first base; but Lasorda took note of my power. Even batting left-handed, I'd muscle the ball high in the air, and Tommy would nod like he knew something. Through the good graces of him and my dad, I had now, at the age of seventeen, batted in three major-league ballparks.

I was in my element during those weeks with Cresse. Mark's son, Brad, was around ten and loved professional wrestling as much as I did. Naturally, we went at it. Brad would try to put the pretzel hold on me, and I'd respond in the spirit of Randy "Macho Man" Savage, who, as Randy Poffo, had actually played minor-league ball with Cresse in the Cardinals' system. It was all good until one day I thought I'd really hurt Brad with a pile driver. I guess he wasn't damaged too badly, though, because, as a catcher, he went on to become a two-time All-American at LSU, leading the nation in home runs. I'd like to think he took after me a little bit, hitting-wise. He certainly had me down pat when he mimicked my routine at the plate, which involved tugging on my shirt and holding up my hand for time until I was good and ready—trying, you know, to put the confrontation on my terms. I got it all from watching Juan Samuel with the Phillies.

While I was in Los Angeles, I had a very welcome visitor. Fraser had sent one of his assistants, Dave Scott, to take a look at me. The tryout was at Dodger Stadium, which was a nice advantage in itself but not the biggest one. I also had the good fortune of getting to take my cuts against one of the best batting-practice pitchers in the big leagues. Cresse was laying them right in there for me, and I was crushing the ball with a wooden bat. I thought I did okay at first base, too, but Scott didn't give a hoot about my glove. He was actually kind of freaking out about the way I hit. Knowing I didn't have the grades to get into Miami, he said, "Okay, this is what we're going to have to do. First, you have to go to this freshman seminar . . ."

It amounted to a couple of classes I was required to take before the semester started, in order to qualify. So I went home, got my stuff, and headed down the coast to be a freshman All-American.

Yeah, right.

There was no big scholarship waiting for me. And not much playing time. Miami had been to the College World Series the previous spring and had *won it* the year before. I needed to be pretty damn impressive to turn the heads of the coaching staff and earn a spot in the lineup, even for the exhibition schedule we played in the fall. I wasn't. Fraser asked my dad, "Didn't you ever put a *glove* on his hand?"

In one of the fall scrimmages, I was relishing the rare chance to play first base when a batter hit me a high chopper off the turf. The sun was setting directly behind home plate and I botched the play when the ball was momentarily caught in it. As I reached the dugout after the inning, the bench coach, Brad Kelley, asked me what happened. I told him. He thought I was being a smartass. He said, "You lost a *ground ball* in the *sun?*"

That set the tone. Kelley knew his baseball—he later became the head coach—but he and I saw eye to eye on practically nothing. The Miami style called for everybody to sprint to their positions, sprint off the field, and sprint back to the dugout after an out. My attitude was, I had seen a lot of big leaguers make outs, and they didn't run back to the dugout. Admittedly, I was a little too big-league for my britches.

It was especially bad form for a guy as overmatched as I was. I hit bombs in batting practice—my teammates called me the best five o'clock hitter in the country—but still had to *learn* how to hit. I was totally unprepared, for instance, when, in an intrasquad game, I had to face a senior named Kevin Sheary, a good, polished pitcher who got drafted by the Mariners. It was the first time I'd ever seen a slider. I almost shit my pants. I was like "What was *that?*" It was the slider from hell.

But if I was taken aback by the talent around me on the baseball team, I was almost in awe of Miami's football team. That was the year the Hurricanes were ranked number one in the country, went to the Fiesta Bowl against Penn State, and got off the plane wearing army fatigues. Vinny Testaverde, Alonzo Highsmith, Michael Irvin, Melvin Bratton, Jerome Brown, Gregg Rakoczy, Brian and Bennie Blades . . . they were monsters. It was impressive just to walk into the cafeteria, down by the athletic department, and see them all at the training table. It was even more impressive to see them in the weight room.

I kind of clicked with the football mentality and began to embrace it. I went so far as to have a barber buzz my hair, marine-style, and shave grooves into the sides, like Brian Bosworth, the controversial All-American linebacker from Oklahoma. The Boz. When I flew back to Philly for the holidays and Dad picked up me at the airport, he took a look at that haircut, flew into a rage, and threatened to leave me there.

The baseball season started shortly after I got back to school, and I settled into life on the bench. One day, though, after watching me mash the ball in batting practice before a game against Creighton, the coaches went ahead and let me start—probably out of curiosity. I think I swung at the first pitch I saw. Ended up 0 for 4. I was *way* too anxious. Had no concept of taking a pitch; no concept of hitting in general. No approach. I was just *swinging*. If a guy had thrown me a first-pitch meatball, I might have sunk a sailboat on Biscayne Bay; but why would they?

I didn't play for weeks after that. I thought, well, there goes my one shot to be an All-American. I just wasn't ready. I was probably the youngest guy on the team and extremely inexperienced, not to mention immature. In my six games, I had one hit in nine at-bats, a single against Georgetown.

My single highlight was a tournament at the Superdome in New Orleans. I got to stay at the Hilton, take in Bourbon Street, meet a couple of ballgirls from the University of Florida, and enjoy a few adult beverages because the drinking age there was eighteen. I was quite pleased with myself when I had a hurricane for the first time and didn't get sick. New Orleans, for me, was not just the coolest trip of the season, but the *only* trip, unless you count the quick one to DeLand, Florida, to play the Stetson Hatters. The first time they left me behind, I was the only guy who hadn't made the traveling squad. I called my dad to moan about it, and he said, "That's not right. That's not gonna happen next year. We're gonna talk to Tommy and get you transferred out of there."

But while Miami was all wrong for me, baseball-wise, it wasn't a lost year, by any stretch. I learned humility, among other things. I really thought I was the cat's meow in high school and figured I'd bust through college with everything going my way. My rude awakening made me think, hmm, maybe I'm not cut out for baseball. Maybe I should actually *study*. I was getting a little financial aid—maybe a thousand dollars a semester—but twelve credits at the University of Miami cost a lot of money. I realized that, hey, my mom and dad are shelling out quite a bit for this school; I should probably try to get something out of it. I won't say that my grades were good, but for the first time I started to apply myself academically.

To that end, one of my ballplayer roommates set a good example—a little first baseman with glasses named Bobby Hernandez, who was a premed student. We called him Stump. Stump clearly possessed the heart and stomach to become a doctor. He had a little dissecting kit, and—I still can't believe he did this—he'd sit me down, sterilize his scalpel or probe or whatever it was, and lance the pimples all around my back and shoulders. It was disgusting. One time I had a big boil that he jabbed and popped, and the thing squirted all over his glasses. Stump goes, "Oh, look! It got on my glasses!"

Aside from pimple popping, the biggest physical benefit of my time at the U was the weight program. As fanatical as I'd always been about getting strong, I was brand-new to sophisticated weight training. In high school, I did curls and whatnot on one of those sit-down stations with the stacks, which was all we had. My dad had bought me a set of cement-filled weights for Christmas one year, and every night, before I went to bed, I ripped off fifty curls and fifty presses with the dumbbells. During the day, I'd do bench presses with the bar. But as far as training systematically at a serious, vibrant, well-equipped gym, alongside motivated, high-level athletes, I'd experienced nothing remotely resembling Miami.

The football guys had their own time set aside, and if they happened to be in there when we were, obviously we were second fiddle. The baseball team was on a totally different program, but it was specific and probably pretty advanced for the times. I thought, What do I have to *squat* for?

I followed the script, but also did my own thing. I loved the steel sound of the weights knocking against each other, that *clink, clink, clink*. The first time I bench-pressed 185, I felt like I was really *doing* something. That propelled me. I got stronger and liked it. For me, though, weight training was about more than just adding muscle. It was a way to build up stamina for the wear and tear of a season. Not that there's a whole lot of wear and tear in nine at-bats . . . but I was hooked. I started reading magazines about proper training and the right supplements to take. With the training table available to us, I ate more. It was the first time I'd ever gone so heavy on salad, fish, and meat—all the food they liked to serve the football players. I'd also run out to the health food store for protein powder and the original Joe Weider vitamin packs. To this day, I believe in protein, supplements, and shakes.

There was another little training device I came up with after watching one of the backup quarterbacks, a black guy with huge hands, throw the football in a way I couldn't believe. It just impressed me somehow. So I went to a guy I knew on the football team and gave him twenty bucks to steal me a football. The Wilson 1001 with the half stripe. I bought a couple, actually, and loved to toss them around with other baseball players. There's no question that it improved my throwing.

Since I was only eighteen at the end of my freshman year, I had one more season of Legion ball left and finally made the Pennsylvania East-West all-star game. I also hooked up with the Skippack Skippers again, essentially regrouping while I tried to figure out what was next. Accepting the fact that I was miscast as a Hurricane and wouldn't be missed, I had cut my ties with Miami U—but not with Miami the city. This time, when my dad talked to Tommy, Tommy said, "Well, what about Miami-Dade?"

Back then, it was officially Miami-Dade North, a busy community college with an excellent baseball program and another coach—Demie "Doc" Mainieri—who knew the right people; a lot of his players had signed professional contracts. So I started a dialogue with Doc Mainieri. I think he might have been a little annoyed at being put on the spot. He wanted to accommodate Tommy but didn't know the first thing about me. Kind of grudgingly, Doc said, "Well, I've got some pretty good players down here, but come on down."

By then I'd finagled a car out of my dad, a red Honda Prelude, so I drove south to the beats of heavy metal and took a one-bedroom apartment on Sans Souci Boulevard in North Miami, directly across the bay from Bal Harbour. I'd walk over the bridge to Bal Harbour, stare into the windows of those fancy stores, and think, I'm never going to be able to shop here. I couldn't even eat lunch in that neighborhood. Every day, I'd have one meal in the school cafeteria and gobble down a Subway sandwich for dinner. I knew the Subway lady by name. Once I had tuna sandwiches two nights in a row and she said, "You on a diet, big boy? You're eating a lot of tuna fish lately."

We started right off with fall practice, and it was evident from the outset that I was in a great environment for baseball. The first time we took infield, I thought we looked like a pro team. We had kids from Hialeah, Miami Lakes, several Cubans—no shortage of talent, including a good catcher, Pete Gonzalez, who was of Cuban descent and would become a teammate of mine in the minor leagues. There was something pure about the program. Miami-Dade was a fun place to play. I was encouraged.

That, in fact, was by design. Doc Mainieri maintained a climate of encouragement, and I got some more of it from his son, Paul, who was coaching at St. Thomas University and eventually won a national championship at LSU. Before a practice game against Florida International, Paul gave me a perfect pep talk. He knew I'd been disheartened by my experience at Miami and told me that there's simply no way of knowing how things will play out in baseball; you've got to just keep plugging. It was exactly what I needed to hear. I'd expected everything to come fast and easy, and Paul was educating me to the hard fact that sometimes—*most* of the time—the game doesn't work that way. By the time spring came around, I was in good shape, physically and mentally, and it showed.

At one point, Doc actually scheduled an exhibition game with Miami, and as I was taking batting practice, Ron Fraser walked up to my dad—it was amazing how many games Dad was able to make—and said, "He looks pretty good." The way my father tells it, Fraser's assistant, my old nemesis Brad Kelley, strolled by at just that moment and muttered, "Yeah, he's a five o'clock hitter."

Later in the day, Fraser made a point of asking my dad where I'd be going to school the next year and mentioned that he'd like to have me back at Miami. Dad told him he wanted to talk to Tommy about the chances of getting me drafted. Fraser shook his head and said, "I don't think he's ready for that yet."

I probably wasn't, but my father was undaunted and unremitting in those days. He was like the Wizard of Oz back there behind the curtain, pulling the strings. In the fall, through Tommy, he had arranged a day for me at the Orioles' Instructional League camp in West Palm Beach. The connection was Tommy's (and his) buddy Eddie Liberator's, who was now scouting for Baltimore after a long career with the Dodgers. They fed me some soup and an apple—I thought, man, is *this* what they get in the minor leagues?—gave me an Orioles hat, put me in an Orioles uniform, and stuck me in one of their instructional games. I didn't knock anybody's socks off. No matter: when my dad came down in the spring, he was at it again. This time he packed me into the car and took me around the state on the Tommy Lasorda Tour of spring training. The first visit was Port Charlotte, where the Texas Rangers trained. Their manager was Bobby Valentine, who was a protégé and favorite of Tommy. Bobby pitched to me in the cage, which went well, then took me out to the field for some defensive drills at first base, which didn't.

But the key stop was Dodgertown in Vero Beach, Tommy's personal playground. This was 1988, the year the Dodgers would beat Oakland in the World Series with Kirk Gibson limping up to pinch-hit and somehow coming through with the walk-off home run against Dennis Eckersley to win game one. The Dodgers had signed Gibson as a free agent that winter, and he asserted his will immediately. When I visited Vero Beach, it was just a few days after a teammate had put eye-black in Gibson's hat and Gibson had gone off, screaming at everybody that this wasn't how it was going to be, that he wasn't there to screw around but to work like hell and win a World Series. Or something like that. He backed it up by earning the National League MVP award. Anyway, I took some batting practice and people seemed to be impressed.

Then Tommy walked over and brought up the notion of me becoming a catcher. He had discussed it with my dad and Joe Ferguson, who had caught for Tommy and was now coaching for him. They were all gathered around and Joe said, "Well, let's see him throw." So I went behind home plate and Ferguson told me not to bother crouching, let's just play catch. He kept backing up until he was at second base, at which point I let it rip a few times. I think I was seeing the results from throwing the football so much. Afterward, Joe walked up to my dad and said, "Hey, he's got a great arm!"

At Miami-Dade, though, I was still a first baseman, and hit well enough to justify it. Midway through the season, I was rolling along—batting around .360 with a few home runs, including a walk-off against Indian River Junior College—and positioned to attract some attention heading into the main scouting weeks. Then, on a play at first base, a runner bashed his knee into my left hand and split my knuckles apart. Tore a ligament. The doctor put me in a cast for three weeks or so. I wanted to get back on the field so badly that I threw batting practice with my cast on. There wasn't much rehab involved after it came off, and I was hitting again by the end of the season. I finished at .364.

Miami-Dade was only a two-year program, which meant that I was done there. I didn't see myself heading back to the University of Miami—I suspect that when Fraser had brought up the idea to my father, he was just being polite—so Doc said he'd help me get into another four-year school. Then he told me he wasn't having any luck. It so happened, though, that he had a backup plan. He suggested I go to St. Thomas, a Catholic university in Miami that had a strong NAIA baseball program, to play for his son, Paul.

Of course, my dad was involved with these discussions, and he had two things to say about it. One, he still wanted to see if I could get drafted. And two, if I went back to school, he wanted me to catch. Honestly, I had worked hard on my defense at first base and thought I was halfway decent at the college level, but I guess nobody was confusing me with Keith Hernandez. My dad thought I might be more appealing to the scouts if I projected as a catcher. Doc said, okay, if I went to St. Thomas, I could catch. They wanted my bat. As it turned out, Paul Mainieri got a job to coach at the U.S. Air Force Academy the next year and Al Avila took over as the St. Thomas coach. His dad, Ralph Avila, was the Latin America scout for the Dodgers, so—through Tommy, of course—there was still a connection. Ralph called my dad to suggest that their sons get together.

I liked the idea of staying in Miami and figured that was probably what I'd do. My dad, however, had already checked out the Phillies' schedule to see when the Dodgers were coming to town.

To my knowledge, the first time the concept of a courtesy draft pick came to public attention was in Kevin Kerrane's book, *Dollar Sign on the Muscle*, published in 1984 as an inside look into the world of baseball scouting. The arrangement is that, as a favor, a team will devote a low-round pick to a player who's important to someone in or close to the organization. It's done not with the intention of actually *signing* the player, necessarily, but perhaps to make him more attractive to college recruiters.

Ed Liberatore—who, by bringing Ted Williams to our house, had already blessed me with the favor of a lifetime—told my dad that maybe the Orioles would do that for me. Dad had called Eddie to advise him that I was going to be *catching* a game for the Skippack Skippers, the grown-up team I occasionally freelanced for, and to offer him a ride, which was accepted. Unfortunately, we were playing Norristown, a team that knew what it was doing. Norristown ran wild on me, stealing base after base. But I smoked a long home run to center field and then another one over the pavilion, and Liberatore said something like "I don't know about his catching, Vince, but damn, that kid can *hit*."

That's when he mentioned about the courtesy pick. First, though, he would have to call Roland Hemond, the Orioles' general manager, to sell the idea.

Since my dad was the one in the middle of all this, I'll just let *him* tell the rest:

I said, "Oh, Eddie, you'd do that?"

He said, "Yeah."

So then I called Tommy Lasorda and told him I'd just talked to Eddie Liberatore and what he was going to do. And I told him about Mike catching a little.

Tommy said, "Catching, huh? Well, all right, wait till I come in [to Philadelphia, with the Dodgers]."

So sure as hell the Dodgers come in and we go down to Vet Stadium. This is a week before the draft. We go into Tommy's office and he said, "Michael, go get set up." You know, put on the gear. And he's asking me, "Do you think he really wants to catch?"

I said, "Yeah, Tom."

So Joe Ferguson was there. Tommy says, "Hey, Joe, come here. I want you to take Michael down to the field and work him out as a catcher and tell me what you think." Then he said, "Hey, Beach." Beach was the bullpen coach, Mark Cresse, and he was really great at hitting pop-ups.

So we go down through the tunnel and I'm sitting on the bench watching and Beach is hitting him pop-ups and he's catching everything. Mike was doing a nice job. So they get him behind the plate and he's throwing down to second base and they're out there about twenty minutes. Afterward, I walked up to Ferguson and said, "Joe, what do you think?"

He said, "This kid can make it as a catcher."

I said, "You serious?"

He said, "Yeah."

I said, "You mind if I tell Tommy?"

He said, "Sure, go tell him."

So I go down through the tunnel to Tommy's office and who's sitting on the couch but Ed Liberatore! Tommy said, "How'd he make out?"

I said, "Ferguson said he could make it as a catcher."

Tommy stands up behind the desk, he looks at Eddie, he's got that crooked finger, and he points that finger at him and he says, "Don't you fuck with that kid, you understand? We're gonna draft him!"

Then he turned back to me and said, "Fergie said that?"

I said, "Yeah."

He said, "Don't bullshit me."

I said, "No, Tom."

So Tommy picks up the phone and dials Ben Wade, who was the scouting director for the Dodgers. He tells Ben, "I want you to do me a favor. I want you to draft Michael Piazza."

I'm sitting there and Eddie's looking at me and laughing a little bit. Tommy says [into the phone], "Here's his father. He'll give you his age and where he went to school and all of that."

We get off the phone and Liberatore says, "Hey, can I go down and say hello to Mike?"

And Tommy says, "Yeah, but don't you fuck with him!"

So we're walking down the tunnel and Eddie puts his arm around me and says, "Vince, I'd rather see him as a Dodger than an Oriole." Eddie had only been with the Orioles for about a year or so at that time. He'd been with the Dodgers for thirty-something years, and Tommy and him were like brothers. He knew about my relationship with Tommy, and Mike's.

Then he said, "Do you mind if I tell him?"

He calls him over and tells him and Mike's all choked up and so am I. We can't believe this. He's gonna play! He's gonna go to the minor leagues!

—Vince Piazza

It was a pretty interesting summer. I caught a few more games for Skippack and actually had the game-winning hit for the South team in the Perkiomen Valley Twilight League all-star game. I also enrolled for the fall semester at St. Thomas University, just in case. And on June 3, in the sixty-second round, the Los Angeles Dodgers selected me with the 1,390th pick of the 1988 draft.

That wasn't the last round of the draft, but it was the last round the Dodgers picked in. If it hadn't been for Tommy, they'd have stopped after the sixty-first.

The way he tells it, "I sent five of my friends from five different organizations out to see Michael play, and nobody wanted to sign him. I *ordered* the Dodgers to draft him. I said, 'I don't give a shit where you draft him, but *draft* him.'

"They weren't doing *me* a favor. I was doing *them* a favor."

CHAPTER SIX

When it came to baseball, I was a hopeless romantic. I played it, practiced it, watched it, read about it, revered it, genuinely loved it, and always assumed it would love me back. Or at least *call* me back.

I thought my fairy tale was beginning on the day I was drafted. Whatever the round, I was rarin' to go—just waiting for the phone to ring or the contract to show up or Sandy Koufax to knock on my door, however it worked. I got my mailgram from the Dodgers telling me I'd been picked. I saw my little name in small type in *Baseball America*. It was cool. I was on my way, feeling good and all set for the next step. Ready to sign, rock and roll. Mentally and emotionally, my bags were packed. Let's get this party started!

. . . Nothing. Silence. Emptiness.

A month went by. Finally, my dad did what he always did when my baseball career was at a standstill. Dialed up Tommy. "What the hell is going on here? Nobody has called."

So Tommy got in touch with Ben Wade, the Dodgers' scouting director, and Ben phoned my dad to say, "Gosh, Vince, I thought it was a courtesy draft." Dad told him that, whatever it was, I wanted to *get going.*

"But we never saw him play a game."

"Well, Tommy told you about him."

"If we're going to sign him, we need to see him play."

That was the opening my dad was looking for. "All right," he said, "I'll put him on a plane and send him out there and you can work him out. If you like him, give me back my money for the plane fare."

By then, I was prepared to follow through at St. Thomas and play NAIA ball if it came to that. I knew the trip to Los Angeles was my best chance—maybe my *only* chance—so I booked a flight and stayed with the general manager of my dad's Acura dealership out there. I couldn't wait to get to

Dodger Stadium, which is probably not a healthy state of mind when you're from out of town and navigating the Los Angeles freeways in a spanking-new Acura. Somehow, it survived.

My nerves settled down when I stepped into the park and saw that Mark Cresse would be throwing to me. It was like the Miami tryout all over again—same place, same pitcher. And I expected the same result. I was more than confident; I was *pumped*. Meanwhile, Tommy was wandering around the outfield, trying not to get in the way, and Ben Wade was eyeballing me skeptically alongside a couple scouts he had brought in, Gib Bodet and Bobby Darwin. Tommy has said that Gib Bodet was the only scout he knew who actually *liked* me back then.

With Cresse serving up cookies to my sweet spots, I don't know how many balls I blasted into the stands. Twenty? Some of them came down in the top rows of the stadium.

There's a special feeling, a surge of satisfaction, that goes along with crushing a ball that hard. At that moment, though, it couldn't match the rush I got from taking the bull by the horns and slamming it to the turf. I knew I had done it. As the balls rattled around the cheap seats and I saw the astonishment on the faces of the Dodger guys, my fading dream sprang back to life. I began to think of myself as a professional baseball player.

Ben Wade, in particular, was beside himself. He didn't know what to do. Fortunately, Tommy did.

When we took a break, I walked over and said to Ben, "What do you think?"

He said, "Get me his schedule. I want to go back and see him play."

I said, "Wait a minute, hold it. You're telling me you're going to go three thousand miles to see a guy play who you drafted in the sixty-second round? Come on, Ben, you're talking to *me*. Let me ask you a question. How about if I brought a shortstop in here and he hit the ball the way that boy just hit the ball? Would you want to go see him play or would you sign him?"

He said, "I'd sign him."

I said, "Okay, how about if I brought a catcher in here and he hit the way that boy just did. Would you want to go see him play or would you sign him?"

He said, "I'd want to sign him."

I said, "Okay then, sign him."

He said, "But he's a first baseman."

I said, "He's a catcher now. Sign him."

—Tom Lasorda, manager, Los Angeles Dodgers

After he talked with Tommy, Wade asked me, "You're going to be a catcher?" When I said yeah, he told me to throw a little bit. I threw so hard my arm *still* hurts. Darwin and Bodet were looking at each other like, "How the hell did everybody miss this guy?"

Then we all went inside and Wade slipped away to call my dad. In one quick conversation, they worked out a tentative deal ensuring that the Dodgers would pay for my education if I didn't stick.

"We've decided we want to sign you," he said when he returned. "We're willing to give you a fifteen-thousand-dollar bonus and we don't want you to play this year. We're going to send you to the Instructional League in the fall and we're going to try to make you a catcher."

Before he even said "fifteen," I was like, "Okay, I'll sign!" He could have said fifteen bucks or fifteen tacos. Fifteen thousand dollars sounded to me like a pretty sweet bonus for a guy drafted in the sixty-second round as a favor.

But even then, in spite of the agreement and the game plan and the baseballs rattling around in the seats of Dodger Stadium, there was no contract presented. Nothing to actually put the pen to and make the whole thing official and get me into a damn uniform.

I flew back home, more time passed, and, once again, with my career in a holding pattern, my dad called Tommy. And Tommy called Ben Wade. And Ben Wade called my dad. It was the same old circle.

"Gee, Vince, I'm sorry," Ben said. "We're signing our first-round pick [a pitcher, Bill Bene, who never made it to the big leagues] and I couldn't get back to you. I'll send Dick Teed to see you."

Dick Teed was an area scout who was on his way to Montreal. He called and told my dad he'd meet us in the Philadelphia airport. Dad didn't care for that. "Dick," he said, "you know, we'd like to have you at the house—get a picture and all that. *Something.*"

"Well, I've got to sign this kid in Montreal," Teed told him. "He's quite a player." He was talking about an outfielder named Marc Griffin, going on and on about him.

"All right, we'll see you down to the airport."

When we got there, Teed was still jabbering on about Marc Griffin, telling us that it was going to take about a hundred thousand and a quarter to get him signed. My dad said, "Dick, do yourself a favor. Forget that kid and give *this* kid the money. You'll be better off."

"Like shit we will."

In three years, Marc Griffin was out of the organization. In five, he was out of the game. Never made it past Double-A.

Of course, I had the advantage of signing in an airport. It's a motivational edge.

The deal was Instructional League, and the drill was to learn how to catch. My instructors were Kevin Kennedy, who had been a minor-league catcher (and would later manage in the big leagues) and Johnny Roseboro, who had caught Koufax and Don Drysdale on some of the greatest teams the Dodgers ever had. It was like the first day of school.

Kennedy was all about mechanics and intensity. Roseboro was just the opposite. He'd mostly sit around smoking a cigarette and talking about Koufax and Drysdale, which had its benefits. With Johnny, there was always a lesson-of-the-day. I still remember a few of them:

"Hey, babe, fifty thousand people in the stands. [Drag on the cigarette.] Don't let them see you throw it into center field."

"Move your feet, babe! Cha, cha, cha! Cha, cha, cha! Move those feet!"

"Hey, babe, sometimes you gotta go out there [to the mound] and let the wind blow a little bit."

"Gotta be a speed cop. [Drag on the cigarette.] Roy Campanella used to say, 'Go ahead and steal. The speed cop'll catch ya!'"

"Hey, babe, you grab that ball, and if someone comes to take you out, you freakin' put that ball right in their chops. [Drag on the cigarette.] I remember one time Frank Robinson was coming around third, and I had the ball in plenty of time and I'm thinkin', he's my homeboy, he's my brother, he ain't gonna do nothin' to me." At that point, Roseboro pulled up the pants of his uniform and showed me a three-inch gash on his leg. "That motherfucker almost *filleted* my ass!"

We were divided into a blue group and a white group, and the catchers would do our early work on the little half field at HoHoKam Park, where the Cubs trained (Instructional League involved multiple teams in one place)— blue group one day, white the next. I thought, why can't I go to *both* sessions? I mean, I had a lot of ground to make up as a catcher. So the second day, when it was supposed to be a day off for our group, I showed up. Kevin Kennedy was like "What are *you* doing here?"

I said, "Can't I work out today?"

He paused for a moment, nodded his head, and said, "I fuckin' like that! Yeah, sure." Of course, a couple of the other catchers heard about it and called me a kiss-ass.

One of the catchers I didn't get along with particularly well was Eric Ganino, the Dodgers' twenty-eighth-round draft choice that year from California, who seemed to me like something of a wiseass. We weren't really enemies, but there was some bickering and jockeying going on between us. One day, during an intrasquad game, I was having a tough time catching and Eric was letting me know about it from the dugout. Being real clever like I am, I yelled back, "Fuck you!" This other catcher, D. J. Floyd, thought I was yelling at *him*, and suddenly charged me from the bench. It was on. We ended up having a full-scale, intrasquad brawl right there on the field. D. J. Floyd fell down at one point and I yelled at him, "Go fuck yourself, D.J.! I could punch you in the face right now!" At the various fields around the complex, the other teams were staring at us and wondering, What the hell is wrong with the *Dodgers*?

I did have a *few* friends. We were scheduled to stay in Phoenix at the Maricopa Inn, and my roommate was a left-handed pitcher named Jim Poole. He suggested we get a couple more roommates and an apartment, so we rented one along with another pitcher, Jeff Hartsock, and a first baseman named Brian Traxler. I remember two things about living with those guys. One was going out with them to a bar, getting drunk, and dancing to the Romantics song "What I Like About You," which was not a proud moment in my life. The other was watching the World Series with them when Kirk Gibson hit that incredible home run. It was one of those "where were you when" moments.

Instructional League was also my introduction to Eric Karros, who would become my best friend in baseball. Eric was one of numerous players there who brought in big credentials from big colleges—he was the sixth-round selection that year out of UCLA—and here I was, a courtesy pick in the sixty-second round from a junior college where I was hurt half the season, trying to cope with a new position and some of the best breaking pitches I'd ever seen. A lot of my teammates wondered what I was doing there, and at times *I* did, too. I wasn't getting a lot of positive reinforcement in those days. So it made an impression when Karros walked up to me one morning after I'd taken a round of batting practice and said, "Man, you've got a lot of power."

The most important thing the Instructional League taught me about catching was that I needed to do a whole lot more of it. That spurred my dad and Tommy into action again.

This time, Tommy's idea was a novel one. For their young Latin American prospects, the Dodgers operated a winter camp in the southeastern countryside of the Dominican Republic. It had been built in a sugarcane field about forty miles from Santo Domingo and was run by Ralph Avila, the Latin American scout who had talked to my dad about me playing for his son, Al, at St. Thomas University. All parties agreed that a little basic training at a Dominican boot camp would be a hell of a way for me to spend the next three months.

That list of parties, however, didn't include anyone in the Dodgers' front office, notably Charlie Blaney, who had just taken over as the club's minor-league director. When Blaney found out I was down there, he put in a call to my dad and played dumb. Asked him where I was. My dad played dumber and said he didn't know. Blaney said yes you do. My dad said, well then, talk to Tommy about it, which Blaney did. I don't know if Tommy and Blaney ever actually came to an agreement on the subject, but the bottom line was that I stayed on as the first American player ever to enlist at Campo Las Palmas.

There were fifty or so prospects in camp, and we slept in a rustic dormitory that was favored by tarantulas. Needless to say, I chose a top bunk. The Latin guys didn't seem to find the tarantulas particularly creepy; they actually *played* with them. I tried to fit in with the culture the best I could, but that was one line I didn't cross. In fact, I never quite came to terms with the whole relationship between Dominicans and nature. There were chickens on the grounds, laying eggs that would be hard-boiled for our breakfast— some of the chickens themselves might have been dinner—and the night watchman's job was to keep the stray dogs away. He was an old guy with a little red hat and a shotgun, and every other night or so he'd shoot down a couple of dogs. I'd be listening to my heavy metal and suddenly hear *Boom! Boom!* Everybody'd go running out to see. One night I watched him blow away a big Labrador retriever. It bled to death right in front of me.

I was happy to find a little gym on the premises, with some old dumbbells, barbells, and benches. I'd go in there and lift after dinner, which upset one of the motherly ladies who worked in the cafeteria. She scolded me: "You're going to get sick doing that!" I didn't have the heart to tell her that I was getting sick, all right, but not from the lifting. Actually, the food was a little skimpy by American standards but not worth complaining about. For most of the Dominican players—there were also a few from Honduras and Nicaragua, among other places—our little dining hall might have seemed like the Four Seasons. Still, whether it was from the lunch meat, the water,

the sugarcane juice, or just the cultural adjustment, there were plenty of times when my stomach had me on the run. I told my mom that I needed some familiar food. When my dad came to visit, he smuggled in a bunch of peanut butter and Carnation Instant Breakfast. Tommy made the trip with him, and I was sitting outside eating my lunch—a bowl of soup and a slim sandwich of mystery meat—when they walked up. Tommy took one look and said, "Jesus Christ! How do you eat this shit?"

My dad also treated me to a few weekends at the Jaragua Hotel in Santo Domingo, where Joe Ferguson stayed while he managed the organization's Licey team in the Dominican Winter League. When I was there, I partook liberally of the pasta, the Friday night meringue music, and the big bottles of Coke you could buy for a dime, although you had to put the bottle back in the rack when you were finished. Periodically, other players would come to town, and we'd hit the disco and drink Presidente beer. Santo Domingo became pretty familiar to me; often, after a long day at the camp, Ralph would drive me down to catch bullpens for the Licey pitchers.

I was grateful for the special privileges I was being afforded, and if my camp mates understandably resented me a little bit, they at least appreciated the effort I gave it. And my struggling attempts at Spanish. Some of the instructors—Ralph Avila, Leo Posada, Chico Fernandez—and the visiting coaches, like Johnny Roseboro, spoke English; but for the most part, I felt like the Latin players must feel when they come to play in the States. When we were riding our short bus to play the Astros or Cardinals and the other guys were telling jokes in their impossibly fast, slang-heavy Dominican Spanish, my couple of classes of foreign language at Phoenixville High gave me no chance whatsoever. I often wondered if the joke they were laughing at was on *me*. Manny Acta, who manages the Cleveland Indians, was an infielder for the Astros—it's hard to imagine now, with his bald head, but at the time he had big, fluffy hair—and years later he told me, "Yeah, I remember you down there. We were all talking about, 'Who's this gringo coming down here to play with us?'"

Among the players in camp was Pedro Martinez, who had just signed and turned seventeen. His brother, Ramon, had already made it to the big leagues, and he'd stop by to work out, as well. I caught Pedro the first time he threw in a game. After one pitch, honest to goodness, I thought I'd broken my hand. For a little guy, he threw so fucking hard I was stunned. He also had a hissing curveball and a nasty changeup. I thought, Who *is* this guy? He's gonna be unbelievable!

In retrospect, the most amazing thing was that, down in the Dominican,

Pedro Martinez was the nicest, sweetest guy in the world, always laughing and joking. When he came to the States, he seemed to turn instantly into something else. He was the most competitive son of a bitch you'd ever see. I mean, he ate gunpowder. More to the point, Pedro was just a little prick; that's about the only way I can describe him. I remember thinking, is this the same guy I knew at Campo Las Palmas? As our careers moved along, I had my issues with Pedro; but I'll say this: I wish the Dodgers hadn't traded him for Delino DeShields right after our rookie years. And I really liked Delino DeShields. I know it broke Pedro's heart to be separated from Ramon like that. He deeply loved his brother.

When I finally got home to Valley Forge, there was only time to catch a little rest, put back a few of the pounds I'd lost—thanks, Mom—and scoot down to Vero Beach for my first spring training.

In the late winter of 1989, I arrived in heaven. They called it Dodgertown.

What a place. The moment you pulled into Dodgertown, it was all baseball. Some guys might have wanted more, but not me. When a workout was over, what I wanted to do was play more baseball. At Dodgertown, you could do that. We'd play a four-hour spring training game, and then Tommy would roll out the cage and pitch to us for as long as we wanted. We worked, man. That was Tommy's philosophy—we fucking *worked*. Sunup to sundown. It was crazy. It was fantastic. These days, you never see anything like that. Guys are out of there by the fifth inning. Five and dive.

Tommy Lasorda was a master at generating enthusiasm—especially among the young players. Right from the beginning, he made us feel like real Dodgers. Tommy would frequently put the greenest kids from the lowest minor-league teams in major-league exhibition games. We'd play, say, a Bakersfield game, and then we'd hear on the walkie-talkie, "Piazza, Karros, Eric Young, up to the big-league field." We'd schlep up to the stadium and the game would be almost over. Maybe we'd hit, maybe we wouldn't; whatever. At the least, we'd sit in a big-league dugout next to pros like Kirk Gibson, Eddie Murray, Mike Scioscia, Lenny Harris, and Rick Dempsey, if they were still around. Then, after the game, somebody would wheel out the cage for extra hitting and Tommy'd be out there dropping pretty good left-handed curveballs on us. I loved it. *Loved* it.

That first year, just when I thought it couldn't get any better, I actually made a trip with the big-league team to West Palm Beach to play the Atlanta Braves in a split-squad game. I was catching and Dale Murphy was batting and I'm thinking, how in the world did I get here? My daydream was

shattered a moment or two later when Dion James came around to score. There was a play at the plate, and he ran me over.

Those were the times when I felt like I was living the fairy tale, just like I'd always imagined it. I still remember driving up the first day and seeing Tommy in the cafeteria, then seeing the *food* in the cafeteria. Big vats of eggs and orange juice and bacon and pancakes. Even my second year, my third year, the moment I got there, the feeling was "Ah, Dodgertown!" I was pumped.

Of course, I'd been to Dodgertown the year before, when I showed off my arm for Joe Ferguson. But I knew it was for real this time when I checked in to get my uniform and the old equipment guy asked me if I was a catcher, grabbed a bag of gear, and threw it at me, as if to say, "Here's your stuff, you piece of shit. Get out of my face." I didn't mind. As soon as I headed out to the field for the first time and laid my eyes upon all the players spread out and stretching, I felt the kind of adrenaline rush I remembered from walking up the steps of the Dodgers' dugout as a thirteen-year-old batboy at Veterans Stadium.

The next thing I knew, Brent Strom, a minor-league pitching coach, was yelling, "Catchers to the strings! Piazza!" I was the first catcher summoned to the strings section, which was Dodgertown oblivion—a bullpen area that Branch Rickey devised back in the day, using thick string or cord to outline the strike zone and encourage pitchers to throw to the edges; actually hit the strings. By the time I got there, it was just a row of mounds and another of home plates. That first day, I did nothing but catch bullpens; must have been ten of them. But that's when I really started learning to catch. I caught good curveballs. I caught pitchers who knew what they were doing.

I learned a lot from being around the pitchers. The pitching coaches— Johnny Podres, Claude Osteen, Dave Wallace, Burt Hooton—conducted meetings on pitching philosophy for the minor leaguers. Once, when they called a meeting, I figured, hey, I'm a catcher, I need to know what they're thinking out there; I should go to that meeting. I was the only catcher there. My old roommate, Jeff Hartsock, and this pitcher from Iowa, Bill Wengert, turned around to look at me, as if a hippopotamus had just pulled up a chair, and one of them said, "What the hell are *you* doing here?"

My response: "What, I can't go to a meeting? A meeting about pitching? And I'm a catcher?"

When I proceeded to follow up on a point that was being discussed, they thought that was revolutionary. Bill Wengert: "What the fuck? Piazza comes to the pitchers meeting and he actually asks a question!"

The catchers were usually with the pitchers anyway, down at the strings. That was our social circle. Our entertainment was the movie they'd show every night in the theater. The only guys who didn't go were the ones sneaking off campus. I never snuck out, because I was a nerd and too tired most of the time, but I had roommates who did. A couple of outfielders, Donnie Carroll and Chris Morrow, got out one night by climbing the fence; but there was always a security guard on duty checking for guys coming back. So they got a cab to drop them off at the tree line, made their way through the woods, climbed onto a roof, and dropped down into Dodgertown like commandos. They called it Rambo-style. It was all good, except that while they were gone, one of the coaches, Tom Beyers, stopped by for bed checks, looked around, and saw there was nobody else in my room. A couple of hours later, here they come. The door opens and they start high-fiving each other, like "Hey hey, we made it!" I said, "No, no, you guys are screwed. They had a bed check." Reggie Smith, the great switch-hitter from the old Red Sox and Dodgers, was in charge of running the players who had been caught the night before on bed check. They were known as Reggie's Runners. Carroll and Morrow were active members of the club.

In a lot of ways, it wasn't very smart to go out in Vero Beach. The local guys were always mad that the Dodgers would swoop down and take their girls, so there were plenty of fights. It wasn't like you could avoid the locals, because there were only a few bars in town. The best one was Bobby's on the Beach, but we couldn't go in there because that was the coaches' bar. Kevin Kennedy and Dave Wallace were responsible for holding up the walls at Bobby's, and if they saw you in there, you earned yourself a morning reservation with Reggie's Runners.

But Tommy took us out from time to time. Once, a few of us who had done something or other exemplary went to dinner with Tommy and Steve Boros, who was the minor-league field coordinator. Across the room, we spotted a cute blond girl with what seemed to be her family. Her brother or whoever it was came up to our table and said, "My sister is here and she would be very interested in one of these young men taking her out for the night."

Tommy said, "Which one?"

"She said the guy in the red shirt."

That was me. I gave out a little "woo!" Pretty girl from Canada, it turned out. I felt like it was quite an accomplishment when I made it to second base that night. I hate to sound juvenile about it, but at that time I *was* juvenile, in a lot of ways. For one, my father considered girls to be among the distractions that he needed to keep out of my path. I also had my mother's sense of morality instilled in me. I'd been sheltered, somewhat. Combine all that with my focus on baseball, and there were a lot of elements working together to make me socially tentative.

I can't deny that Tommy looked after me in those years—socially, to a small degree, and definitely, in a big way, on matters of baseball. I'll deny all day that I was ever handed anything I didn't deserve; but indisputably, he was the steward of my entry into pro ball and conversion to catching—my enabler, so to speak. For those first few spring trainings, Tommy took the extra step of putting Joe Ferguson in charge of my catching education, although Ferguson was certainly not the only one who played a part in it.

Tommy himself actually had some hands-on input with my catching skills. When he threw BP, he usually wanted a catcher behind the plate. I'd go back there and he'd bounce the ball in the grass and shout, as only Tommy could shout, "Come on, Michael, block that ball!" He was as much a cheerleader as an instructor. But there was no shortage of coaches on call to teach me the mechanics of the position. It was a collective thing between Fergy, Johnny Roseboro, Kevin Kennedy, and Mark Cresse. Ferguson had a body type similar to mine—he was tall—and was able to show me a particular technique of blocking balls in the dirt. Most catchers kick their leg out to stop the ball, but because my legs needed more room I had to angle my feet a little differently. Joe understood that.

Cresse's big contribution was the Catcher Olympics. He set it up for competitions in things like blocking balls, fielding bunts, and throwing to second base—you'd get points for hitting a bull's-eye affixed to a screen in front of the bag—and the grand finale was always the pop-up-catching contest. It would go six rounds and involve all kinds of circus catches. To make it more interesting, Cresse would sometimes toss your mitt on the ground so you'd have to find and grab it before chasing after the pop-up. The all-time best performance was put on by a guy named Ken Huckaby, who eventually reached the big leagues in his thirties. Huckaby came out wearing a tie and carrying a briefcase. While the ball was in the air, he slipped into a suit jacket and pulled his mitt out of the case. He called it "the executive catch." All the major-league and minor-league catchers were involved, and the judges gave the scores by holding up playing cards. Tommy was always a judge, of course. One day, when it was extremely windy, I ran about forty yards and slid another five to snag a really high pop-up, and Tommy erupted: "Jesus Christ, what a great catch! That was one of the best fucking catches I've ever seen!" I never won the Catcher Olympics, but the most important thing was not to finish *last*. For the guy with the lowest score, Cresse would paint the top of a swim cap like a certain part of the anatomy. The prize was called the Dickhead Award, and the winner had to wear that swim cap for an entire day of practice.

What a blast it all was. At Dodgertown, I was completely, blissfully, wholeheartedly in my element. Especially that first year. In the spring of 1989, there was only one small thing that might have spoiled the mood for me—if my dad had actually told me about it.

He and Burt Hooton had a pretty good relationship. Hooton came from Texas and he liked to talk to Dad in a Philly accent. He'd go, "Yo, Vince!" My father would answer, "Yo, Burt!"

So Hooton meant well, I'm sure, when he approached my dad a few days before we broke camp and said, "Vince, I don't know what he's doing here. He's not ready for this. He should be in school."

CHAPTER SEVEN

My first club assignment was Salem, Oregon, of the Northwest League, which didn't begin until June. So I reported to extended spring training in Port St. Lucie, Florida, living at the Holiday Inn on U.S. 1. Even *that* seemed romantic to me.

I was working hard to progress as a catcher, and no doubt making progress, but, by all accounts, Ted Williams had been right when he told my father that "hitting's going to be his big suit." That much was pretty obvious when, at the age of twenty, I arrived in Salem. Our manager, Tom Beyers, got tired of watching me chase balls to the backstop, so I split the catching duties with a guy from Puerto Rico named Hector Ortiz, who eventually spent some time in the major leagues but put in *eighteen seasons* at the minor-league level.

My batting average was nothing special, but my power attracted a bit of attention. The Dodgers' owner, Peter O'Malley, flew up to Oregon to watch us (I had the feeling that he came to watch *me*, but more likely, it was to check on our top draft choice, Bill Bene), and with him looking on, I hit one of the longest home runs they'd seen at Chemeketa Community College, where we played our home games. One of our pitchers, Larry Gonzalez—we called him Lar—had become a good friend, and I can still hear him saying, "Man, that was a *bomb!*" Before long, I actually developed a little fan following. Made the all-star team.

My father came out for some games late in the season, and he was sitting along the third-base line one night when Burt Hooton—he was our pitching coach—walked over to shoot the breeze with him.

"Yo, Vince!"

"Yo, Burt!"

Dad had been stung by Hooton's remark back in March—more specifically, by the friendly, professional opinion that I didn't belong—but he didn't let on. He just said, "Well, Burt, I've been sitting here for six innings, and I've got to say, I don't see too many prospects out there."

As my dad remembers it, Hooton's reply was "You know, Vince, I've got to apologize for what I said during spring training. If there's anybody here who's got a chance, it's your son. He works longer and harder than any player we've got."

My dad said, "Don't worry about it. I'm glad it's working out."

I was still on my baseball honeymoon when I arrived in Vero Beach for my second spring training. And this time, I reported as an all-star. Not as the last guy taken. Not as the courtesy pick. Not as the kid who never caught before. An *all-star*. It was a powerful feeling.

That was followed by a painfully *un*powerful feeling. Before our noses had a chance to peel, about a dozen of us got sick with the flu—so sick, cafeteria workers delivered Jell-O and chicken soup to our rooms for nearly two weeks. It ate me up to be back in Dodgertown, the place that brought out my best, and spend beautiful day after beautiful day in bed.

But I'd get my fill of Dodgertown that summer. My assignment was the Vero Beach Dodgers, the organization's Class A affiliate of the Florida State League. Unfortunately, the Florida State League was known, and still is, for being merciless on hitters. I didn't find it particularly kind to catchers, either.

My defensive difficulties were not lost on our manager, Joe Alvarez, a Cuba native and former minor-league infielder who made his home in Miami. He found a convenient solution when I got sick again—this time, mono. I was only out of action for about a week, but when I was ready to play again, Alvarez informed me that I'd be putting in some time at first base because I'd lost my starting catcher's job to Pete Gonzalez, who had been the catcher when I played first at Miami-Dade. Pete was also from Miami, of Cuban ancestry, and Alvarez was sort of incestuously tied to him—knew the family and whatnot, sort of like Tommy and me, I suppose. Pete was definitely more advanced defensively than I was at the time, and seeing as how we had some pretty good pitching prospects on the club, I'm sure Alvarez wanted a good receiver back there handling them. On the other hand, Gonzalez wasn't such a wonderful hitter, and I didn't see how I could lose my job by getting sick for a week.

Neither could my dad, who hadn't suddenly gotten shy about making his opinions known. His grumbling got back to Alvarez, who gave me a message to pass along: come on down to Vero so we can get all this shit behind us.

I went down there and we talked it out and I said, "Okay, we've got an understanding here, but you've got to promise me you'll catch him."

He said, "Oh yeah, I'll catch him."

So now he's still catching Gonzalez and I'm really pissed. He and the dad are buddies from Cuba. I was just finding all this out, and I realized there was no way Mike's gonna catch. This guy is trying to bury Mike, trying to get him out of the organization. And he knew I was pissed. I was staring at him and he's looking the other way.

The politics were playing a part, too. The manager didn't like Mike's relationship with Tommy. That was really starting to pop. I think the minor-league people resented Tommy's involvement. Between me and Tommy, they felt like there was too much going on. My friend Al LaMacchia, the scout with Toronto, told me, "Vince, you got to slow down. Some of these guys are saying the father is a little bit of a pain in the ass."

I said, "Yeah, I can understand that. I've been making a lot of noise and maybe I shouldn't, but it pisses me off that he's not catching. He's a catcher; he's not a goddamn first baseman."

—Vince Piazza

One night, when we were in Baseball City playing the Kansas City Royals, I was batting, man on first, and Joe gave me the bunt sign. I bunted and fouled it off. He gave me the bunt sign again and I think I fouled it off again. Then I look down and he's giving me the bunt sign with *two strikes*. I'm like, what the hell, nobody gives the bunt sign with two strikes. I didn't know if he made a mistake or if he thought I was trying to show him up by not giving an honest effort on the bunts or what; so I said to myself, fuck this, and hit away. Grounded out, I think. He pulled me from the game and aired me out. The whole thing just seemed weird.

Dave Wallace was our roving pitching coach and a person I could talk to, so I said to Dave, "I don't know what it is with this guy. We definitely don't mix. He doesn't like me and I don't know why. Maybe it's political, because of Tommy. Maybe he's just very partial to Pete Gonzalez. I have no idea. The guy gave me a two-strike bunt. What the fuck is that?"

"Please, Mike, just be patient," he told me. "Hang in there."

I was willing to do that, hard as it was. Through the whole scouting and drafting drama, I'd developed some calluses on my pride. I was realistic. Paul

Mainieri's pep talk had stuck with me; helped me understand that it wasn't all going to unfold according to a preconceived script. Considering the skepticism I was up against, my script, in particular, would have to be shopped around for a while before it found a producer. I got that. I wasn't bringing an attitude. I just didn't see the sense of bunting with two damn strikes. I was pretty sure Mike Schmidt never did that.

Then we went to Fort Lauderdale to play the New York Yankees and the same thing happened all over again. Alvarez gave me a two-strike bunt sign. I tried to bunt and fouled out or something. I really don't recall the details, but he yanked me out of the game for the second time.

A short while later, we were playing the West Palm Beach Expos in Vero Beach and they had a left-handed pitcher going. We'd faced the guy before and I had something like three hits. I got to the park, dressed, looked at the lineup, saw I wasn't in it, went berserk, changed again, got in the car, and drove back to the house I shared with a couple other players. It was spontaneous combustion. I didn't stop long enough to think about my dream or my dad or all the winter nights in the batting cage.

As soon as I walked in the door, the phone was ringing.

"Mike Piazza?"

"Yeah."

"This is Charlie Blaney. It's a terrible thing you did, leaving the team . . ."

I said, "Charlie, save it. I'm done. I'm quitting. I'm not having any fun. Do you think I want to fucking bunt with two strikes? What is *that?* I gave it a shot and I'm leaving."

"Where are you going?"

"Home."

"Can you stay at this number for a few hours?"

"Yeah, sure, I'll be here. I'm just packing."

I was still puttering around, waiting for the phone to ring, when my roommates, Mike Wismer and Scott Marabell, got back from the game. Wismer was from Philly—I actually played against him in high school—and he was all fired up. He said, "I can't believe you did that. You gotta be shittin' me. That was the ballsiest thing ever. You should have seen the look on his fucking face!"

I was like, "Why was it so ballsy? Fuck you, I'm leaving. I'll go home and sell cars or something."

I really felt like it was the end of the line—at least with the Dodgers. I'd been sick twice, benched, reamed out, embarrassed in front of my team; I didn't give a shit anymore. I wasn't feeling slighted or bitter or anything like that. Just, fuck it. You know, take your job and shove it. Let Pete Gonzalez have it. The game had beaten me. I was done.

In the meantime, Blaney was talking to Alvarez, Tom Beyers, Reggie Smith, my dad, and I didn't know who else. The way my dad understood it, Alvarez wanted me gone, Beyers told him I wasn't a bad guy but was playing out of position, and Reggie Smith, who was the roving hitting instructor, said something like "I've never had a problem with the kid. But I gotta tell you one thing. I've watched him hit, and he's the kind of kid to me that, if you let him go, he'll turn around and bite you in the ass. I wouldn't let him go."

After Blaney talked to Reggie, he called me again and said, "Okay, we've decided to let you come back."

Let me come back? Like I'd been begging to. I assumed he meant they'd move me up to Bakersfield or even back down to rookie league for a little punishment. No. He was returning me to Vero Beach and Joe Alvarez.

I really don't know why, but I agreed. I think I just had nothing better to do. Baseball had monopolized my ambitions. Pure and simple, life as I knew it revolved around the game. Playing ball was my default position. My identity.

I did know, however, that when I rejoined the team, it would be different. *I* would be different. The whole episode had driven the romance right out of me. It was like I had lost my virginity.

Actually, I *did* lose my virginity that summer, which was probably no coincidence. I won't embarrass her by using her name, but she was a Greek girl from Chicago—a *blond* Greek, a little older than I was, far more mature, and extremely sweet.

My sexual inexperience went a little deeper than just the sheltering and social awkwardness that I alluded to earlier. I wouldn't say that I'd been a prude, but I was directed by a moral compass that pointed me away from things that might be frowned upon by Catholicism. Even when I started in pro baseball, I always found a church to go to. Girls were around in those days, and I sometimes did the bar scene, but I wasn't running around with my choke out.

When I met the Chicago girl—we were in Clearwater, playing the Phillies—not much happened, but we kept in touch. Then she flew down and rented a car, which made an impression. I thought, wow, she's got it going on—her own job, her own money, her own life. I also admired the fact that she cooked for her father, who had a heart condition, and made sure he ate right. Altogether, she was so domestic, caring, and responsible that I think it broke down my moral barriers a little bit. Plus I was now twenty-one, and feeling the urge to be adult. On top of everything else, it definitely aided the cause that this thoughtful, attractive girl was also very patient. Bear in mind, I didn't even *date* in high school. I was nervous as hell, and when we were ready to go, I said, "All right, well, you know . . . I'm a virgin." She was floored.

I guess you could say that I left my innocence in Vero Beach, all the way around. It would never again be my first time; and I'd never again bleed Dodger blue. Even after talking to Tommy about my situation with Alvarez.

I told Michael, "Okay, you go in tomorrow and apologize, because you should have never done what you did by leaving. I know how frustrated you must have been, but you go in and apologize. Give him the benefit of the doubt."

When Michael came back and apologized, they fined him two hundred dollars. I never heard of a young kid being fined two hundred dollars with what they're making. When I talked to Michael, he said the manager had hollered and chewed him out in front of the whole team and said something about him having to go to the big-league manager with his problems. Michael would have never come to me. His *dad* came to me. That's an important point. So I told Charlie Blaney what Joe Alvarez said.

Blaney said, "I don't believe that."

I said, "Charlie, that boy ain't lying to me. He never lies to me."

Leo Posada was right there, and he said, "I was in the clubhouse when Alvarez said it." Charlie's jaw dropped.

Michael went through a lot because of his relationship with me. When he was in the minor leagues, they thought he was there just because of me and he didn't have the ability to play. But they were wrong. I ended up getting into a lot of situations with it. After this happened, I was up having lunch with Peter O'Malley and Charlie Blaney and a couple other guys, and Peter asked about Mike Piazza. Charlie said, "Oh, he jumped the club."

I didn't say anything, but after Peter left I said, "Charlie, do you know what 'jumping the club' means?"

He said, "Yeah, it's leaving the club."

I said, "That's wrong. When you leave and go home, that's jumping the club. He did not do that. He walked out because he was mad and embarrassed. That's not jumping the club. A lot of players have done that."

Then I said, "Charlie, let me ask you a question. Do you think

Pete Gonzalez will catch in the big leagues? The only way he'll see the big leagues is if he buys a ticket."

Charlie said, "Then you think Michael's a prospect?"

I said, "Yes!"

—Tom Lasorda

An apology was appropriate and necessary—no arguments there—so I stood in front of my teammates and said something like "Look, I let the team down by leaving, and it was unfortunate, it was inexcusable. If you have a problem with a coach or somebody, you've got to talk it through. You can't just walk out. I understand that, and I'm sorry."

That's when Alvarez took over and said, in effect, "On the same note, obviously we're not always going to agree on playing time and everything. If you feel you have to, you can call Charlie Blaney, you can call"— he looked right at me—"*Tommy*, you can call whoever you want to call. But you need to talk to me first."

With that, I was back, but wearing an attitude that had been dramatically and permanently adjusted. From then on, I was aloof, detached, a little militant, arriving at the park every day with a fuck-this, who-cares disposition. *Contemptuous* would be a good word for it. My sense of reverence had been wiped out to the point that I no longer gave a damn who was who. I was going to play hard and do my best and be loyal to my teammates, but I could muster absolutely no affection or affinity for the organization anymore.

Believe it or not, when I got back into a ball game—after a little grace period—Alvarez had me bunting *again*. I was furious and confused. I talked to Charlie Blaney and he said something on the order of "We wanted to play a mind game on you. That's why we did that." I felt like I was in the Twilight Zone.

The kooky scene served only to reinforce my new attitude. And you know what? As bad as it was, in the traditional ways, that attitude worked for me. It became my game face. I realized that, if I was going to make it, I had to be a motherfucker. That sounds crude and selfish, I know, but the *other* way hadn't worked. It hadn't protected me from getting benched and screwed with. It seemed to me that the organization had set the terms, and playing by them, for me, meant playing with contempt. Playing *angry*. And believe me, my anger was real. I'd come into professional baseball with a fairy-tale image of how it was going to be, and for a little while it was actually that way. Or seemed to be. When that idealism was blown up, I got a chronic case of the red-ass, as they say in the clubhouse.

My season—hell, my *career*—turned around at that point. From an out-side perspective, it might have seemed like I came back gung-ho and rededi-cated. I've heard it said that the Vero Beach incident made me appreciate what I had; allowed me to turn the page and start fresh and fired up. Nope. That wasn't it.

It did, however, refine my focus, which was no longer fixed on pleasing my manager, my dad, or Tommy Lasorda. Nor on the privilege of being a professional ballplayer. I was locked in now on the baseball itself. Specifi-cally, on hitting the shit out of it.

I was also zeroed in on getting away from the Dodgers, if I could. Right after I came back, we were playing the Phillies in Vero Beach and I found out where they were staying. Their manager was Lee Elia, who was from Philadelphia, so I called the hotel and they put me through to him. I said, "Lee, I'm really frustrated here. I'm not really getting along with the Dodg-ers and I don't know what's going to happen. They might even release me. I was thinking maybe the Phillies would be interested in me. Is there any interest there?"

Elia said, "Let me tell you something. Baseball is like college. If you have the grades, you're going to graduate. It doesn't matter where you are; if you can play, you're going to get to the big leagues." He also told me that the Phillies were cutting back and, in short, weren't interested. That was my mental detachment from the Phillies. Before then, I was thinking that maybe they'd save me.

In the meantime, we had a pretty good team at Vero Beach, starting with Eric Young, who stole seventy-six bases that year. I did my part. Against Dunedin, I hit a walk-off home run, and when I got back to the dugout, Alvarez said something like "You keep working on that and you're gonna be a heck of a hitter."

Gradually, I raised my average to around .300; but a season in Florida takes a lot out of you, and by August most of the players with good averages started sitting on them, claiming little nagging injuries or whatever. Since I didn't give a shit, I went out and played a lot while the other guys were recuperating. My average dropped to .250.

Apparently, that was reason enough to keep me on the bench when the playoffs started. In the first round, we played Port St. Lucie and they had a good pitcher named John Johnstone going for them. I was sitting in the bullpen and said to the guys there, "You watch what happens. We're gonna be losing and Alvarez is going to have to put me in and I'm gonna have to fucking save the day." Wouldn't you know it, I'm warming somebody up, we're behind, it's around the fifth inning, and I hear, "Piazza, come on down!" Alvarez pinch-hits me with two guys on, and I think I knocked a double off the wall.

We won that series. In the next one, against Port Charlotte, I hit a monster home run, over the lights, and walked while I watched it. Probably shouldn't have done that, but it was all part of the new attitude. Port Charlotte's manager, Bobby Jones, told somebody they were going to deck me. I was not well liked in the Florida State League, and I didn't really give a damn. Not as long as I hit.

In the finals we played West Palm Beach, the team we'd finished behind in our division during the regular season. We won again. League champs.

The next day, in the Vero Beach newspaper, there was a picture of me pouring a bottle of champagne over the head of Joe Alvarez.

CHAPTER EIGHT

It's strange, the little things that stick in a person's head. For me, one of those was something that happened during the Instructional League in the fall of 1990, right after my season at Vero Beach.

I attended Instructional League for a few years in a row, and it was always worthwhile. Johnny Roseboro would be there, puffing his cigarette and dispensing his colorful, catcherly wisdom. And Reggie Smith, a guy I could relate to as a hitting coach. Reggie had some advanced ideas but tried to still keep it simple. His philosophy was "Hit 'em like you live—hard and in the alleys."

This particular day, I was hitting in the cage with Reggie and happened to notice that some guys were setting up for a little workout on the main field at HoHoKam Park. I saw Billy Lott warming up over there—he was a big, strapping former football player from Mississippi who had been drafted in the second round in 1989—and also Billy Ashley, who was the third-round draft choice the year I was taken. I thought, great, I'll jump in when I can and get some extra swings. So I walked over and said, "Hey, who's pitching BP? Let me get some cuts in with you guys."

Tom Beyers was there. He was my manager at Salem and would be my manager again the next season at Bakersfield. Beyers was a nice guy and helped me in a lot of ways, but I don't think he was ever my biggest fan. Not as long as I was a catcher.

He said, "Uh, Mike, this is just a special workout for Billy Lott and Billy Ashley."

"Oh, really? Okay, all right, fine. Sorry."

I picked up my bag and bats, slinked back to the cage, flipped on the machine, and hit for two hours straight.

That told me exactly where I stood in the organization. After two years, I was still the sixty-second-round draft choice. The courtesy pick. And I

knew the only way I would change that perception was by hitting the ball so fucking hard that they couldn't dismiss me any longer.

That was my mission at Bakersfield.

To get ready for it, I lifted. I lifted *a lot*.

After being sick twice in 1990 and worn down by a long summer in Florida, I was at my lowest point, strength-wise, since I'd started using the weight room at Miami. I thought, man, I gotta get it in gear. So I hit the weights hard when I got home to Philly after Instructional League, then spent a month or so at our family place in Boynton Beach and hit them even harder, working with a guy who had gone to college with my brother Vince and knew his way around the gym. The more I learned about proper training—routines, repetitions, plateaus, muscle groups, nutrition, the whole bit—the more enthused I became about it.

My workouts that winter left me in great shape for spring training, 1991, which went well. For that I could also thank Reggie Smith.

Reggie was an unorthodox batting coach who had learned a lot in Japan from Sadaharu Oh and brought some Asian, martial-arts philosophies into hitting, like thinking of the bat as a sword. His basic approach was to cut the ball in half. But he was also a disciple of Ted Williams—which was where I came from—and it all tied in. Minimizing movement. Keeping the head still. Tucking the elbow. A slight uppercut. Essentially, a short swing. That spring, Reggie showed me one particular drill that opened up my world. He brought a pitching screen to the plate and placed the nearest edge behind my hands, a little closer than the catcher's mitt would normally be. All I had to do was hit the ball off a tee. But when I swung, my bat smacked that vertical pole and stung the hell out of my hands. I didn't see how I could possibly get to the ball with that damn screen there.

Reggie laughed, walked up, grabbed the bat, stood where I stood, and smoked a line drive. Then he explained that I was swinging *around* the ball instead of through it. With a shorter, tighter, and consequently quicker stroke, he said, I'd have more time to recognize the pitch before committing to my swing. He was so right. The extra split second made me much better at identifying not only the types of pitches coming at me but the strikes, as well. As a result, I was less likely to get *myself* out and more likely to put the head of the bat on the ball. And here's the beauty of it: at the same time, I became more explosive at the plate, with the power now packed in close to my body.

The whole concept really hit home in an intrasquad game, when I was

facing a guy named Javier Delahoya, who had been a fourth-round pick out of Los Angeles in 1989. Delahoya threw me an inside fastball and I just tucked in my elbow, kept my hands in tight, took the bat straight through the ball—boop!—and drove it out of the park. I was like "It's that fucking easy?" It was a watershed moment for me. I kept working with Reggie on that drill, and by the end of the spring I was actually squaring up the ball with my eyes closed. Muscle memory, Reggie said.

Spring training ended on a high note when I accompanied the Dodgers to an exhibition game in New Orleans. I'm pretty sure that was Tommy's doing, and I appreciated it; but it demonstrated, on the maturity front, that I wasn't ready to hang with the big boys. As a preview of the years to come, I found myself with Eric Karros—who would spend the season at the Dodgers' Triple-A club in Albuquerque—and on the town, in the presence of refreshments and single women. In particular, there was a very attractive blonde whom we were sparring over, and as the evening moved along, she asked if we'd be coming back to New Orleans anytime soon. I sensed that I had the edge on Eric, so I said, "Oh yeah, we'll be back." And Eric, in a dry, bitter voice, muttered, "We'll probably never see this town again for the rest of our lives." I tried to play it down at the time but told him later, "You dick. You're such a sore loser."

The next day, we were joking about it in the clubhouse, and John Candelaria, who was playing out the string with the Dodgers, cornered us and said, "Hey, when you're in here, don't ever talk about the night before. That's your own business. Nobody wants to hear that shit."

But I *was* ready for Bakersfield. My extra muscle proved to be a nice complement to the friendly dimensions of Sam Lynn Park and the desert wind of the California League. (One night, the tin roof blew off our dugout.)

We had a stacked team that year. Billy Lott was on it, but most of the hype was over Raul Mondesi and Pedro Martinez. In our first win, I homered with Mondesi on base and Pedro threw a two-hitter. In our second, I hit a grand slam for my roommate, a tall right-hander named Greg Hansell. The next time Pedro pitched, I hit two homers. Hansell took a no-hitter into the seventh on his second victory, and I crushed a 430-footer, according to the local paper.

In spite of being a pitcher and a couple of years younger than I was, Hansell was a good roommate from the day we moved into our apartment. That's because his parents, who had driven up from Los Angeles County— where his father was a sheriff—met us there with silverware, a TV, and everything else we needed packed into their Camry. His mother, Margo, had

been a professional housecleaner, and she had our place looking about as good as it could for a couple of guys making twelve hundred bucks a month. Almost immediately, she became my West Coast mom, more or less. After I got to the big leagues and came to public attention, I hired Margo to handle all my fan mail.

My little flurry of home runs gave me the league lead and a more regular place in the lineup. For the first couple of weeks, Beyers had been splitting the catching between me and Ed Lund, a good defensive player from Notre Dame. On the days I wasn't catching, I'd sit or DH or play first base, where Beyers believed I should have been on a regular basis.

It was easy to see how he thought that. My Johnny Bench imitation left a lot to be desired. I threw some balls away and spent quite a bit of time at the backstop. But my defense didn't prevent our pitching staff from finishing second in the league in ERA. I was getting better and picking up the support of at least a few people in the organization. Mel Didier was a scout for the Dodgers, and he did me a good turn by telling Beyers a story about when he was working for the Expos and they drafted a high school pitcher whom they converted to catcher. He said the kid wasn't much of a catcher at first, and his manager insisted on playing another guy instead. Didier told the manager, "If you don't catch that kid every day, I'm firing you and getting somebody in here who will." He was talking about Gary Carter. It was Mel's way of suggesting that Beyers let me catch.

My competition for the league home run title came from Jay Gainer of High Desert, who had the advantage of playing in a park where your hat would blow into the bleachers. I hit one over the scoreboard there. In Bakersfield, I hit four balls over the sun screen in center field. They said that nobody else had ever done that more than twice. Beyers was impressed, and kind to me in the papers. He said, "That kid has some devastating power. When you hit a ball 400-feet-plus, let alone to center field, let alone on a breaking pitch, that's power. . . . You couple bat speed with Piazza's strength, and you've got what you're seeing now."

Going into the final month of the season, I was sitting at around twenty home runs and Hansell had fourteen wins. Feeling cocky, I wagered him that I would end up with at least two homers for every victory of his. It kept things interesting around the apartment—especially when I got hot and he kept piling up no-decisions. He'd thought he was on to a sure thing, and it was my pleasure to make him squirm.

My only real issues with Hansell, though, had to do with dinner and snacks. He always wanted to grab a pizza or a Big Mac and fries after a ball

game. Carrying forth in the image of my dad, I was more particular about
what I ate. But we could deal with that. More important, Hansell had the
good sense to steer clear when I wasn't feeling sociable, which was too much
of the time. Even *more* important, he didn't mind when I cranked up the
stereo in the car. He even came along with me to local concerts. Over a
summer in Bakersfield, Hansell got an education in heavy metal and I got a
good taste of his new-wave and alternative stuff—bands like Depeche Mode
("Personal Jesus," "People Are People"), Oingo Boingo, and the Smiths,
with Morrissey.

I remember going with him to see Dangerous Toys. There was all
this screaming, and all of a sudden a guy sticks a microphone in
Mike's face—and Piazza knew all the words! For the most part,
though, you couldn't tell he was a heavy-metal guy if you didn't
know that it was usually Metallica playing in his headphones.

I'll never forget the day [August 13, 1991] when Metallica's
new album—the Black Album—was released. He woke me up early
and told me he was going down to the record store because he had
to be the first one in line to get it. He got it, came back, put his
headphones on, and disappeared into his room. Three hours later,
he came out pretty upset. I asked him what the problem was. He
said, "They sold out, man." He didn't mean the store was out of
albums; he meant that Metallica had lost its soul and gone mainstream. The album wasn't hard enough for him. I listened to it, and
when I was done I told Mike that I thought it was really good. He
said, "Exactly." I guess a guy like me wasn't supposed to think that.
He was almost in tears.

There were just a few things Mike really cared about. First was
his family, then music, then cars, then food. He stuck to himself
pretty much. I didn't realize the kind of background he came from
until we went down to the dealership in Torrance one day and they
hooked him up with a brand-new Acura. I said, "Wow, your dad
must have some good friends there."

He said, "Well, he owns the dealership."

He didn't advertise that part of his life. In fact, Mike wasn't a
real social guy. He worked out and listened to his music and that
was about it. When he listened to music, he was doing one of two
things. Either he was playing the air drums or he was squeezing his
hand grippers. He had those grippers in his hands all the time. The

steel ones. He worked at it nonstop. Once, he squeezed one of them so hard he broke it, and he was really upset about that. I remember him saying, "Man, those things cost me fifteen bucks." I was in awe because I could barely squeeze it with both hands. He'd leave them on the coffee table in our apartment and people would pick them up and try to squeeze them and they wouldn't budge. They thought it was a practical joke.

—Greg Hansell

Meanwhile, as we proceeded to clinch our division, Hansell's streak of no-decisions continued all the way to five and the end of the regular season. He never got off of fourteen wins. And my home runs kept coming. The last one was my twenty-ninth, making me the insufferable winner of the bet, which, although I don't recall exactly, was probably for a lunch at Olive Garden. We used to tear that place up for the free salad and bread sticks.

My home run total was two short of Jay Gainer for the California League title, but the fourth highest in all the minors. I made the all-star team again and led the league in slugging percentage. In short, I had accomplished what I profoundly needed to—put up numbers that the Dodgers couldn't help but notice. I know for a fact that my season got the attention of Fred Claire, the Dodgers' general manager. In his words, I was now, for the first time, "a legitimate prospect."

I was pleasantly surprised to find out, also, that the Dodgers weren't the only ones who had made a note of my breakout. Around the time I was overtaking Hansell in our little wager, I started hearing from agents suddenly interested in representing me. Among them was Hansell's guy, Dan Lozano. One day, Greg was meeting Lozano for lunch at Marie Callender's and asked me to come with him. Danny still rags me about showing up with "the best bed-head ever." But he obviously had no bias against bad hair. We got along. He didn't pressure me. He didn't even try to recruit me.

For the league playoffs, Beyers wanted me to shuffle over to first base because our regular guy, Rex Peters, was hurt. That was fine. I knew it was a tough situation for Beyers because a lot of people were in his ear about me catching. It undermined his authority and probably offended him, to some degree. To his credit, Beyers never took it out on me. But he did bring it up in a way that was probably for my own benefit. He said something like, "Geez, Mike, I just don't understand the way Tommy interferes in your career . . ."

Whether the chirping came from Tommy or my dad, it wasn't going to stop until I was either out of the game or catching on a regular basis. My dad, especially, would see to that. As the playoffs moved along, Ed Lund may have gotten nicked or something, I don't recall, but I was behind the plate one night against High Desert and happened to throw out a bunch of guys—I think it was four in a row—trying to steal. They were probably running because it was me back there, but I *did* have an arm. Sometimes I'd hurry and lose my mechanics, but I definitely had enough on the ball to throw people out. This time, my father was there to see it, sitting with Johnny Roseboro, who, like everybody else, knew how frustrated he was about the organization's reluctance to leave me behind the plate. My dad recalls Roseboro grabbing his arm afterward and saying, "Goddamn, what a game he caught!"

"Don't tell *me*," my dad replied. "Tell *them* son of a bitches."

But he wasn't finished. At the hotel that night, one of our roving instructors approached my father and remarked that my throwing performance had been embarrassing for the people who didn't want me catching. Dad's response: "Look, if you guys aren't going to catch him, why don't you release him?"

The instructor said, "If we catch him a hundred games next year, will you leave us alone?"

"Hey, you got a deal. That's all I want."

If my dad was making a nuisance of himself with the Dodger people—and there's no doubt that he was—he had his reasons. He knew full well that my only chance to make it to the big leagues would be as a catcher. And he also knew that it wouldn't happen, *couldn't* happen, until I got a lot more games under my belt. At one point, he asked Joe Ferguson how many games he thought it took for a young catcher to ready himself for the major leagues. Fergy's answer was five hundred.

"Five hundred games!" my father blurted out. "He can't get fifty a year! This kid'll be thirty years old before he catches five hundred games!"

When we were eliminated, the Dodgers asked me to fly to Florida along with a couple of pitchers—Jody Treadwell and Gordon Tipton—to help Vero Beach in the playoffs. There was no issue to consider between me and Joe Alvarez, because the organization had let him go after my season there. Charlie Blaney later told the *Los Angeles Times* that the situation with me played a part in that decision. At any rate, it was common for the Dodgers to shuffle players around to make the strongest possible playoff rosters. They placed an unusual emphasis on winning minor-league championships. The rule was that you couldn't move *down* a level to play with another team in the postseason, but since Bakersfield and Vero Beach were both in Class A ball, Blaney figured it was okay. As it turned out, I wasn't allowed to play. The Dodgers were one of the first organizations to get flagged for doing that.

I wasn't finished for the year, however. Raul Cano, the general manager of the Mexicali Aguilas (Eagles) of the Mexican Winter League, had come to scout us during the California League playoffs because the Dodgers had just entered into an agreement with Mexicali to provide some players. Cano watched one game and decided that I would be provided.

I signed for eleven hundred dollars a month and played with guys making three to five times as much. Most of them were higher-level minor leaguers. Some were washed-up major leaguers whose wives followed them around, pulling U-Hauls, with two kids in the backseat. It made me think, man, I never want to be that guy. That was something I actually feared. I was dead set on being established financially before I started on a family.

For that reason, I welcomed the advice given me by Warren ("the Deacon") Newson, an outfielder who joined us from the White Sox. He said, "You owe it to yourself, if you ever get to the big leagues, to be single for at least one year while you're up there." (In fact, that ranked with the wisdom conferred upon me later by Lenny Harris, the great pinch hitter and very funny man. Lenny told me, "When I was younger, you didn't worry about nothing. Now you gotta wrap that thing up. You go out tonight, something can jump into your system and kill your ass.") I acknowledged the Deacon's counsel in spades, and only wished that he had shared it with the very nice Mexican girl who followed me home one night, then another, and wrote me—in English— the most heartfelt love letters I've ever read. That girl was *serious*.

Mexicali is tucked right against California, and three of us—Jim Tatum and Jason Brosnan were my roommates—rented an apartment across the border in El Centro, California. Right off, we had a scrimmage against a semipro team called Joe's Car Wash, I think it was—*somebody's* car wash, or maybe it was a diner—from the border town of Calexico, California, which sort of bleeds together with Mexicali. Joe's Car Wash had this little pitcher throwing from all different angles; slider, slider, slider, then an eighty-mile-an-hour fastball, up and in, that blew right past me. I couldn't believe I'd struck out on an eighty-mile-an-hour fastball. The guy embarrassed the hell out of me. But that's what playing in Mexico was all about: deception, finesse, speed changes, arm slots, whatever. We used to say that a Mexican pitcher will shoot the ball out of his ass if he thinks he can sneak it by you.

The Aguilas had two capable catchers and a good first baseman from Mexicali named Guillermo Velazquez, whose nickname was Memo. Later in the season, I filled in for Memo when he was hurt. Early on, though, before we hit the road for the first time, the manager, Frank Estrada—everybody called him Paquin—said to me, "I need you to play right field."

I said, "Right field? I haven't played right field since ninth grade."

He said, "Well, that's all I can do right now. You can either play right field or I'm gonna have to put you on the bench. I have no choice. I have two good catchers."

I said, "Well, I'm not playing right field."

So we get on the bus, and I see there are nine bunks in addition to the straight-back seats. And the shortest trip we had in that league was about eight hours. I looked at the bunks and I looked at the bus driver and I looked around at my teammates and I said, "What's the deal with the bunks?"

Somebody said, "If you're starting the game, you get a bunk. If not, you get a seat."

With that, I walked right up to Paquin and said, "Here's your right fielder, right here. No problem." Suddenly, I'm a team guy.

Opening night, I'm out in right field, runner on third, I get a fly ball, come up throwing, and damn near gun the guy out at the plate. He thought he was going to cruise in, and it was a bang-bang play. So I get back to the dugout and everybody's like, whoa, where'd that come from? I mean, I wasn't Vladimir Guerrero, but I could throw a little. Around that time, I'm thinking, hmm, this might not be so bad. Then they started hitting long flies over my head, and the truth came out. I couldn't go back on a ball. And if the play happened to be out there along the wall, forget it. Those suckers were concrete and steel, no padding, and I didn't think it was in my best interest to break my wrist or neck in the Mexican Winter League.

As you might imagine, conditions in general were interesting down there, and so was the way the Mexican players dealt with them. The bus, for example. There was one very long trip, in particular, for which Cano told us we'd bus to Hermosillo, leaving around midnight, and then fly to Mazatlán. I was a little skeptical about the flying part, and sure enough, when we arrived at the airport in Hermosillo the next morning, there was no flight for us. As soon as we found out we'd be driving the rest of the way, which would add up to about a twenty-six-hour bus ride, one of the Mexican guys said, "Let's go to the store." I figured I'd pick up some chips and maybe a big bag of M&M's. What they had in mind was a few cases of Modelo, Tecate, and Dos Equis, which they wheeled to the bus in a hand truck. We drank the whole way down there. I have to say, the Mexican players could drink and smoke at a high level, and then go out and play a damn good game of baseball.

There was another American on our team, a left-handed pitcher from Louisiana named Dave Lynch, who was pretty entertaining, and both of us were amazed at the changes in temperature that could clobber you in just one December bus ride. From Hermosillo to Mazatlán, driving through the desert, I went from being the coldest I'd ever felt to the hottest. There was no heat or air-conditioning on that bus. The windows were open as the sun went down, and an hour later my teeth were chattering. After a while, I either fell asleep or passed out, not sure which, and around the time we got to the Los Mochis area, I woke up drenched in sweat. Lynch had finagled a bottom bunk because the guy who had it was off somewhere playing cards, and just as I leaned over to talk to him, he rolled out and said, "Dude, I'm fucking boiling!" The next day it rained, so they poured gas on the field and burned it dry. That might have been the game we won in some controversial manner and the locals—I mean, *lots* of them—ran after us throwing mud balls at our bus as we pulled away.

In one particular respect, however, the experience closely resembled the minor leagues: I didn't catch much. To be honest, that probably bothered my dad a little more than it did me. He urged me to talk to Paquin about it. A little reluctantly, I did. I explained that if I wasn't going to catch, I preferred to move on. Paquin told me that, since he already had two good catchers and would have to let one of them go to accommodate me, I should give him some time to think about it. A few days later, he came to me with his answer: he was going to release the backup, who was the younger of the two. I happened to know that the kid's wife had just had a baby, so I said, thanks, but no, I can't take that guy's job; he needs the money. Paquin was only about five foot eight, at the most, but he had been an excellent catcher who played one game for the Mets in 1971. He could throw out anybody at second base. The ball would just parachute down there, but he'd get rid of it so quickly, and his arm was so accurate—kind of like Bob Boone—that nobody would run on him. Knowing that, I pondered the situation for a minute and asked him, "How about this? If you'll work with me before and after the games on my catching, I'll stick around and try to help you win." Paquin was happy to do it, and he taught me a lot.

In the end, going to Mexico was absolutely the best thing I could have done that winter. It was the time of my life. But more important, it was when I started to become a polished hitter.

In fact, I can almost pin it down to a moment. I struggled badly for a while, barely hitting .100, and one day some veteran reliever was working me over pretty good. It was three and two and I fouled off about six pitches.

Then something clicked and I got hold of a slider for a home run that won the game. It just seemed like I'd finally figured it out. I ended up with about sixteen homers—had a great season—and in the process kept my end of the bargain with Paquin: we made the playoffs. Meanwhile, I came away *knowing* that I could hit in the big leagues; knowing, in fact, that I *would*. I felt like I'd seen everything a pitcher could throw or do, and there wasn't much I couldn't handle. Bring it on.

Eventually, Paquin let me strap on the gear now and then. Looking back on that winter, it was probably a blessing that I didn't spend too much time behind the plate and put more wear and tear on my body—an aspect of catching with which I would become well acquainted later on, when I was back there for 140 games a year in the National League.

CHAPTER NINE

Tommy was like a little kid sometimes, which was probably one of the reasons I enjoyed him so much and a lot of the organizational people didn't. And I liked him best in spring training, when he was at his youngest. Like the night in 1992 when Burt Hooton challenged him to a ball game.

This was at the end of the day, after the regular Grapefruit League game had been played. Even at that hour, Burt knew there was no way Tommy would turn down the challenge. So they chose up sides, with the two of them pitching, of course—Tommy tossing up his big lefty roundhouse and Burt countering with his famous knuckle-curve. The only concession was that they moved the pitching rubber a few feet closer and threw from behind the protective screen. Otherwise, it was the real deal—three strikes, four balls, run it out, everything. Tommy took me as his catcher, but I don't recall the rest of the teams, except that Burt chose Eric Young, who had stolen 146 bases over the previous two minor-league seasons. Naturally, Eric made it to second base somehow—probably stole it—then took off for third. I nailed him, and Tommy was beside himself. He's out there on the mound, screaming, "Attaboy, Michael! Attaway to throw him out!" He was *into* it. After three or four innings, Burt and Tommy were sucking the oxygen out of the stadium. This was during the period when Tommy was making his Slim-Fast commercials ("If I can do it, *you* can do it"), but he was sixty-four years old, for Pete's sake, and he was sweating his ass off. Finally, Peter O'Malley shut off the lights to make them quit.

It wasn't the only time that Tommy got himself worked up on my behalf that spring. Hitting-wise, I was able to build on my experiences in Bakersfield and Mexico and capitalize on some opportunities to play with the big-league club. I homered three times. One of them was on a big breaking ball from Jose DeLeon, a pitch I couldn't possibly have done anything with before I went to Mexicali. And one—the big one—was a pinch-hit grand slam to right-center against Paul Gibson of the Mets. On that occasion, it was like a flash of light exploded in Tommy's head; as if he had seen the future and been startled by the speed at which it was approaching. As soon as the ball landed, he ran up to Mark Cresse and shouted, "Get him down to the bullpen! Get him to start blocking some balls! Work with him!"

That game was in Port St. Lucie, and my dad was taking it all in next to a Cubs scout named Ed Lyons. When I came up to bat with the bases loaded, Lyons asked him, "Is that your kid? Who the hell scouted him?" My dad turned halfway around and pointed to Tim Thompson, a Cardinals scout from Pennsylvania who was sitting a couple of rows behind them. Thompson was one of the scouts who had advised me to get an education instead of worrying about being drafted.

"Tim Thompson? He's a hell of a scout," Lyons said.

"I know. He's a friend of mine. Please don't say anything."

"Oh hell no, I wouldn't say a word."

My dad claims that he called the grand slam, even the spot where it cleared the fence. The moment it did, Lyons stood up, turned toward Thompson, and bellowed, "Hey, Tim, did you have a chance to sign this kid?"

Thompson just looked at my dad, shook his head, and said, "So, Vince, you finally got even with me, huh?" It was all good-natured, but there might have been more truth in that remark than my father would ever admit.

It was an important Grapefruit season for me, because I was on the Dodgers' forty-man roster for the first time. That didn't mean I'd make it to Los Angeles—or even to the Triple-A club in Albuquerque—but it protected me from being taken by another team in the Rule 5 draft, and it indicated, finally, that the organization saw a little value in me. At least, *some* people in the organization did, although I was never quite sure which.

On that front, I was interested, years later, to read an article in the *Hardball Times Baseball Annual 2009* that was written by Craig Wright, an analyst who had been employed by the Dodgers as an advisor to Fred Claire. Wright wrote,

> During my 21 years working full-time with the major league teams, I was asked to make evaluations or recommendations involving several future Hall of Famers. It was fun to see their careers fulfill their promise, but I rarely felt like I had done anything to help their careers along. Players with Hall of Fame talent are generally so obvious that they rarely need any help in getting their careers

on track. Mike Piazza was a very different case, perhaps the most unusual in the history of great players. Unlike most Hall of Famers, Mike Piazza was far from a scout's dream. No one drafted him out of high school; no one considered signing him as an undrafted player. He didn't throw or run well, and he played first base, a position where you had to hit like Ted Williams to get noticed. And there was always something about Piazza's stance and swing that bothered a lot of visual scouts. He was abnormally upright in his swing with little bend in his knees, and his swing seemed a tad long. His hands were way down on the bottom of the bat with the pinky over the knob, and he would stand a little far off the plate. While other hitters with that stance would dive into the plate to compensate on certain pitches, Piazza seemed to be just reaching out to cover the plate, almost flicking at the outer pitch, though with surprising pop. It was different, and it was easy to be concerned that he might eventually hit a wall—that he would start to be overwhelmed by power pitchers, that against good pitchers he'd have a big hole low and away, and that he wouldn't be able to generate power on quality pitches away.

. . . I personally started to get excited about Piazza's big league prospects during his 1991 season in the California League. . . . When I expressed my excitement about Piazza that off-season to general manager Fred Claire, I was surprised to hear that the assessments of Piazza by our scouts and player development people were very mixed, and the consensus was, at best, lukewarm about his prospect status. Some felt he would never be more than a "minor league hitter," and some also thought he would never make it as a catcher and would have to move back to first base. . . . Fred indicated that he was encouraged by Piazza's 1991 season, but with so many conflicting views, and with the prospects we had in front of Piazza, we could not be making any plans around him. That disappointed me.

At the time, it seemed to me that Tommy had been beating the drum as a one-man band on my behalf. Not that my viewpoint is objective, but I really believe that, in an ironic sort of way, Tommy, unlike most of the nonplaying personnel I'd come across in the organization, considered my prospects without the clutter of bias, without being hung up on draft positions, prototypes, pedigree, politics, jealousy, resentment, or any of the stuff that packed my minor-league years with so much tension.

I was never certain which factor actually hammered me the hardest: the skepticism over my catching skills or the animosity over Tommy's meddling. It was no secret that he and a lot of the minor-league people weren't the best of pals. Tommy and the Albuquerque manager, Terry Collins, hated each other, simple as that. At organizational meetings, Tommy would complain that the minor leagues seldom sent him anybody he could work with, and Albuquerque's general manager, Pat McKernan, would stand up and argue that Tommy didn't know what to do with the talent he got. What I didn't realize until later, though, was the size of the rift between Tommy and Fred Claire. Those two couldn't have been more different in background and style. Fred had started out writing for newspapers, then joined the Dodgers as a public relations assistant and methodically worked his way up to GM. Tommy was all baseball. Fred was slim, buttoned-down, and soft-spoken. Tommy was Tommy. Tommy thought Fred was a pencil-pusher. Fred thought Tommy was a loose cannon.

So, while Tommy was having visions of me behind the plate at Dodger Stadium—not right away, because Mike Scioscia was the most respected player on the team, but soon enough, because Scioscia was thirty-three years old—the front office had me ticketed for the Double-A team in San Antonio, with a guy named Bryan Baar scheduled to be the catcher in Albuquerque. My dad, of course, grumbled to Tommy that I should be the one in Triple-A because I'd outplayed Baar the year before. (Baar, however, had spent the season a level higher.) Tommy told him not to worry about it because if something happened and he needed a catcher, I'd be the one coming up to Los Angeles. I wasn't complaining, anyway, because Baar had pretty decent credentials, for one thing—good arm, good power—and for another, Greg Hansell was also going to San Antonio, which meant I'd have a first-rate roommate and an apartment all tidied up by his mother. Besides, being a history buff, I was happy to find myself in the city of the Alamo—and possessed, no less, of a fresh affinity for the Mexican influence, since I could now hit breaking pitches.

The effects of my newly acquired aptitude showed up, big-time, in the Texas League. When the season got cranking, I was hitting about a hundred points higher than I ever had before. Meanwhile, I found that, in baseball, nothing acts in a vacuum: I carried a greater sense of confidence to the plate, and that confidence served to raise not only my batting average but also my expectations—which, in turn, wound me a little tighter still.

Once he was able to do in the Texas League what he had done in the California League, people recognized that he was legitimate.

But he still had something to prove. His anger was probably directed toward management. He wanted to prove to a lot of people that he was there because of his own merits, not because of anything given to him. I think that escalated his intensity to a level where he literally couldn't hold it in. He was kind of a red-ass, frankly.

Of course, his favorite word was the f-word. He would go three for four and that fourth at-bat, if he struck out, it would probably weigh on him a little harder than it should have. It wasn't a nice, soft, to-yourself kind of curse. It was people in the cheap seats hearing the f-bomb. It's not fair to say that Mike wasn't a team player, but when you do those things, that's what people are going to think. It makes you look a little selfish. But the fact is, he never gave an at-bat away. He just had that drive. He took it to the next level. Even after games that most people would celebrate with a beer, he'd go back to the gym and have a protein shake while the other guys were out in the bars.

— Greg Hansell

In San Antonio, thankfully, I was able to loosen up at a nice apartment. Instead of staying at the nondescript complex where the players usually lived, Greg and I found a place with a pool, mixers, and a date night. The lady in the office kind of liked me, and she gave us the furnished model, complete with potted plants. I'd never had plants before. It was a great setup until Hansell was called to Albuquerque.

Then, about thirty games into the season, with my average at .377, the manager, Jerry Royster, summoned me into his office to tell me that Bryan Baar was coming down and I was moving up. I said, "Oh, shit." Not that I didn't want to go to Albuquerque. It was just that Hansell usually took care of the bill-paying and utilities and whatnot, and with him already gone, it meant that I had a lot to do before I could leave the next morning.

My flight took me from San Antonio to Dallas to Salt Lake City to Seattle, and I grabbed a cab to Tacoma, where we were playing. I pulled up to the ballpark on two hours of sleep. To borrow a phrase from Tommy Lasorda, I looked like I'd been welding all night without a helmet. Bill Russell was the Albuquerque manager, and when I saw him I said, "Man, I hope I'm not playing tonight. I'm exhausted."

He said, "You're playing. We've got a doubleheader and nobody else to catch."

I dragged myself out for infield practice and one of the coaches hit me a high pop-up. I looked up, got dizzy, saw two or three balls in the air, and collapsed. Everybody had a good laugh, the first game started, and I went three for four. Had three more hits in the second game. After one of them, I was standing at first and the Tacoma first baseman, Dann Howitt, said, "Hmm, I see you're really having a hard time making that adjustment to Triple-A."

But my odyssey wasn't over yet. We bused back to Seattle, flew overnight—Seattle to Salt Lake to Phoenix to Albuquerque—and landed around noon. I was staying at the Howard Johnson's (most of the players already had their own places, of course), and when I got there they said my room wasn't ready yet; all they had available was one suite. I said, I'll take the suite. They said that wasn't authorized. I said, it's authorized, give me the suite. When I got to the ballpark that night, Pat McKernan's assistant said something like "Oh, you're going to take the suite, huh?" I'm sure they thought I was being a rich-boy prima donna. Around that time, my dad was in the news a lot because he was bidding to buy the San Francisco Giants. People knew my story. What they didn't know was how desperate I was for a few good hours of sleep.

In just under four hundred at-bats for Albuquerque, I hit .341, with a twenty-five-game hitting streak and sixteen home runs on top of the seven I had for San Antonio. Defensively, my progress was apparent in one sequence when I blocked a curveball in the dirt, called for another, and blocked that one, too, which impressed one of our scouts so much that he phoned Fred Claire to tell him about it. I was smelling the big leagues at that point—so close, so focused, so locked in that I could think of nothing else, other than the chords and lyrics pounding in my headphones. I had no idea, however, that the Dodgers had been kicking around the idea of bringing me up since midseason. In the *Hardball Times* article, Craig Wright provided a firsthand account of the internal debate:

> Shortly after the 1992 All-Star break, just a half-season further in Piazza's development, Fred Claire asked me to review the team and make recommendations as to what we should do with the rest of our season. I wrote: . . . *We have been given a golden opportunity to gamble on a catcher with exactly what this team is crying for, power. I know when I have asked about Piazza, you have shown little interest in making him part of the mix, but I'd be doing you a grave disservice if I didn't fight and fight hard on this point. . . . My absolute #1 recommendation is that we promote Piazza and play him.*

We weren't ready to do that—or at least it was explained to me that the field staff wasn't ready to do that. Tommy Lasorda genuinely loved Mike as a person and was plenty willing to help him along up to a point, but contrary to legend, Lasorda was far from fighting to pave the way for Piazza to be a big league regular. . . . Lasorda was [sixty-four] years old, and he had already shown signs of a common affliction that creeps up on older managers, a tendency to overplay veterans at the expense of young players. Scioscia was a Dodger institution and very popular with the field staff who had already demonstrated . . . that they were willing to play him as a #1 catcher even though he had nothing left.

. . . A further sign of my faith in Piazza came a month later when in mid-August the Pittsburgh Pirates sought to make a trade with us that would include Mike Scioscia, and as part of the deal the Dodgers would get catcher Mike LaValliere, whose contract had gotten too expensive for the small-market Pirates. On the surface it was a very good deal, but when asked to analyze it I concluded: *[At this stage of their careers] I personally consider LaValliere a . . . better catcher than Scioscia. Yet I can see refusing to make this deal if we have to take on LaValliere. We don't need what LaValliere can offer us as a catcher; what we need is what Mike Piazza can offer us as a catcher. And if Piazza were a bust—which would surprise the hell out of me—Carlos Hernandez [a highly rated prospect who was in his rookie year with the Dodgers] has a better chance of giving us what we need from our catcher. . . . I am in favor of anything that will clear the deck for Piazza, and I find I can't endorse any move that will make it harder for him to establish himself in the majors.*

Fred Claire was steadily becoming more enamored with Piazza as he continued to play well, and he declined the Pittsburgh deal.

All the while, my mission was to hit the ball hard enough that the decisions would make themselves. I was named the organization's Minor League Player of the Year, and the call-up came on the first day of September.

There was a little bit of buzz over my arrival in Los Angeles. Tommy took care of that, of course; and, of course, he also reminded my dad of what he'd said in the spring—don't worry, it'll happen. But it wasn't just Tommy anymore. By proving that my Bakersfield season hadn't been a fluke, I had become the Dodgers' top prospect. The prevailing school of thought was that, if I made a good account of myself in September, I'd take over for Scioscia as the starting catcher in 1993.

The worst team in Major League Baseball was waiting for me in Chi-cago. I could have, *should* have, arrived in style. Actually, four of us were pro-moted at the same time, the others being Billy Ashley, Rafael Bournigal, and Kip Gross, a long-haired pitcher who had been up and down and knew the drill—or at least convinced me and Ashley that he did. We all had first-class tickets, but Gross advised us that if we downgraded to coach, the Dodgers would reimburse us in cash for the difference in price. Apparently, Bournigal was not quite the dumbass that Billy and I were. (You might know Ashley from the Fox reality show he starred in, *Househusbands of Hollywood*.) To us, Gross's scheme sounded like a shrewd move. That is, until we got to the Hyatt on Wacker Drive, asked for our reimbursements, and Bill DeLury, the Dodgers' traveling secretary, shook his head and said, "No, no, no, no . . ."

I made a better account of myself the next day at Wrigley Field, bat-ting sixth in the lineup between Karros and Dave Hansen, catching Tim Crews, and facing a big right-hander, Mike Harkey. Wrigley, of course, is a gorgeous, resonating ballpark that strikes a chord with anyone who loves the game, but the awe factor didn't hit me too hard. I'd been taking BP with big leaguers since I was barely a teenager, and my spikes had already dug into the grass of the Vet, Shea, and Dodger Stadium. Plus, you know, I was committed to not giving a shit. Like they say, you gotta dance with the one that brung you.

Determined not to make an out on the first pitch I ever saw in the major leagues—which came with one out in the second inning and Karros on first base with a single—I took strike one right down the middle. Ended up walk-ing, anyway. The next time up, I *did* swing at the first pitch, and stroked a double to right-center. I followed that with two singles; I was three for three altogether, until Eric Young pinch-ran for me in the eighth. Before Eric got out there, Mark Grace, the Cubs' first baseman, leaned toward me and said, "Hey, it ain't that fuckin' easy."

I must have looked like I knew what I was doing behind the plate, because only one guy, Dwight Smith, tried to steal against me. My throw bounced to second base but got there in time. Ryne Sandberg hit two home runs for the Cubs, Karros tied the game with a homer in the ninth, and we won in thirteen. And my father was there to catch it all, snapping pictures and crying into his glasses.

My next at-bat came three days later in Pittsburgh, a single against Randy Tomlin to make me four for four in the major leagues. That would have been great for my confidence if I'd been lacking in that department; but I *knew* I could hit. And so did Tommy. From the start, he was telling people that, if I stayed healthy, I would hit more home runs than any catcher ever had.

Another encouraging endorsement was thrown my way when I caught Bob Ojeda, a veteran lefty who was the kind of pitcher a catcher enjoys working with, a guy who could dot an *i* and knew what he was doing. Afterward, Ojeda was downright lavish with his praise of my receiving. *That* was where I needed confidence. It gave me a lift. I was feeling it. Between Tommy and Ojeda, I figured I was right on track for the Hall of Fame.

My high lasted for exactly two days—until I got the assignment for Orel Hershiser's next start. I'd actually caught Hershiser once before, when he was rehabbing at Bakersfield after shoulder surgery. He had been very complimentary of me at the time, but the pleasure was all mine: Hershiser had that good sinker, could spot the ball anywhere he wanted, brought a plan to the mound, and was an incredible athlete. Orel could pull back on the bunt and slash the ball through the hole better than anybody I've ever seen. Once, in Montreal, he said, real casually, "Hey, Mike, can I use your bat? I need one with some power in it." I flipped him my Mizuno and he cracked a double off the wall. You couldn't help but admire the guy.

This time, the opponent was San Diego, and it was 1–1 in the top of the seventh. Jerald Clark was on third base for the Padres, and I needed to talk to my pitcher. So I glanced back at the umpire, Joe West, said, "Time," and ambled out toward the mound.

Before I got there, Orel was screaming at me and pointing furiously at home plate. I turned around just in time to see Jerald Clark stepping on it with what turned out to be the winning run.

I was stunned. I ran to West and said, "Joe, didn't I call time?"

He said, "Yeah, but I didn't give it to you."

Naturally, Hershiser was upset with me, and so was everybody else—except Tommy. He told the media that, before it was over, I was going to win a hundred more games for the Dodgers than I would ever lose. It was nice of him, but not much consolation at the time. I was so distraught that I actually chain-smoked a few cigarettes after the game. Leave it to Lenny Harris to turn my misery into a great impression: me sitting in front of my locker, dragging on a cigarette, moaning, "Man, I fucked up . . . I fucked up . . ."

That was a bad day for the Piazzas all-around. While I was fucking up at Dodger Stadium, the major-league owners were meeting in St. Louis to discuss my father's bid to buy the Giants. During one of the breaks, Fred Kuhlmann of the Cardinals, who was chairman of the ownership committee, blurted to the media that the sale was being rejected because my dad had not passed a background check.

The entire situation, to me, was bizarre on several levels. I'd been striv-ing my whole life—with the intense, complete, sometimes controversial sup-port of my father—to reach the major leagues, had navigated through the peaks and valleys of a very stressful minor-league experience, had worked my way from Phoenixville to Miami to the Dominican Republic to Mexico and finally to Los Angeles, with all the organizational stops in between . . . and the moment I arrive, reporters are asking me if my father's in the Mafia. They're asking me if he's ever been involved in "unscrupulous activities." There was a writer from the *Los Angeles Times*, Ken Daley, who might have been the first to question me about it straight-out. I didn't tell him to go fuck himself, but that was the general idea that he picked up on.

My dad had put the deal together pretty much on his own. The Gi-ants were languishing at Candlestick Park, and their owner at the time, Bob Lurie, was looking for a buyer. No locals were coming forward, so Lurie re-ceived permission from Major League Baseball to entertain offers from parties outside San Francisco. The ownership group my father mustered up started with his partner in the computer service business, Vince Tirendi, and other investors were based in the Tampa Bay area. They made no secret of their intention to move the franchise there. Dad negotiated with the pertinent government officials, found minority ownership, worked out a stadium deal, left 'em laughing, everything. It all came together around midseason, 1992.

He was visiting me in Albuquerque at the time, and at one point re-ceived a phone call, finished it, and told me, "I gotta go, I gotta go. This thing is happening." A couple of months later, here I was on the Dodgers and our owner, Peter O'Malley, stood prominent among the opponents of the sale because it would take away his biggest rival. Los Angeles hates San Francisco and San Francisco hates Los Angeles, and they *need* each other. Other owners objected to putting the Giants in Tampa Bay, specifically. A lot of dynamics were working against my dad—and then they come out and say that he has been turned down for reasons of "background."

> We had a hell of a deal, a hundred and ten million dollars. We had the stadium for a dollar a year. Little did I realize that Baseball didn't want to move the team because they had Tampa Bay earmarked for expansion. So they'd do anything to stop me from putting this deal together. That was embarrassing, when they made that comment about my background. Mike was just coming up, and it embarrassed the hell out of him.
>
> What happened was an unfortunate situation. Through a very

prominent attorney in Philadelphia who was doing a lot of work for me in acquisitions with dealerships and all that, and his son, who was also an attorney, I got involved with this guy who said, "I own this company down here, Vince, and it's doing well, and if you've got some money, I'd like to invest it for you and get you a good return on your money."

I said, "All right, I'll give you around ten thousand bucks."

So I gave him ten thousand in cash that I had over the years, that I'd just saved. I gave him some money, too, out of the business. They come to find out that this guy was embezzling money out of the company, so they grabbed him and threw him in jail for embezzlement. At the time this is all occurring, he probably read in the paper that I was applying to buy the baseball team. He thought he'd found a way to get out of jail. So he calls Baseball and tells security that the one individual who's investing in that team, he was laundering money. He told them he had this business and I put a lot of cash in there, overstating what I gave him.

This all was taking place while they were getting ready to approve the deal. Now the security people call the owners at the meeting there, telling them there might be a little problem and we've got to hold up and find out what the problem might be with Mr. Piazza. And the guy from St. Louis, Fred Kuhlmann, was half shot in the ass, from what I understand. So Kuhlmann goes to the bathroom, walks out, and there's a reporter there. The reporter asks him how the meeting's going. He says, well, we've got a problem with this Piazza person; he might be involved with the Mafia. He's laundering money or something; we're trying to check it out. [White Sox owner] Jerry Reinsdorf was standing there, and he said, you can't say that. And he said to the reporter, he [Kuhlmann] didn't mean what he was saying; we haven't even had a chance to check it out.

After all the investigations through the depositions, they come to find out it was all bullshit. I hired Bruce Kauffman from Philadelphia—now he's a federal judge—to file a lawsuit against Baseball. He said, "Look, I'll take this case and I'll take it on contingency. I want this case." Because he'd checked it out and knew everything I was telling him was true. Finally, they settled. They gave me a nice piece of change. And I got a nice letter from Major League Baseball saying anytime you want to become an owner, you're automatically approved.

—Vince Piazza

My dad's case is actually taught in law classes. He did some television interviews, and kind of liked that. He also liked the $6 million he received in the settlement. What he *didn't* like was the insinuation that any Italian-American with enough money to buy a baseball team must be in the mob.

A few days later, when another rookie, Pedro Astacio, was shutting out the team that my father hadn't been allowed to buy, I delivered my first major-league home run, and my last of the season.

Bud Black started for the Giants, but my long ball came off Steve Reed in the fifth inning, deep to right-center at Dodger Stadium. I believe it would have cleared the street next to Phoenixville High and probably landed on Mr. Thompson's driveway; maybe even dented the roof on his garage. It was one of four home runs I would hit against Reed over the years, in only seventeen at-bats. All of those came in the first dozen or so times I faced him, when he couldn't get me out. Then he hit me in the elbow, and after that I had one little single against him.

As the 1992 season wound down, I was expecting some grief from the veterans, for at least a couple of reasons—one, on general principle, since I was a rookie; and two, because I was a threat to the job security of a guy who had earned their loyalty. Traditions were changing, but the old-school custom amounted to completely ignoring rookies unless the opportunity arose to humiliate them. Eric Anthony once told me that when he got called up to the Astros, they were a predominantly veteran team with well-established players like Mike Scott, Terry Puhl, and Alan Ashby, and for a long time nobody said a word to him. That same year, 1989, Dennis Cook—nicest guy ever—pitched a couple of games as a rookie for San Francisco, even won one, and the Giants made it to the World Series; but Dennis Cook didn't even get a T-shirt. It wasn't like that for me, but there were moments that called for thick skin.

On one particular bus ride to the airport, Billy Ashley and I were on the receiving end. Some of the older players, mostly pitchers—guys like Ojeda, John Candelaria, Kevin Gross, and Roger McDowell—would sit in the back of the bus and get blasted, and on this night we were coming off another ugly loss. Billy had been having some defensive issues in the outfield—one ball had bounced up and nailed him just below the mouth—and they started cracking on him. "Hey, Ashley, why don't you put a glove on your fuckin' chin?!" He was visibly shaken. I could see his lower lip start to quiver.

Then Bobby Ojeda turned to me and said, "And you, fuckin' Piazza! Takin' Scioscia's job!" Thankfully, Scioscia was laughing.

Mike had been the Dodgers' starting catcher for most of his thirteen years, his entire career, but even he was not exempt from the kind of jocular abuse that baseball is famous for. He was known to have a pretty fair appetite—I can just imagine some of the pasta dinners that he and Tommy put away on the road—and with that in mind, a couple of the Dodgers would bring a little kitchen timer and a bunch of bananas to team meetings and set them next to Scioscia. The timer would go off in the middle of the meeting and somebody would announce, "Snack time, Scioscia!"

But Scioscia, who by that time was making over $2 million a year, was a consummate pro, a rock of a catcher, and extremely kind to me. As tough a time as it must have been for him, he never showed a trace of bitterness about turning over his position. Maybe it was because we're both Italian Catholics from Philadelphia.

The move became practically inevitable when his batting average dropped to .221 that year. I didn't do much better, at .232, but I was a hell of a lot cheaper. With that factor in the mix, I was pretty sure I finally had the front office behind me. I'd shown that I wasn't overmatched in the big leagues, and I was holding my own defensively. The fairy tale appeared to be back on track.

Before the season ended, though, I was in store for one more little dose of disillusionment. This one had nothing to do with *me*, per se, but reminded me, once again, that professional baseball is not always the sport for romantics.

It was the last day of the year, at Houston, and it would be our ninety-ninth defeat, the most games the Dodgers have lost since they moved to Los Angeles; and tack on a half century to that: the most since they dropped 101 as the Brooklyn Superbas in 1908, the year the *Cubs* won the World Series. But that wasn't what bothered me so much. Astacio was pitching for us, Pete Harnisch for the Astros, and the guy behind *me* was Doug Harvey, the umpire who was referred to as God—probably because that's how Harvey referred to *himself* when he called balls and strikes. It was an interesting dynamic: over the shoulder of the most impressionable rookie loomed the most grizzled guy on the field. Harvey had been in the National League for thirty years, and by that time was considered probably the greatest umpire of the second half of the century.

Starting time was one o'clock. Before I had a chance to pull down my mask, Harvey informed me, "This is the last game of my career. We all have four-thirty flights, and we're gonna be on that plane." It didn't take me long to find out what he had in mind. When I'd drop down into my crouch to give the target, he'd bark at me, "Get out there, get out there!" Put my *mitt* out there, he meant—place the target *outside* the strike zone, and he would take care of the rest. I was actually setting up behind the opposite batter's box, and Harvey was calling strike after strike. Apparently, he had given the same instructions to the Houston catcher, Eddie Taubensee. Astacio was shouting at me to get my target behind the plate, and Harvey wouldn't even let me take the time to walk out there and explain to Pedro that everything would be fine if he'd just throw the ball to the mitt, no matter where it was. On the bench, we described the strike zone as "dugout to dugout." Looking back on it, I don't believe that the events of that day represented a true reflection of Harvey's integrity or personal character. As far as I'm concerned, all of that is intact. The man was simply ready to go home. At the time, though, that very short afternoon did make a small contribution to my growing cynicism toward the industry.

In my second at-bat, I swung at a pitch that was practically over my head and somehow grounded out. When I came out to catch the bottom of the inning, Harvey greeted me with something to the effect of "That was great, Mike. That's what I'm talking about."

I came up one last time in the ninth, with us down 3–0, two outs and nobody on. As I'm setting up, Harvey tells Taubensee, "You know what? I'm gonna give him a real at-bat now." So Taubensee passes that along to Doug Jones, who was on in relief, and I strike out anyway.

The game was over in an hour and forty-four minutes, at which point Harvey removed the chew of tobacco from his mouth, placed it on home plate, and walked away. Eighteen years later, he was inducted into the Hall of Fame.

My first big-league crush was over a beautiful green-eyed brunette named Christina. Actually, even though I'd made my major-league debut, I was playing at the time in the Arizona Fall League, which was making *its* debut. The previous couple of years, I'd been in Arizona for the Fall Instructional League, but had finally outgrown it. My education continued, however. The experience with Christina was highly instructional.

The rationale behind the Arizona Fall League was that the major-league organizations wanted to keep some of their best prospects in one general spot, closer to home, instead of seeing them scattered all over the Americas. We were the Sun Cities Solar Sox, and would become the AFL's official first champions. Hansell was on the club, and Jeromy Burnitz. I split the catching with Derek Parks, who had been a first-round draft pick of the Twins.

The signature feature of the AFL is that all the ballparks are within easy driving distance. One night I was at Christina's house, which was closer to where we were playing the next day than the place I shared with Hansell in Glendale; so I asked her if I could crash there. We weren't sleeping together, because, in spite of losing my innocence, I was still very mom-and-church about that sort of thing. Anyway, she didn't want me to stay. I said, "What's the big deal? We're dating, we're on our way to becoming boyfriend-girlfriend . . ."

Finally she relented, and I curled up on the couch. But I evidently wasn't sleeping very hard, because after a while I thought I heard a window open. Turned out, I *did* hear a window open. Christina had crawled through it to go meet some other guy—one of the Phoenix Suns, I found out later. (Being from North Dakota and everything, she eventually married a hockey player.)

Now, you would think that I'd give it up after the window escapade. Nope. I was seriously infatuated with this girl. Hansell liked to point out that Christina's answering machine was always a lot fuller than mine; but I just didn't get it, even though everybody else did. She bartended at a place in Tempe, and after the infamous sleepover I went in there to see what was up. She gave me a hug and said she really liked me and whatnot, so I figured everything was cool. Then she said, "You're the nicest guy . . ." Uh-oh. Red flag. And *still*, I soldiered on. I went with her to a fraternity bar called the Dash, and a couple of the frat dudes were checking her out. They were eyeing me and I was balling up like, "I'm gonna kick your ass." It was almost like a swordfight thing.

A week or so later, Jeromy Burnitz was at Christina's bar and saw a friend of hers, who said, "What's up with Mike? Is he out of his mind? Christina doesn't even want to see him anymore." I grilled Jeromy about it afterward, and he basically told me, "Dude, come on, turn the page. Snap out of it, man."

I finally did, but I was hurt. Hurt and prepared, in a way. From Christina, I learned a little bit about what it's like to play in the big leagues.

Along those lines, it was also time—*past* time—that I hired an agent. I'd felt for a while that I wanted to take my business to Dan Lozano and his group. Danny had once called the apartment I shared with Hansell in Bakersfield, and to my surprise actually wanted to speak to me. That got the dialogue started, and we talked periodically, but mostly as friends. I was putting off the big decision.

For one thing, there were also other agents to consider. In the following year or so, I had some contact with the cousin of Rafael Bournigal, who was the agent for Rafael and Ramon Martinez, among others. There was also a dude from Minnesota who kept calling my parents' house—bad idea. And Tommy was pushing me toward somebody he knew. "You should sign with this guy John Boggs," he kept telling me. My preference remained Lozano, but, still stalling, I told him that I planned to play through Triple-A and check out my options before I committed. And explained about my dad.

My dad insisted that I didn't need an agent. He never really said it, but the implication was that *he* could do my negotiating. He was also going on advice that Tommy gave him: "If a team offers you five million dollars and your agent gets you six million dollars, you should only give him five percent of that extra million dollars he got for you, not five percent of the whole six million." But agents do more for players than just negotiate contracts. They help with managing money, endorsements, channeling media requests, and all sorts of details that require time and attention. I just felt that I needed representation from an outside party, which was the very thing my father was leery of. He didn't want to lose his influence over me. I was very aware of that, and consequently the decision to finally hire an agent was a significant one in my life. It was a show of independence. I wouldn't say that I made it in *defiance* of my father, but it was probably the first time I'd acted against his strong advice in an important matter.

After the Arizona Fall League, I'd returned briefly to Philadelphia, then headed back to Los Angeles and stayed with Hansell's family. I'd lived with them during my call-up in September and felt at ease there. Ate well, certainly. But it also put me in closer proximity to Lozano. He and an agent he worked with, Brian Cohen, took me to a basketball game at the Forum that winter, ostensibly just to watch James Worthy, Byron Scott, Vlade Divac, and the rest of a mediocre Lakers team. But the night had a good feel to it, and afterward, in the parking lot, I said, "You know what? I'm gonna sign with you guys." I knew I'd have some talking to do with my dad, but my mind was made up. Brian Cohen went rummaging through his car, tossing things all over the trunk, trying to find the paperwork he needed to make it official. Danny was laughing. I said, "Take your time, dude, it's cool."

There was another small convenience to being in Los Angeles that winter. In those days, the Dodgers maintained an unusual tradition by which they'd hold informal workouts at Dodger Stadium in January, before spring training, and top them off with an exhibition game against the University of Southern California. It was a big deal. Most of the top minor-league players would be there. One year I got into a home-run-hitting contest against Bret

Boone, when he was playing for USC, and the whole lower level of Dodger Stadium was packed.

But January 1993 was different for me. This time, I felt like I was playing in my home ballpark. The organization had allowed Scioscia to become a free agent, and he had signed with San Diego. The stars were now aligned so clearly that one of Danny's partners, Dennis Gilbert, was able to call Fred Claire and say, in effect, "Look, we all know that Mike's going to be your starting catcher this year . . ." To which Fred replied, "Okay, fine, what do you want?" Instead of the $110,000 minimum salary, I got a raise to $126,000.

In baseball terms, it wasn't a lot of money. But if my negotiations with the Dodgers had always gone that smoothly, I'd have probably retired in their uniform.

CHAPTER TEN

Late in spring training, 1993, when I was batting around .500 with a few home runs and appeared to have ended any remaining suspense concerning the starting catcher's job, Tommy sent me up in extra innings to pinch-hit against Steve Bedrosian, the veteran reliever for the Braves, with a couple of runners on base, and I lined a single to win the game. Afterward, in a live interview, a prominent Los Angeles television reporter named Jim Hill asked Tommy if I was earning the position legitimately.

In retrospect, that's when I should have clung to the advice of Roy Campanella, the great catcher who had been paralyzed in an automobile accident after ten Hall of Fame seasons with the Brooklyn Dodgers. Campy had first played in the Negro Leagues, but his father was a Sicilian immigrant and Roy had grown up in Philadelphia, so we had quite a bit in common. He'd helped Scioscia when Mike was a young player, and over the previous couple of springs had adopted me as his latest protégé. From his wheelchair in Campy's Corner, as it was called—where catchers and others collected for his benevolent counsel and soft-pedal storytelling—Campanella favored me with practical guidance on the defensive and psychological demands of the position I was still learning. I'd already been privy to a lot of Campy's theories through Johnny Roseboro, who was probably his first disciple. On the subject of blocking balls in the dirt, for instance, Rosie, passing along Roy's concept of "body follows glove," would repeat the same thing again and again, just like he'd first heard it from the Hall of Famer: "Turn the glove over, and the body will follow. It's like a backhand in Ping-Pong. Just play Ping-Pong." Adding those lessons to the techniques that Joe Ferguson had taught me, I felt that my ability to receive low pitches was equal to anybody's. I'm confident in saying that, when I caught, no pitcher on the Dodgers' staff was afraid to bounce his wickedest pitch with the tying run on third base. Campanella had a lot to do with that.

But as much as Campy helped me with mechanics, his most indelible lesson was even more fundamental. "Just play baseball," he would say, urging me to block out any and all of the peripheral things that made a hard profession so much harder. "Just keep it a game." Roy encouraged me to handle a nineties sport with a fifties mentality, and I wished like hell that I could. I wished I could deal with everything *his* way.

For starters, Roy Campanella wouldn't have been the least bit bothered by what Jim Hill said and plenty of others were thinking. He'd been in professional ball for a decade before Jackie Robinson broke the color line, and the slights and hardships that Campy endured were immeasurably more severe than the comparatively trivial stuff I encountered—the doubts of a couple of minor-league managers and the skepticism of the major-league media. But I hadn't acquired tolerance in the doses that Roy had, nor any semblance of his serenity. At the age of twenty-four, those things consumed me. Only the people closest to me would have known it—Karros, my family, Greg Hansell, Danny Lozano—but I seethed over Hill's insulting question and the disrespect it represented on a much wider scope. The fire had been flickering inside me since Vero Beach, if not before, and this was the sort of thing that made it rage.

Hell, yes, I earned the position legitimately. I had been the organization's Minor League Player of the Year. I'd played practically around the calendar for five years in a row. For the second straight season, I'd put together an outstanding spring training; led the team in hitting this time. I was throwing so well that Mark Cresse said I had the best arm of any Dodger catcher since Steve Yeager (which, truth be known, was only about eight years). Most important, nobody questioned that I'd outperformed my competitors—Carlos Hernandez, who was the primary challenger; Lance Parrish, an eight-time all-star whom they'd brought in for insurance in case I proved to be not ready; and Don Wakamatsu, a proficient knuckleball catcher who could handle Tom Candiotti if need be. As it turned out, I handled Candiotti just fine, for the most part, and the other starting pitchers—Hershiser, Kevin Gross, Pedro Astacio, and Ramon Martinez—as well.

Still, I knew that my *defense* hadn't won me the job. In a backward, ironic sort of way, the uncertainty about my catching skills might have actually worked in my favor; may have been one of the reasons the Dodgers didn't bring back Scioscia for a fourteenth season. They wanted me in the lineup, and they didn't want their pitchers complaining that they'd rather throw to Scioscia. It was a show of faith on the organization's part—possibly the very first I'd received, of any consequence.

I'd begun to carve out a little reputation as a hitter. Not a *big* one, mind you—certainly not to any celebrity kind of degree. Los Angeles is, of course, a city of stars, and I wasn't one. It seemed like nobody in L.A. even knew how to pronounce my last name until Vin Scully, the Dodgers' famous announcer, started saying it with the proper Italian inflection—Pea-OT-za. In one of my first games at Dodger Stadium, they showed an interview with me on the JumboTron and identified it as Eric Karros. (Some people thought we *did* resemble each other. Tommy used to look at me, then look at Eric, then look back at me and say, "Where was Vince Piazza in 1967?") But I was gaining some traction within the organization. During that spring training of 1993, teammates would gather around the cage to watch me take batting practice. It was good for my ego.

When the team plane left Florida, I was on it. Nevertheless, I wasn't about to take anything for granted. I knew damn well that I wouldn't have the job for very long if I drove in forty runs a year, like Scioscia did. No long-term leases for me; I'd seen enough guys yo-yoing between L.A. and Triple-A to know better than that. Rather than rent an apartment I might have to vacate, I decided to just move back in with the Hansells (even though Greg was in Albuquerque).

We actually opened the regular season on the road—straight back to Florida—but first, there was the annual end-of-spring, home-and-home series with the California Angels. I homered off Mark Langston at Dodger Stadium, and the swell of the crowd just surged through me. That was the start of a special relationship I would enjoy, for quite a while, with the fans of Los Angeles. I still refused to romanticize the game; but at times like that, I couldn't help but love it. The fact is that, in spite of my attitude, I never lost my infatuation with the sport itself, at the organic level. My beef was with the petty, stupid stuff that mucks it up in the organized version.

From Miami we flew to Atlanta, where I got into a little home-run battle in batting practice with Darryl Strawberry, who was one of the players I held in awe when I was younger, and Eric Davis, a teammate I really enjoyed. In spring training, when Eric commented on the way I was mashing in BP, my response had been, "Yeah, I'm dropping some skull on the ball." I'd picked up that expression in the minor leagues from Brian Traxler, who'd always say, "Come on, man, drop some skull. Drop some head." You know, the *bat* head. Eric Davis liked that and nicknamed me Skull: "What's up, Skull?"

I was launching the ball into the seats before the first Atlanta game, trying to outmuscle Davis and Strawberry, getting a little carried away, and on one swing I felt a tweak in my oblique. I told Eric, "Man, I think I pulled something."

He said, "Where is it?"

I showed him, and he goes, "Oh, man. Go get checked out by the trainer."

First, I hit a few more bombs, which only verified that my side felt a little weird. Eric said, "Hey, man, if your shit ain't right, don't play. Go in there and get some treatment."

I finally went to the training room and got some ice, and the trainer asked me if I was going to play. I said I didn't think so, but first I'd talk to Tommy. So I walked into his office and said, "Tommy, I don't know, I tweaked something in batting practice."

In a calm, reassuring voice, Tommy told me, "Now, Mike, it's okay. Let me know if you feel like you need a rest. It's not a big deal. It's early in the season, and we're going to need you for the long haul, so you do what you feel like you need to do. Just play it day by day."

I appreciated his compassion. "Well," I said, "I really don't think I can play tonight."

"Jesus Christ! You don't think you can play?! *What the fuck?*"

I held the ice in place and went back to the trainer, who suggested I get a shot of novocaine and Xylocaine, with some cortisone in there. They called in the doctor, a surgeon from Atlanta who was the nicest guy in the world, and he pulled out this long needle, loaded it up with cortisone and Xylocaine, asked me where it hurt, and said, "I don't know what's going to happen, but whatever." I missed two games—Tom Glavine and Pete Smith—but was good to go after that. The doc hit the spot.

At any rate, I learned my lesson about trying to power up in batting practice, and another about being a piece of meat. But in the greater scheme of baseball, the strategy worked. I got off to a good start with the bat and even shot down eleven of the first sixteen runners who tried to steal on me. Of course, as soon as I cooled off in the throwing department, there was talk about moving me to third base.

Our first home stand began with three games, all losses, against the Cardinals. For the finale, Tommy moved me up from seventh in the batting order to third, which felt good. I came up in the first inning against Rene Arocha, a right-hander from Cuba, and got a pitch I could handle.

I'll never forget his first home run in 1993. Mike hit a ball no more than ten feet off the ground, a line shot to right field, way over the fence at Dodger Stadium. We're all watching, and Tommy's telling me, "Jesus Christ, that's how you drive that outside pitch!" And I'm thinking, you know, that didn't really look like an outside pitch. So I go into the video room and pull it up and I'll be darned if that pitch wasn't six inches off the *inside* part of the plate. It was incredible. That was the sort of stuff that separated Mike as a hitter. There were three things I've seen him do as well as anybody. One, hit a golf ball. Two, throw a football. And three, hit with power to right field as a right-handed hitter.

Mike subscribed to that Ted Williams hitting philosophy. But I read that book a thousand times, too, and it didn't do for me what it did for him. Mike worked his ass off. He was passionate about hitting. He knew his swing and he knew what he needed to do to fix his swing, as well. For him, a lot of it had to do with his ability to keep his hands inside of a baseball. He kept his hands close to his body, didn't let them get away from him. Barry Bonds is probably the best I've ever seen at that. The closer you stay, the stronger you are; but it's very difficult to do. What was really weird was that I used to hit behind Mike a lot, and I swear that guy would get more broken-bat flares over the second baseman's head. The first couple months I'm watching this shit, I'm thinking, this guy's the luckiest motherfucker I've ever seen. But after watching it for a year or two, I realized it had nothing to do with luck at all. It was his ability to fight off pitches that got everybody else out. I think I marveled more at those kinds of at-bats than how hard he hit the ball, or how far he hit it.

—Eric Karros, teammate

The promotion in the batting order afforded me a better sense of security. I was flattered to hit between Davis and Strawberry. When we swept the Pittsburgh Pirates in the next series, I felt the situation had stabilized enough that I could move out of the Hansells' house and into Karros's condo in Manhattan Beach.

Eric had been National League Rookie of the Year in 1992, and he'd taken me under his wing when I was called up in September. His place was on Eleventh Street, in the front unit of a duplex, about a mile from the beach. One of his roommates had just moved out, and another took care of the money matters, so I was just assigned a bedroom and a cut of the rent; let the good times roll.

With the way I was playing and the response from the fans and now my connection to the larger world through Eric, I began to see it all as my window of opportunity. Socially, I mean. Not that I had ambitions to be another Wilt Chamberlain in that respect. It wasn't about conquest or even promiscuity. I just wanted to be *that guy*. I wanted to date Michelle Pfeiffer, and if not her, whoever was the hot star at the moment. I guess it was the last vestige of my romanticism with baseball, the image in my head of life in the big leagues.

When I moved in with Eric, I was introduced to the fruits of the game. Not that he was a bad boy, because he wasn't; but I started to comprehend what was available for a guy in my position. Then I made adjustments, like a batter does when he gets a better look at what the pitcher has. Since this was happening in Los Angeles, I'd been thinking Hollywood. But Eric set me straight on that. His advice, in a paraphrase, was "What do you want to run around in Hollywood for? Why would you go fishing in those waters when everything's right here in front of you?"

Manhattan Beach was more like a college town—young, casual, and ready to party, with a lot of hockey players, Los Angeles Raiders, and really tan women. Eric and I weren't beach bums, but on the off days we'd go down and watch volleyball and try to look good. About three or four times a week, we'd eat lunch at a restaurant called Houston's, where I'd order orange roughy. I didn't mind the steak, either, but I was hitting the ball well, so I got a little superstitious about orange roughy. Our routine also included driving home slowly from the ballpark in Eric's BMW, which had a pretty good stock sound system, and cranking up some Dr. Dre—his debut album, *The Chronic*. "One, two, three and to the four./ Snoop Doggy Dogg and Dr. Dre is at the door." We played that gangsta rap a lot. Eric also loved a band called Live.

After the games, we liked to unwind at Harry O's on Highland, which was like our second home. It was an easy, breezy, T-shirt and flip-flops kind of place, and we had the run of it. If there was a band that night, I'd occasionally sit in as the drummer for a few songs. The proprietor, Dougie, would let us bartend whenever we wanted. I was into Rolling Rock beer, old 33, made in Latrobe, Pennsylvania, "from the mountain springs to you," so I asked Dougie if he could stock some Rolling Rock. He said, "How the fuck am I gonna get Rolling Rock in here?" But he got it, and I drank it, and then I'm looking around seeing all these other guys in there drinking it. Dougie saw it, too. After a while he said to me, "Fuck that Rolling Rock. I need you to start drinking some Bud Light. I got cases of Bud Light back there, and nobody's drinking it." Eric and I sold a lot of Bud Light for Harry O's, and we never paid for a single beer. Three years straight. I think it was a record.

Harry O's had a back room, and sometimes we'd duck back there to keep from being mobbed. I know, it sounds crazy. But it *was*. Mostly, it was people—men and women both—just talking about the game. The majority of them were from around the area, and as a rule they weren't the type to fuss over anybody, but *some* did. There were also the women who had followed us home from Dodger Stadium. That happened every single night we played at home. One night, Eric looked back and counted six cars following us from the ballpark, all the way down the 110 to the 405 and then on to Manhattan Beach. "Look at this shit," he said. "It's like a fucking parade." When we walked out of the stadium to the parking lot, there would be people ten deep yelling, cheering, clamoring for autographs. It was like U2 coming out of the Hollywood Bowl.

Honestly, there were times that year when I felt like Elvis Presley. Girls were flashing us, throwing their bras at us. When they followed us home, we'd try to shake them on the freeway. Once, Eric pulled over to see what was going on and three or four girls came up to the car. A really cute one started stroking my arm, but if she was eighteen I would have been surprised. I told Eric, "Dude, we'd better get the hell out of here." People would knock on our door and say their cars broke down. It was usually a girl, but now and then there'd be a guy with a pack of baseball cards in his backseat. "Oh, we didn't know it was you. Would you mind signing these cards?"

At Harry O's, we'd sometimes stay after hours drinking a little in that back room, where they stacked the money. I recall one night, in particular, when Eric and I were having a beer and there were about a dozen women waiting for us. Finally one of them said, "Are you guys gonna take one of us home, or two of us, or what? What's the deal? Because if not, we can all get out of here." But it wasn't like it sounds. Occasionally, we'd invite ten or twelve people over to just hang out at our place after hours. We had a strobe light, kind of a disco ball that we'd fire up, for a party effect. Truthfully, though, there wasn't any debauchery going on. We tried to keep it light and laid-back. And yet, any way you slice it, here I was, a guy from Philly who made it through high school without so much as a date, with a whole corral of California women, right in my house. It occurred to me that, yeah, this baseball thing is okay.

Without much of a strain on our social lives, Eric and I were always well aware that we had a ball game to play the next day. One time, we might have been a little *too* aware. It was a Friday night, and Saturday we'd be facing Ken Hill of the Expos. He was a short-armer with a wicked splitter, and frankly, neither of us was looking forward to that. So we arranged a ride ahead of time and dedicated ourselves to getting messed up. I'd just gotten my first credit card, a white MasterCard from Charter Pacific Bank, and Eric had a fine suggestion. He said, "Let's go out and break this thing in." We started out at Harry O's and then moved on to Sunsets, by the Manhattan Beach pier—which happens to be where Eric eventually met his future wife one night. She was a college basketball player, and they ended up hopping a fence at an elementary school and playing on eight-foot rims at one o'clock in the morning.

On this night, we were drinking sex-on-the-beach shots. That's kind of a fruity, wimpy cocktail, with vodka, and for the full effect we had about thirty apiece. After a few hours of that, I was sitting on some steps just off Manhattan Beach Boulevard—the main street—throwing my guts up. I'd bought a pair of suede and leather Bally shoes at an outlet mall in Pennsylvania, and Eric gave me a lot of grief about those shoes. He called them elf boots. I still don't have much style, but back then I had considerably less. I thought those shoes had a nice Italian look. Anyway, according to Eric, the best thing about that night was that I puked all over those elf boots and had to throw them away. The *worst* thing was that Kevin Gross was our starting pitcher the next day.

We walked into the clubhouse Saturday afternoon looking a little lethargic—my ribs were actually sore from throwing up so much—and Kevin Gross glared at me and said, "What'd you guys do? Did you go out last night? You motherfuckers went out last night? I'm fucking pitching!"

We replied with something smart-ass and brilliant, like, "Uh, ya, uh, ya . . . yabba-dabba-doo," and that set him off all over again: "If you guys don't get some hits today, I'm gonna kill you!"

I looked at Eric sort of sheepishly and said, "Uhhh, I think we better get a couple hits."

I ended up with two, including a two-out RBI single in the first inning on a three-two pitch. I felt better then. Kevin Gross was a big guy to start with, and he'd been studying karate with Jim Gott, one of our relief pitchers. I really wasn't looking forward to him kicking my ass. *That* was pressure.

Mike really didn't have that much of a normal college life, and that's where your social life is usually developed. Now, all of a sudden, he's a single, good-looking guy in L.A., the face of the Dodgers, and he felt like he had to act like it. I think he almost felt like he had to live up to other people's expectations. From the social standpoint, it seemed like, hey, this guy should be out there banging everybody

around. But when you got down to it, I'm not sure that was him.
Mike was the kind of guy that, whoever he's with, that's who he's
with. When he had a girlfriend, he would never mess around, and
I don't remember any year when he didn't have a girlfriend. The
minute the season ended, he'd break up with whoever he was with
and go back to Philly. I know he'd been hurt by that girl from North
Dakota, but once he got to the big leagues, there wasn't anybody
from North Dakota. It was all L.A.

 We were just a couple of jackoff ballplayers who had life by the
balls. It was good to be us.

—Eric Karros

On the first of May, after pressing a little hitting third in the order, I settled
into the five hole and started to relax and roll. It was the last of May when,
after making progress as a catcher, I hit Candiotti in the ass on a throw to
second base.

 We were well ahead of the Cardinals in the eighth inning, with Ozzie
Smith on first base. Knuckleballers are traditionally easy to steal against,
since the pitch comes in slow and cuckoo and isn't easy to handle cleanly,
so Ozzie broke for second. I stabbed at a low knuckler that left me fading
away from the throw, and came up firing without having my feet set. Unfortunately, Candiotti's feet were set. He would tell you that his ass was not
an insignificant obstacle, but it was embarrassing nevertheless. I cursed and
stomped around and generally made myself the biggest ass in the play, but of
course, since it was 5–0 at the time, my teammates thought it was hilarious.
The next day, the entire pitching staff showed up in the dugout with targets
that Orel Hershiser had taped onto the seats of their pants.

 Generally, though, I didn't have a lot of trouble catching Candiotti . . .
until June 12, when we beat the Padres, 6–4, in spite of my four—yes, *four*—
passed balls. His knuckleball was the devil itself on that night. I tried calling
for curveballs, but there was no way he'd go for that. The way he saw it, if
I couldn't knock down his knuckler with a special mitt the size of a sofa
cushion, what chance did the batter have to square it up with a twig of ash?
There was another occasion, though, when we had a big lead and just for the
hell of it—or maybe it was for my sake—Candiotti decided to throw nothing
but his lackluster fastball for a while. It worked for a couple of batters, and
then they started lighting him up. So he called me out to the mound and
we kicked at the dirt and let the wind blow a little bit, as Johnny Roseboro
would put it, and then Candiotti looked at me and said, "Forget Plan B."

There were fewer complications on the batting end of it. Later in June, in Cincinnati, I clobbered a ball that the *Los Angeles Times* reported might have gone five hundred feet, maybe even 550, if it hadn't been stopped by the upper deck. Eric Davis said, "That guy is from another planet." When we returned to Chavez Ravine and I was introduced with the lineups, I was greeted by a rousing reception that was something new for me. Then I hit a three-run homer and caught Ramon Martinez's shutout.

"It's kind of cool, and it's a little flattering," I was quoted saying in the *Times*, concerning the cheers. "In my last at-bat, they were really charged up. I think it's neat." Yeah, I said "neat." I wasn't *always* a badass.

That was the series in which *Sports Illustrated* came out to do a cover story on me. It was a heady time, and I'm afraid I fell into the trap of getting too full of myself, which led to a regrettable error in judgment the following week. Roy Campanella died on June 26 and I didn't show up for his funeral in Hollywood Hills on the morning of the thirtieth.

McDowell and Gott made it, and without a doubt I should have, too. Ross Newhan of the *Times* let me have it at the bottom of a notes column, under the heading of "Where's Piazza?":

John Roseboro, Joe Ferguson, Steve Yeager, and Mike Scioscia—an impressive string of Dodger catchers who were all helped and influenced by Roy Campanella—attended Wednesday morning's memorial service for the Hall of Famer, but Piazza, the new Dodger catcher and another visitor to Campy's Corner in Vero Beach, was conspicuous by his absence. Of course, Piazza had a night game Tuesday and another Wednesday, a pretty tiring schedule for a 24-year-old who noted the other day that he's getting sick of all the media questions and attention regarding his rookie-of-the-year chances. . . . Piazza has come a long way from the 62nd round of the 1988 draft, but it can be a short trip back.

Newhan's item came out on the Fourth of July, and the *SI* story—"Blue Plate Special"—was dated the fifth. I was playing defense in the cover photo and swinging the bat in the two-page spread inside, accompanied by the headline, "A Piazza With Everything." The article quoted Greg Maddux— Greg Maddux!—saying, "He's one of the better hitters in the game right now. . . . A lot of people have trouble in their second or third year after a really good first season, but I would be really surprised if he did." Among the pictures was one of Tommy pinching me on the cheek.

I have to say, the photo made me cringe a bit. It was more ammunition for well-informed, opportunistic fans like the ones at Shea Stadium. I was walking out to the bullpen to warm up the pitcher before a game there one night, and the loudest people in the house—God love 'em—are yelling stuff like, "It's not who you know, is it, Mike?"

Honestly, I was bitter about that subject. Wherever we went, I kept hearing it over and over, in all forms—the godson (which I wasn't), nepotism, the silver spoon, growing up as a dilettante, all of that. People assumed I spent my childhood taking violin lessons; that somehow my family *bought* my way to the major leagues. Nobody would give me credit for, one, being a pretty good ballplayer, and two, working like hell to get there. I know that credit shouldn't matter, really. But it did. In my experience, it would always be the hardest thing to get.

Otherwise, there wasn't much to gripe about in my rookie year. That didn't stop me, however. I was committed to the art.

For starters, I couldn't tolerate anything that distracted me from playing baseball. I mean, *anything*. Like kids in the clubhouse. I'm ashamed to admit that, now that I have two daughters of my own, but the fact is, I had a hard time drawing the line between focus and selfishness. I was so single-minded about my job that it was all about me—my meals, my sleep, my privacy, my rights—and I *hated* it when teammates allowed their kids to run around when we were putting on our game faces, or taking them off. Cory Snyder was Mormon, and he had a gang of them. At one point, we actually held a team meeting to talk about day care. I think Orel, Jim Gott, and Tom Candiotti organized it. The discussion was that there were going to be new babysitters in the wives' room, and they were going to supply toys and coloring books. This went on and on until finally Tommy couldn't stand it anymore and blurted out, "What the fuck? A fucking day care? Let's get some fucking runs!" Best meeting ever.

Of course, I don't mean for that to reflect poorly on good fathers in general or Cory Snyder in particular. Cory was a good teammate, and, in fact, one worth fighting for. Especially if it meant fighting the *Rockies*. I hated them about as much as kids in the clubhouse.

We had some battles with those guys. Literally. Once, at Mile High Stadium, Ramon Martinez buzzed Andres Galarraga, who led the league that year with a .370 batting average. Galarraga ended up singling for his fourth hit of the game. Then Ramon tried to pick him off first base and hit Galarraga in the neck. On the next pitch, Galarraga took off for second, and I threw him out by twenty feet. But while he was being tagged, Galarraga kicked Jody Reed in the elbow and put him on the DL. The next batter was Charlie Hayes, and Ramon, doing his duty, drilled him in the back. Hayes just erupted, screaming, "I'm gonna kill him! I'm gonna kill him!" He tore out for Ramon before I had a chance to even slow him down. On one hand, it's the catcher's job to protect his pitcher whether or not he agrees or gets along with him. On the other hand, we're not the speediest class of athletes. The system works best when it's another catcher we're trying to get our hands on. Anyway, Ramon runs off the mound like a gazelle and Tim Wallach dashes in from third base and takes down Charlie Hayes with a sliding tackle. We all jumped into it, and then suddenly I felt like a little kid being picked off the pile. It was big ol' Don Baylor, the Rockies' manager, telling me, "That's enough, that's enough."

The next inning, I caught hold of a fastball from Keith Shepherd—I was *on time* for that one—and crushed it way the hell out to center field for my second home run of the game. The next batter was Cory Snyder, and Shepherd hit him. Shepherd was a boxer, and after he nailed Snyder he stood out on the mound staring into our dugout going, "Come on! Come on!" We all looked at one another, nodded, then charged out there at the same time and kicked his ass. Bloodied his lip, at least.

That brings me to pitchers. Since it's so vital for a battery to be of the same mind in the course of a ball game, I wish I could say that I got along famously with every pitcher I ever worked with; that they were my best friends on the ball club and my special guests for Thanksgiving dinner. Not the case. Right from my rookie year, I picked up on a pattern in the clubhouse: pitchers on one side, everyday players on the other. Or, more to the point, pitchers on one side, *me* on the other. And among the pitchers, Ramon and Pedro Martinez tended to be front and center. That was why, privately, I was so pleased with Eric one day when he blew up Ramon.

Ramon had gotten knocked around a couple times and simply left the ballpark after he was taken out of the game. So Karros calls a meeting and he stands up, looks at Ramon, and goes, "I just want to ask this: Why the fuck are you leaving, dude? We're out there busting our asses trying to get you to spit the fucking hook and you're walking out the tunnel in the fucking fifth inning and getting in your fucking Ferrari and driving home?" Poor Ramon was shaking, almost crying. Then Orel got up, and it turned into a pitchers-against-hitters thing. He was really just trying to be the peacemaker, but I didn't want to hear it. That day, I was proud to be the friend of Eric Karros.

Needless to say, however, I was always on my pitcher's side in any dispute with an umpire. Most of it was general principle, but now and then a particular ump—Paul Runge, for example—would afford me another reason.

We were playing the Florida Marlins, and early in the game there was a play at the plate. I put the tag down but Runge called the runner safe, which I disagreed with. I said something like, "Aw, come on." He didn't answer— just stared at me with cold, penetrating, Charlie Manson eyes. I thought, oh shit. Later, I was batting against Ryan Bowen, three-two count, and I just sort of twitched a little bit toward a ball in the dirt. I trotted off to first base, and before I could take two steps Paul Runge's yelling, "Yeahhhh! Ouuuttt!"

I knew he was baiting me, so I didn't utter a word. I sat down in the dugout, strapped on my shin guards, went back out there, and Runge said, "You know, Mikey, Johnny Bench used to try to steal pitches from me all the time, and I told him, 'Johnny, just catch the fucking ball. Don't try to pull it back and snatch it back and frame it and all that bullshit.'" I think he was passing that along in a friendly, helpful sort of way, as if to say, okay, I tested you and you passed, so I'll give you a little tip. Yeah, thanks, pal.

Frankly, though, it was out of character for me to respond so placidly. Playing angry had become a basic part of my game, and I didn't feel compelled to change. After my Vero Beach drama, when I'd been driven to the brink of quitting and came back with my teeth bared, I was self-indulgent about my anger. As often as not, if I didn't get a hit, I'd pitch a fit. I mean, I'd go *off*.

I know it rubbed a lot of guys the wrong way. My temper made me look immature, which I was, and all about me, which I also was, but with a purpose. I truly believed, and still do, that a ballplayer can be selfish and still be a team player. Joe Morgan once shared with me his philosophy on how a team wins: by having a bunch of players who produce career years at the same time. I wanted every year I had to be a career year, and for that to happen, I felt like I needed every at-bat to be successful. If it wasn't, I was incensed. It was as if something was always chasing me and I had to just keep going, keep going, no failures, no stopping, keep going, gotta have a hit.

I'm sure a lot of players hate it when they squander at-bats, but they don't destroy the dugout; so, yeah, I confess to pushing it too far. I'd throw bats and helmets. I'd scream and cuss and make a scene all-around. When I'd see a great player like Fred McGriff strike out with the bases loaded, walk back to the dugout, lay his bat down, put away his helmet, and trot back out to play defense, I'd think, hmm, maybe I need to control myself. The idea never lasted long. That just wasn't how I was wired. Like it or not—and frankly, I liked it—a baseball game brought out in me what Al Leiter, my future teammate, describes as "that controlled rage that practically everybody who's worth anything plays with."

On one level, most of my teammates understood; on another, they just shook their heads; and on *another*, they thought—some, if not most of them—that I was just a total, self-absorbed, narcissistic, red-assed jerk. A few of them called me Snapper, in reference to my temper. Tommy would ream me out over the stunts I pulled in fits of rage. He was afraid I'd hurt myself, because I'd kick and punch things as hard as I could. He told me that Frank Howard had once banged his elbow on the bench after making an out, and it really set him back. Eventually, I stopped kicking stuff because I'd screwed up my toe by trying to punt the dugout; but I had better technique with punching.

When I was a kid, I was a Bruce Lee guy and always watched *Kung Fu Theater* on Saturday mornings. I also read a book in which he talked about disciplines called "kungs." There was a speed-running kung, an eyesight kung, and an "iron-fist kung," in which a guy broke his knuckles on a big rock, then allowed the knuckles to heal and proceeded to punch and punch the rock until ultimately it would move. The principle is that you have to clench your fist as tightly as you can and be committed to the punch—drive straight through it, even if you're hitting a concrete wall. When I punched the wall of the dugout, it was an iron-fist kung. I'd never catch it at an angle or off center. Never with a haymaker. Always short and flush.

I may have actually broken my knuckles a few times doing that, but I never said anything. I just varied my routine a little. Once, I messed up a shopping cart in the clubhouse. In Atlanta, I threw a water jug. In Montreal, I slammed my helmet against the wall and it bounced into the stands, where a fan grabbed it and wouldn't give it back. At Dodger Stadium, I struck out and tried to fire my helmet into the little slot in the dugout by the bat rack. I missed the slot and the helmet ricocheted and nicked the head of one of our trainers, Dr. Bill Buhler. I rushed up and apologized to him, and he said he was okay, not to worry about it; but that incident made me less dangerous with a helmet in my hand. Still, my anger didn't fade. Maryann Hudson, the beat reporter for the *Los Angeles Times*, wrote of me, "He likes to play baseball as if he is tearing somebody's head off." She had it right.

"People are always telling Mike that he should smile more," Lasorda told her. "But I say leave him alone. This is how he got here."

That was just his nature, and it probably allowed him to achieve the success he achieved. He wasn't that way off the field. But if that's all you're seeing, I could understand how, as a teammate, you may not be feeling like really rooting for this guy. Nobody felt like he's the underdog, let's pull for him. It wasn't jealousy—just, I'm not pulling for this guy; he's a pain in the ass. He'd sit in the dugout going, "Fuck! Fuck! Fuck!" I used to watch and cringe when he'd make an out. He'd say, "Fuck! Fuck! Fuck!," then hit his fist on the concrete. It wasn't with the open palm, just for show. He would literally smoke the concrete top of the dugout with his closed fist. How he didn't break his hand in fifty different places ten different times, I'll never know. That was his greatest achievement in baseball.

—Eric Karros

The baseball life had its effects, as you might expect, and they were magnified by my immediate success. So, for that matter, did the culture of Southern California.

There's no disputing that California changed me. I loved growing up in Phoenixville and I give it credit for my drive, work ethic, and value system; but after I'd been in Los Angeles long enough to get the hang of it, I was thinking, well, let's see, I've got the beach, I've got Hollywood, I've got Sunset Strip . . . I don't think I'll be going back to Sal's or Nardi's anytime soon. I guess that's how your mind works when you're twenty-four and the good life is coming at you in waves.

I have to say that California style was not something I came by naturally. I had to step it up. One of the girls I dated said I dressed like a redneck. I wouldn't have minded, except that I was feeling the need to be more like what I thought I was *supposed* to be like, now that I had sand in my shoes, money in my pocket, and press at my locker. At one point, I was talking to a friend back home about my first season in the big leagues and he said, "I don't care about that. Have you slept with Pamela Anderson?" That was an epiphany for me. Is this really what guys expect out of me? And yeah, I was influenced by that. Maybe if I'd been more confident outside of baseball, maybe if I'd been more social in high school, maybe if I'd have completed college, maybe if everybody outside my family (or so it seemed) hadn't doubted me from the time I was seventeen years old, I wouldn't have cared what people *expected* of me. But I cared. I cared deeply. A couple of decades later, with the advantage of perspective, my best advice would be to shut out all the noise and make your own personal choices; to seek after what *you* think is important, not some shallow, superficial, popular concept of status and satisfaction. Young men are being taught and tantalized by the wrong things. I certainly was. I was sold the whole bill of goods. I wanted to be the rock star.

Thankfully, Eric was there to help me with the particulars, like clothes. Eric actually had a clothes guy. *Everybody* had a clothes guy—not to mention a car guy and an electronics guy and a pay-my-bills guy. I could hold my own with cars and electronics, but I needed some sartorial expertise in a big way. The Dodgers didn't allow us to wear jeans on the road; always a suit and tie. Not only that, but the players had this thing going where they'd all try to outdo each other on the plane, as far as looking good. I had no suits and no chance. So Eric introduced me to the clothes guy whom Hershiser had introduced *him* to, Alex of Best Dressed by Alex. He made me three suits, two sport coats, and some slacks, and I wrote him a check for around thirty-two hundred dollars. My hand was actually shaking as I cut that check. But I knew I had to step it up. I was severely style-challenged. A few people seemed to think I acquired some, soon enough, but that was only because there were professionals around to see to it. Even when I was in New York, playing for the Mets, the famous designer Joseph Abboud told one of my teammates, Robin Ventura, that "we need to get Piazza into some of our clothes. He dresses like a monkey."

In that respect, Manhattan Beach was my refuge. I didn't have to dress up to sit in the sand or have a beer at Harry O's. And it didn't take long to become well stocked in casual wear. The president of Quiksilver, Bob McKnight, was a huge sports fan, and he'd invite me, Eric, and Raul Mondesi to his warehouse in Huntington Beach and say, "Pick out what you want. Go crazy." We'd load up on T-shirts, shorts, sunglasses, flannels, hats, whatever. I once brought along a friend named Eddie Braun who was a stuntman. Eddie called it "the rape-and-pillage store." We also got a lot of gear from No Fear. I was all set.

I did take a stab at style by picking up a Jaguar convertible as a loaner car. I thought I was becoming a big deal, but the first time I heard somebody yell "Hey, Mike!" at a stoplight, I took the car back. I suddenly realized I didn't *like* being a big deal, if that's what this was. To put it another way: I didn't care for the demands of the spotlight. For one thing, I didn't like people calling my hotel room—usually when I was still trying to sleep on the morning of a ball game. Often, it was media. Once, though, when I was in New York for a TV appearance, a woman I knew from Los Angeles called thirty-four hotels to find me. That's when I started checking in under an alias. My favorite was Hugo Boss.

I also never understood or had much patience with the autograph phenomenon. When people crowded around the fence of the player parking lot after a game, I couldn't help but wonder why they were there. I no longer placed baseball people on pedestals and didn't wish to encourage it. I'd just slip into my car—or more often, Eric's car—and get the hell out of there. I received hate letters from fans asking why I couldn't at least wave at them. After a while, the Dodgers' public relations guys prevailed upon me to give a nod or a wave or something—anything to show that I wasn't a total jackass. So I did better. I signed a few autographs. I'd never be Ernie Banks, and I had no tolerance for so-called fans who exploited the situation for their own profit, but I was well aware that my livelihood depended on the popularity of the game and the players. No doubt, I owed the paying customers. What I felt I owed them, though, was good, hustling baseball and, to the best of my ability, a team deserving of their support. They responded to that.

Some, I might add, responded a little too brazenly for my taste. Aggressive women didn't really turn me on. If a girl followed me home, it didn't mean that I had to take advantage of it. Don't get me wrong—I wasn't an angel. But from a spiritual standpoint, that sort of thing just left me feeling empty, incomplete. Obviously, premarital sex was morally objectionable to the Catholic Church, which, like my very Catholic mother, was still a major influence in my life. That said, my world had been rocked, and there was a battle going on inside me. On one hand, as a young, single, Rookie of the Year candidate in the most glamorous city in America, I felt I had an image to live up to; the rock-star thing was a powerful temptation. And let's be real—a little late-night adventure with a beautiful, willing woman was a pretty powerful temptation, too. I was not only human but a physical, previously sheltered, highly visible, glaringly eligible human with a sudden and extraordinary degree of opportunity along those lines. I was floating between two worlds, following my moral compass one night, and the next, the macho beats in my headphones. There were some very compelling, confusing contradictions that I had to deal with constantly. On the occasions when I *did* step out, I made a point of going to confession afterward.

At any rate, I wasn't all-in. I'd go through my mail and see the female handwriting and the hearts on the envelope, and then the photos inside, the sweet letters . . . and generally, I'd toss them. They tended to blend together. Once, though, won over by the picture, I called the girl, asked her to come to the ballpark one night, and put her on the guest list. After the game I walked out to meet her and learned my lesson about going by photographs. Another time, before a home game against the Marlins, I was warming up Candiotti in the bullpen, which I usually did to get accustomed to his knuckleball du jour. It was a cool thing, because the fans would crowd around and get me pumped up for the game. This particular night, I noticed a girl walking down the aisle, tracking me like a laser beam. With the way she filled out her jeans, it was all I could do to keep one eye on the knuckleball. I mean, she was *gorgeous*. Then I hear, "Mike! Mike!" and she's handing me a little packet. I went back to the clubhouse and everybody gathered around, like little kids in a tree house: "Let me see! Let me see!"

It was a picture of her in a bubble bath, and a dorky poem. Something like: "I'm in the bath, and I want to go fishing, too. But I don't want to catch Marlins, I want to catch you." Everybody was grabbing at the picture, asking, "You gonna call her?"

The jeans were in my head, but the poem was in my hands. The jeans . . . the poem . . . the *poem* . . .

"I just don't think so."

I suppose I was a difficult case. I wasn't a one-night-stand kind of guy, and I wasn't in a marrying frame of mind, either. Not at that point. I was smack in between—all about the girlfriend. Somehow, I felt much better about suspending my Catholicism with a girlfriend. Plus, I craved the companionship. My teammates were tired of hearing me bitch and cuss; I needed a sympathetic ear, preferably attached to a beautiful face. I didn't get into a relationship for the wild side of it. I just liked having somebody to share my life with—on a short-term basis. The biggest compliment Eric Karros ever paid me was when he said he'd give me permission to date his daughter. Actually, he said that all the time.

My first major-league girlfriend was a flight attendant who worked the team plane one night. I stopped seeing her after the all-star break, when I heard she was talking to Roger McDowell, one of our relief pitchers.

Then there was Debbe Dunning. You might know her as the Tool Time girl on *Home Improvement*. We were introduced by Brian Cohen, who worked with Danny Lozano and had met her at a ball game. She was beautiful, obviously, and we had a nice thing going over the second half of the season. She even met my dad. He came out to Los Angeles and we had dinner together, and Debbe's saying Michael and I did this and Michael and I did that, and I could see my father silently flipping his lid. Later, when we were alone, he made no attempt to keep quiet about it. He was clear and very stern: "Don't get married. Don't get married. Don't get married." But it wasn't that he didn't like her. If she had been a movie star who came from a billionaire family and gave up her career to work with underprivileged children, that still wouldn't have been good enough. He just didn't want anything messing with my career.

After the season, I had a promotional trip to Hawaii and took Debbe along. Then it was my mom's turn. She didn't care for that *at all*. But I was flaunting my independence in those days. I even turned down an appearance on David Letterman's show to make that trip. It was a good time, and we were still together until around Halloween, when one night she brought over some pumpkins and her dog. I'm not quite certain how it turned bad, but I'm pretty sure it involved me suggesting that it was time to move on. That was just my rhythm. When the off-season came, I needed to break free of my regimen and cut loose a little. Evidently, that wasn't what Debbe had in mind. There was screaming and crying, and then the Tool Time girl waffled my ass. She'd been doing this Tae Bo boxing thing, and she had a huff worked up, and I hadn't taken a punch like that in a long time. Then she and her dog were gone.

A few months later, I saw her at an MTV rock-and-jock softball game. Darren Daulton, the Phillies' catcher, was there, and he said, "Hey, that Tool Time girl is hot." I mentioned that we had dated. I don't think he believed me, but just then Debbe walked up and said, "Mike, you don't have to ignore me," or something like that. Very gracious. When Eric got home that night, he told me that Debbe and Daulton had hooked up. So I guess it worked out pretty well for everybody.

Anyway, my dad was happy.

Daulton was the starting catcher for the National League in the 1993 All-Star Game, and Bobby Cox, the manager, picked me to back him up. Given my hunger to be recognized on my own merits, it meant a lot to me.

I was the first rookie catcher to make the team since Gary Carter in 1975, and that was not my only distinction. I was also the only player that year not to hit at least one ball over the wall at Baltimore's Camden Yards during the home run derby. I crushed a bunch of them in the warm-up round, but in the regular contest they threw some lefty coach I'd never seen before. The guy was cutting and sinking the ball—not on purpose, I'm sure—and I couldn't elevate it. After about five or six pitches, I was thinking, get me the hell out of here.

I already had some bad karma going, because I'd brought along the flight attendant I was dating and, at an event the night before, she sort of offended Barry Bonds's wife, Sun. My girlfriend asked how long they had dated before they married, and when Sun said six months or whatever it was, she said, "Oh, that's not very long." I was just a rookie trying to blend in with the scenery and I figured she'd be happy to do the same, and here she is popping off to Barry Bonds's wife. The next day Barry came into the clubhouse and said, "Who the hell was that girl?" It wasn't really a problem with Barry, who was always friendly with me, but it made me want to go sit in a corner, which I did, more or less. From that point on, I pulled off a really good rookie routine by keeping my mouth shut, except to laugh, as I listened to Daulton, Mark Grace, and John Kruk—who looked like he'd just climbed out of a coal mine—bullshitting in the players' lounge.

In those days, fraternization was discouraged during the season, which was how I liked it. There was a bunker mentality, a strong sense that the other team was the enemy. I thought it added a little bit to the game when Tommy Lasorda would be hollering insults at the guys in the other dugout, or at least making sure we knew what assholes they were. He was that way even in *spring training*. We'd be getting ready for the game and he'd be telling us about the other pitcher and say, "Let's get this motherfucker." Tommy absolutely hated the opposition and made that perfectly clear to anyone within range of his voice, which carried well.

(As a point of information, Tommy's disregard for social graces, once the game was on, was applied to his *own* players, as well. Mark Cresse told me that, before I got to Los Angeles, a couple of the Dodgers' outfielders had once collided chasing a fly ball and were sprawled on the ground as the batter circled the bases. Tommy was very concerned. "Get the ball!" he shouted. "*Then* die!"

Don't get me wrong, though; Tommy really did care about his players. He just cared more about winning, and it didn't matter to him how it sounded. Once, when things weren't going well for us, he hit the team with a speech that went something like this: "If you don't like me because I want to win, and if you don't like me because I want you to concentrate and do your best, and if you don't like me because I tell you to stop staying out all night, then fuck you. I don't like you, either.")

But the All-Star Game was different. Marcus Allen, the Hall of Fame football player, once said that a good player could always muster up enough hate for the other team to get him through the day; so, in that respect, the All-Star Game didn't compromise anybody's basic competitiveness. It was just your chance to see what these guys were *really* like. That was the coolest thing about being an all-star, especially a young one. That and the grab bag full of great stuff from the sponsors—shoes, bats, you name it. The uncoolest thing, especially for a young player, is a toss-up between offending Barry Bonds's wife, taking an oh-for in the home run derby, and striking out to end the game. I pulled off the hat trick.

Back with the Dodgers, though, I was playing well enough that Tommy bent the club policy and let me keep my mustache an inch or two below my lip. He busted my balls about it but didn't press the point, which was a good thing, because I'd become superstitious about the mustache—which was really just a prop—and wouldn't have cut it even if he had insisted. I was leading a third-place team in average, home runs, and RBIs. It was all about swinging the bat.

Along those lines, out of the blue, Mizuno sent me a batch of new ones to try out. When I'd been a batboy in Philadelphia, I'd picked up some heavy wood that the players used. The power hitters, especially, would walk up to the plate with bats that weighed thirty-eight or forty ounces. That had changed by the time I got to the big leagues. I started out with a thirty-four-inch, thirty-two-ounce Louisville Slugger that was one of the biggest bats in the rack. The ones that Mizuno gave me, late in the year, had been made for Jose Canseco—they actually had his name on them—but he had switched to another brand. They had thinner handles than the ones I'd been using, and I decided to take some hacks with them on September 14 in San Diego. When I hit two homers that night, I became a Mizuno man.

A week and a half later, my thirty-third home run broke the rookie record for a catcher, set by Matt Nokes of the Tigers in 1987. A week after *that*, my 107th RBI, on a double against the Giants' John Burkett, broke the Dodgers' rookie record.

The world seemed to be mine for the taking. Dan Lozano believes that, maybe in a James Dean kind of way, people were somehow attracted to my anger and my attitude of not giving a shit about anything but baseball. Almost in spite of myself, life just kept getting better. After the *Sports Illustrated* piece, I shot a commercial for ESPN—the only ballplayer they used that year, I was told. It was taped at Blair Field in Long Beach, and they had me steal home, which asked a lot of the imagination. The commercial showed my grandmother—not my real one—watching on TV and cheering me on. They paid me something like fifteen grand.

But the topper came with the final game of the season, Fan Appreciation Day. It was the last of four against San Francisco, which arrived in town trailing the Braves by one game in the NL West. The Giants beat us the first three, which gave them 103 victories, but the only thing that mattered to them was winning one more than Atlanta; it was the last season of only two divisions in each league, with no wildcards, which meant that you had to win your division to play in the postseason.

Bonds claimed his third MVP award that year, and the Giants had a lot more going for them than just him. Matt Williams had a big season, too, and their rotation included a couple of twenty-plus-game winners in Burkett and Billy Swift. Rod Beck was a tremendous closer, but the guy in their bullpen who frightened me was Mike Jackson. He was a menacing-looking dude, with the bill of his cap creased down over his eyes to the point that it looked like he couldn't see, and he had an intimidating motion that came from way the hell over on the right side. He was also a little bit unpredictable, which is what makes a pitcher scary. I'd go so far as to say that Mike Jackson was the only guy I ever faced who scared the shit out of me. I actually fared okay against him—four for nine, with just a couple of strikeouts—but it didn't feel like it. On one of my hits, I broke my bat in three places. When I came up against him, my objective was not to lose my face. Of course, I found out later that he was the world's nicest guy.

Fortunately, when I stood in against him in the sixth inning of the season's 162nd game and lined out to left, we were already up 6–1. The Giants needed to win to keep pace with the Braves, who were sweeping Colorado, and we needed to win to finish the year at .500. Considering that we'd lost ninety-nine games in 1992, that would mean a lot to the organization. Fred Claire had made a rare appearance in the clubhouse that day to give us what sounded like a World Series pep talk. It must have worked. The Giants started a rookie, Salomon Torres, and we knocked him out in the fourth inning. I homered in the fifth against Dave Burba, and when I came to bat against Dave Righetti in the eighth, I was caught off guard by a standing ovation.

I still have the video of that. It includes the home run I crushed to right-center, my thirty-fifth of the season—the most any Dodger had hit since Duke Snider in 1957; more, incredibly to me, than even Steve Garvey, Frank Howard, or Pedro Guerrero. The crowd kept at it until I came out of the dugout for a curtain call. I felt like John, Paul, George, and Ringo, all bundled up in blue and white. After I trotted to home plate to catch the ninth inning, Tommy sent out Carlos Hernandez to take my place so the fans could give me *another* standing ovation. When I watch that tape, even now, I get the chills. We won 12–1 behind Kevin Gross, broke even on the season, and had the satisfaction of knocking a great team out of the playoffs.

Most of the crowd stayed after the game because they were giving away a car. Our PR guy told me to get out there: Karros and I were going to raffle off our game shirts. I grabbed the microphone and said, first, that Eric and I were all set to party that night, and then that whoever holds this number will win a signed jersey from last season's Rookie of the Year, Eric Karros.

The place went wild. Then Eric took the mike and said, "And the next winner will get a signed jersey from *this year's* Rookie of the Year, Mike Piazza!"

Of course, that hadn't been announced yet, which made it even cooler. In all my time with the Dodgers, that may have been my greatest moment. Throughout the last month or so of the season, I'd felt a warm wave of fan support and affection, and that was the day it all washed over me.

Right about then, I loved L.A.

CHAPTER ELEVEN

I was able to publicly thank Roy Campanella when the Rookie of the Year award was announced in late October. The Dodgers were in Taiwan at the time, playing a series of exhibition games, and Maryann Hudson of the *Los Angeles Times* reached me with the news that it had been a unanimous vote. While acknowledging Campy, I also expressed my appreciation for Eric and the rest of my teammates, trying to play nice and do all the right things for a change.

But I couldn't finish the deal. For reasons I don't recall—apathy, irreverence, ignorance?—I neglected to show up for the Baseball Writers' dinner where they handed out the actual awards. In the years ahead, when I came up short for various honors that I thought I might have deserved, I often wondered if it had anything to do with blowing off that banquet.

In the start of a private tradition, I also won the Silver Slugger award as the best hitter at my position. What made me proudest, though, was catching 141 games as a rookie and throwing out fifty-eight runners trying to steal—the most in the major leagues and in Dodger history. I wouldn't go so far as to say that I should have won a Gold Glove that year (instead of Kirt Manwaring of the Giants), but Karros was kind enough to say it for me.

Other than the games in Taiwan, it was my first off-season as a pro in which I didn't keep playing. Around the holidays, I spent some time in Philly and stopped in to see my friend Joe Pizzica at his parents' house. He showed me the scrapbook that his mother was keeping on me and I signed a bunch of stuff for his family, which was cool. I couldn't have known it then, but it was essentially the last time we'd hang out together; although, over the years, I periodically left him tickets when we played the Phillies. Even when he had his own, he'd stop at will call and see if there were any being held in his name. Sometimes, confused by "Pizzica," the window clerks would hand him the envelope with "Piazza" written on it, which contained the tickets I'd left for one or more of my brothers; but he wouldn't take them.

About thirty minutes from our house in Valley Forge, I found a gym in Collegeville where the owner, Marc Polignano, would work with me privately every night after the place closed. There was another one in Jeffersonville with brand-new equipment, and the owner was kind enough to give me a key, since my dad owned the building. I'd go in late at night and have it all to myself. Once, the cops drove by, saw the lights on, and came in to check it out. I thought I was about to get arrested, but they were like, "Hey, Mike! How you doin'?" That gym was perfect until the power lifters took it over. I'd spend an hour or two there every Christmas Eve, after it closed early and everybody else had gone home.

Weight training had become an important part of my baseball routine, but I was pulled deeper into it by the California factor. It's my observation that Californians take better care of themselves than people anywhere else in the country, if not the world. Even though I'd been lifting on a regular basis for quite a while, I couldn't help but feel inferior when I walked into a Gold's Gym anywhere in Southern California. I developed a mild case of muscle envy. For the first time, I started working parts of my body that had nothing to do with baseball. It was intoxicating. I admit, I wanted the women to like what they saw. When I walked the beach and out of the corner of my eye caught a girl checking me out, I dug that. Between the beach and baseball, I had no problem motivating myself to get into the gym. Even on New Year's Eve, I went straight from the gym to the batting cage in our basement. For a long time, I made it a point to be in the cage at midnight of December 31, so that the very first thing I did in the new year was hit a baseball.

That year, I stuck around home long enough to drop by Phoenixville High School and talk to the baseball team on the occasion of its first meeting. My brother Tony, the second youngest, was trying out for the varsity, and I could tell he was uncomfortable with me being there. So I gave some autographs, told them all to work their asses off and read everything they could on hitting, advised them to go ahead and drink beer if they wanted but to keep their dignity, and got the hell out of there before my brother and the coaches threw me out. On that note, it was back to Los Angeles. And back to business, among other things. There was a contract to be negotiated.

As a rule, I hated contract time, but this round figured to be interesting, at least. Normally, players don't have much bargaining position after their first year because they're not on the open market and aren't yet eligible for arbitration, which leaves the minimum salary as the default position.

Sometimes, especially when the player is obviously a big part of the team's foundation, the organization will attempt to sign him for multiple seasons so that it can avoid arbitration when the time comes. Then there are the occasions when a team will offer above the minimum simply to act in good faith and maintain amicable relations with a player it hopes to keep around for a long time. The Dodgers had been fair to me when they kicked in an extra sixteen thousand dollars for my rookie year, but both sides knew that sixteen thousand wouldn't get it done this time.

There were at least three fresh developments working on my behalf. The first, of course, was that I had batted .318 and set records in home runs and RBIs while manning the most demanding position on a ball club. Statistically, it was the best season a rookie catcher had ever produced. Second was the fact that the Dodgers had paid Ryan Luzinski—Greg's kid—a bonus of six hundred thousand bucks after drafting him in the first round of 1992. He was a catcher. It stood to reason that if Luzinski could demand that kind of money coming out of high school in New Jersey, a significant investment would certainly be in order for their starting catcher and Rookie of the Year. And in January—this is the third thing—the club shelled out more than a million to sign Chan Ho Park, a free-agent pitcher out of Korea. I felt I had a boatload of leverage.

And I knew I'd need it, because I had designs on a multiyear contract and the Dodgers had never awarded one to a player headed into his second season. After winning Rookie of the Year in 1992, Karros had played the 1993 season for just over four hundred thousand. As expected, the club made me a preliminary offer—the usual one year—citing Eric's precedent and setting my figure just a tad higher. But I was not of a mind to let the organization stand on its own self-serving tradition, and neither was Danny Lozano. He identified Frank Thomas as a sort of template for me. Frank's 1991 season, his second, had been very similar to my rookie season, and the White Sox had rewarded him with a three-year contract for around $4.5 million.

That was the ballpark we had in mind when Danny, Dennis Gilbert, and I sat down with Fred Claire and Sam Fernandez, who was the Dodgers' legal counsel and did a lot of their negotiating. Ordinarily, the player doesn't participate in those discussions, but Sam and Fred had requested that I be there. It was a mistake on their part. Apparently, they had misread me. I was carrying a grudge from the way the organization had treated me in the minor leagues and felt strongly that the front office owed me a show of respect.

We laid out the Thomas example and made the appropriate comparisons, and then Sam Fernandez went into his spiel. Something like "Well, if you bring a Martian down from Mars and try to explain the system to him, he won't understand . . ." I'm looking at Danny like, a fucking Martian from Mars?

At that point, I couldn't hold back. I didn't like what they'd done with Eric's contract, and I didn't like what they'd done to Jody Reed. Jody had been our starting second baseman in 1993, earning around $2.5 million, and the Dodgers made him an offer—a pretty good offer, I think—for the next three years. They gave him a certain number of days to accept it and then pulled the offer off the table. He ended up signing with Milwaukee for about $750,000. I can't really blame the Dodgers for any of that, but afterward, I saw Fred Claire on a few television shows almost reveling in the fact that, after they took back their offer, Jody Reed never did get his money. That just didn't strike the right chord with me. So I was pretty well whipped up into a frenzy by the time I got into that meeting and saw that Fred and Sam had every intention of signing me on the cheap, figuring I had no other option. I said, "You guys paid Chan Po Park a million-two from Korea, and you paid Ryan Luzinski six hundred thousand, and you're trying to tell me that you're going to renew me at four hundred?"

I went on for a while, with feeling, and threw some other names in there, too, which surprised even Danny and Dennis. But I wasn't finished. When it was apparent that I was getting nowhere, I stood up and said, "If you guys do that, don't fucking expect me at camp, because I ain't showing up." And I walked out of the meeting.

Lozano told me later that Sam Fernandez turned white when I left the room. Dennis couldn't believe it, either, and said, "Danny, go get him!" By that time, I was already gone. I was serious about this.

Eventually—a week before spring training—the Dodgers capitulated on their philosophy. I got three years and $4.2 million, starting with $600,000 the first year and ending with $2.7 million for the third, which would have been my initial year of arbitration. It was not only the first multiyear contract the Dodgers had ever given to a player after one season, but also the largest; and in fact, the second-largest in baseball history. I think Fred understood that I had it coming, but it was harder for Sam to take. The way he saw it, Danny and Dennis had beaten him. Not only that, but I had failed to show a sufficient level of Dodger blue in my bloodstream. The club wanted unconditional loyalty and couldn't seem to comprehend that it works in both directions, or that I might not feel so all-fire beholden to the organization that gave me a chance. For some crazy reason, I sort of thought that 112 RBIs would wipe out any debt.

My contract was also a painful admission on the team's part that Tommy had been right about me, and that a lot other people in the organization—some of whom couldn't stand him and even thought he was maneuvering to become the general manager—had been severely wrong. I sensed that the grudge I'd held since Vero Beach was no longer a one-way affair. The relationship between the Dodgers and me had become personal, with tension under the surface and Danny forever in the background protecting me. The way things were playing out, he wasn't at all sure I was going to be the Dodger-for-life that everybody assumed I would. Gradually, he was conditioning my mind to that possibility.

In the meantime, I didn't have to miss any training camp, except for one long day in New York. I'd been selected by the ESPY Awards as Breakthrough Athlete of the Year. The event was held in Madison Square Garden, and I originally told ESPN that I couldn't make it because the travel back and forth would knock out two days of spring training, which my obsession wouldn't permit. To solve that little problem, the producers actually sent a private jet to fly me up in the morning and back the same night, after the show. They also rented me a tux. So there I was, all cleaned up and bullshitting with Emmitt Smith and Jimmy Johnson, thinking, ah, now *this* is the big leagues.

In 1994, we could have been a contender. In fact, we *were* a contender—leading the National League West by three and a half games on August eleventh when the world, as we knew it, stopped. It was a labor strike, which meant no playoffs and no World Series and, when you get down to it, no real meaning to anything that happened over 114 games.

For a while there, in the first couple weeks of April, I was almost hoping the season would get wiped out altogether. I was batting .086 going into a series in Pittsburgh, but broke out of it by going seven—all singles—for thirteen. A lot of power hitters turn up their noses at bloops and bleeders, but, depending on the situation, I was generally just as happy with two loopy singles to right as one bomb into the bleachers. Honestly, I never really considered myself a power hitter. I was just a hitter with some power. Those singles in Pittsburgh meant a lot to me, because I proved to myself that I could adjust, cut down my swing, and turn things around when I was going bad. From that weekend on, I hit in 1994 just like I'd hit in 1993.

At that stage of my career, I felt I was so focused, so locked in mechanically, that there were times when I could pick up the pitch right at the release point; I could detect just a small manipulation on the ball in the pitcher's hand. Actually, Karros was one of the best I've ever seen at reading the pitcher—looking for tells, we called it, like the way he held his hand or his glove for a certain pitch. Eric was the kind of hitter who always wanted to know what was coming, and he made a science of studying the pitcher with that in mind. He was frequently in the on-deck circle when I was at the plate, and sometimes he'd try to help me out by watching the *catcher*. Once, at Olympic Stadium in Montreal, when Darrin Fletcher was catching for the Expos, Eric said that he could tell me whether the pitch was coming inside or not. If it was, he'd just say, "Come on, Mike." So I'm digging in and I hear, "Come on, Mike," see a fastball headed for the inside half of the plate, and knock it off the wall for a double. Next time up, "Come on, Mike." Boom, base hit.

Then Eric steps in to bat, and Darrin Fletcher goes, "You wouldn't happen to be telling Mike what's coming, would you?"

Eric said, "What are you talking about?" But for the rest of the series, he was screwed—scared shitless that they were going to drill him.

I always figured that if I knew my *swing*, and kept it in good shape, everything else would take care of itself. For a long time, I wasn't much of a video guy, like so many players were. Tony Gwynn started that trend, and ultimately it became so sophisticated and easy to use that I succumbed to it. But a lot of the younger players were addicted to video—and not just for studying pitchers. They'd get called out on strikes, then run down to the video room and have the guy in there rewind for the last pitch. After they saw what they wanted to see, they'd sprint back through the tunnel to the dugout and start yelling at the umpire: "That was a fucking *ball!*"

Karros even stayed up to speed on all the umpires—their patterns for balls and strikes. I got to know the umpires well enough by feeling their breath on the back of my neck for 140 games a year. By and large, instead of bringing too many elements into it, I preferred to keep hitting as simple as possible. In spring training one time, a few of us were sitting on a stage speaking to some minor-league players about hitting, and I was thinking hard about how to boil it all down for them. When it came around to me, I said, "I go up there looking for a pitch. I'm looking for *my* pitch, and when I get my pitch, I'm trying to knock the third baseman's dick off." I thought that pretty much explained it. And then Eric says, "I don't see too many dickless third basemen walking around."

Eric was a tough audience, but there was one theory of mine that he bought into. I pointed out to him that you get four at-bats every game, so, unless you hit the ball first, you're going to get twelve strikes. To succeed, all you have to do is make good contact with four of those twelve. That shouldn't be so hard, should it? If you hit the ball hard four times, you're bound to get a hit or two, and at that rate you'll make the Hall of Fame. If I had a mantra, I suppose that was it.

Of course, for every grudging shred of respect that Karros would give me about hitting, he'd make up for it by piling on the shit about my baserunning. He complained that it was practically impossible to drive me in. I argued that I was on base all the time, so what's his problem? But he had a point. Once, in Cincinnati, I was on second and Eric hit a ball that landed on top of the center-field fence and actually rolled along the ridge for about ten or twelve feet. Thomas Howard chased after it until it finally dropped back in play. Somehow—I guess I was confused—I got stuck at third. Eric rounded second base and couldn't believe I was standing there ninety feet in front of him. He just put his hands on his hips and stared at me, like he often did. He'd stay mad for about twenty minutes at a time.

The ideal solution, for me, was to just knock the ball out of the ballpark. In June, at Joe Robbie Stadium in Miami, against Mark Gardner, I hit 1) the first grand slam of my career, 2) the longest home run that had ever been hit at that park, and 3) the longest home run I had hit, according to the unofficial measurement: 478 feet. A lot of people, including me, think the ball I got hold of the year before in Cincinnati went considerably farther, but whatever.

I hit another grand slam two weeks later against the Rockies, ten rows into the upper deck at Dodger Stadium. From there, it's a quick, short-season summary: I started the All-Star Game in Pittsburgh and was shut out in the home run derby for the second time in a row (in subsequent years, I excused myself, occasionally joining Chris Berman and Joe Morgan for the blow-by-blow instead). Raul Mondesi gave the Dodgers their third consecutive Rookie of the Year. On August 11, Ramon Martinez shut out the Reds, 2–0, in Cincinnati, without shaking me off a single time, if I recall correctly, to put us two games above .500.

And then it was over.

The strike was a bad time in the game. It alienated the players from the owners, the owners and players from the fans, and even players from other players. But we'd known it was coming, and inevitable, because our collective bargaining agreement had expired and management was insisting on a salary cap for the next one. In fact, after we struck, the owners went ahead and imposed a cap, then withdrew it and did away with arbitration. From our perspective, the only encouraging thing about the whole ordeal was the impressive display of solidarity among a lot of players making a lot of money.

We weren't opposed at all to competitive balance; we just felt that that was the owners' concern. It wasn't our job to worry about who was competitive and who wasn't. If George Steinbrenner didn't care about the Reds or the Royals, the solution was for *us* to accept a salary cap?

Of course, not all the players were on the same page. During the strike, Eric and I went to a union meeting at the airport Hilton in Los Angeles, and found it interesting, to say the least—starting with Tim Leary. He was a veteran pitcher, thirty-six years old, playing out the string with Texas. Actually, Leary would never pitch again in the major leagues, and he probably sensed it. He really wanted to finish the season, which was still a possibility as late as early September. Leary said, basically, "You guys, I'm just being the devil's advocate . . ." And then Glenallen Hill, a big outfielder who was playing for the Cubs at the time, yelled out, "I don't like him!" Glenallen proceeded to stand up and deliver what was almost like a Baptist revival speech about sticking together and staying strong. After that, it was Mark McGwire—a side of him that a lot of people haven't seen. He had the owners' proposal in his hand, and he goes, "Look at this! It's fucking bullshit! We're not gonna fucking do this!" Then he slammed it down. For my money, he and Glenallen Hill were the heroes.

For whatever reason, a lot of the dissent on our side came from the Phillies. There was a meeting in Orlando that I didn't attend, but some of the guys there were under the assumption that the Phillies' management wanted Lenny Dykstra to be a shit disturber. His voice certainly didn't blend into the chorus. Players were imitating him, going, "I'm just sayin', dude, this might be the best deal we can get, dude." (I know: who am I to point out somebody else saying "dude"?) The word was that Dykstra was going to cross the line, with teammates like Dave Hollins and Darren Daulton right alongside. But the weirdest thing of the whole off season was the talk of Cal Ripken Jr. walking a picket line.

In 1995, spring training started with replacement players. That was a gigantic bone of contention, because it meant that the owners were actually planning to open the regular season without us. At the very end of March, we sought an injunction to stop them. The National Labor Relations Board had asked a federal district court to support its petition charging the owners with unfair labor practices, and the players had voted to go back to work if the court came through. The judge was Sonia Sotomayor, and it took her about twenty minutes to rule in our favor and restore all the terms of our previous collective bargaining agreement. Fourteen years later, when she was nominated for the Supreme Court and was getting crushed by conservatives—whom I generally count myself among—I thought, Hmm, Soto-mayor . . . she's not that bad a lady.

Her decision cleared the way for the 1995 season to start about three weeks late, even though a new labor agreement wouldn't be reached for another couple of years.

For me, the silver lining of the strike was the chance to spend some time on the beach. Not that I made a beeline for it. In the beginning, we figured the season would pick back up anytime, so Eric and Billy Ashley and I worked out every day at the gym. I wouldn't let myself believe we were done for the year because, for one thing, we had a great shot at making the playoffs, and for another, my whole deal, as far as an annual goal, was thirty homers, a .300 batting average, and a hundred RBIs. I had the batting average, but was still six home runs and eight RBIs short. By pumping weights every day, I was trying to *will* the strike to end.

We stayed with our regimen for two or three weeks, but finally one day, in the middle of our workout, Karros said, "Dude, we're not going back." I kept lifting on a regular basis—it extended into the longest stretch of weight training I'd ever been through—but the urgency wasn't there anymore. With the sun and sand in mind, I turned to beefing up my bird legs.

I got into volleyball games whenever I could and became friends with Gabrielle Reece through Nike promotions, which were always a day at the beach. We staged our own goofy Olympics. They were sort of like a Southern California citizenship test. I once threw a Frisbee into a bucket from thirty feet, thirty consecutive times. Another time, there was a televised spot in which I dove into the sand and guided the volleyball just over the net into the corner, as if I knew what I was doing. Truthfully, I wasn't bad at volleyball—a hell of a lot better than I was at basketball. It might have been Gabrielle who was teaming with Holly McPeak when I played against them with football star Jerome Bettis—the Bus—as my partner. I believe we actually won. Gabrielle tended to come at things from the athlete perspective, but I had some good discussions with her about my dating habits. From those, she was the one who came up with the term "season girlfriend."

My girlfriend for that season was an actress and stuntwoman named Anita Hart. During the strike, she was doing an episode of *Baywatch*, and I guess that's how I got involved in it. Season five. "Deep Trouble." Anita was the girl I saved. I'm swinging a baseball bat on the beach, in full uniform—yeah, whatever—and Pamela Anderson walks up to me and says, as I remember it, "What are you doing?"

I say, "I'm a baseball player."

Pamela: "Why are you swinging a bat on the beach?"

Me: "I'm working on my swing while we're on strike."

Right then, Anita starts yelling "Help!" and I run out into the bay with Pamela to save her. When we pulled her in, Anita looked at me and said something like "You're cute," and my response made it pretty clear that we'd be hooking up. It was a tough assignment for me, playing myself. I went Method.

There *was* method, though, to my silliness. I hoped it would show that I could lighten up a little bit and didn't take myself too seriously. For that gig, the only thing I was serious about was meeting Pamela Anderson. Took one for the boys back home.

And then, for the *girls* back home, I struck up a friendship with Fabio.

I'm a high-end audio geek and happened to see an article about the stuff Fabio collected, which was the same kind of stuff I collected, mostly from a company called Krell. The article said that Fabio had spent about a million dollars on amplifiers, preamplifiers, speakers, digital-to-audio converters and such, and he had a full mixing board in his house. Not long after, I met him at a Super Bowl party in California that my stuntman friend Eddie Braun had gotten me and my dad into. We started talking about audio and Krell and before you know it, lo and behold, I'm at Fabio's house. I walk in and there are three Great Danes and about thirty motorcycles. His kitchen was stuffed with dirt bikes. In the living room, where he kept the stereo equipment, he had a big-ass, three-gun projector—some incredibly cool stuff.

We hung out a few times. Nice guy. Fabio told me he was one of only three people in the world who had an American Express card with a single name on it. The other two were Cher and Madonna. He pulls out his wallet and says—he's from Milan, you know—"Mike-a, here it is, a-my American Express-a card. It has-a my one a-name: Fabio." One time he calls me, and he goes, "Hey-a, Mike-a. Let's-a go get-a some a-breakfast, and then we'll-a listen to some-a stereo." He always ate breakfast at this little café on Sunset Boulevard; so I meet him there, and as we're eating, a tourist bus pulls up. The driver slows down and I can hear the guy saying, "There's Fabio . . . There's Fabio eating breakfast with Mike Piazza." All the tourists are snapping pictures and I'm thinking, is this really happening? I was on the tourist tour.

Needless to say, it was an off-season like no other. I also appeared on *Married with Children* and *The Bold and the Beautiful*. I was a presenter for the MTV awards show. I met Eddie Van Halen and played golf with Charles Barkley. Tommy took Eric and me down to the Doral Open in Miami and made Jack Nicklaus feel my forearms. A woman in Bakersfield named her horse after me (and I'll resist the corresponding joke).

But I was still in my batting cage on New Year's Eve, still obsessed with crushing the baseball.

It was April by the time we got to spring training. Most of the replacement players had already left, but enough remained to make it contentious.

For that matter, it was contentious before we even showed up. Karros had taken some heat about disparaging remarks he made in the press concerning the scabs. He felt terrible about it, so I said, all right, dude, I'll get you off the hook. I was ready to let it rip, because some of the replacement players—mainly, a pitcher named Rafael Montalvo, who had pitched one inning for the Astros back in 1986 and hadn't played organized ball in the States for three years—were saying things like they were going to have us five games in first place by the time we got back and we'd probably want to thank them. Bob Nightengale of the *Los Angeles Times* got hold of me and I said, "Who's going to care if we have a five-game lead in scab games? That's ridiculous. Does someone really think we'll be rooting for these guys? What do they think we'll do if we win it, give them a playoff share? Do they want rings? We'll give them rings, all right—made of tin."

When the season finally started, there were no replacement players on the roster. There was, however, an import who helped us into first place. A year after reeling in Chan Ho Park out of Korea, the Dodgers had turned to Japan and snatched-up Hideo Nomo, a pitcher more accomplished and much readier to contribute. The signing showed some impressive enterprise on the organization's part. In Japan, Nomo had been involved in an unusual contract squabble that resulted in him being declared a free agent prematurely. Peter O'Malley was on the prowl for international players, and when the opportunity presented itself, the Dodgers made Nomo the first native of Japan to come over from the Japanese major leagues and play in ours. O'Malley may not have struck many people as a pioneer, but he was ahead of the game when it came to finding players in foreign countries. It was a structured philosophy on his part. At times, I suspected that O'Malley's appetite for international talent—especially as an alternative to free agency—was so strong that it took precedence over winning. But the organization deserved nothing but credit for this acquisition. Nomo—the Tornado—turned out to be the leading edge of a wave of excellent Japanese players to bring their skills to America. He became the Dodgers' fourth straight Rookie of the Year. Plus, a good friend.

As it happened, the Tornado wasn't the only one who relocated that year. When I arrived back at Eric's condo from spring training, I found that Billy Ashley had been staying in my room. I was a little peeved about that, and decided it was time to get my own place. I bought a small town house close by, still in Manhattan Beach, on the edge of both the village and the golf course. As the first order of business—I knew my limitations—I brought in an interior designer and asked her if she knew anybody who could run errands and do laundry and basically hold the place together. She recommended her niece, Teri O'Toole, who happened also to be an artist. So Teri took care of not only the housekeeping but the paintings for the walls, as well.

Of course, Dodger Stadium was my second home in Los Angeles; but it had been so long since we'd played that I'd actually forgotten the combination to my locker. For a while that year, everything was just a little out of whack, in fact.

I tugged a hamstring in our second game and had to miss a few, including the home opener. But I came back whaling and was hitting .537 on May 10 when I smoked a ball to the right-field wall in San Diego and thought it was gone. Out of the box, I Cadillac'd a little bit, and when I saw the ball hit the wall I had to accelerate. Then I realized I'd missed first base, hit the brakes to go back, slipped, put my hand down to get my balance, and landed clumsily on my left thumb. Tore the ulnar collateral ligament, an injury known as gamekeeper's thumb (named for the affliction that was common to Scottish gamekeepers when they killed rabbits and such by pushing down really hard to break their necks). Reggie Smith was coaching first base at the time, and I looked at him and said, "I just fucked up my thumb." He told me to yank it out. When I did, I wanted very badly to scream, which of course, like crying, is not allowed in baseball. In denial, I caught another inning. Ramon Martinez was pitching, and his ball moved a lot, so my hand was getting pummeled. When I got back to the dugout, it was badly swollen. I told our physical therapist, Pat Screnar, that I couldn't handle any more. My batting average would have to hold at .537 for a while.

The thumb was placed in a cast, and as soon as it was removed, Screnar got me working with putty and rubber bands to build the strength back. After about a week of that, I tried to hit off a tee. On the first swing, I took a big rip and the bat went flying out of my hands. I actually did scream that time—it was okay because it wasn't a game—and hopped around and undoubtedly swore a good bit. Pat said, "What are you doing? Take it easy."

Late in May, the club left for a ten-game road trip and I worked out at the stadium with Mike Scioscia. It felt downright eerie to be in there when the place was so empty and quiet, with the grass uncut. But it was a good working environment, and when I got to the point at which I could at least hold on to the bat—around the time the team was returning to Los Angeles—I suggested to Fred Claire that I go down to Albuquerque for some rehab. He said, "That won't be necessary." So Pat designed a support system with tape, strips, disposable wrap, and more tape. He did a good job.

I didn't argue with Fred, because I desperately wanted to be back in the lineup. Of course, Tommy was all for it, as well. We were 8-14 while I was on the DL (9-17 counting the games I'd missed earlier with the hamstring problem), and Tommy, on general principle, didn't care to see me sitting. He had a favorite expression he'd recycle every time the subject of me taking a day off came up. He'd say, "I don't have a bat long enough for you to hit from the bench." I couldn't complain. I was young, I liked being in the lineup, and I especially didn't want to miss the day games after the night games, which is when catchers and old guys usually rest. Dodger Stadium was a pitcher-friendly park, but the ball carried better in the daytime and I wasn't interested in wasting that good, warm air making small talk in the shade of the dugout. It was, in fact, a day game when I came off the disabled list—Sunday, June 4, against the Mets. The crowd was humming and my adrenaline was revved up. I homered against Pete Harnisch and caught Candiotti without a passed ball, which was probably a bigger accomplishment.

The home run was a little misleading, as it turned out. It took a few more weeks for my power to make it all the way back. In spite of how I felt about it at the time, I had probably come off the DL too early. But by June 26, I was strong enough to hit a ball clean out of Dodger Stadium in batting practice. That didn't happen often. We were playing the Padres that night, and a few hours later, with the score tied in the ninth inning, I was due up third against Trevor Hoffman, who proceeded to hit Delino DeShields and walk Jose Offerman. He probably wasn't too worried, considering that he had gotten the better of me all three times we'd previously met, with two strikeouts. Before I stepped to the plate, I told Karros, "Just kill me if I get cheated up there." I lived. Hit the first pitch on a line and over the right-field fence to end the game.

The next day, Tony Gwynn and some other Padres started talking about me being the MVP, which seemed a little premature considering how many games I'd missed. But I appreciated it. Nobody on the *Dodgers* was saying that, with the exception of Joey Amalfitano, our third-base coach.

That was around the time we were jockeying with the Rockies for first place. On June 29, Nomo shut them out, 1–0, to put us up by half a game.

Colorado loaded the bases in the eighth inning, with one out, and Nomo threw a splitter that Andres Galarraga nubbed back to the mound. Hideo brought it home and I threw a rocket to Karros at first base to complete the double play. Tommy went nuts: "Jesus Christ, you threw the shit out of that ball!" That was fun, and so was catching the Tornado. He was sensational that year—led the league in strikeouts, shutouts (tied with Greg Maddux), and fewest hits per nine innings.

Part of Nomo's success stemmed from the fact that, unlike a lot of modern pitchers, he wasn't afraid to keep the batter off the plate. A couple of years later, after Scott Rolen of the Phillies had touched him up for a couple home runs, Hideo hit him three times. After the third time, Rolen—a big guy whom I'd definitely put in a category with Brooks Robinson and Mike Schmidt as the greatest defensive third basemen I've seen—showed up at our clubhouse door looking for him. Nothing came of it, but it was clear that Nomo had made his reputation. With *us*, though, he already had one. When Nomo pitched, it was *his* game. We had a left-handed reliever named Mark Guthrie, whom I really enjoyed because he was hilarious and a huge hard-rock guy and shared my affinity for cigars, and Gut would walk into the clubhouse on a day when it was Nomo's turn and go, "Why am I here? It's Tornado night. I don't think I'm even gonna get dressed."

Obviously, there was a language barrier between Nomo and me. But as a catcher for the Dodgers, there was almost always a language issue with the starting pitcher. Over the next couple years, Chan Ho Park (Korea) would complete our United Nations rotation, which already included Nomo (Japan), Ramon Martinez and Pedro Astacio (Dominican Republic), Ismael Valdez (Mexico), and Tom Candiotti, who spoke knuckleball. It was so confusing that I once walked out to the mound to talk to Nomo and started jabbering in Spanish.

Hideo and I, however, understood each other in the ways that counted. After his games, when he would retreat to a separate locker room at Dodger Stadium (where I used to dress as a batboy) and answer questions for the hordes of Japanese reporters that followed the team all year, he was always very gracious about shooting credit in my direction. His generous words had an unexpected benefit. Nomo's agent, Don Nomura, was friendly with Danny Lozano, and they landed me a three-year endorsement deal with Komatsu, a Japanese heavy-equipment company. I also did a Japanese underwear commercial for Gunze that showed me sliding into home with my feet in flames, then reclining on the plate in nothing but my briefs. I was the Jim Palmer of Japan.

Martinez was also an ace for us that year, and on July 14, at Dodger Stadium against the Marlins, he happened to get plenty of latitude from Eric Gregg, the home plate umpire. Gregg's strike zone was so generous that, after the third inning, I called for nothing but fastballs, which Ramon was spotting crisply off both corners. He sliced through the Florida lineup in twenty-eight batters, without giving up a hit.

I took some special pride in catching that game, in light of the fact that, in other ways, Ramon and I had trouble finding a comfort level with each other. Among the many examples was a game the year before in which Ramon had covered first base against the Giants and bobbled the toss from Karros. That prompted our former teammate Darryl Strawberry, who had been on second base, to round third and barrel toward home. I didn't block the plate, because that's a bad idea when the runner's legs are eight feet long and you don't know where the throw is going to be. Strawberry came in standing up, and was pretty much past me by the time the ball arrived. Afterward, Ramon got all over me: "Why didn't you block the plate?" I said, "Why didn't you catch the ball?" Ramon also grumbled sometimes about the way I called games, but there was none of that on the night of his no-hitter.

Two weeks later, Ramon beat the Reds, 4–2, to keep us within range of the Rockies, who had been threatening to pull away with the NL West. But the memorable aspect of that game had to do with Cincinnati's final relief pitcher. Rick Reed had been a replacement player, and we all knew it. A bunch of us—admittedly, I was front and center—crowded the railing of the dugout and yelled, "Scab!" I'd like to say it wasn't with malice, that we were just trying to start a rally in a close and important game, but it was a volatile time.

Tommy had that game in mind when, a month down the road, he tried, unsuccessfully, to talk the front office out of calling up a big first baseman named Mike Busch. Busch had been a tight end at Iowa State and was a pretty good power prospect. For most of us, though, the operative fact was that he had crossed the line in spring training. He had a wife and a baby and a ranch in Missouri and had given us the whole I-have-to-cross-because-I've-got-a-farm-payment-to-make-and-my-mother-is-elderly thing. Our thing was not only did we have bills to pay, too, but there were a lot of minor-league lifers with wives and kids of their own who had honored the strike. When Busch came up, Brett Butler, whom we had just picked up in a trade with the Mets, made some remarks to the press about him being a scab. I went on a radio show and was asked about having Busch as a teammate. I said I didn't respect his decision but what am I going to do, not throw him the ball?

It turned ugly. The *Los Angeles Times* dredged up some of our quotes about Busch from spring training. Then the fans started booing Brett Butler. The Dodgers even held a press conference to handle the situation. At that point, I said it shouldn't have become a public matter, that it was our dirty laundry and wasn't for the media to wave around. That was not well received. The whole thing was a spectacle.

Personally, I didn't think a distraction like that was going to do us any favors in a pennant race, and I sure didn't want anything messing with my focus and timing. Two nights before Busch's debut, in a getaway game at Philadelphia, in front of my family and no doubt some friends, I'd gone four for four with two doubles, two home runs, and seven RBIs. My man Delino DeShields told the *Times*, "He hit the ball tonight as hard as I've ever seen in my entire life. Did you see those balls he hit? Damn, that's crazy right there." Until that night, I didn't have enough plate appearances to qualify for the batting title. Suddenly, at .367, I popped right into the lead, with Gwynn—who'd already won it five times—trailing by ten percentage points. No catcher had won a batting title since Ernie Lombardi in 1942, and he caught only eighty-five games.

Of course, I knew damn well that Tony Gwynn was not the guy you wanted to challenge in a batting race. He was the greatest high-average hitter of my generation, by far—the greatest since Ted Williams, for that matter—and dedicated himself to being just that. It seemed to me that Gwynn could have hit with more power if he'd wanted to, but that wasn't his game of choice. He was all about spoiling pitches and finding holes. There was a general belief among pitchers, catchers, managers, and scouts that the better the pitches you made to Gwynn, the more he'd hurt you. Many times I stretched my mitt far to my left to catch a ball below and beyond the strike zone, and before it got to me, Gwynn had simply served it into left field, nice as you please. Now and then we'd run out of ideas for him and say, what the hell, let's just throw it in there and see what happens. He was so geared to handling supposedly unhittable pitches that it sometimes seemed as though he didn't know what to do with a ball right down the middle. He'd pop it up. As a rule, though, you weren't going to prevent Tony Gwynn from getting his hits.

Two weeks after I jumped into the batting lead, I was down under .360, Gwynn was up over .360, and I was smacked on the wrist by a pitch from Mark Leiter of the Giants, who called the next day to apologize. I left that game but didn't miss any others. We were going stride for stride with the Rockies, and Tommy's no-bat-long-enough principle was in full effect.

When the Giants left town, San Diego assumed their place. All things considered, I thought I was well within my rights to take a personal moment when Gwynn dug in to hit in the first inning. I told him it was time he stepped aside. He cracked up and had to walk out of the batter's box.

We played two series with the Padres in the final week and a half, separated by only three critical games at home against Colorado. The Rockies came to Chavez Ravine a half game ahead of us, but we were playing well, having won three in a row. In the series opener, we were down 3–2 in the sixth when I reached on an error and Karros slammed a huge two-run homer that won the game and gave Martinez his seventeenth victory. We split the next two and jogged down the road to San Diego with a half-game lead. Thousands of Dodger fans came with us, and we wanted nothing more than to clinch the division in front of them.

By that time, Gwynn—whose brother, Chris, played for us that year— had easily wrapped up the batting title, but I was more than happy with the trade-off: we beat the Padres the last two games of the season to wrap up the NL West by a single game over the Rockies, who also won their last two. I homered in the Saturday game—my thirty-second of the year—and in the finale, Mike Busch, of all people, struck the big blow with a tiebreaking three-run blast in the seventh.

Although he had batted only seventeen times on the season, Busch was a hero to Dodger fans. The players, meanwhile, acknowledged his role in helping us to the title; but that didn't matter much when we held our meeting to divvy up the playoff shares. We were a strong union team and felt like we needed to make a statement. We voted him nothing, not even a partial share. The way we saw it, that was money that the union had negotiated, and Busch was a scab. He had acted *against* the union, not with it. So now we're going to vote him a share? Nope. Can't have it both ways, pal. Fred Claire thought we were wrong in what we did, and he called in Eric and me to ask us to reconsider. "I just think it's bad," he told us.

I said, "Well, then, *you* give him a fucking share." Then we walked out. For what it's worth, Busch was not on the postseason roster.

In the meantime, we partied at Prego in San Diego. The star of the evening was Tim Wallach, who hadn't made it to the postseason since 1981 in Montreal. Wallach got so drunk that four guys had to carry him to his car. The whole time, his wife is going, "Oh God, Timmy."

The division series pitted us against the Reds, led that year by Barry Larkin, who had always been a great shortstop, and Pete Schourek, who had never been a great pitcher. In his prior years with the Mets, Schourek, a left-hander, was the kind of guy who was actually fun to hit against. He gave up some of the longest bombs of anybody in the league. Then he went to Cincinnati in 1995 and all of a sudden you couldn't touch him. He never pitched that way again.

In the first game of the playoffs, in Los Angeles, I reached Schourek for a home run but we fell short, 7–2. In the second game, Karros hit two home runs, I went 0 for 5—including a strikeout, looking, in the ninth, against Jeff Brantley—and we lost, 5–4. Butler and Chad Fonville were on base all day in front of me, and Eric was crushing the ball behind me, so you can imagine how I felt—especially having it go down that way in our own ballpark. The strange thing was, though, that Dodger Stadium felt different in the playoffs. Since the games started at five o'clock for national TV, the sun would be setting for a good portion of them, and it wasn't the same hitting atmosphere that we were accustomed to. That's not an excuse, because the other team played in the same atmosphere, but the upshot was, we didn't feel too badly about having to go to Cincinnati for game three. Besides, we had Nomo lined up. David Wells blew us away, 10–1.

The sweep was a miserable end to a season that I felt pretty good about, otherwise—which, of course, only made it worse. Had we won or even made it to the World Series, I could have relished the facts that I'd put up the highest slugging percentage (.606) in Dodgers history; that, after three years in the big leagues, nobody but Babe Ruth and my hitting idol, Ted Williams, had ever hit more home runs (91) with a higher batting average (.327) than I had; and that I'd finished a very close second to Barry Bonds (1.009 to 1.006) in OPS (on-base percentage plus slugging percentage), a favorite statistic of the sabermetrics people. The great Jim Murray of the *Los Angeles Times* wrote a column comparing me favorably to the most renowned catchers in history. With the MVP vote coming up, I liked my chances.

The irony, though, was that they would probably be compromised by my best friend in baseball—as would his by me, for that matter. Karros and I had the same number of home runs that year, and he actually drove in more runs. He was also in better graces with the press. There was some consensus among the Dodger media to push Eric for MVP. That was all good, except that I couldn't agree entirely with the rationale. Writers kept saying that Eric had held the team together when I was hurt. He did hit well in those times—he hit well *all year*, especially in the clutch—but the fact was, we had a losing record when I wasn't in the lineup. From my perspective, that seemed to underscore my value to the ball club. I guess it was a matter of how you looked at it.

At any rate, I thought we both had better seasons than Barry Larkin, who, after a full frontal assault by the media starting in early September, ended up winning it, with Dante Bichette of Colorado—who led the league in home runs and RBIs—second. And Greg Maddux (19–2, with a 1.63 ERA) third. I finished fourth, one place ahead of Eric.

That was the beginning of a growing cynicism I nurtured over the years toward the MVP award. And the writers, too.

CHAPTER TWELVE

Hideo Nomo shut out the Braves, 1–0, in our first home game of 1996, outpitching Tom Glavine. As great as Glavine was, somehow I went three for three against him, all singles, to make it eight for sixteen in my career. I suspect it's because I was willing to be patient and take the ball to right field. That year, I would actually lead the major leagues in opposite-field hits, which served me well against craftsmen like Glavine, who will abuse impatience. In any case, we took two out of three from the Braves, which was a good sign, seeing as how Atlanta set the standard in the National League.

It wasn't long, though, before the season took a grim turn. Early in May, Brett Butler left the team to have a cancerous tumor removed from his throat. Butler was still one of the best center fielders and top-of-the-order hitters in the game, but he was almost thirty-nine and would have to undergo intensive radiation treatments. Most people figured he was through as a ballplayer.

We never found a long-term replacement for Brett in center field, but Todd Hollandsworth, a rookie playing mostly in left, picked up a lot of the slack in the batting order. Amazingly, he would become our fifth consecutive Rookie of the Year (following Karros, me, Mondesi, and Nomo).

Eric, Mondesi, and I did our parts, as well, in holding things together. I was leading the league in hitting late in May, when I slid clumsily into second base—the only way I knew how, it seemed—and hyperflexed my knee. Players don't ordinarily admit this, but I badly wanted to win a batting championship. I would have preferred it even to a home run title. As I've noted, I didn't like to make outs.

My knee was swollen and sore, but it was playable, and we were straining to hang close to the Padres, of all teams. In June, we asserted ourselves by taking three out of four in Atlanta, the last of them coming behind Candiotti, 3–2, when I hit a couple of homers. That finally pulled us even with

San Diego. We then won two out of three in Chicago, wrapping up the final game in thirteen innings after some strong relief work by Chan Ho Park, who actually drove in the winning run with a bases-loaded walk.

Afterward, Park was having a wonderful time talking to the writers when one of them glanced into his locker and noticed that the sleeves and pants of his suit had been chopped off. Raul Mondesi was the perpetrator in an act of good-natured rookie hazing, a tradition we observed to make new players feel like part of the ball club. Chan Ho didn't see it that way. He went into a rage, flinging a chair across the clubhouse. Apparently, sophomoric humor wasn't cool in Korean clubhouses, but showing up your teammates in front of the media wasn't cool in ours. I kind of ripped him in the papers for that, and he, in turn, made a public thing of it. I suppose I should have been more sensitive to the cultural considerations, but the bottom line was, I didn't click with Chan Ho the way I did with Nomo.

Nevertheless, we arrived home in first place, looking good and gathering steam. That Sunday, we came from behind to tie the Astros with two runs in the eighth and beat them in the bottom of the ninth on my one-out home run against Xavier Hernandez.

It was June 23. After that date, nothing was ever quite the same.

For all of the difficulties I had with the Dodgers over the years—from their lack of interest in me after the draft to the minor-league drama to the contentious contract negotiations—I always appreciated the fact that they weren't just another baseball team. The Dodgers had a soul.

Actually, they had *two* souls. One belonged to Peter O'Malley, the family-oriented owner and gentleman whose father, Walter, had brought the team over from Brooklyn in 1958, ten years before I was born; and the other—proud, public, loyal, loud, and a little chaotic—was, unmistakably, Tommy Lasorda's. Tommy, of course, had replaced Walter Alston, who had accompanied the club from Brooklyn and managed it well for twenty-three years. Alston went about his business in a strong but quiet and conservative style, which fit right in with the O'Malleys—especially Peter. When the time came, credit Peter for having the self-assurance to hire a flamboyant Italian cut from a drastically different cloth. Between them, O'Malley and Lasorda *were* the Dodgers, as we knew them.

That lasted until the moment I stomped on home plate to put away the Astros.

Sometimes, it seems like the game of baseball is out of our hands. We think we're swinging a thin-handled bat at a two-seam fastball, taking

Glavine the other way or going deep against Xavier Hernandez, and really, it's some other power taking over—God, fate, poetry, whatever you want to call it. The victory on June 23 was the 1,599th of Tommy's incredible, Hall of Fame career as a major-league manager. And the last.

That night, he attended a charity dinner at the Century Plaza Hotel and complained to his wife, Jo, about abdominal pain. She took him to the hospital the next day, an off day. On Tuesday, he was diagnosed with an ulcer. On Wednesday, he underwent angioplasty surgery. Tommy had suffered a minor heart attack, and the doctors weren't sure when.

Billy Russell, his old shortstop and coach, took over the team, expecting to return it to Tommy in a week or two. Tommy expected the same. Meanwhile, the docs were telling Tommy to start taking things a little easier. He knew that wasn't feasible as long as he was managing the Dodgers. Maybe somebody else could take it easy in that job, but not Tommy Lasorda. About a month later, there was a press conference at Dodger Stadium, and Tommy's voice was shaking when he said, "For me to get into a uniform again—as excitable as I am—I could not go down there without being the way I am. I decided it's best for me and the organization to step down. . . . That's quite a decision."

Yeah, it was. I wished I could have lightened the moment somehow. In the best tradition of Tommy himself, maybe I should have pulled him aside and jumped all over him the way he always jumped on me when I felt like I shouldn't play: "You mean to say you can't sit in the fuckin' dugout and tell Billy Ashley to go up there and pinch-fuckin'-hit? You can't walk out to the fuckin' mound and hold up your right fuckin' hand for Todd Worrell? What the fuck? I'd love for you to get some rest, Tommy, but we don't have a lineup card big enough that we can read it from your fuckin' house in Fullerton."

On one hand, even though he was sixty-eight, managing the Dodgers was everything to Tommy, and I'd always thought they'd have to haul him out of the dugout in a box. On the other, I suppose we could see it coming while he was convalescing. He was scheduled to coach at the All-Star Game, which was in Philadelphia that year, and there was no way he'd miss the trip back home if he could help it. But he watched from his couch in California.

Tommy was the only thing missing from that night. There were about fifty family members and friends of mine in the crowd, and I had a good time with the whole scene. The year before, at the All-Star Game in Texas, I'd taken a batting-practice ball to the outfield and had Barry Bonds and a few other guys sign it. When it was covered with autographs, I held it up to one section of the crowd and got everybody cheering and screaming, then took it over to another section and got the people worked up over there. Whichever section made the most noise got the ball. When I tossed it into the seats, it turned into a scrum to see who could come up with the prize. I reprised the act in Philadelphia, and they went wild over it.

I'd been the leading vote-getter for the game—I was hitting .363 with twenty-four homers at the break—and found that immensely gratifying. Even so, it didn't quite equal the honor of catching the first pitch from Mike Schmidt, the guy I'd always wanted to be like. At that instant, it hit me that I really *was* like Mike, in a superficial, just-getting-started sort of way. (Thankfully, I was booed less—although, within a couple years, I would make up a lot of ground in that department.) To top it off, he signed the ball: *Mike, I think you're the best.*

That was the greatest moment of the evening . . . until the bottom of the second inning, at least, when I cranked a long home run off Charles Nagy, the American League starter. According to Bob Nightengale of the *Los Angeles Times,* Tommy sat up and screamed when the ball came down in the upper deck of Veterans Stadium. *That* was the greatest moment of the evening . . . until we'd completed the 6–0 shutout and I was named the game's MVP (I also had an RBI double).

At the end of the night, though, the greatest moment might have been seeing my mom crying tears of joy as I held up the MVP trophy. Or watching my dad accept congratulations from half the population of Chester, Montgomery, Delaware, Bucks, and Philadelphia counties. He was beaming and bragging so much, I finally had to say, "That's enough, Dad."

In the postgame interviews, I told the writers, "This is a small tribute to my dad." I meant that, of course. But if I'd known what was going through Tommy's head at the time, I could have dedicated my award to him *and* my father. I think they both would have liked that.

After four losses, Billy Russell's first win came in Colorado on a night when I homered three times and drove in six runs. We led 13–0 going into the bottom of the eighth, behind Ismael Valdez. The final score—classic Coors Field—was 13–10, with the tying run on deck.

At that time, I was having more trouble than ever throwing out runners, which my pitcher friends were not reluctant to point out. They didn't have a lot to say when I homered three times and drove in six runs, but I'd hear from them on days like the very next one, when the Rockies embarrassed me by stealing ten bases, six of them by my old teammate Eric Young. We lost that one, 16–15. For what it's worth, I homered in that game, too. Just saying.

Russell had been my manager in Albuquerque, and he was a good bench coach for Tommy, but after he took over the Dodgers, he and I didn't gel. I'm not sure what the problem was. There were some strange dynamics running through the organization in those days. Tommy became a vice president when he stopped managing, and a lot of people seemed to be afraid that he would take their job, or that associating with him would somehow put them on the wrong side of something or other. My dad once walked into Billy's office and was appalled to find no trace that Tommy had ever been there. All of the old pictures had been taken down except for one of Walter Alston. Russell had actually played more for Tommy than he had for Alston, not to mention the fact that Tommy was the one who had hired him. It seemed like a slap in Tommy's face, which of course my dad couldn't tolerate. He said, "Billy, what the hell are you doing? How can you have that picture up there and nothing of Tommy to go with it?"

According to my dad, Russell told him, "I've got to protect my own ass."

That's the way it was around there. Billy had been warned to steer clear of Tommy. He wanted my dad to convey that message to Tommy, but my dad didn't think it was his place to do that, per se. What he said to Tommy was, "That stupid ass is telling me that Fred Claire said he should stay away from you."

Later in the year, when reporters asked Russell who he thought deserved the MVP award, he answered, "Ken Caminiti." It was hard not to take that personally, as much as I admired Caminiti. A tough-guy third baseman, Caminiti was carrying the Padres while battling through a barrage of hardship. At various times in 1996, he dealt with injuries to his abdomen, biceps, elbow, groin, hamstrings, and back. Then, on August 18, a day after we'd taken over first place, San Diego was playing the Mets in Monterrey, México, when Caminiti had a bout with nausea, dehydration, and Montezuma's revenge. They put him on the training table with an IV and a Snickers bar, and he got up, marched out, and hit two home runs to bring the Padres back into a tie with us.

Meanwhile, I was still limping around with a gimpy right knee—torn cartilage, it turned out. It must have happened when I hurt myself sliding in May, but I never knew it until an MRI on the knee showed a "minor disruption" about the size of a pebble. The doctor said I could play on it if I could handle the pain. I figured I could handle pain better than surgery. I was terrified of knee surgery. I'd seen too many catchers who were never the same after it. Anyway, the knee didn't bother me in the batter's box—and my comparative health is not the point here. The point is, I was a *Dodger*, and the Dodgers' manager was lobbying, at my expense, for a player on the team we were dueling for the division title. I don't know if Billy was instructed to say that or not, but I got the distinct impression that the organization was trying to suppress my value. We were due to negotiate a new contract at the end of the season.

I sometimes had my issues with Tommy, too, but for as long as he was my manager, he was always an ally. I couldn't say that about Billy Russell. There was a game, for instance, when Ramon Martinez had two outs in the ninth and two strikes on Ryan Klesko—we were way ahead of the Braves—and threw a nasty cutter that I missed, which allowed Klesko to reach first base. Ramon got the next guy, no problem, but when I walked out to the mound he wouldn't shake my hand. I don't expect a pitcher to give me a hug and kiss for doing what I'm paid to do, but from my perspective, I've busted my ass back there and a "hey, good job, way to work hard" isn't too much to ask. I loved catching Jim Gott, for instance, because he'd get genuinely excited about any little thing I did to help him out: "Good job, Mike, way to go! Way to block that ball!" But Ramon . . . Sometimes, I'd start toward the mound and he'd just turn his back on me. This time, I was so incensed I wanted to kick his ass right on the spot. Russell could tell I was furious about something, although he wasn't sure what, and got in my face about it. I could understand that he'd have problems with my temper, but at that moment he was only making it worse. We came very, very close to fighting.

In spite of the O'Malley influence, the Dodgers were not a big-happy-family kind of ball club, and after Tommy retired, the rift between pitchers and hitters only grew wider. Both Ramon and Ismael Valdez went anonymously to Maryann Hudson of the *Times* and said that I didn't know how to call a game. I have to acknowledge that, at times, I was hard on Ramon in the media, so it worked both ways. As for Ismael—he was a guy who, when the game reached the later innings, was usually looking at the bullpen, and he knew that I thought he should suck it up more often. He certainly knew *Eric* felt that way, because one night after a bad loss in Florida we had a team meeting and Karros spoke his mind about it. Basically, he called Ismael a pussy. Valdez confronted him outside the shower, of all places. They started fighting, the only problem being that Eric was in his towel and shower shoes. Naturally, the towel fell off, and Billy Ashley said, "What are you going to do now, Eric? Hit him with your cock?"

It's ironic to me that the pitchers I had the most difficulty with were the

Latin guys, whom I'd been catching since I went to camp in the Dominican Republic. I didn't have the same kind of trouble with Nomo, Chan Ho, or Candiotti, even though I'd never before caught a Japanese, Korean, or knuckleball pitcher. One of the complaints was that I obsessed too much over my hitting, that if I struck out or bounced into a double play, my concentration drifted when I was behind the plate. There's a double edge to that. Hell yeah, it bothered me when I didn't come through with the bat, and maybe that showed up in my body language. But there was a lot of pressure on me to carry the club offensively, and I took that responsibility very seriously. I never consciously let a bad at-bat affect my defense, but sometimes it's inevitable. Pitchers are sensitive, and they pick up on those things. In addition, some pitchers are insecure to the point that they're eager to blame anything but themselves for their failures. I've had pitchers who were getting lit up tell me that the other team had my signs. No, dude, they don't have the signs.

And then, thankfully, there are those who put the whole thing in perspective. Candiotti used to say, "I don't give a shit if you ever throw a guy out. Just hit me a three-run homer."

I was well aware that I needed to straighten out my throwing. To that end, I watched some tapes of myself from 1993 and put in some dedicated sessions with Mike Scioscia. He pointed out a couple of technical flaws, but throwing is not an easy thing to fix. When guys started to steal on me, I tended to rush my throws, and that led to bad habits. Plus, because of my bat, I was playing nearly every day, which meant my body was tired and beat-up most of the time. I'm not offering excuses—just saying that there was a lot going on, a lot of moving parts. I told Jim Murray that year, "You have to remember, we have a staff that includes Candiotti, who throws a knuckleball, and Hideo Nomo, who throws the ball out of a corkscrew and the forkball sometimes goes in the dirt."

That said, I concede my shortcomings as far as throwing out base stealers—I guess I *have* to, considering that I missed 155 of them that year, the most in the majors—but I'll also argue that that's only a small part of what a catcher does defensively. The primary task is to coax the best game possible out of the pitchers. I did that by knowing their strengths, studying the hitters, and being aggressive in the strike zone—especially early in the count. I made sure, as much as I could, that we didn't fall behind in balls and strikes. I insisted that our guys pitch with confidence, whether they had any or not. It worked. Pitchers didn't walk as many batters when I caught. And I'll point out, proudly, that in 1996 the Dodgers led the National League in ERA.

There's a lot of chemistry and trust involved in the pitcher-catcher relationship and I embraced that part of the job. I also welcomed the break that conscientious catching provided from the pressures of hitting in the middle of the lineup. By nature, I was so consumed by hitting that, with idle time on my hands, I'd have been inclined to overthink my approach to it. I believed in going to the plate with a clear head so that I could focus on simply seeing the ball—on freeing up my swing, letting it come naturally—and the constant demands of catching helped me do that.

> Mike as a receiver . . . this never gets mentioned, but in my view he always caught the ball extremely well. He never got credit for what he accomplished as a catcher. There were a lot of people who said, let's move Mike to first base, as if it would be an easy transition. I never really thought that was in the best interest of our team or Mike. I just tried to look at what the player brought to our team, and Mike was so much on the plus side that I never thought about making a change. As a catcher, he hit in record proportions. There was never anybody better.
>
> —Fred Claire

That whole summer, we continued to shuffle back and forth with the Padres. One of the more interesting games came against Montreal at the end of August, when Ramon faced off against his brother, Pedro, whom we had traded because, as I heard it, the Dodgers thought he might be too small for a heavy workload.

I only wish I'd gotten along with either Martinez half as well as they got along with each other. They really did have a special relationship. Pedro was known to sit in the dugout and pray for Ramon when his brother pitched against his team—or slip back to the Montreal clubhouse, where he could cheer more openly. On the night they opposed each other, Pedro was asked what he was thinking after Ramon walked three straight batters in the bottom of the third to let in the first run of the game. He said, "I was hoping he'd make some adjustments." Ramon did, and we won, 2–1, on back-to-back homers by me and Eric in the fourth.

We were playing great ball in that stretch—I had a nineteen-game hitting streak at one point—and kept it up into the final month of the season. On September 1, in Philadelphia, I crushed one of my favorite home runs ever. It was off Mike Williams, a reliever who became nastier later when he developed a split-fingered fastball, and it disappeared into a tunnel in one of the upper decks in left-center. We lost that game, but less than two weeks later, Nomo beat the Cardinals, 4–1, to put us half a game ahead of San Diego.

In his next start, following a shutout by Valdez, there was a tricky, unexpected element to work around. The mound at Coors Field was slippery and Nomo had a little trouble with it early on. I talked to our pitching coach, Dave Wallace—people might not realize that the catcher and pitching coach work together closely—and before the second inning we convinced Hideo to pitch out of the stretch all the way. We started out with mostly fastballs in the first few innings, but Nomo's forkball was so evil that night that we went to it heavily in the latter stages of the game. We were both feeling it.

That was an example of a ball game in which I didn't get a hit and didn't really care. When a guy has it working the way the Tornado did against the Rockies, the catcher gets into a rhythm just like the pitcher does, and probably enjoys it just as much. There's a satisfying sense of control, empowerment, and total involvement—putting down a sign and a target and watching the pitch pour into your mitt exactly the way you had in mind. Nomo walked four batters but he never did make a mistake in the strike zone. His masterpiece was the second no-hitter I'd had the privilege of catching in as many seasons. More important, it came at a critical time, stretching our lead in the division to a game and a half with less than two weeks remaining in the season.

We lost the series finale and carried a half-game advantage to San Diego for an enormous four-game series that didn't change a thing. We had a chance to take three out of the four going into the last one, but the Padres got to Nomo for three runs in the fifth inning. I hit one of my longest home runs in the eighth—they measured it at 446 feet—to make it 3–2, and that was it. The San Diego crowd was chanting "MVP!" for Caminiti—who had an incredible second half of the season—when he hit two singles and made a great defensive play in the ninth, all with a torn rotator cuff. I seemed to be losing out in the suck-it-up-and-play competition, even though the cartilage tear in my knee was making me pop Advil every day. But I continued to lead the league in hitting (only because Gwynn didn't have enough at-bats to qualify) and felt like I was still the front-runner in the MVP race—that I *had* to be—in spite of all the noise to the contrary.

Back at home, we took two out of three from the Giants to go up two games with only three to play. Against the Padres. With a single victory, the division title would be ours.

Valdez started the first game for us and led, 2–1, going into the eighth, when Caminiti tied it with a homer to center field. It seemed like every time he did something against us that year, Vin Scully would go, "Ken Caminiti, everybody's MVP!" Thanks, Vin. But Caminiti had a compelling case, obviously, and added to it in the tenth inning, doubling home Steve Finley with the winning run.

Meanwhile, everybody seemed to think I was packing it in because I openly speculated that the series wasn't that big a deal: if we won the division, we'd play the Cardinals, and if we didn't, we'd be the wildcard and face the Braves right away in a five-game series instead of—inevitably—a seven-game set in the next round. I thought that was a very pragmatic perspective. Fred Claire went nuts.

After the Padres beat Nomo on Saturday, it all came down to the final game. Russell and Claire spoke to the team beforehand, urging us to have some pride, lay claim to the NL West, and for Pete's sake, don't get swept. That was well and good, but the theme was watered down a little bit when we pulled out Ramon Martinez after one inning so we'd have him ready for the first game of the playoffs. Kind of a mixed message, I'd say. Ironically, the strategy worked out to the extent that Pedro Astacio took over and shut the Padres down.

It was still 0–0 in the bottom of the ninth. Wayne Kirby led it off for us and walked, then Hollandsworth reached when they misplayed his sacrifice bunt. That brought me up against Dario Veras with two on and no outs. A base hit would win the division. I struck out. Then Karros grounded into a double play. In the top of the eleventh, Finley doubled against Chan Ho Park, Caminiti singled him to third, and, wouldn't you know it, Chris Gwynn—Tony's brother, who had come up in the Dodger organization—smacked a changeup into right-center to bring them both home. Trevor Hoffman got us one-two-three in the bottom of the eleventh.

So the Padres sprayed their champagne right in front of us, Tony Gwynn picked up enough at-bats to clinch the batting title again, and Caminiti, with forty home runs and 130 RBIs, was a unanimous choice for MVP. I was second in the voting with a .336 average, thirty-six homers, and 105 RBIs.

To that, my emotional reaction was pretty much the same as it had been in 1995: fuck the MVP. I was already jaded by the voting process. Six years later, after Caminiti admitted in a controversial *Sports Illustrated* story to using performance-enhancing drugs, a lot of people thought that it tainted his award; but I couldn't get worked up over that. From my point of view, it wasn't steroids that won it for Caminiti; it was the popularity contest. It was the legend of getting off the training table, pulling out his IV, polishing off his Snickers bar, and clubbing two home runs against the Mets in Monterrey.

This is a cliché, I know, and perhaps a rationalization, but what mattered more to me than even the MVP award was the respect of my peers—which was why I was so offended by the indifference of the Dodgers on my behalf. The highest compliments I got seemed to come from San Diego. The Padres' manager, Bruce Bochy, told the *Los Angeles Times*, "Being a former catcher myself, I can't tell you how impressed I am. For him to catch a hundred and forty games and hit like he has all season is absolutely unbelievable."

And then there was the official endorsement of another guy from San Diego, one whose authority was unsurpassed, in my book, and whose approval meant more to me than that of anyone else connected to the game. Ted Williams operated a museum and Hitters Hall of Fame in St. Petersburg, Florida, and in 1996, for the first of three consecutive seasons, I was honored by it as the Most Productive Hitter of the Year. Me—the kid with the batting cage!

When we lined up before the first playoff game, most of us were wishing that we had, indeed, won the damn division and were looking across the field at the Cardinals (who, incidentally, swept the Padres). The Braves' *reserves* included the likes of David Justice, Terry Pendleton, Andruw Jones, and Luis Polonia. As they were being announced, Mondesi nudged Karros and whispered, "Holy shit, they've got two teams!"

They also had a nice late-season pickup in Denny Neagle, one of the league's best left-handed pitchers. It seemed like we were always getting outmaneuvered in the way of ad hoc acquisitions. It seemed, also, that our roster was perpetually young, which was not really the perfect prescription for a postseason matchup with Atlanta. As much as we fought the feeling, there was no denying a certain sense that we were doomed in that series.

Even now, I can offer no other explanation for game one. Ramon pitched well, and of course John Smoltz pitched well for the Braves. It was 2–2 in the bottom of the eighth inning when I came to bat with two outs and nobody on. I squared the ball pretty well to right field—well enough to get it over the fence at Dodger Stadium. I'd hit enough home runs over that fence to know what one felt like, and *that* was a home run. Except that Jermaine Dye backed up, reached up, and, to my astonishment, caught the damn thing.

To this day, I don't know how that ball stayed in the park. And I wasn't the only one. Guys said it to me, and they said it to the *Los Angeles Times*.

Bobby Cox: "I thought Piazza's ball was out. Way out."

Smoltz: "I thought it was gone. It was one of the worst sliders I'd thrown all year."

Tim Wallach: "What happened to Mike's ball? I don't understand it. . . . It was weird."

What was even weirder was that, leading off the tenth inning, Javy Lopez, Atlanta's catcher, hit a ball to right-center that *didn't* look like it was going out. And, of course, it did.

You can imagine how disheartening it was to come off a game like that and have to face Maddux in the next one. Valdez actually outpitched him into the seventh, but then Fred McGriff and Dye hit home runs and they beat us, 3–2. The last game was less suspenseful. Nomo wasn't at his best, and Glavine was.

And so, we had once again fallen short. Everybody said so. We had five Rookies of the Year on our club; we were *supposed* to win. Making the play-offs two years in a row wasn't good enough. Raising our winning percentage for the fourth consecutive year wasn't good enough. After losing to the Braves, we heard the same refrain that we had heard before and would hear again, over and over: the Dodgers were chronic underachievers. Eric and I talked about it all the time because it drove us crazy. If having a bunch of Rookies of the Year means you're supposed to win in the postseason, then I guess we were supposed to win in the postseason. But it also means you've got a young, inexperienced team.

After the season, I found out what it was like to play on a club that *wasn't* young. MLB put together an all-star team for an eight-game series in Japan. Alex Rodriguez was still a young guy, but we also had Cal Ripken Jr., Barry Bonds, Gary Sheffield, Ivan Rodriguez, Andres Galarraga, Juan Gonzalez, John Franco, Jeff Brantley, and Sammy Sosa. And Nomo, which was interesting. Now, *that* team was supposed to win. Sure enough, we kicked some ass.

On the first Monday of 1997, six months after Tommy stepped down as manager, Peter O'Malley announced that he would be selling the Dodgers. It's hard to overstate the magnitude of that development.

No matter how our personal circumstances had played out, those of us who were Dodgers realized that we were part of a special organization. Tommy hammered that home in his inimitable way, but Peter was the man who made it so. He was the one who set the tone by serving ice cream to club employees every time we took over first place or widened our lead, by entertaining us in Dodgertown with barbecues and hay rides and a huge St.

Patrick's Day party and even a visit from Santa Claus, by allowing family members to fly free on the team plane anywhere we went, by actually listening to our suggestions about things like flight food and room arrangements, and, most important, by maintaining his dignity at every turn. Not only were the Dodgers considered a family, but they were, in fact, the last entirely family-owned team in the game.

Ultimately, that was the reason O'Malley felt compelled to sell. As he said at his press conference, "Professional sports today is as high-risk as the oil business. You need a broader base than an individual family to carry you through the storm." In the attempt to broaden his base, Peter had wanted to build a football stadium at Chavez Ravine and lure the NFL back to Los Angeles; but the city opted to use the Coliseum for that purpose. I think that took a toll on him, and so did baseball's latest collective bargaining agreement, which had been signed in November.

The new collective bargaining agreement included a luxury tax imposed on the well-heeled teams, to be distributed among those in smaller markets. It wasn't just the principle of revenue sharing that bothered O'Malley, but the peculiar position it put him in. He could have been obligated to cut a check to the Anaheim Angels, who competed against him for the same market. It would have amounted to the O'Malley family handing out money to the Disney corporation, which was in the process of taking over the Angels. That was hard to swallow. At the same time, however, the five-year agreement gave baseball some much-needed stability, which made it a good time to sell.

In order to soften the shock of the sudden announcement, the press conference conveyed the message that everything would continue on, business as usual. We knew differently, of course. There'd be no more Santa Claus in Dodgertown, and it was not likely that I'd see the new owner at Mass every Sunday, as I did O'Malley.

As if to prove their point, though, the Dodgers did some very important business just two days later. They signed Eric Karros to a four-year, $20 million contract, making him the club's highest-paid player. Eric was due to become a free agent after the 1997 season, a year before I was. But my contract had expired, as well, and by signing Eric first, Fred Claire and Sam Fernandez appeared to be doing one of two things: declaring him as the top priority or setting some kind of precedent for me. Either way, I didn't find it warm or particularly fuzzy.

I'd asked for a four- to six-year deal at $10–13 million a year, which was somewhere in the range of what Albert Belle had just received from

the White Sox; probably a smidgen less. I figured the organization would be motivated to dodge arbitration—I had two more years of it—and, at the same time, tie me up through my early seasons of free agency. It made perfect sense to me. Nevertheless, Eric's contract, whether calculated to do so or not, made my request look a little out of whack, if not outrageous. The Dodgers were aiming to give me four years at about $30 million, total, which seemed pretty damn generous by comparison. Those numbers also fell in line with the $6,665,000 for which the Rangers signed Ivan Rodriguez about ten days after Eric's deal was done, avoiding arbitration by giving Pudge the biggest one-year contract in history and more money than a catcher had ever made in a season. Even so, Dan Lozano and I had our own calculated notions of what I had coming to me, and we weren't daunted by any of that.

When it became painfully obvious that our attempts at a long-term deal were going nowhere, and since I'd hit more home runs and driven in more runs over my first four years than any other catcher, ever, we decided to go for a record arbitration bid. Nobody had ever requested more than $6.5 million—Jack McDowell in 1994—but we hinted to reporters that we'd be shooting for around $8 million, which was roughly Ken Griffey Junior money. The way baseball arbitration works is that the player will submit his figure and the team will submit its own, and rather than arrive at a number in between, the arbitrator must choose one or the other. We hoped that by throwing eight million out there, the Dodgers would be nervous enough to nudge their offer a little higher. I truly didn't want to go through the arbitration process, but we had arrived at that point and we had a game plan in place. When we submitted the official asking price, we set it at $7,650,000. It wasn't the $8 million we'd floated to the press, but it was still a record arbitration figure, and it was enough to get the club off its duff.

In no time at all, we'd settled for two years and $15 million. Sam and Fred were willing to go to three years for a little less money per season, but that third year would be my first crack at free agency. I didn't see any reason to sell it out for a salary I was sure I could beat, by a lot, when the time came.

In the end, the deal left the Dodgers at significant risk of losing me after my sixth season. Needless to say, they knew that. Or at least they *should* have.

Then again, ownership of the club would soon be changing. Whose problem was it, really?

CHAPTER THIRTEEN

Early in spring training of 1997, Bob Nightengale, the Dodgers' beat writer for the *Los Angeles Times*, approached me to ask about the rumors. Apparently, it was unimaginable that a sixty-second-round draft choice—and a courtesy pick, at that—could legitimately hit .326 and average a hundred RBIs over his first four seasons of Major League Baseball. Apparently, it was all but impossible for a guy who wasn't a particularly gifted athlete—couldn't run, not especially graceful—to be strong, quick, and skillful enough to drive so many balls out of so many ballparks. Apparently, it was not plausible that the son of a prosperous businessman with friends in high places would actually put in the work required to make himself—at the rate I was going—the best-hitting catcher in the history of the game, according to the numbers.

Apparently, my career was a story that nobody cared to believe. Apparently, my success was the work of steroids. *Had* to be. Those were the rumors.

I didn't mind that Nightengale asked the question. He was ahead of the curve on the steroids issue. In 1995, he'd written a story in which Randy Smith, the general manager of the Padres, estimated that 10 to 20 percent of major leaguers used steroids. Tony Gwynn was quoted saying, "It's like the big secret we're not supposed to talk about, but believe me, we wonder just like the rest of the people. I'm standing out there in the outfield when a guy comes up, and I'm thinking, 'Hey, I wonder if this guy is on steroids.'" Bear in mind, too, that in 1996 the Orioles, Mariners, and A's had all exceeded the previous single-season record for home runs, and more than twice as many players as ever before had hit forty—including Ken Caminiti and Mark McGwire, who reached fifty for the first time. Those two had not yet been implicated, but steroids had become part of the conversation. And in the course of that conversation, my name was being dropped. This was a chance to speak for myself.

"They're saying, 'Piazza is on steroids. Piazza is doing this, Piazza is doing that,'" I told Nightengale. "People can say what they want, but I don't use steroids. I'm not upset by the rumors, but I'll be upset at myself if I ever start listening [to them]. . . . I think if people saw how much work I put into this game, those rumors would stop. And it's not only training. It's my diet."

Nearly everything I put in my mouth was gauged for its muscle-building value. That was a habit I'd picked up from my dad and the Joe Weider magazines, way back when, and refined through my associations with trainers and nutritionists on the teams I'd played for and the gyms I'd lifted in. There were a lot of supplements available that didn't have to be acquired illegally or through a prescription. You could walk into GNC and buy androstenedione, or "andro." Or you could pick up the Monster Pak, with those intriguing before-and-after pictures. There was clearly a line that had to be crossed to get from the Monster Paks to the controlled substances classified as performance-enhancing drugs. For those, essentially, you needed a dealer. You had to seek out somebody to supply you with something you couldn't get at the mall. You had to break the law. I was interested in power, but not prison.

The Monster Pak served my purpose. It included andro, creatine, and various types of amino acids. In the off-season, I'd eat eggs and whole wheat toast, take the stuff in the Monster Pak, and head to the gym to train. Or go to Bucky Dent's camp in Boca Raton, Florida, and work out there. I do believe that supplements make a difference, but they have to be used in conjunction with serious training and a good diet. I always included protein shakes in the mix, as well—and still do. I never bought andro separately in a bottle, like the one that was spotted in McGwire's locker in 1998, but frankly, I never made a point of *not* buying it that way. I just didn't need to, because it was part of the Monster Pak. Andro was so accessible, and so common, that it never occurred to me to consider it cheating. When we heard about McGwire's locker, players didn't think of him as a cheater. But the media made such a commotion about it that the perceptions shifted. As a result, I felt compelled to phase andro out of my routine. Of course, it was later (in 2004) banned by the Food and Drug Administration and baseball as a "steroid precursor."

I'd disagree with anyone who says that there was a steroid culture in the game—at least, there wasn't one on the teams I knew—but there was a *drug* mentality, and it blurred the lines between what was acceptable and what wasn't. With the Dodgers, and I'm sure with most teams, you pulled a hamstring and boom, there's the Vioxx. We had a big trunk full of drugs for your aches and pains and inflammations. Charlie Strasser, the trainer, always said that if somebody really wanted to rip off the ball club, he shouldn't go for the bats or balls or gloves but for that big trunk with all the drugs in it. They had Vioxx, Indocin, Voltaren, you name it. As soon as you yanked a muscle, they'd bring you a cardboard sheet with the foil in the back and they'd punch out whatever pills you needed. But I should add that medications weren't abused by the players. The trainer was the only one who could dip into the trunk. On the other hand, the stuff was there for us and we weren't reluctant to take advantage of it. I used Vioxx because it was an intense anti-inflammatory and it made me feel good. When I'd caught for twenty-two straight days and could hardly drag myself out of bed to get to the ballpark, Vioxx picked me up. I'd sing, "It's gonna be a Vioxx morning . . ." Vioxx was ultimately associated with heart-attack risk and was pulled from the market by the manufacturer.

I also took greenies a couple times. A lot of guys couldn't play without them, but I didn't care for the feeling they gave me. Raul Mondesi would snap off a couple of greenies in a big cup of coffee and say, "Mike, take this!" They left me too jittery. I preferred Dymetadrine, which is a very light asthma medication that sends more oxygen to the brain. Dymetadrine made me alert and focused, which helped for day games after night games. Occasionally I used ephedra for that purpose. It was a fat burner, like drinking ten cups of coffee, and another supplement you could easily buy at GNC. Nobody was concerned about the propriety of it until an autopsy revealed that Steve Bechler, a young pitcher for the Orioles who was trying to lose weight, had ephedra in his system when he died of heatstroke after a spring training workout in 2003. It was then added to the banned list.

The banned list keeps growing, which I suppose is not surprising. In some fashion or other, aren't all modern medicines performance-enhancing drugs? Johnny Bench told me he'd get a cortisone shot every two weeks in his thumb. Is cortisone a PED? No, not officially. You get a cortisone shot so you can go out and play, and that's being tough; that's manly. But if you take a PED before you go out and play, that's cheating. I'm not making excuses for guys who do steroids; that's not my point. My point is, there's a drug culture in sports.

As to when our collective consciousness was actually raised in regard to PEDs, it's hard to say. The Caminiti article in *Sports Illustrated* (2002) by Tom Verducci is generally credited for opening the game's eyes. It certainly spoke loudly to a lot of players. But I think the impact of steroids was impressed upon me by Mark McGwire—although, when he came over to the National League in 1997, I really didn't know what I was looking at, other than raw, mind-boggling power that absolutely blew me away. Like everybody else, I'd make sure to be out on the field when McGwire was taking batting practice, just to get my world rocked. He was hitting balls in places where I'd never seen them hit. Freaking Scud missiles. My only thought was, holy shit! Whether his capacity to crush a baseball was artificially flavored or not—the guy did hit forty-nine home runs as a *rookie*, back in 1987—it was fucking impressive. I was awestruck.

Not long ago, I saw an interview with Reggie Jackson in which he said that players used steroids even in his day, but that not much was made of it because those guys weren't changing the game. When home run records started to fall, it was a different matter. That's what brought on all the scrutiny and led, eventually, to McGwire's admission that he was taking them when he hit seventy home runs in 1998. Maybe the PEDs helped him break Roger Maris's record; I can't say for certain. But I can say this: Mark McGwire knew how to hit. He understood the strike zone and had a clear idea of what he was trying to do at the plate. He was an unbelievable low-ball hitter. When I was catching and he laid into one, it sounded to me the way that twenty-ton howitzer must have sounded to my dad when he was standing next to it back in Germany.

I wasn't sure exactly what, other than great technique and incredible strength, allowed McGwire to hit a ball so astonishingly hard and far, but I knew it wasn't andro. I also knew that there was a buzz going around the game, and I had a pretty good idea that, real soon, I'd have to make a call— either cross a line or don't. I chose not to.

In the meantime, I had no problem telling Bob Nightengale I was clean. I was also in great shape after another winter of hard training, and ready for the best season of my career.

We expected a lot out of 1997. So, by midseason, when we were playing .500 ball, trailing the Rockies and losing sight of the Giants, there was some explaining to do.

I was not a politically correct kind of guy and never sought the position of clubhouse leader. My pattern was to leave my heart on the field and pick my spots with the press. But after four good seasons that kept jacking up my profile, my locker had become a gathering place for the local and even national media. Whether I liked it or not, I had become a spokesman for the ball club. As its catcher, that was part of my job description, anyhow. What's more, I was having a big year, hitting around .360 and competing again for a batting title. For a variety of reasons—among them, relative health, better mechanics, and my sessions with Mike Scioscia—I was also throwing out base stealers with more frequency than any time since 1993. I was leading the voting for the National League all-star team. The platform was mine.

The subject was team chemistry. We'd never been known for it, but the '97 season was feeling less lovey-dovey than most. In late April, we'd aired everything out in a team meeting that ended in a team scuffle. As usual, we were divided between hitters and pitchers, but the splits went deeper than that. Several of us, including me, had our differences with our manager, Bill Russell. (To start with, he'd made me catch the full nine innings of the first televised spring training game, presumably because he wanted so badly to win it. My blood was boiling by the sixth.)

And then there were the cultural fractures that resulted from a global roster. When we ate in the clubhouse after road games, for example, the American players sat at one table, the Caribbean guys at another, and the Mexicans at a third. That was right there for the writers to see; but the underlying language differences had less conspicuous, more problematic effects. Once, after Chan Ho Park suffered through a rough outing, our pitching coach, Dave Wallace, instructed him to control his emotions. The next day, Chan Ho, ever dutiful, was off by himself practicing his *motion*. Sometimes, when our communication broke down, Park would throw a two-seam fastball when I was expecting a four-seamer. I'd get ticked off and vent it in a snippy Philadelphia manner that offended his Korean sensibilities. Our backup catcher, Tom Prince, had a similar situation with Nomo. One night, when they couldn't get their signs straight, an interpreter had to walk them through it after the game.

Meanwhile, from where I stood, the most significant cultural difference might have been the one in competitive spirit. I'll admit that I took losing harder than most guys, American or otherwise, but it seemed to me that the overseas players weren't as hell-bent on winning as I expected a good teammate to be.

Those were the points I was trying to make in an interview with Ross Newhan of the *Times* in the last week of June. Newhan had come to me to write a fairly lengthy profile, but in the course of our discussion he asked if I thought the Dodgers' unusual multinational makeup had an impact on our performance. I said, "Without a doubt, because you really don't know what guys' agendas are. You would like to think that everybody has that same common goal to win, but there may be guys just interested in staying here, guys just interested in putting certain numbers up." That became the focus of the article, which was printed under the headline OPEN MIKE.

It was a frank discussion—probably *too* frank, in retrospect—about the dynamics of diversity on a ball club. "The backgrounds are so different on this team," I told Newhan. "I mean, you've got Nomo from Japan, Chan Ho from Korea, you've got guys from the Dominican Republic and Mexico . . . so what do people expect? That all of a sudden we're going to be one big happy family? Of course not . . . Sure, I hang out with Mondesi once in a while, but for the most part, you're going to gravitate to the guy you have most in common with . . . and I don't think there's anything anybody can do or say to change those cultural or background differences.

". . . I have to say that's where not only Peter (O'Malley) but the fans should realize that because of the (diversity) there's going to be problems just as far as guys being able to relate to each other on a daily basis. It seems like that's the way Peter's direction has been the last couple years. . . ."

There was a deluge of fallout from the "Open Mike" story—so much, so immediately, that I had to hold a press conference the next day to set some things straight. I was furious over the fact that my comments were being construed and discussed as racial. What I said in the interview was that the game was changing and we, as a team on the leading edge of that change, were having a little difficulty dealing with some of the very human issues that had come along with it. But what people heard was something on the order of, what are *these* guys doing here? I was only two generations removed from Sicily, the son of a high school dropout who had to fight his way through Norristown and was denied a chance to own a major-league ball club basically because he was Italian. Why would I, of all people, discriminate against somebody from a different kind of background? (Hell, at the time I was dating an actress named Lisa Barbuscia—she went by Lisa B— who was an Irish–Italian–Puerto Rican from Brooklyn who considered herself British.) How could my meaning get so distorted? I had simply addressed the challenges of trying to win baseball games in the National League when the catcher has to talk to his pitcher through an interpreter.

In any event, the little firestorm didn't set back the ball club. We entered July eight games out of first place and left it tied at the top with the Giants, with a couple of nice winning streaks in between.

Pennant races were hard on me. They meant that I couldn't get the rest a catcher craves and genuinely needs. My performance had suffered in the final weeks of 1995 and 1996, and I badly wanted to turn that around. By 1997, I was determined to dominate the last couple of months of the season and will my team to the World Series.

It helped tremendously that we began interleague play that year. In those games, I was able to stay in the lineup as a designated hitter without having to catch. It felt like a few days in the Bahamas, and it got me through the schedule much fresher. Another source of relief was the best lineup I was ever a part of. Karros, Mondesi, and Todd Zeile, whom we had signed as a free agent, all hit thirty or more homers, the most impressive being one that Zeile hammered into about a forty-mile-an-hour gust of wind one night at Dodger Stadium. We were loaded and dangerous.

In August, we traded for Otis Nixon. By September, we were thanking him for coming on over. Delino DeShields was off to St. Louis and Brett Butler, while back in action, wasn't up to the workload he'd once carried, so Nixon brought a needed blast of speed to the lineup. A week after he arrived, we traded Pedro Astacio to the Rockies to bring back my old minor-league teammate Eric Young, who added another great set of legs. We also signed Eddie Murray for a month. He was forty-one years old and had just been released by the Angels; but still, he was Eddie Murray. Meanwhile, our pitching was second only to the Braves. We thought it was our year.

For that matter, I thought it was *my* year. Tim McCarver—leave it to a catcher—touted me as the MVP choice on national television, and it pleased me that Fred Claire and Billy Russell spoke up for the cause, as well; not to mention Karros, of course. At the same time, Don Baylor, the Rockies' manager, lobbied hard for his own guy, Larry Walker, who was putting up huge numbers in Coors Field. Baylor described me as one-dimensional. Mike Scioscia—another old catcher, naturally—answered by saying that we wouldn't be in first place without me, and Russell told Ross Newhan, "Our guy might not have the numbers that (Walker has), but he's more valuable to our team than Walker is (to the Rockies). They could win without Larry, but we couldn't do that here. For us, the game doesn't start until Mike starts it."

I'd waited a long time to hear words like that from my own organization. They gave me the sense that everything was coming together. It sure seemed that way on September 16, when, in the top of the first inning at St. Louis—after we'd won in fifteen the night before, the opener of a two-game series—I cracked a two-run homer to put us ahead. Then, in the bottom of the inning, Mark McGwire made me feel like a skinny backup shortstop.

The Cardinals had traded for McGwire at the end of July but weren't expected to re-sign him. That day, however—on his way to fifty-eight home runs for the season (he had thirty-four in Oakland)—there had been a press conference before the game to announce that he had agreed to a four-year contract. The deal included the creation of a foundation to combat child abuse, to which he would donate a million dollars a year. It was a cause that McGwire felt strongly about, and the weight of the moment moved him to tears. When he came to bat against Ramon in the first inning, the St. Louis fans were already on their feet. They were still standing on the fifth pitch, which McGwire lofted over the scoreboard high in left-center field, at the time the longest home run in the history of Busch Stadium. It seemed almost superhuman that he could crush a ball like that in those circumstances. When we got back to the dugout, Karros walked up and said, "Are you shittin' me? We should have given him high-fives when he went by."

We trailed, 6–3, going into the ninth, with Dennis Eckersley on the mound to close for the Cardinals. I led off with a single, Karros followed with a double, and Mondesi and Zeile kept the rally going with singles. We tied the game on an error and went ahead on a sacrifice fly by Eric Young. Scott Radinsky struck out the side in the bottom of the ninth—McGwire wasn't involved—and we headed off to San Francisco with a two-game lead over the Giants.

It was another two-game series, but this time we lost the first one, 2–1, as I went 0 for 4 and Barry Bonds hit a two-run homer in the first inning off of Chan Ho Park. We all noticed that Bonds did a little pirouette on his way to first base, possibly because we'd plunked him a couple of months before— Antonio Osuna got him in the ribs and the Giants had charged the field. Anyway, a series split would serve our purposes just fine.

The second game was 5–5 in the tenth inning when I singled on a tough pitch by Rod Beck and Karros followed with a solid hit that moved me up a base. It was a great chance for us to go in front and get back our two-game lead. Mondesi was next, and he proceeded to hammer a screaming line drive to right field. It froze me for a moment or two. The ball fell in for a single and Joey Amalfitano held me at third, which was the right move with no outs and my dial-up speed. The bases were loaded and life was getting good. But Zeile struck out looking and then Murray, pinch-hitting, tapped into a home-to-first double play. Brian Johnson won the game for the Giants with a leadoff home run in the twelfth. The race was tied.

That little sequence might well have cost me the MVP award. As Tom Verducci wrote in *Sports Illustrated:* "Either way you slice it—that Piazza should have scored [on the single] or that he should have been replaced—the episode is a black mark against the Dodgers' catcher in a contest so close that the smallest of blemishes is scrutinized." In the same article, Verducci laid it on thick for Walker: "Larry Walker of the Colorado Rockies had a season that, were it an oil painting, would be immediately hung in the Louvre. In some ways, it was a season that comes along once every two generations. . . . Except . . . Didn't Walker play his home games in a hitter's paradise, and didn't his team fail to contend for a playoff spot? True enough, but Walker overcame both understandable prejudices."

Returning home, we dropped the first two games against the Rockies, to fall one behind San Francisco. In the finale of that series, I got hold of a changeup from Frank Castillo and it landed on the pavilion roof, then caromed into the parking lot—the first time a ball had ever left Dodger Stadium via left field. A headline in the next day's *Los Angeles Times* read, PIAZZA'S HOMER DENTS SOME CARS. The home run was my thirty-seventh, a career high, and, at 478 feet, matched the distance of the one I'd hit in Miami three years before. Two batters later, Mondesi added another blast to give us a 5–1 lead in the third inning. Ramon Martinez couldn't hold it. Meanwhile, the Giants were winning in San Diego.

We went down swinging, at least. My next home run came five days later in Colorado, against a right-hander named Darren Holmes, and was recorded as the longest ever hit at Coors Field—somewhere around five hundred feet. I've seen it listed as 504, but more often as 496. According to the records, it was also the farthest I ever hit a baseball, although I suspect that the Colorado air played a part in that; it didn't *feel* like my longest shot.

I can't say for certain which of my home runs *did* feel that way, but there's definitely a different sensation involved with the ones that are truly crushed—when you catch a pitch out in front of the plate and meet it square with all the leverage of a perfect swing. The homer off Holmes came on another changeup, which was no coincidence; an off-speed pitch allows a hitter to maximize his bat velocity and complete his transfer of weight. When you can wade into the ball and lift it right out of your wheelhouse, the mechanics are almost like a punt. Practically every muscle in your body is working toward the same purpose, which is where the hours and hours in the batting cage come in. I was a grinder. All my life, I hit and hit and hit, and in that way developed and refined the relationships between my feet and hands, my hips and head, my forearms and eyes. Leverage—in effect, power, when you factor in physiology—results from the harmony of all those parts. If a pitch you anticipate happens to sit on a tee in front of the plate, and you see it well and time it right and bring enough strength to bear, your bat becomes a catapult. The bat will actually *bend* an inch or so when you address the ball with the full force of a sublimely coordinated rip. I've felt that. The visceral response is close to euphoria. It's a power hitter's sense of perfect.

Of course, it lasts only for a moment. A season lasts half the year, and for the Dodgers in 1997 that was just a little too long. It didn't matter that we won four of our last six games, because the Giants matched us and closed out their division title. We were five days late and two games short.

Our failure was blamed, predictably, on an absence of leadership. References were made in the media to Kirk Gibson and 1988. I guess I was supposed to play the Gibson role. Batting .362 with 201 hits, forty homers, and 124 RBIs wasn't sufficient; I should have set the tone in spring training by reaming out the ball club in four languages. It would have also helped if I'd talked one of our pitchers—presumably Nomo or Park, who led us in victories with fourteen—into winning twenty-three games like Orel Hershiser did in '88. Maybe I could have been a better leader by picking up a little speed in San Francisco.

The Florida Marlins, who went on to beat Cleveland in the World Series, were the wildcard winners that year, which meant that we had nothing to show for a pretty damn good season. Nor did I personally, even though my batting average tied Bill Dickey (1936) for the highest mark a catcher had ever produced. (If you'll indulge me, I'll point out that Dickey caught 107 games that year; I caught 139.) Tony Gwynn won his eighth batting title by hitting .372, with Walker second and me third. I would never come that close again.

The record I shared with Dickey was broken in 2009 by Joe Mauer, who batted .365 while starting 105 games as Minnesota's catcher. Since I'm a member of the catchers fraternity, it does my heart good that Mauer has won three batting titles. It's a remarkable accomplishment that stamps him as a great hitter. That said—and without taking anything away from Mauer—I didn't have the DH position available to me once a week, and he didn't have to beat out Tony Gwynn.

In the matter of stats and records and the like, I can't deny a certain measure of selfishness. It was an acquired quality, I think, brought on by equal parts ambition and pressure. Even in a season like 1997, when my teammates were flashing around the bases and banging the ball out of the park, I couldn't shake the feeling that, if we were going to get where we all wanted to be, I was the guy who would have to put up the big numbers and deliver the big hits. A lot of that burden was probably self-imposed, but not all of it. To some degree, the Dodgers put it on me, inadvertently, when they kept me in the lineup at a rate well beyond what was required of most catchers, and when they rushed me back from an injury, like they did in 1995. I was good with all of that, and wouldn't have had it any other way, but it did turn up the pressure. I especially felt the heat when we struggled. I knew that if we weren't successful at the end of the season, my critics would attribute it to the fact that I didn't carry us like the superstar I was supposed to be. To a certain extent, that went with the territory. But I also knew that if we *were* successful and I *did* carry the club, I wasn't likely to be acknowledged with an MVP award. Blame seemed a lot easier to come by than credit.

Of course, some might say that the slights were imagined on my part, or at least exaggerated. Maybe so. Maybe I *needed* to feel disrespected, because that was what fed the beast inside me. Maybe I *needed* the extra pressure, because that was just the right current for my kind of wiring. I can't complain about a burden that I actually craved. If, under the weight of that burden, I carried myself in a way that made me seem self-absorbed to my teammates, I regret that part of it. But I can't apologize for the way I had to play; for the way I *chose* to play. I subscribed to what Joe Morgan told me: winning is the product of players playing well. It was in everybody's best interest—not just mine—that I perform at a high level. The way I saw it, the more I hit, the better chance we had of winning, which I coveted. And the more I failed, the better chance we had of losing, which I couldn't stand. That year, I didn't fail often, but we lost when we could least afford to.

In the tally for MVP, my grand total was three, one of which came from Kevin Acee, then of the *Los Angeles Daily News,* who was kind enough to stop by my locker one day in September and say, "I voted for you, because I watched you every day. I witnessed it. You're the MVP of this league, and I don't give a shit what anybody says." Jeff Bagwell had three votes also. Walker had twenty-two. With all respect to Larry, who was a great all-around player and whose raw numbers were admittedly better than mine (409 total bases? are you kidding me?), I can sincerely say that I felt cheated—more so than in 1995 or 1996. In those years, the rap against me was that I faded down the stretch. This time, I took the Triple Crown for the second half of the season, batting .367 with twenty-four home runs and seventy-three RBIs after the all-star break. It made no difference.

But at least there was a distinction attached: Bagwell and I are the only players ever to lose an MVP award to a guy who played at Coors Field.

By the time of our season's premature conclusion, Peter O'Malley had found a buyer. The sale hadn't been approved and consummated, but Rupert Murdoch and News Corporation—effectively, the Fox Group—had won the sweepstakes by meeting the highest price a professional sports franchise had ever been sold for, a figure reported to be as large as $350 million.

Meanwhile, I had my own business to take care of. There was one year remaining on my contract, but it was my last year before free agency and I didn't want to play it while trading punches with Fred Claire and Sam Fernandez (the Dodgers' negotiator) over a long-term deal. So, at the end of October, Danny Lozano and I established a signing deadline of February 15. If we didn't have an agreement by then—by spring training, in other words—we'd shut down the discussions and file for free agency after the season. In the accompanying story in the *Los Angeles Times*, Danny said that if I signed a multiyear deal by the deadline, it would be my intention to finish my career with the Dodgers. If not, the same would apply to whatever team I signed with as a free agent.

No sooner had we set our deadline than Fernandez called to say that we'd have to hold off on that because they expected Fox to be approved around the first week of spring training. We understood that O'Malley might be reluctant to put such a large obligation on the books—I was looking for a package of seven years at approximately $15 million a year, over $100 million total—at the very moment he was trying to complete a sale. Without saying so publicly, we agreed to relax the deadline. In retrospect, that was a mistake. I think the Dodgers detected it as a sign of weakness, which it wasn't. I was firm and confident about my asking price, and certainly not of a mind to cut the club any slack. I felt that they'd missed chance after chance to do right by me, and the time had finally come.

As recently as July, they'd had an opportunity to sign me for considerably less. The Texas Rangers had completed a contract with their catcher, Ivan Rodriguez, for five years at just over $8 million each. Pudge was the best in the game defensively, but his offensive numbers didn't compare to mine. I couldn't understand why the Dodgers didn't come to me the very next day and say, okay, we'll give you five years at *nine* million each. It would have been a hell of a bargain: less than half what I wanted by the end of the season, after batting for the highest average in Los Angeles history and finishing off the best five-year stretch of hitting that a catcher had ever racked up. I'd have probably taken the deal. But they had made no effort in that direction.

It didn't escape my notice, furthermore, that they'd signed Karros through his first three years of free agency. Then, in January, they signed Mondesi for $36 million over four years, which would cover his first two years of free agency, with a club option for the next two at $12 million each. It appeared that I was their lowest priority. Lozano described it to me as a slap in the face. At the same time, though, I was picking up interesting signals from the Fox people—indications that signing me would be their first order of business. I wondered if perhaps the O'Malley administration was delaying the deal as a favor to Fox, to allow the new owners to kick off their regime by announcing the biggest contract in the history of the game.

The whole thing made my head hurt. I could hardly keep track of all the angles and personalities involved. There was O'Malley representing the old organizational style: we're the Dodgers, and you should be happy to play for us; we'll pay you well, but not Yankee-well; we're not getting into those stratospheric salaries, no matter who you are. It was because of the modern economics that O'Malley was getting out of the game, so he certainly wasn't looking to violate that philosophy on his way out. Meanwhile, with Fox about to take over as the new sheriff in town, maybe, rather than making a splash by trotting me out in front of the cameras all signed and sealed, the team president, Bob Graziano—who had been a longtime aide to O'Malley—was eager to draw his six-gun and demonstrate just who was in charge now. Then there was the personal war playing out between Danny and Sam Fernandez, who was a two-time loser in their previous skirmishes. On the periphery, of course, there was also Tommy in his new management role, sorting through his deep-seated interest in me, his professional loyalty to O'Malley, and his working role with the new ownership group. And finally, there was my father, torn between his allegiance to the Dodgers, the possibility of bringing me closer to home, and his highly developed instinct for deal making.

Over the winter, I worked through my funk in the usual way—went to the gym and wore myself out. Because of the negotiations, I spent more of the off-season in Los Angeles than usual, and devoted it to getting stronger. I hired a nutritionist, who made me six meals a day, high in protein; lots of eggs, pancakes, tuna, chicken, steak, and creatine shakes. A trainer named Mike Ryan, who works with a lot of Hollywood and high-profile types—his client history includes Karros, John Elway, Mark Wahlberg, and the Rock, among others—took a look at my diet and recommended a supplement regimen.

In March, the steroids issue was brought into the spotlight when Tom Verducci wrote about it in *Sports Illustrated*. He reported that I had put on twenty pounds and gotten up to 240 over the winter, which may have been a bit exaggerated since my weight generally remained steady around 230 to 235, and quoted me saying, "Let's face it, guys get paid for home runs. If you hit 30 home runs, nobody cares if you hit .250 doing it. That extra strength may be the difference of five to 10 feet—the difference between a ball being caught or going over the wall. Why wouldn't you lift and take supplements? You've got one time in your life to get it right. I want to get it right." I stand by that, and point out that I didn't say *illegal* supplements. I played by the rules, as hard as I could.

All in all, it was not a standard-issue spring that year. For starters, the sale of the Dodgers had *not* been approved by the first week of training camp, in spite of what Sam Fernandez had told us. But the Fox people were on the scene, nevertheless. One of their public relations guys, Vince Wladika, approached me at a restaurant in Vero Beach and said something like "Yeah, we know you want a hundred and five million for seven years. I think we can do that." I didn't know if he was serious, sarcastic, drunk, or what.

Around that time, I sat down with Vin Scully for a television interview and his first question was on the order of "What's this deadline thing?" I was like "Uh, well, Vin, we just wanted to kinda make sure we were focused on baseball. . . ." He wasn't happy about it. And Scully's voice carried a great deal of authority in Los Angeles.

A few days later, Bill Plaschke of the *Los Angeles Times* reached Brett Butler in Atlanta, where he had retired after the 1997 season. I guess the conversation got around to my contract situation and leadership skills, because, "answering a general question," as Plaschke put it, my old teammate went off. "Mike Piazza is the greatest hitter I have ever been around," he said, ". . . but you can't build around Piazza because he is not a leader. . . . You know all that stuff that went down last year about Mike being the leader, calling out the team, all that stuff? It was all fabricated. Mike Piazza is a moody, self-centered, 90s player. . . . We're in (crunch) time during pennant races the last two years, and all Piazza seems to care about is winning the MVP from Larry Walker or the batting title from Tony Gwynn. We'd be winning games 8–0, but if he isn't getting his knocks, he'd be all ticked off, walking up and down the dugout all mad. Do you want to spend $100 million and build your team around that . . . or pay for a less talented guy who is more of a leader? . . . You know why Ken Griffey is a leader, why Barry Bonds is a leader? It's respect. They are respected because they are team players. We didn't have any of that on the Dodgers. . . . Mike doesn't want to be a leader, he just wants to play."

The last statement, I agreed with. In fact, I didn't express a lot of disagreement publicly with any of it. Thankfully, my teammates did. Eric Young and Todd Zeile were vehement, and even Billy Russell came to my defense. Not surprisingly, Tommy led the charge.

"This is totally uncalled-for on Butler's part, and I'm very disappointed he did this," Tommy told the *Times*. "I've known Mike Piazza since he was nine years old, and nobody wants to win more than Mike. Believe me, these are totally erroneous statements. The audacity for him to say this . . . It's just crazy."

He spoke in even stronger terms to the *New York Post*. We were playing the Mets in an exhibition game, and a writer named Tom Keegan took the opportunity to ask Tommy which of us—Brett or I—was the more self-

ish player. "Butler, without question," Lasorda said, according to the *Post*.
"He'll tell you what his average is against right-handers and what his average is against left-handers. This guy wasn't well-liked by players, you know.
Whatever his reason for saying the things he said, it was stupid. . . . Piazza
wants to win. When his pitcher pitches a good game, he's the happiest guy in
the world. . . . Terrible, terrible statement, and a very erroneous statement.
What does he mean Piazza's not a team man? He plays hard. He gives it all
he's got. How can a guy who hits .330 with 40 home runs and knocks in 120
runs not be good for a team? No catcher has ever done what he has done."

In the same story, Tommy also mentioned a testimonial dinner at which
he had sat with Whitey Herzog, who asked him which current player he
would pick to build a team around. Tommy suggested they both write a name
on a piece of paper. In Tommy's words, "He turned his paper over and it said
Mike Piazza. Mine said the same thing. He sure as hell didn't put Brett Butler on it, and neither did I."

Still, Butler's assault seemed to be what a lot of Dodger fans wanted to
hear. The way the whole contract drama looked to them—many of whom
were taking their cue from Scully—was that, by setting a deadline and insisting on so much money, I was demonstrating a conspicuous lack of loyalty
to the ball club. I understood that. I don't profess to have been driven by
loyalty, except to say that I was willing to give up my free agency and stay in
Los Angeles for the rest of my career. On the flip side, though, how hard had
the Dodgers tried to tie me up for the long term? What loyalty did they show
Karros that winter, when they left him unprotected in the first round of the
expansion draft for the Arizona Diamondbacks and Tampa Bay Devil Rays?

All those factors took a toll on my attitude. While I liked and respected
Peter O'Malley, I felt very little chemistry with the front office. All along,
I believed that we could get a deal done if O'Malley, perhaps as a final gesture of his ownership, would simply invite me to lunch so we could talk it
through. That never happened.

As I saw it, there were three sticking points in our negotiations—three
important items on which the Dodgers weren't about to budge. One was the
money, of course. It wasn't in their DNA to give out Steinbrenner money;
or, for that matter, to appear like they had capitulated to a player. The second point was the length of our demand. They wouldn't go beyond six years
and I wouldn't accept fewer than seven. And finally, I was insisting upon
a no-trade clause, which the Dodgers never gave. This was about loyalty,
right? If I was to forgo free agency and commit my future to the Dodgers,
I wanted that commitment to work both ways, and I wanted it in writing.

For me, Exhibit A was Eric Karros. After signing him to a long-term contract, the club had not only exposed Eric to the expansion draft but—according to what Danny kept hearing from baseball officials—had attempted to trade him to the Devil Rays for another player who had been left off the protected list (the plan being that Tampa Bay would first draft that player). It was exactly the sort of thing that hardened my position. In my history with the Dodgers, everything had always been on their terms. It was as if they felt entitled to treat me in whatever manner they chose, as if I should feel privileged to wear their particular shade of blue for less than my market value. Well, at long last, I had worked myself into a position where I no longer had to do business that way, *their* way.

The sale came through on March 19, at which time the old Dodger traditions became a moot point. We were now dealing with Fox.

But we were still dealing with Sam Fernandez. He called Danny and set up a meeting after work at the Ritz-Carlton in Marina del Ray, which was peculiar. Fred Claire was not present, which was even more peculiar. Although Sam was the lead negotiator, Fred had always acted as a facilitator of sorts. He was the one who would say, in effect, "Let me put this thing together because I can see it's not getting done." Now, without Fred *or* O'Malley in the picture, the discussions took on a different tone. Danny tried to impress upon Sam the importance of star quality in a city that had lost the Rams, Raiders, and Wayne Gretzky. Unmoved, Sam showed Danny an offer sheet for six years and $76 million, without a no-trade clause.

I truly believe it was an offer calculated to make me turn it down, while, at the same time, good enough—a million more than Pedro Martinez was making in Boston as the highest-paid player in the game—to convince the fans of the club's sincerity and generosity. Danny asked for a *limited* no-trade clause, a handful of teams that they couldn't send me to. Nothing. He asked for a seventh year. No. He then asked for a $3 million buyout for the seventh year. That would put the package at $79 million and I'd sign it the next day. Uh-uh.

Incentives? Nope. A hotel suite on the road? No. Four box seats for family and guests? No, no, no. The media widely reported the offer at $80 million—a figure they didn't hear from us—but it never got there. Meanwhile, Bob Graziano stated publicly that signing me was not an urgent matter because I was already under contract for the season. And that's where it stood on Opening Day, 1998, when we played in St. Louis.

"Mike," Danny told me, "they don't want you to sign. You have to say something. This is making you miserable. If you need to vent, go to somebody you trust and tell your side of it. Get it off your chest. It's time."

I reluctantly agreed. I'd been deliberately avoiding the subject with the beat reporters, but I couldn't let it fester any longer. My position all winter and spring had been that I didn't want to drag the negotiations into the season. Well, the season had arrived.

So, after we'd been shut out by the Cardinals and the clubhouse had finally emptied, I sat back and opened up to Jason Reid of the *Times*. "I'm not going to lie and say I'm not concerned about this, that I'm not confused and disappointed by the whole thing, because I am," I said. "I'm mad that this has dragged into the season, and that it now has the potential to become a distraction.

"How can I not think about this? If they say they have the intent to sign me, then sign me. But if they don't have the intent to sign me, then just let me know. Just let me know, so at least I'll be able to start to think about having a future somewhere else after the season. But what they're doing now, the way this is going, I just don't get it."

CHAPTER FOURTEEN

The fans of Los Angeles were beating me up on a daily basis. That wasn't characteristic of them, but my spiel in St. Louis hadn't gone over well with the nine-to-five shift. On top of that, Vin Scully was crushing me, we'd lost our first four games, and by the time we got to Dodger Stadium for the home opener I still hadn't driven in a run.

The crowds booed me. Booed me hard. They chewed me out harder. One guy was screaming at me, "You're no Steve Yeager!" In a letter to the *Los Angeles Times*, another fan wrote, "Rupert Murdoch, you would be better off spending your millions producing a sequel to the Spice Girls movie rather than re-signing the poster child for the Generation-X ballplayer." People were siding en masse with Brett Butler.

It hurt, but I could see it coming. Understandably, the paying customers didn't care about no-trade clauses, fair market value, and my personal history. They found it hard to sympathize with a ballplayer who feels disrespected by $80 million and the biggest contract in the game. I got that. What I didn't get was the ball club's response to my remarks in the *Times*.

The Dodgers answered with a statement of their own, issuing a press release in which Sam Fernandez said this: "Unfortunately, to date, we have not been able to bridge the wide gap that exists between our respective positions, primarily because, at this point in the negotiations, there is no good way for either side to accurately assess the level of compensation that a player of Mike's caliber can command in today's market."

What?

They couldn't accurately assess the level of compensation that I commanded in the market? That was their business! That's what Sam was paid to do! They had at their disposal the terms of every contract of every player on every team. And from that, they couldn't figure out what I was worth? Why? Because they didn't *want* to? Or maybe because they couldn't find a good comparison, seeing as how no other player had batted .334 in his first five seasons, averaging thirty-three homers and 106 RBIs, while catching 140 games a year? How in the hell could Danny and I negotiate with a man who had no idea what his offer should be and seemed to think that we didn't, either? Believe me, we were having no trouble assessing the appropriate level of compensation. None at all.

I was dumbfounded. In my response to their response, I told Jason Reid of the *Times*, "The Dodgers' actions are making it clear to me that they really aren't interested in having me here much longer. From what I've been hearing, that is becoming painfully obvious."

To someone removed from the situation, the Dodgers' company line may have sounded like merely a negotiating ploy. But I wasn't removed from the situation, and to me, it was the latest of a numbing series of incidents over the years in which the organization had tried its damnedest to put me in my place. It felt like not getting a phone call after being drafted. Like being benched in Vero Beach and ordered to bunt with two strikes. Like being humiliated in front of my minor-league teammates. Like being told that I couldn't take batting practice with the *real* prospects. To my ears, Sam's ridiculous remark had the same offensive ring as all the doubting that I could make it as a catcher and all the unsubtle hoping that I wouldn't. It came from the same place as making me file for arbitration. As not having my back in the MVP races. As coming to terms with everybody but me.

In the papers and on the talk shows during those days, I was criticized for, among other things, characterizing myself as "unappreciated." I may well have said that, but I don't recall it. I do recall a radio interview in the dugout with Jim Rome before the home opener, when he asked me if I felt appreciated and I replied, "That's not relevant." I recall, while venting in St. Louis, using the words "confused and disappointed." At any rate, whether or not I referred to myself as unappreciated, I hate that term. I reject it.

That said, I don't find it easy to describe my prevailing emotion toward the Dodgers at the time. It was complicated. But I can trace the path to how I got there, how the journey generally *felt*, which was this way: that, from the day I was drafted all the way through that final contract negotiation, they were invariably reminding me, in one form or another, that I was nothing. Or at least, not all that my dad or Tommy or, most important, my accomplishments would suggest. You could pin my perception on too much pride, too narrow a perspective, or any personal peccadillo that you choose, but that's the dynamic by which my disposition toward the Dodgers was defined. I found myself constantly striving for the breakthrough moment when, in the organization's eyes, I was no longer nothing but really, truly, *something*. I never got there.

On the second day of our first home stand, we shut down the negotiations. It was decided: I would play the season, hopefully help the Dodgers to the World Series, and then file for free agency.

The next night, with all the commotion out of my head, I hit a grand slam off Jeff Suppan—Devon White went over the wall in center field and almost made an incredible catch on it, but the ball glanced off his elbow—and drove in six runs against the Diamondbacks. The night after that, I hit a grand slam against the Astros, 443 feet to right field, on a 3–0 pitch from Mike Magnante. As I trotted by Jeff Bagwell at first base, he said, "Holy moley, that was a bomb." The Los Angeles fans actually cheered me out of the dugout for a couple of curtain calls.

Suddenly, I wasn't such a monster. A few weeks later, I hit my third slam of the month, just down the right-field line against Kerry Wood of the Cubs. I remember a girl calling in to *Dodger Talk* after the game and saying, "Give him what he wants!" The tide was turning. I was winning the people back with my bat.

On Wednesday, May 13, we beat the Phillies behind Chan Ho Park and a big night of hitting from Todd Zeile, who had started every game for us at third base. I celebrated at Harry O's, jumping onto the stage and playing some drums with the Fish Tacos, who were the basis for a band I loved called BulletBoys. Life was pretty good at that moment. The next day, after hanging out with my stuntman buddy Eddie Braun, I got to the ballpark early to film a promo for Classic Sports Network. Then I went 0–4 as Mark Portugal shut us out with relief help from Mark Leiter. In baseball, things change on a daily basis.

But I had no idea how much.

I was strolling out of the shower when our trainer, Charlie Strasser, approached almost giddy, it seemed to me, and said, "Fred wants to talk to you in the back." In the training room, he meant—actually, Dr. Frank Jobe's medical office inside it. I threw on a Pittsburgh Penguins jersey, and when I walked in, Zeile was already there, along with Billy Russell and Derrick Hall, the PR guy.

Fred cut right to it: "We made a trade. We traded you to the Florida Marlins."

Holy shit, I'm not a Dodger anymore . . . I'll never be in this clubhouse again . . . I'm leaving Eric. Nomo. Mondesi . . . I'm leaving Tommy . . . I'm leaving Los Angeles . . . I'm done here!

I took a moment—maybe a few—to let it sink in, and then asked Fred who Todd and I were traded for. He said he couldn't answer because it wasn't a done deal. I was thinking clearly enough to figure out that, if the details were still being sorted through, it must mean that Gary Sheffield was involved, since he had a big, complicated contract with a no-trade clause, which meant there would be further negotiations.

I told Fred, "I wish I could say it's been a little slice of heaven," and walked out. There was a lot to process. Dodger Stadium was no longer my summer home, but what was, really? I knew, Todd knew, and most everybody else knew that we wouldn't be long for Florida; that the Marlins, who had won the World Series the year before and were dumping salary to start over, would flip us for cheaper players as soon as they could. One teammate predicted I'd wind up with the Yankees. Somebody else guessed the Phillies.

I shrugged and said, "I'm with the Fishes."

In a few slow-motion minutes I was sitting in my car, talking on the phone with Danny, trying to make sense of it, trying not to cry. We felt there was a remote chance that it was all a scare tactic on the part of Fox, that Fred would call me in the next day and say, hey, you won't believe what happened, but the whole thing has fallen through. And then, of course, I'd be spooked enough to go ahead and sign for the latest offer. Quite a scheme. Except that we were way off.

The next day was nuts. In the morning, there were TV news crews at the gate of my development in Manhattan Beach; my clothes guys were packing three big boxes of shirts, suits, and shoes they'd picked out—all Italian, of course—to send to Miami, and a suitcase to send with me to St. Louis, where the Marlins were playing; Jim Rome was on the radio hollering that you don't trade a Hall of Famer and joking about Fred Claire waking up someday with the head of a horse in his bed; my housekeeper, Teri O'Toole, was screening the phone calls (Rome and Fabio got through); my buddy from the clubhouse, Bones Dickinson—I called him "the night squire," for his skills in social brokering—was at the front door with three equipment bags of my baseball gear; and a writer from *Sports Illustrated*, Michael Bamberger, was taking note of the whole wacky scene. Then Teri handed me a phone that Lozano was screaming into.

"As of eight this morning, five teams had called Dombrowski [Dave Dombrowski, that is, the Marlins' general manager] wanting to make a deal," he told me. "It gets better. The Dodgers want you to dress for tonight's game. They say that until the deal is done, until Sheffield makes up his mind, you're a Dodger."

"This is such bullshit," I said. "Who knows when Sheffield's gonna make up his mind? He's got a ring, he's got a house in Florida; maybe he doesn't *want* to go anywhere. He's got the Dodgers by the balls. What are they gonna do—say the deal's off? And have all that egg on their face? No way."

It was a hellish state of limbo. In addition to the no-trade clause, Sheffield had taken a large advance from the Marlins. That would now be negotiable. There was also the matter of the extra income tax he would have to pay in California. That would be negotiable, too. By the time everything was added up, Sheffield, who would play right field in Los Angeles, would be making about twice as much as I was for 1998. Meanwhile, I was just learning that the Dodgers would also be taking on the salaries of three other veterans—Bobby Bonilla, a strong hitter who played mostly third base (and could thereby replace Zeile); Charles Johnson, an outstanding catcher; and Jim Eisenreich, a reserve outfielder. In addition, they'd receive a minor-league pitcher, Manuel Barrios. All for me and Zeile, who, with his wife, Julianne McNamara—the gold-medal Olympic gymnast—and two young kids, had just moved into his Southern California dream house.

Anyhow, Danny and I agreed that I had to report to the ballpark. But I didn't have to talk to the media. Having already been down that road, I didn't want to say anything I'd later regret. So, after I parked my Cadillac, I took the stealth route into the stadium, through the yellow seats on the 100 level. It didn't work. I suddenly heard a stampede of footsteps coming from down the corridor. When I turned around, they had me surrounded. I said I'd talk about it in St. Louis, when everything had settled down. Have a nice day.

In the relative safety of the clubhouse, I went straight to Russell's office, separated from the press by a closed door and a couple of security guards. It was a matter of waiting. We heard that Sheffield and his agent were in the building, negotiating. Karros came in and said, "You know what's strange? You're the marquee player in the deal, but you're not the one holding it up." Tommy was next. He kissed me on the cheek, pulled me up close, and said, "Before you're out of this game, you'll break every offensive record ever set by a catcher, you'll have a harem, and you'll have more money than you'll know what to do with." Then came my man Nomo, nodding, with a jersey to sign. There would be more of that before the night was over.

Finally, approaching game time, Zeile and I got word from Fred that we didn't have to dress. The thing was getting done.

Hugs all around. Autographs for my teammates. Photos with the clubhouse guys. Then the players made their way to the dugout, leaving the locker room to me, Todd, and the strange, dense silence.

It was the first inning when I got out of there. As I came into view walking down the runway toward the parking lot, fans in left field began to cheer and clap. I didn't want to look back. I raised my hand in appreciation and kept going.

My car radio was already tuned to the game. I slid in a tape, then pulled out for some pizza at Paisanos in Hermosa Beach. Before it arrived, a cute little girl on Rollerblades skated up and said, "Aren't you supposed to be at the ballpark tonight?" I said yeah, and signed a paper plate.

They officially announced the trade after the game. Fred Claire had the honors, which was odd, because he hadn't been much involved in it, which was odder. Tommy hadn't, either. It turned out that Bob Graziano had engineered the deal, acting on behalf of Chase Carey, the CEO of Fox Television. Fox happened to be in discussions with the Marlins about purchasing their TV network, SportsChannel Florida, which was controlled by the Marlins' owner, Wayne Huizenga, who was a matter of months from selling the team to John Henry. The cable discussions proved successful, and so did the Marlins' effort to dramatically reduce their payroll. Apparently, somehow, I helped make it all happen.

"[The trade] had nothing to do with the team itself or any type of normal move that's ever been made," Claire said years later in an interview with MLB.com. "You can't go back in time and show me a player of [Piazza's] magnitude traded in May. That shows how out of balance it was. It was made for non-baseball reasons."

Claire had been in on some of the initial trade talks, but was ambushed on Thursday night when they told him the deal was almost done. Graziano called from the Dominican Republic to let him know. Fred assumed they'd already worked out the complication of the no-trade clause, because he was certainly aware of it, but evidently not. The final details were nailed down by Carey. It was a different way of doing things.

Bob Graziano told me that there would be a press conference to announce the trade, and I said, "Then there will be two announcements, because you don't need me. I'm not going to stand for this, not going to be a part of this."

My objective (had been) to sign Mike and have him continue and hopefully finish his career as a Dodger. That's what I wanted to have happen, and that's what *should* have happened.

—Fred Claire

On their front cover, next to my full-frame, unsmiling mug shot, *Sports Illustrated* called it "The Trade of the Century." In terms of total salaries, it was the biggest ever made. The Dodgers took on $83 million in payroll and sent about $26 million to the Marlins—a net cost to them of around $57 million. Graziano told the media that the deal "helps improve our chemistry, helps improve our hitting, and helps improve our defense. I think the team is markedly improved."

Jim Murray, for one, disagreed. "The Dodgers always have adhered to the Branch Rickey theory of roster cutting that it's better to deal a player a year early than a year late," he wrote in the *Los Angeles Times*. "But in Piazza's case, 10 years early? . . . The Dodgers traded away more than a part of their team. They traded away part of their soul."

Dave Dombrowski of the Marlins called that night and told me to take another day before flying to St. Louis to meet his team. Todd did, but I had no interest in sticking around Los Angeles any longer. I'd been kicked out of the nest and needed to start flapping my wings before I crashed to the ground. I was staggered and disoriented, in serious need of something tangible to do. All along, I'd kept the faith that the situation would eventually be worked out, one way or another. The concept of being traded by the Dodgers was so crazy, so unthinkable, that I had hardly entertained it—in spite of Danny's warnings. I *couldn't*.

Maybe that was my mistake. Maybe I overestimated myself and underestimated the organization. But how could I not see it that way? I'd just had my best year, one of the best years—maybe *the* best—in the history of baseball, for a catcher. In spite of everything we'd been through, I honestly believed that I was going to be a Dodger for life. There was no way the club could let me go.

When it did, I felt like the stone rejected. Get me on a plane.

Los Angeles was all I knew as a major leaguer. I took out an ad in the *Times* thanking the fans for five years of fantastic support. I would genuinely miss them, and the city, too. L.A. was my comfort zone. There was a lot of anxiety over leaving it.

After a couple days had passed, however, I was amazed by how quickly the emotional ties had been snipped and the good times forgotten. Ramon Martinez, for instance, told *Sports Illustrated*, "You're not going to see teams running on us so easily anymore. And we can be more confident about throwing breaking balls in the dirt with men on base. Charles [Johnson] will block

them. It's very good news for the pitchers." He told the *Times,* "Everybody
can see the difference in the team. Everyone is excited again, and we feel good
about the team. You can see a big difference on the bench in the games . . .
the way we're acting even when [we're trailing]. Everything is better now."

> The ironic thing was, I remember that the first day, Charles Johnson
> was walking in from warming up the pitcher in left field before the
> game. As he passes each section on his walk to the dugout, each sec-
> tion stands up and starts cheering. And I'm thinking, wow: Argu-
> ably the best hitter who's ever played on this team, and arguably the
> most beloved player on the team, is gone, forgotten, just like that.
>   Within the organization, I think that, initially, people were ex-
> cited about the changes. But at the end of the year, it was, oh wow.
> The trade was like an earthquake. It shook everything. It changed
> everything about the Dodgers. . . .
>
>   —Eric Karros

My connections were mainly to Eric and Tommy, but Eric was engaged to
be married and Tommy appeared to be *dis*engaged, in spite of his title. I appreciated the sensitive position Tommy was in and understood that he couldn't stick
his neck out for me during the negotiations, which weren't really his jurisdic-
tion. Nevertheless, I was disappointed in what he had to say after the trade. His
message was that the Dodgers had tried their best to sign me. In other words, it
was all my fault. I'm not sure what I wanted to hear from Tommy, and I'm not
sure what I *needed* to hear from Tommy; but what I *did* hear made me sad. I guess
I'd expected some sadness from *him,* but got the company line instead, spoken
with a stern voice that could have come from Sam Fernandez or Bob Graziano.

That effectively ended my relationship with the Dodgers, and it strained
my relationship with Tommy at the same time. To make it worse, it was impossible to untangle my relationship with Tommy from my relationship with
my dad. From a personal perspective, *that* was the fallout from the trade.
Almost a decade and a half later, I still love Tommy and I'm pretty sure he
feels the same way about me; but the fact is, although we talk and see each
other now and then, we haven't been as close as we should be since I left the
Dodgers. Time has mended our feelings somewhat, but I think, deep down,
the whole episode still hurts all three of us. I often wonder how different
things might have been between Tommy and me if I hadn't been traded.

Ironically, I'd barely slipped into my black and teal before rumors started
up that the Dodgers would re-sign me as a free agent after the season. A

month later, when Fred was fired, Tommy took over as interim GM and made some efforts to get me back before the July 31 deadline with another trade. As far as I was concerned, though, that door was closed. I had no desire to return to the Dodgers. It just wouldn't have been the same.

Bill Russell was canned on the same day as Claire, who, fighting his instincts to quit, had stuck around to help with the messy transition. In his book, *My 30 Years in Dodger Blue*, Fred said, "My reaction to the trade cost me my position with the Dodgers. The trade cost the Dodgers much more: their franchise player, and, more importantly over the long run, their credibility. . . . On May 15, the new owners unleashed a tsunami from which the Dodgers have yet to recover."

Whack by whack, Fox was severing all bonds to the old Dodger culture—with the exception, of course, of Tommy, which would have been disastrous for public relations. Like Fred, Russell, too, had been with the organization for thirty years. Mickey Hatcher and Mike Scioscia were axed. Instructors, scouts, coaches—Eddie Bane, Gary Sutherland, Dino Ebel, Ron Roenicke—nobody was sacred. A week after he took over from Fred, Tommy fired two of my favorites, Mark Cresse and Reggie Smith.

Before the summer was out, the general manager's job had been turned over to Kevin Malone. He dealt Johnson and Bonilla, waived Barrios, and chose not to pick up the option on Eisenreich, leaving Sheffield as the only player from the trade who lasted into the next season. The talent base was deteriorating, and the pressure was on Malone to make his mark. By December, Kevin Brown, a thirty-four-year-old ace, was the last big-time free agent available. The Dodgers signed him for seven years and $105 million—exactly the money and term that I'd asked for.

When I heard about the Kevin Brown contract, the first thing I thought of was my press conference in St. Louis when I joined the Marlins. Somebody had asked me if I thought signability had anything to do with the Dodgers trading me. I said no. A few of the media guys had gone, "Yeah, right." Well, the signing of Brown reinforced my original reaction: it wasn't the money that made them deal me away; it was all about the relationships—Danny and Sam, Fox and the Marlins, the Dodgers and me. As if to prove the point, for the next four years the Dodgers piled on the payroll. They signed Sheffield, Todd Hundley, Jeff Shaw, Carlos Perez, Shawn Green, Marquis Grissom. . . . From 1997 (my last full season in Los Angeles) to 1999, the club increased the player budget by 58 percent; from 1997 to 2000, the bump was 96 percent; from 1997 to 2001, it was 127 percent, all the way from $48 million to $109 million.

Meanwhile, through friends like Karros and Bones Dickinson, I was kept apprised of all the grassroots ways in which life with the Dodgers had become different. When Sheffield refused to cut his goatee, they changed the facial-hair policy that I'd been skirting for so long. They allowed players to wear jeans on the road. To appease Kevin Brown, they even fixed the showers at Dodgertown. We all understood those showers. When the water pressure dropped, they'd get intensely hot; so the players simply stepped aside for a moment or two. The first time it happened to Brown—I don't know, maybe it was the second—he grabbed a bat and beat the shit out of the showerhead. After all those years, the team brought in plumbers to fix the water pressure problem.

I held on to my condo in Manhattan Beach, and that winter I found some solace in reading the local year-end reviews of what the Fox people had done to the Dodgers. One in particular helped me, perhaps, to move on. Or at least made me smile. It was part of a column in the *Times* by Bill Plaschke, who, in my perception, had always seemed to operate with an agenda when it came to matters about me, as if he preferred that I fall on my face. This time, though, with more than half a season to look back on what he had wished for, presumably, he wrote, "The difference between this trade and one of Carey's hot projects—the movie 'Titanic'—was that the movie eventually sailed. . . . The Piazza trade will be forever viewed as concrete shoes."

Ultimately, I felt like I came out on the winning side of the titanic trade. It sure didn't hit me that way in the moment; but like they say, a baseball deal can be properly judged only over time.

I'd say that thirteen years is long enough. In 2011, when the Dodgers were wallowing around in the marital and financial mess surrounding Frank and Jamie McCourt—who had bought the club from Fox in 2004—Chris Dufresne wrote this in a lengthy *Times* story about the team's slow, sad surrender of the city: "The Dodgers' reign lasted, unchecked, for about 40 years. The headstone would read 1958–1998. . . .

"You can town-track the sea change, Dodgers to Lakers, to a period between March 1998 and June 1999. It began with Peter O'Malley selling ownership to Fox, much more interested in Murdoch Green than Dodger Blue. News Corp. then made the cataclysmic misjudgment, in the spring of 1998, of thinking it could trade Mike Piazza and not pay a price for it."

CHAPTER FIFTEEN

Nothing against the Marlins. I liked Miami well enough that I've made my home there. The franchise itself is sharp enough to have won two world championships in the first eleven years of its existence. The one in 1997, the year before I arrived, came in only its fifth season. It was pretty remarkable. In certain ways, Florida was an admirable organization.

But I was miserable.

It was a bad time for me and the ball club both. My pride was smarting and my head was spinning. And, although it was only mid-May, it seemed to me that the Marlins had practically packed it in. The first time I ventured into their clubhouse, in St. Louis, it felt like a morgue. I was trying to put on a good face and be all gung-ho, like "Hey, guys, let's go, let's *go*," but the atmosphere sobered me up in a hurry. It was quiet, lifeless, *depressing*. Cliff Floyd was the only guy I recognized. I went up to Cliff and said hello, and that was about as lively as it got.

Right off, Jim Leyland, the manager, called me into his office and said, "Mike, I've got to be honest with you. We don't know how long you'll be here. We're talking about a possible deal. But let me tell you something: There's no doubt in my mind that you're going to get your money. You've earned it, and don't let anybody tell you otherwise. I'll do the best I can to keep you in shape." I took that to mean I probably wouldn't be playing much, if at all, because, for one thing, he wasn't going to disrupt his lineup for a temp who wouldn't be there long enough to do laundry, and for another, the Marlins didn't want me getting hurt while they were trying to trade me.

So I was sitting in the dugout in my turf shoes when Mark McGwire caught a pitch from Livan Hernandez and launched it against the *St. Louis Post-Dispatch* sign in center field. They measured it at 545 feet, which was almost unimaginable to me, because I knew how special it felt to hit one 445. A few innings later, I looked up at the scoreboard and happened to see that

that Expos and Dodgers were getting started in Los Angeles. That's when it really sunk in that, wait a minute, hold the phone, I've been *traded*. . . . What the hell just happened?

As the weird reality swept me up, I slipped into a narcissistic haze, more or less, so caught up in my own situation that it felt like I was the epicenter of the universe. In my efforts to maintain a positive spin, I'd told myself that it would be nice to move into our family house in Boynton Beach, on a golf course and close to the ocean, and let Zeile stay there for as long as we remained with the Marlins. I'd told the press that we had golf clubs, Jet Skis, and no worries. Half of me even *believed* it . . . until I saw that the Dodgers were batting in the bottom of the first without me. I didn't snap out of it until, in the top of the seventh of the game at hand, Dave Berg was on first, Craig Counsell was on third, Hernandez was due up with us trailing 4–3, and from the end of the dugout I heard, "Piazza!"

Shit. I wasn't even wearing a cup. Thankfully, Todd Stottlemyre gave me a first-pitch slider and I lined it to center field for a sacrifice fly that tied the game. We lost it in the bottom of the inning on a home run by Brian Jordan.

The next day, Sunday, I started against Kent Mercker, went one for five, and we got hammered. On Monday—it was an odd four-game series—McGwire amazed me with another ridiculous blast and I did something even more incredible: hit a triple. We actually won. Afterward, headed home to Miami, we walked onto the bus for the airport and one of my young teammates got up to give me his seat. I didn't know whether to feel flattered or old.

A couple of days later, though, after two losses to the Diamondbacks, I had no trouble at all figuring out how to feel about my new life. In the second one, a day game, it was blistering hot and Amaury Telemaco, whom I was always leery of, fired a ball behind my back. Then I broke my bat on a grounder between first base and the pitcher's mound and wanted *so badly* to run him over at the bag, but he took a sharp left turn as soon as he touched it. I stranded four runners that day and let one in when I threw the ball into left field as Devon White stole third. Do you know what's worse for a ballplayer than having a miserable game? When nobody cares. It was probably my self-absorption speaking, but it seemed like I was the only guy in town with any feelings whatsoever about how we played.

That was my low point. That was when humiliation overtook me. I slumped back in the dugout thinking, what am I doing here?

My only solace was the prospect that it wouldn't be for long—with one caveat. My dad was thinking that he might get involved with the group negotiating to buy the Marlins from Huizenga. The Marlins' president, Don Smiley, was heading up that party, and if my father purchased an interest in the team, it was of course unlikely that I'd be traded. But that would probably take months to play out, and Dombrowski wasn't waiting around.

Meanwhile, Dan Lozano was staying with me and Zeile in Boynton Beach, ready for anything. We had no idea what was next or when it would come. The situation was complicated by the fact that I'd be eligible for free agency at the end of the season. Some of the teams asking about me were thinking only of the current pennant race, but others didn't want to do a deal unless they could sign me for a few more years. Then there were teams like the Angels, who said they weren't in a position to trade but would go after me in the free-agent market.

Baltimore was a player, but, as I understood it, didn't want to give up a young third baseman named Ryan Minor. The Rockies were talking. The Red Sox were very involved but preferred not to trade a lot of talent if they were going to have to pay me a pile of money after the season. I would have been interested in going to the Yankees, but they were in good shape, catching-wise, with Jorge Posada. On WFAN in New York, Mike and the Mad Dog (Mike Francesa and Christopher Russo) were campaigning for the Mets to trade for me, but I wasn't seeing it. Fred Wilpon, one of the Mets' co-owners along with Nelson Doubleday, went on their show and said, nah, the club was going to stand pat. Then Doubleday went on and said, oh yeah, the Mets would love to have me. What was up with *that*? All the while, Steve Phillips, their general manager, was telling the media that if he were to part with prospects, he'd do it to fill a position not already equipped with his leading power hitter (Todd Hundley had hit thirty homers in 1997). My guess was the Cubs, who seemed to be in the picture all along.

On Friday, May 22, exactly a week after the Dodgers had officially traded me to Florida, Danny was on the phone all morning at my place in Boynton Beach. Before I stepped into the shower, he hung up and told me, yep, it looked like I was going to Chicago.

When I stepped *out* of the shower, I walked into a brand-new world. Danny had been on the phone again, and then again. I stood there dripping, half dazed by the news. It was the Mets.

I said, "The *Mets*? Get out of here! Don't they have Todd Hundley?"

I hadn't realized that Hundley was hurt. The Mets needed a catcher, the sooner the better, and they needed some power. It was all good. It was fantastic, in fact. But I hadn't heard it from the Marlins.

When I got to the stadium, Leyland was there to intercept me. The deal had already been announced: me for Preston Wilson, a promising young outfielder; and two highly rated pitching prospects, Ed Yarnall and Geoff Goetz. I did an impromptu press conference, and Danny, who had come to the park with me, worked his own session. He'd been talking to reporters in the tunnel when somebody told him to just come on into the clubhouse and do it there. The papers took note of that, making the point that we'd reached the age of agents in the clubhouse. That was one way of looking at it. Another was that we'd reached the age of all-star catchers being traded twice within eight days of May.

> When they made the trade, John Franco and I were like little kids, like twelve-year-olds trading our baseball cards. We're going, "We got Piazza!"
>
> —Al Leiter, teammate

The Mets were playing at home on Saturday, a four o'clock game against the Milwaukee Brewers. I planned on making it, and after a mostly sleepless night I got to the West Palm Beach airport in time for a mid-morning flight. The trouble was, my flight was actually leaving out of Fort Lauderdale. I caught a later one, and the guy I sat next to on the plane told me all about this new catcher the Mets had traded for.

It was around two o'clock by the time I got to New York. Immediately, I was dumbstruck by the difference between arriving there and arriving in Miami. A crowd was actually waiting for me at the airport. "Yo, Mike! Go get 'em, Mike!" It was crazy and phenomenal.

Another crowd was standing in line at Shea Stadium to buy tickets. Next thing I know, I'm dumping my equipment bag at a locker next to John Franco's, meeting and shaking the hand of Al Leiter—the starting pitcher that day—and being escorted to a press conference by Jay Horwitz, the Mets' PR guy. My locker, incidentally, already had my number 31 uniform hanging in it, courtesy of Franco, who was in his ninth year with the Mets and fifteenth in the big leagues. Franco was the National League's career leader in saves by that time, and of his own accord had given up his number so I could wear it, graciously switching to 45 in honor of Tug McGraw, one of his childhood idols. I had fond memories of McGraw from his days with the Phillies, but he carried significance with the Mets as the lefty reliever who had popularized the phrase "You gotta believe!" when they went to the World Series in 1973. Franco's gesture made me feel wanted and recognized in a way that I really needed right about then.

That seemed to be the theme for the day. The trade had been made at the urging of Nelson Doubleday, but it was evident that even Fred Wilpon had come to believe in what I could mean to the Mets. He told Bill Madden of the *New York Daily News,* "Look, I'm a businessman, but I wasn't able to sell this team to the public without Mike Piazza. They weren't buying it. . . . Nobody can say we're not a better team with Mike Piazza. Now maybe our fans will start believing in us." Steve Phillips said it was the most exciting day of his career.

And then there was my new manager, Bobby Valentine. While never at a loss for original thoughts or words, Bobby's image and personal style were cut from the mold of his mentor. Tommy Lasorda had been his first minor-league manager. Bobby was Tommy's guy. And he was pleased.

I was in the bathroom of my office and Steve Phillips yelled into the bathroom to say we had gotten Mike. I think we got instant credibility with that trade, and we began to build an identity around Mike. The Mets had not had a player of Mike's star quality in many years. For a couple years, since I'd gotten there, we'd been in search of an identity and credibility. But the instant impact was the fact that the Mets would make such a deal and Mike would actually be in our uniform. From the first day, everything about it was rather bigger than life.

—Bobby Valentine, manager, New York Mets

The revitalization of the Mets had already brought Leiter and another left-hander, Dennis Cook, by way of the Marlins. I'd never really crossed paths with Leiter, who had an earned-run average under two and a cut fastball that took some getting used to. We huddled for a brief meeting before the game with Valentine and the Mets' pitching coach, Bob Apodaca, but for the most part we would depend on veteran instincts. It was complicated, highly technical stuff: when I walked out to the mound in the second inning, Al pointed out where Jerry Seinfeld was sitting. I told him that he'd probably develop some whiplash from shaking me off so much. Later, when Leiter and I became good friends, our mound conferences deteriorated further. One time, he was getting knocked around a little and I walked out there, glanced around at the runners on base, and gave him the Chevy Chase routine from *Caddyshack.* "You're not that good," I told him. "You suck."

This time, we at least came up with a plan, simple as it was. We stuck with fastballs for a while and moved on to his off-speed pitches later in the game, when we had the lead. Thankfully, I had contributed to that with an RBI double against Jeff Juden in the fifth. Leiter finished with his first shutout in two years, in front of a crowd numbering nearly thirty-three thousand—about half again as much as the night before. Talking to the writers afterward, Bobby described the occasion as so energizing that even John Olerud, our silent first baseman, had gotten caught up in it: "In the fifth inning, he said, 'Let's go, guys.'"

Franco was kind enough to let me stay with him for a few days, until I got settled, and it was in the wee hours that night when the gate closed behind us at his place in Staten Island. As soon as we stepped into the house, the bell rang. It was a carload of fans at the gate, just letting us know how excited they were about the trade; letting me feel the love.

By then, it was abundantly clear that, whatever else it might bring, life with the Mets would be interesting.

But not easy. Nothing in New York is easy.

In the words of Bobby Valentine, "The six-hundred-pound gorilla in the room was Todd Hundley. What do we do now?"

Coming into the season, Hundley was not only the Mets' catcher and leading slugger but also their most popular player. In short, he was everything but healthy. After off-season elbow surgery, he was expected to be on the disabled list until July. It put the Mets in a tough spot, especially when the media was clamoring to trade for me and stick Hundley in left field when he was ready, which would be easier on his elbow. The last thing the ball club wanted to do was alienate him. And so, about the time Phillips was publicly saying that they didn't need anybody else at Hundley's position, he was also assuring Todd that I wasn't coming to the Mets. I'm sure he meant it, at the moment. Having been put at ease, Hundley made light of the situation when the Mets reporters asked him what he'd do if the team made a deal for me. He said he'd empty his locker and get the hell out of there. It seemed to be all in good fun until the thing he had been told wouldn't happen actually did.

Under the circumstances, Hundley was very cordial to me when I joined the club. Then, a few days later, rumors leaked that the Mets were displeased about his rehabilitation and concerned that he might have a drinking problem. In spite of that, he was back in the lineup about the time they expected him to be, just after the all-star break. He played mostly left field, and had a tough time with it. Todd was a hard-nosed guy, but it seemed as though all the drama took a toll on him. Some uneasiness developed between us, compounded by the fact that I was struggling, too, leaving more runners on base than I ever had—a point that the New York papers hammered home on a regular basis. Given his track record with the Mets, I could understand that Todd might have thought he should still be catching.

Whatever he thought, it nearly came to a flash point on a team flight. The Mets were a team that drank on the plane—there was always beer available—and he'd had a few. I was listening to my Walkman when Hundley sauntered up and said, "What's up, dude?"

I said, "What's up, Hot Rod?"

Then he punched me in the arm, a little harder than I thought he should have, and I said, hey, take it easy. Then he punched me in the arm again. By that time, I was definitely getting ticked. I kind of pushed him away and thought we were going to fight. Fortunately, it didn't escalate. You can't fight on an airplane.

At any rate, I wasn't concerned about being moved out of the catcher position; not at that time. I knew the Mets hadn't brought me in to play first base or left field. I also knew that, after trading away those pitching prospects, they weren't eager to watch me walk off to free agency after the season. The media saw it the same way. Like they are with any story line in New York sports that involves even a trace of controversy, they were all over the contract angle. From the moment I got there, hardly a day went by without some reporter or another asking me, "Did you talk to Danny today? Did Danny talk to Steve? Any progress?"

Before they would discuss a long-term deal, the Mets sent me off for an intense, full day of physical examinations. Among other indignities, I had to duck-walk, practically naked, in front of two surgeons, so they could look for signs of arthritis in my hips. I must have proved myself physically capable of swinging a bat and waddling after bread crumbs. Danny came to New York to stay with me for a while, and during our first road trip after the trade—which, wouldn't you know, was to Miami, the third time I'd played there in three weeks, for three different teams—he and Phillips finally sat down for their introductory discussion. But there was no progress to report.

From that, I think, the fans of New York took their cue. It wasn't that they didn't *care*. There was none of that Miami apathy. In a short time, in fact, average attendance at Shea Stadium virtually doubled, from around eighteen thousand a game to roughly thirty-five. But people weren't coming to the park for the purpose of showering me with hospitality and affection. Hell, no. They were looking for reasons to disapprove of me, and they found one every time I failed to drive in a teammate. Unfortunately, that happened a lot. It didn't matter that my batting average remained high—the more runners I left on base, the more they called me out; and the more viciously. Ira Berkow of the *New York Times* referred to it as "serial booing."

Deep down, the issue wasn't simply my clutch hitting—that I hadn't come quite as advertised—but the fact that I hadn't declared my unconditional loyalty to the cause. I hadn't signed with the Mets or promised that I would. Privately, I wasn't too enamored of the prospect. The fans, sensing that, considered me a hired gun. A mercenary. It offended them and set in motion a wicked cycle: I'd ground out to short with a man on second and the crowd would clobber me with boos. The more I was booed, the less I felt like staying in New York for the long term. The less I felt like staying in New York, the more it showed. The more it showed, the harder I was booed.

The open hostility made me a wreck and all but a recluse. Each time the cycle spun around, I retreated further into my shell. I'd rented a thirtieth-floor apartment on the Upper East Side, Seventy-second and York, and rarely left it for the first month or two. It wasn't only the treatment at Shea that affected me; the entire scenario—the whole New York thing—seemed overwhelming. As badly as the Mets wanted me to turn around the franchise, I wanted just as badly to turn it around, and the last thing I needed was extra pressure from the biggest, loudest, most demanding city in America. I put more than enough of it on myself. Bad nights only got worse when I replayed them in my head. I'd often give Al Leiter a lift home from the ballpark, and if we'd lost or I'd struck out with two guys on base, I was horseshit company. Al would try to lighten the mood with small talk, but I had nothing to say. Certainly nothing pleasant. After a while, he stopped trying.

Even the basic logistics of the city took their toll. As a visiting player, I'd never had any difficulty navigating New York—after a game, I'd just go for a steak at Peter Luger's in Brooklyn—but dealing with it in an everyday capacity, there were so damn many restaurants, and so damn much of everything, that in the beginning it just locked me up. It might have been different if I'd arrived in the off-season or been producing the way I wanted to; if I hadn't been distracted, daunted, and depressed. As it was, I couldn't cope with New York *and* leaving runners in scoring position. The simplest things seemed forbidding. I was paying more to park my car in a garage than it cost me for a place on the beach in Los Angeles. My dad had a friend in the automobile business named John Bruno who was kind enough to show me around the town—we had some nice Sunday nights in the West Village—but I didn't feel like a part of it, or particularly care to. My defense mechanism was kicking in.

In more general terms, an inner voice told me never to get too attached to a city. During my time in Los Angeles, I'd been friends with one of the goalies for the Kings. He had been traded as soon as he bought a house. He convinced me that, in professional sports, investing in a place to live is the kiss of death; or the kiss of trade, as it were. In Los Angeles, I'd gone ahead and bought one anyway, established some roots, connected with the town, and suffered the consequences. In New York, in 1998, I wouldn't be making the same mistake. Not without a long-term contract, at least. Any major commitment would have to be a two-way proposition.

I really wasn't sure how the Mets felt about that. During the trading process, they hadn't been one of the teams that predicated their interest on signing me to an extension. And it wasn't like I was fast becoming a local icon or anything. Negotiations were uneventful. In general, the organization seemed to be as leery about the situation as I was—in which case, why not test the market?

We were in a holding pattern, and my state of mind was stuck on gloomy. New York, frankly, was beating me. At one point, I told my dad that I didn't give a shit anymore. He grumbled back at me, blaming anyone he could think of for the mess I was wallowing in. I'd thought he'd be happy, at least, that I was closer to Philadelphia. *Nobody* around me was happy.

Even my housekeeper was depressed. Teri O'Toole had moved east with me from California but was jolted by the brusque, snappish style of New York City. She eventually went into the convent.

There was at least one way in which New York embraced me without reservation. Unwittingly, and with startling regularity, I seemed to feed the city's craving for drama. As soon as the narrative threads had been established for the Hundley controversy and the negotiations watch, Pedro Martinez went ahead and hit me in the hand with a two-seam fastball on a Friday night in Boston. This was early in June.

According to the papers, there was no way that Pedro would deliberately put me on first with two strikes already, even though there were also three balls and the base was open, with a runner in scoring position. I suppose there was a slight chance of that being true. It's also true that he disliked me, he had exceptional control, I'd knocked him around in our previous meetings (seven for seventeen with three home runs), and it hurt like hell. I might have been hypersensitive to that sort of thing because it was my free-agent year, but it *felt* like a knockdown pitch. In the baseball tradition, I usually made a point of not rubbing the spot where I'd been hit or in any way acknowledging the power of the pitcher, but that time, halfway to first—after pausing to stare at Pedro for a couple seconds—I doubled over in pain. They took me straight to the hospital for X-rays. The hand, my left, was badly swollen but nothing was broken.

I returned to the ballpark in time to tell the media, "He's been known to do that. . . . He's buzzed a lot of guys. I'm not the first and I won't be the last. . . . Obviously, this year he doesn't have to hit so he can be a little bit more liberal in there. . . . Draw your own conclusions."

At the same time, in the other clubhouse, Pedro was telling the *Los Angeles Times*, "He was my teammate and an acquaintance. But we were definitely not friends."

Needless to say, the story was not over. Reporters were carrying our quotes back and forth between the clubhouses. When the Boston guys asked Pedro for his response to my statement, he said, "Fucking Piazza."

My response to *that* was, "All the money in the world can't really buy any class."

Then it was Pedro's turn. As recorded in the *New York Post*: "He's talking about class? He was a millionaire since he was a kid. . . . He's not a better person than me."

Me: "If he's got a problem with me, he knows where to find me."

Pedro: "What does he want me to do, go and fight him? Go in and start throwing punches? That's not me. That's where I have my class."

And to think we were grown men, leaders in our industry, making $20 million between us.

I missed only a couple of games; but after we lost on Sunday, we were eight behind the Braves. We were nine and a half behind them a month later, when we went to Atlanta and took a beating in more ways than one. We lost all three games, and in the second of them, on the Fourth of July, I was off again to the hospital. Gerald Williams conked me on the head while following through with his backswing.

The next day I wore a hockey mask for the first time. Meanwhile, my hand was still sore from Pedro and my shoulder was tender from when Gregg Zaun of the Marlins had slammed into me in a collision at the plate. It was hot. It was the getaway day before the All-Star Game. We went into the eleventh inning. When the Braves loaded the bases with one out against Franco, I walked out to have a talk with him. The instant I got there, the umpire, Angel Hernandez, was saying, "Let's go! Let's go!" I was like, "Dude, can we have a meeting? The winning run's on third base."

So Walt Weiss hits a shallow fly ball to left field and Michael Tucker, the runner on third, decides he's tagging up no matter what. Our left fielder, Bernard Gilkey, was a little surprised, I think, and his throw came in on the short hop. I managed to block the plate and snag the ball before Tucker got there, and he came at me with the dirtiest slide I've ever witnessed. He literally jumped into my thighs with both spikes. Didn't even hit the ground. Left about a six-inch gash in my right leg. After the collision and tag, it took me a moment to gather myself and raise my head up. As I did, I held the ball in the air, then turned toward the dugout, hoping to get a chance to hit in the twelfth.

I couldn't believe what I saw. Angel Hernandez had actually called Tucker safe.

I slammed the ball into the ground and started to give him hell, but Franco was already doing it. When I couldn't even get Hernandez's attention, I kind of spun him around. Somehow, I avoided a suspension. Franco, who bumped the ump a time or two, was not so fortunate.

Afterward, Valentine told the media, "I had a front-row view. The throw beat him. He fell into Mike's lap with a lousy, illegal slide. He cut him up, never touched the plate, got tagged out and they boarded the plane. I saw what everyone else saw. No marks on home plate. A lot of marks on Mike's leg where the cuts are."

And my two cents: "That was the most ridiculous call I've ever seen in my ten years of pro baseball; in my twenty years of baseball, period. It was just beyond belief. I'm completely flabbergasted."

We never did make a run at the Braves—I have to say, they were *damn* good—but we still had a shot at the wildcard. That's why I was there.

For months, however, I simply didn't help much, as the crowds were more than happy to point out in unison. There were times when *I* felt like booing me, too. Like the last day of July, the first time we'd played the Dodgers since the trade. I went 0 for 4, hit into two double plays, and allowed the Dodgers to tie the game in the ninth when I failed to block a wild pitch from Franco. They ended up scoring three to beat us, 4–3. But while I expected to be held accountable for my bad nights—after all, I'd grown up in Philadelphia—the New York fans were so enthusiastically brutal that any lingering prospects of me re-signing with the Mets looked pretty damn bleak. Speculation picked up that I might return to Los Angeles as a free agent.

There was a measure of humiliation in all of that—an implication that I just wasn't cutting it in New York and might as well go back where I came from, with my tail between my legs. Maybe, as a challenge to my pride, that was the thing that got me going. Or maybe it was the fact that, around the same time, the Mets announced they would postpone any additional contract talks until after the season, which cleared my head quite a bit. I homered and drove in three runs in the series finale, the first day of August. Later that month, I drove in three in a game at Colorado, three against the Rockies at Shea, four at home against the Diamondbacks, and three in San Francisco.

August got the crowds off my back and put us smack in the playoff picture. The three RBIs against the Rockies came on a pinch-hit double off Chuck McElroy that cleared the bases and completed a doubleheader sweep. Shea Stadium rocked. When I crushed a long home run off Darren Oliver to help beat the Cardinals, the fans actually asked for a curtain call. And I actually gave it to them. A page had been turned. When I hit a grand slam off Andy Benes to help bring us from behind against Arizona, the applause was no longer out of place.

There was even a standing ovation from a sellout crowd in Los Angeles—over the top of my jeering detractors, who still remained—when, at the end of August, I returned for the first time and homered in the sixth off Carlos Perez. In the tenth, I singled to start the winning rally. The Dodger fans didn't seem too concerned about the loss, since their team was under .500 and well out of the wildcard race by that time. In the *Los Angeles Times*, J. A. Adande wrote, "It was a giant wave of forgiveness for the month of April. . . . As tough as it might have seemed the last time he was here, things sure seemed better than they do today." I was eight for thirteen over the four games. We won three of them and left L.A. tied with the Cubs for the wildcard lead. In spite of our success, though, the whole series, to me, had a strange vibe. Through it all, there were rumors that Lasorda, who was still acting as the Dodgers' general manager, would come after not only me at the end of the season, but Valentine, too.

By early September, I'd homered eight times in two weeks. In Houston on September 14, batting in the first inning against Jose Lima, I crushed a 480-footer to straightaway center field that is considered the longest home run in the history of the Astrodome. Two days later, I hit a two-out, three-run shot in the ninth off Billy Wagner to give us a 3–2 lead in a game we ended up winning in eleven on a pinch-hit blast by Todd Hundley (who, when he started, was usually in left field).

I'd been amazed by Wagner the first couple of times I'd seen him. I just didn't expect *anybody*, much less a little left-hander, to throw that hard. But I had good results when I started taking his fastball to the opposite field, and was pleased to be able to say that the two hundredth home run of my career had come against him. More important, it kept our momentum going. Heading into the season's last two series—five games—the wildcard was ours to blow. We led the Cubs by a game and the Giants by three and a half.

Incredibly, we lost all five, the final three to the Braves in Atlanta. Even the Giants passed us by, forcing a playoff between them and the Cubs for the wildcard, which the Cubs won. After overcoming my clutch-hitting problems to drive in 111 runs for the season, I left fifteen men on base in the Atlanta series. It seemed like nothing good ever came out of playing the Braves.

It would have been nice to find a little solace in the RBIs, or in my third straight Most Productive Hitter of the Year award from the Ted Williams Museum & Hitters Hall of Fame—in *something*—but honestly, there wasn't any. Not with that abysmal finish. Not with the playoffs going on without us.

To me, in fact, the whole 1998 season had the feel of failure. I had failed to reach an agreement with the Dodgers, failed to lead the Mets into the playoffs, and failed to master New York City. I was haunted not only by our collapse in Atlanta, but by the notion that New York had proved to be too much for me. I didn't want to be remembered as just one more guy who couldn't play there.

The more I pondered it, the more I believed that there was a reason I'd been traded to the Mets. I didn't really know what the reason was, but I knew I couldn't walk away from it, just because New York was difficult. I decided that if the Mets wanted me and the contract was acceptable, I'd stay.

Danny agreed. He respected my motive and was quick to point out the earning potential of that particular choice, as well.

From the moment I'd arrived in New York, Danny had encouraged as much buzz as possible. When Howard Stern invited me onto his radio show during the season, for instance, Danny was all for it. (Of course, he didn't have to answer Howard's questions. We talked about when I'd dated Debbe Dunning, the Tool Time girl, and Howard asked me, "Did you bang her?" I laughed it off and told him I only dated nice girls. Evidently, I handled it okay, because I received a roundabout message that Debbe thought I'd been sweet to her.)

For that matter, Danny was almost always on the side of publicity, one memorable exception being the *Penthouse* interview I'd been asked to do the year before, in the fall. He'd reminded me that I was a proud Catholic and shouldn't go anywhere near that interview, but I did it anyway, without him knowing. I think it was a case of wanting to have my voice heard, to assert my independence a bit, and to squirm out of the grasp of my background, my parents, my agent, whatever. What I ended up asserting was my immaturity. I said some unenlightened things about women and spouted a stance on abortion that was the polar opposite of what I was brought up with and actually believe in. As soon as I said those things, I was pretty sure that I'd screwed up, and my mother erased any remaining doubt. She made it abundantly clear that she was disappointed in me as a Catholic, a man, and a Piazza. But at least that debacle prepared me for Howard Stern. I'd learned my lesson.

That said, I'd been raised in a capitalistic household and was well aware that New York presented opportunities no other town could match. Image was important to me. On the other hand, so was privacy. The classic New York dilemma. I began to think that, if things worked out with the Mets, I ought to live away from the city, somewhere with personal space. And driveways.

After the season, I headed back to my condo in Manhattan Beach, where I could hang out with Danny and get all this resolved. My dad had assumed I'd spend the off-season in Philadelphia, which was one of several points that we saw differently in those days. He was also looking into an arrangement by which I might end up in Philly full-time. He'd gotten a call from Sidney Kimmel, the philanthropist (namesake of the Kimmel Center for the Performing Arts in Philadelphia) and founder of the Jones Apparel Group, who was interested in buying the Phillies. Kimmel was inquiring about whether my dad might want to be a partner in the franchise, and whether, if he was, he could persuade me to sign with the Phillies as a free agent. My dad's answers were yes and yes. In fact, it had been a dream of his.

Not of mine, however. I would go to great lengths to make my father happy, but I simply couldn't see this one his way. It was a huge relief to me that it didn't work out—the Phillies weren't really for sale—because the game was hard enough without the complication of my dad as an owner. First of all, it would have been a nightmare from a media perspective, inviting all manner of questions, sidebars, and snide remarks. What's more, there undoubtedly would have been conflicts of interest that neither of us needed. What if the manager wanted to sit me down or the GM thought it best to trade me? What about contract negotiations? What about the perceptions of the other players? Would they consider me a spy for the front office? The thing was, I'd been busting my ass all these years to prove that I *wasn't* my father's puppet. It would have been a very sensitive and thankless situation.

When those discussions broke down, my dad poked around the Dodgers, heard what he wanted to hear, and told me that they were willing to bring me back at a discount—for less than they'd offered me in April. I insisted I wasn't going back there, and *especially* not at a discount. After the word got back to Tommy, I heard he was upset, on a personal level, that our relationship hadn't meant more. Going back to the spring, that made two of us. As far as I was concerned, the Dodgers were the one team that was definitely out of the bidding. And the Mets were the one team that was definitely *in* it.

Steve Phillips did the negotiating for the Mets, the problem being that he had different marching orders in each ear. Just like May, Fred Wilpon was the conservative voice and Nelson Doubleday the enabler. But Doubleday was on safari in Africa. From there, he went quail hunting in England. The way I heard it, Phillips or somebody reached him on the plane and told him that I wanted a shitload of money and Doubleday said, "Fuck it, sign him!" and hung up the phone.

When he was in San Diego for the World Series (Padres and Yankees), Phillips drove up to Los Angeles to sit down with Danny. It was obvious from the start that he was serious about getting something done. Danny called me and said, "You know, we could send a nice message to everyone in New York that, 'Hey, this is where I want to be; I'm not interested in going anywhere else.'" I was on the same page.

So they began talking in earnest, and Danny was amazed: Phillips had it all laid out already. He named the teams that would probably get involved with me and the ones that wouldn't and who might sneak in late as a dark horse. Danny had been talking to a few of those clubs, and he knew that Steve had it nailed. Phillips also had phone contact with Fred Wilpon whenever he needed it. He'd step outside, make the call, come in, and report the conversation, and then Danny would step outside and call me. The first offer was a package of $82 million for seven years, a pretty good starting point.

I really didn't know if it was going anywhere from there—or if so, when—so after a while, I headed to the gym in Venice Beach. Danny reached me on my big, clunky, analog cell phone and said, "Hey, the Mets have ninety-one million on the table. I think you should hold off on your workout." The deal being offered was almost exactly what I'd wanted from the Dodgers in the spring.

I said, "You think you can get ninety-three?"

All this time, the press was going nuts with rumors: I'm leaving, it's not getting done, whatever. When Danny called back again, he and Phillips were on a break. The numbers were still at seven years and $91 million, but the Mets had been talking about a limited no-trade agreement, which was another thing the Dodgers hadn't been willing to do. Plus a half-million-dollar relocation bonus if they *did* trade me. A hotel suite on road trips. A luxury box at Shea. After a while I just said, "I'll take it."

We never even talked about making me the highest-paid player in baseball history at the time (surpassing Pedro Martinez). It just happened, in one day.

I flew to New York to sign the papers and be there for the announcement. The Mets said they'd never had so many credential requests for a press conference. It was also one of the very rare occasions on which Wilpon and Doubleday were pictured together—one on either side of me. Caught up in the moment, I referred to New York as "the capital of the world" and said that if I were ever fortunate enough to be elected to the Hall of Fame, I'd go in wearing a Mets cap.

That night, I went out with Danny for dinner at Asia de Cuba, where we ran into Jeff Bagwell and his wife. I'd become friends with Jeff from all-star games and whatnot. He was a hell of a hitter and blatantly unorthodox; he'd "crab," I called it—squat way down and stay close to the ball. Bagwell and Craig Biggio, his running mate with the Astros, were among the first players to switch over to tiny bats. (Biggio's had a weird shape that, to me, resembled a mushroom.) Those two had some serious symbiosis going on, to the extent that a lot of guys thought they relayed signs to each other when one of them was batting. I don't know about that, but I do know that they won a lot of games for Houston; and I know that, if the 1994 schedule had played out to its completion, Bagwell would have put up one of the best seasons in modern history. At any rate, we got along, and Jeff's wife had set me up with a friend of hers, a model named Monica Mesones, who was from Uruguay and had been the first *Playboy* playmate from Latin America. Originally, I was supposed to meet the three of them after a game—this was in Los Angeles—but that night Bagwell barreled me over on a play at the plate. He was out, and I was seething. I was a moody son of a bitch, and I didn't care if my date was Miss America; I wasn't going. As it turned out, Monica and I ended up dating for a while anyway . . . which has nothing to do with seeing Jeff and his wife at Asia de Cuba, except for the fact that it might have made me a little uncomfortable. Or a little *more* uncomfortable.

In spite of all the ceremony surrounding the contract, and notwithstanding all that it represented for me, I wasn't truly at peace with it. When Bagwell offered me congratulations, something pounded me in the stomach. I came down with a terrible case of panic and anxiety. That night, I didn't sleep a wink, wrestling with the gravity of what I'd just done and the expectations that I'd have to deal with. I was thinking, goddamn, this is *seven years*. What if I don't play up to the contract? What if I end up hating New York? What if New York ends up hating me? What the hell did I just *do*?

Thankfully, Danny talked me down, as he often did. I leaned on Danny for intervention in a lot of different areas. He spoke with my dad, for instance, when I started thinking seriously about buying a house in Alpine, New Jersey, a very nice suburb in Bergen County, roughly ten miles from Manhattan.

My dad thought I should just rent a place in the city for the season, since it would be so easy to come home when it was over. He had guided me through virtually every step of my life and career, and I appreciated it profoundly. I took my father's advice to heart and still do. But the events of 1998 had been life-changing for me. The misery I'd felt for most of the year was closely tied to confusion, which stemmed, in large part, from the conflicting counsel of so many well-meaning people. It wasn't so much that I had to *stop* listening to my dad, but I had to *start* listening to myself. I wanted to live in New Jersey, where I could park in my own garage, tool down to Starbucks for breakfast, and otherwise be left the hell alone. If that meant standing up to my father, well, it was time. Danny felt the same way about *his* relationship with my dad. So he called him, told Dad how badly I wanted this house—the owner, a guy who had managed Mike Tyson, was offering it for a steal—and added that I'd really like his blessing. My father didn't appreciate Danny's involvement, and it caused some tension between them for a while. But they got over it. And I moved to New Jersey. I'd like to think my dad respected me for that.

Meanwhile, two days after the Mets announced my contract, they announced Al Leiter's. Then they signed Robin Ventura. They signed Rickey Henderson. In a three-way deal, they also picked up reliever Armando Benitez from the Orioles and traded away Todd Hundley. To the Dodgers, who had decided they needed a catcher who could hit.

CHAPTER SIXTEEN

Like a lot of people in the game, my impressions of Bobby Valentine had not been favorable. When he managed the Texas Rangers, he had been called the most hated man in baseball. Opponents found him arrogant, smug, annoying, and sneaky. Valentine had been known to stand on the top step of the dugout—Chris Wheeler, the Phillies announcer, called him Top-Step Bobby—and cuss at players on the other team. There were rumors that he had a spy planted in the visiting clubhouse. He was the ultimate micromanager, the intuitive type who had his hand in every pitch and every twitch, it seemed like. The year before I got to New York, he used 131 different lineups. Nobody questioned that Bobby was smart; they just wished he didn't remind you at every opportunity. Or sweet-talk the media the way he did.

I was probably more inclined than most players to cut him some slack, because he reminded me so much of Tommy; but I'd had my own little run-in with Bobby. It was during the last spring training before I was traded to the Mets. They were crushing us one day. I think Rico Brogna had three home runs. One of their guys stole a base, which is considered bad form in that situation, and Billy Russell gave Bobby a hard stare from the other dugout. Bobby responded with something like "I'm trying to do you a fucking favor and get you some fucking outs!" Then I glared at Bobby with that "what an asshole" look—I was catching at the time—and he glared back at me with a "what are *you* looking at?" look. A week or two later he approached and said, "You're not still mad at me, are you?" Whatever.

But he treated me well when I joined the Mets. I'm sure that Todd Hundley wasn't as thrilled with him, but I certainly had no complaints. For one thing, I was pleasantly surprised to find that he didn't try to call the game for me when I was catching. My only issue with Bobby was the incestuous relationship he maintained with the media. The players were frequently puzzled by leaks that we couldn't trace to any other source. Of course, the writers and broadcasters loved Bobby. He understood the way New York operated and was only too happy to play that way. He embraced it. In fact, that was part of the reason why he embraced *me*.

> I think the team needed somebody like Mike. We needed to be able to have that celebrity status because, a) we were in New York, and b) we were competing on a daily basis with a celebrity team across the borough. There was no other chance for us to compete on Page Six [the *New York Post* gossip section] or on talk radio without the celebrity status of Mike.
>
> It was a very demanding situation for him. I'm not sure that anyone deserved to be put in such a role of responsibility. He was being asked to catch every day and hit the home run in the ninth inning and say and do all the right things in the biggest city in the country, every day.
>
> — Bobby Valentine

I was generally moody with the media, as I was with everybody else, but I understood what came with the territory and served my time in front of my locker. What I *didn't* understand was the full sweep of the public spotlight that bears down on a well-paid ballplayer in New York City. It didn't hit me too hard during the 1998 season because, in my misery, I didn't go out much. Then, when I moved to New Jersey, I figured I'd bought some privacy. And I had. But I still tried to sneak into the city, unnoticed, from time to time. It was difficult.

In February, I checked out a club in SoHo called Varuka, where some Yankees hung out. I was wearing sneakers at the time, which didn't meet the dress code, but the guy at the door said, "If I let David Wells in here almost naked, I guess I have to let you in with sneakers." The next day, I read in the paper that I was kicked out of the place because no Mets were allowed. Sometimes, when New York is being New York, all you can do is laugh.

On another occasion, I was driving to Shea Stadium and heard some girl on the radio berating a ballplayer for making a fuss about something or other. I had no idea what it was all about until I got a call from Danny saying that the singer Usher's people had phoned to apologize. I said, for what? Turned out, there had been a story that I'd shown up at Usher's private party, couldn't get in, and made a scene over it. When I arrived at the ballpark, one of my teammates, Benny Agbayani, said, "Why didn't you tell me you were trying to get into the party? I was there. I could have gotten you in." I

still don't know where all that came from. Just New York being New York,
I guess.

The city never takes off the full-court press, even when it's in foul trouble. Drivers would jump out of garbage trucks to shout something at me or
talk baseball. Cars would pull up to the curb and guys would lean out the
window for autographs. A kid would open his jacket to show me his Mets
jersey—and of course, have me sign it. Random people would remark on
my mustache. And the national media were always just down the block.
On that front, I played along, for the most part. I became a semiregular on
Howard Stern's show. I dressed up as a city slicker—silk handkerchief and
everything—for the cover of GQ, April 1999.

Needless to say, there's a useful side to all that attention. For a few years,
I was going strong on the commercial circuit. I filmed a series of them for 10-
10-220, a long-distance service, with Emmitt Smith, Terry Bradshaw, Hulk
Hogan, and my good friend Alf. (I also did one with John McEnroe that
didn't air, for whatever reason.) AutoZone had me trying to start a car with
a dead battery. And at one point, I had a contract with Claritin, which one
or two of my teammates resented: "Why the fuck is Piazza doing Claritin
commercials? He doesn't have allergies!"

Meanwhile, the local sportswriters did their jobs in ways that weren't really objectionable or even unprofessional, necessarily, but kept me on edge.
Joel Sherman of the Post liked to write about how much money everybody
was making and what they were doing to earn it. I recall one game, early in
1999, in which we were down 3–2 in the bottom of the ninth, with Trevor
Hoffman closing for the Padres, and John Olerud singled to lead off the
inning. I'd been scuffling a bit and as I headed to the plate I was actually
thinking, "All right, I need to come through here or Sherman's going to rip
me for being overpaid." Thankfully, I ended the game with a two-run homer,
which, for the bucks I was making, was apparently what I was expected to
do. About a month later, I snapped out of a slump with a big series against
the Brewers and the headline over Joel's column read PIAZZA BREAKOUT
MORE LIKE IT. (Sherman also belonged to the camp of New York writers
who seemed to take delight in reporting my failures, and he waited patiently
for the opportunity to do so. One year, when my numbers were down, he
showed up at a series in Philadelphia ready and eager to write about it. Right
about then, I went on a tear. He finally approached me in the clubhouse and
said something like, "So, you've had a good week or so . . ." I had stolen his
thunder, and the disappointment showed on his face. He never wrote the
story.)

Then there was the *Daily News* beat writer Rafael Hermoso, who asked me straight-out if I had used andro. I told him I'd bought it over the counter at GNC as part of my Monster Paks. Then he said, in so many words, "So you did steroids?"

The question irritated me, but I tried not to be confrontational. My reply was something like, "Did I tell you I did steroids? What are you talking about? Andro is over-the-counter."

But the landscape was shifting, as far as the way in which certain supplements were being regarded. As a team, we'd had an informational session about steroids, and that was the first time I'd heard andro referred to as a precursor to testosterone. (Creatine, on the other hand, is an organic acid, a naturally occurring substance that you consume when you eat salmon or steak, although, obviously, not in the same amounts that you get from purchasing it as a supplement.)

Around that period, we were also hearing more and more about human growth hormone (HGH). Guys were going to these life-extension or wellness clinics that offer hormone therapy, where you can get a blood profile and recommendations on supplements that will increase your hormone level, and the corresponding prescriptions. It didn't seem much different than a woman going in for a face lift or a boob job. All the noise surrounding HGH—it was supposed to give you a vigorous, youthful feeling—made it sound as though it was on the verge of becoming mainstream. If you could get a prescription at a clinic, it wasn't illegal. On the other hand, it did have to be injected with a needle. I absolutely detested needles. I once passed out in spring training when they drew blood for a simple blood test. The times I didn't pass out, I always felt woozy and just plain lousy.

Anyway, I wanted to get the lowdown on HGH—like a lot of players, I was trying to sort all this stuff out—so I did a little reading on the subject, then went to Fred Hina, the Mets' trainer, and asked him, "Fred, what's the deal with this growth hormone? Are the teams going to be giving it out?" I figured, if it was so good and generally accessible, why wouldn't the ball clubs make it available just like Vioxx, Indocine, Voltaren, and cortisone? I assumed HGH was simply the next step in the evolution of medicating the ballplayer, the latest drug that teams would use routinely for rehabbing injuries. Standard procedure.

When I inquired about it, Fred was sort of speechless for a moment, then said, "I'll check around and get back to you on that." I think he was genuinely curious about it. A day or two later, he came to me and said something about the feds, like it was some big thing, and that was the end of that. Fred made it clear to me that HGH was considered a controlled substance—although it wasn't officially banned by MLB until 2005. The whole episode was kind of amusing, actually, and more than a little bewildering. Like creatine, HGH is made up of amino acids and is produced naturally in the body. The problem lies in the fact that people pig out on the stuff. That's when it becomes unhealthy. At the time, though, so little was known about supplements and such, and the scene was changing so fast, and baseball's policies were so ambiguous, that players often found themselves on unmarked trails, trying to navigate a hazardous (but promising) new frontier. It wasn't simply a steroids issue. On a broader scale, guys were trying to figure out what they could do nutritionally in terms of supplements, sorting through the fitness magazines and health food stores for something that might help their games yet respect the rules and not create a firestorm like the one over McGwire's bottle of androstenedione. A power hitter, in particular, was simultaneously teased and taunted by a general, growing premise that there was some sort of magic formula, a secret of unlocking athletic potential, to be summoned from the inside of a can or some other product easily found at the mall. There's no such thing; but there was certainly the *rumor* of it, the tantalizing, unremitting murmur. It was an age of exaggeration, misinformation, and, most of all, confusion. It could be disorienting.

Given the nature and abundance of the New York media, it was surprising that more wasn't reported on PEDs in those days. I suspect that the writers were as bewildered about the whole subject as we were. It certainly didn't come up often in my experience, which is why the instance with Hermoso stands out to me.

At any rate, when New York got in my face, whether it was the fans, a newspaper guy, or the city itself, I had a refuge. And I'm not talking about New Jersey.

I mean music. My answer—especially before a ball game, in the car and the clubhouse—was to crank it up and drown out the rest of the world: Anthrax, AC/DC, Boston, Bad Company, Van Halen, Yesterday and Today, Zebra; everything from A to Z, as it were.

After he sent up Todd Pratt to bat for me in the ninth inning of an 8–3, early April game in Montreal in which I had three hits, including a home run, and five RBIs, Bobby told the press that he did it so "Todd Pratt could tell his grandkids one day that he pinch-hit for Mike Piazza." Actually, it was because I slightly tore the medial collateral ligament in my right knee—although we didn't know the exact nature of the injury at the time—in a rundown between second and third after Brian McRae missed a bunt. Bobby initially wrote me into the lineup the next day, but he took me out after Fred Hina observed how much the knee had swollen. Then they put me on a plane to Newark, so I could get an MRI. I missed a couple of weeks.

It wasn't much of a problem for the ball club, because we had a hell of a lineup in 1999, starting at the top with Rickey Henderson. (Now that I think of it, I still owe Rickey a pair of headphone amplifiers. I had a nice set that he envied and I told him I'd pick one up for him. Never did. Sorry about that, Rickey.) It's common knowledge that Henderson was one of the greatest leadoff hitters of all time and also one of the greatest characters. I didn't know him well before the season, because he'd spent most of his career in the American League, but whenever he'd come up to bat against us he'd turn around and say, "Whaddup, P?" He could make you smile.

So many Rickey stories made the rounds that you were never sure what was true. Rick Rhoden, one of his teammates with the Yankees, told me that Rickey had had some issues with their manager, Lou Piniella, and after they met in Piniella's office one day somebody asked Rickey how it had gone. He said, "We agreed to let bye-byes be bye-byes." Most of the lines, though, involved Rickey referring to himself as Rickey—such as "Rickey don't like it when Rickey can't find Rickey's limo." A lot of that might be urban legend, but this much is definitely true: Rickey Henderson was a consummate pro, a bighearted guy and a player I really appreciated as a teammate. For starters, he was always on base, even at the age of forty. That's a big part of the reason why we got outstanding seasons that year from so many people—namely, Edgardo Alfonzo, Robin Ventura, John Olerud, Roger Cedeno, and Benny Agbayani. We scored nearly a run a game more than we had in 1998. With all that production across the board, we played through my injury and were doing well . . . until we somehow lost eight straight games in late May and early June.

The last two of those were my introduction to Yankee Stadium. For the most part, I enjoyed the hell out of playing there. The first time I walked into the park, fans were lined up outside chanting, "Piazza sucks! Piazza sucks!" I got a chuckle out of that. But I wasn't laughing after we dropped the first two games of that weekend series, and neither was Steve Phillips. In New York, you don't lose eight straight without consequences.

The consequence, this time, was that, on June 5, Phillips and Bobby engaged in an hour-long meeting/argument, during which Phillips fired three of Bobby's coaches—the pitching coach, Bob Apodaca; the hitting coach, Tom Robson; and the bullpen coach, Randy Niemann. So we now had two owners who didn't get along and a serious split between the manager and

GM. And Bobby saying that he didn't deserve to keep his job if the ball club didn't pick up the pace over the next couple of months.

And Roger Clemens pitching against us the next day.

At age thirty-six, it was Clemens's first season with the Yankees after thirteen in Boston and two in Toronto, where, both years, he led the American League in wins, ERA, and strikeouts. In my only previous appearances against Roger, the season before, I'd had a couple of singles in a game at Toronto. I remember thinking, hmm, I see the ball pretty well off this dude. I could pick up the split-fingered fastball coming out of his hand—because I was blessed with great eyesight, I could actually see the spread of his fingers—and was able to eliminate that pitch, which he depended upon heavily.

That was my plan when I faced Clemens leading off the second inning on that Sunday in '99, with Al Leiter going for us. The result was a double over Bernie Williams's head in center field, which got us started on a four-run rally. In the third, Olerud singled and I made it 6–0 with a home run. Four batters later, we'd knocked the big guy out of the game.

That got us going on a roll in which we won fifteen out of eighteen, and had some fun doing it. Bobby saw to that. I'm referring specifically to June 9, an extra-inning game against the Blue Jays at Shea Stadium.

Joe Ferguson had taught me how to subtly cheat on pitchouts by running into the ball to shorten the pitch and build up some momentum for the throw. I tried it in the twelfth inning that day with Pat Mahomes pitching, Shannon Stewart on first base, and Craig Grebeck at the plate. I suppose I might have taken an extra step forward to try to nail Stewart, and the umpire, Randy Marsh, called catcher's interference on me. It was an unusual call, which prompted Bobby to come rushing out of the dugout and get himself tossed. The next inning, I looked over and did a double take. There he was—we all knew it instantly, which he'd fully expected—leaning against the ledge alongside the steps that led to the tunnel. He'd taken two of those strips that players use for eye-black and made a mustache out of them. He'd also put on a Mets T-shirt, a different cap, and dark glasses. I don't know if he was trying to masquerade as a grounds-crew guy or what, but of course the cameras caught him, and the league wasn't as amused as we were. He got suspended for two games and fined five thousand bucks.

But he had succeeded in loosening us up, which was very much in order because the dugout had been decidedly tense for a few days: bad vibes between Valentine and Bobby Bonilla. Valentine had benched Bonilla, Bonilla had refused to pinch-hit, there was some shouting, Valentine had snubbed him the next time he needed a pinch hitter, and so on. Anyway, we won the fake-mustache game in the fourteenth with smiles on our faces, completing a sweep of Toronto, then took two out of three from the Red Sox and Reds, three out of four from the Cardinals, and three straight from the Marlins before the Braves—always the Braves—stopped us.

In the opener of the Boston series, the Mets honored my old hero and backyard instructor, Ted Williams. Tom Seaver drove him to the mound in a golf cart, Lasorda introduced him, and it was my privilege to catch his ceremonial first pitch. The guy was eighty years old, so I stepped out in front of the plate. He waved me back and delivered a strike. As you might expect, I was eager to do something noteworthy that night, and tied the game, 2–2, with a two-run homer off Tom Gordon in the bottom of the ninth. But the Sox beat us in the twelfth.

Nevertheless, we were six and three against the American League by the time the Yankees came to Shea to resume the Subway Series on a weekend in July. I continue to watch the Subway Series every year, and it's still a great show; but at that stage it was novel, immensely competitive, and truly special. The modern version of the series had started in 1997, and when they visited us in 1999, the Yankees, predictably, had gotten the best of all three sets. They were also sailing through the AL East, up three games on the Red Sox. And once again, they had the ball right where they wanted it—in the meaty hands of Roger Clemens.

But in the bottom of the sixth on the ninth day of the month, with the score tied 2–2, I had Clemens where I wanted *him*—at two and one, with a couple of runners on base. He served me the slider I'd earned by laying off the splitter, got it up a bit, and I lined it into the temporary picnic area set up beyond left field. Leiter had the situation in hand, and 5–2 was how it ended. It appeared that Al and I *both* had Clemens's number.

In the Saturday game, on a sinker that Ramiro Mendoza didn't get as low as he would have liked, I crushed a higher, longer (measured at 482 feet) three-run homer that landed on top of the picnic tent and put us up 7–6 in the seventh. For the second day in a row, I took a curtain call from a fired-up crowd. Even the Yankees were buzzing about that blast. Jorge Posada said it was the hardest-hit ball he'd ever seen. When Derek Jeter came up to bat in the top of the ninth, he inquired, suppressing a smile, as to whether I'd gotten it all. Still, after I'd been intentionally walked, it took a two-out, two-strike, two-run pinch single by Matt Franco, against Mariano Rivera, to pull the game out in the bottom of the ninth, 9–8.

Sunday, I had three singles, but my old buddy Orel Hershiser—we had signed him as a free agent at the end of spring training—didn't have one of his better afternoons and the Yankees salvaged the finale. Regardless, we'd made our statement, and I felt like I'd made mine, as well. For a while there, I'd started to take some flak again about not hitting in important games and situations. In the Subway Series, I'd proved to New York that I could do that.

And I'd proved to myself that I could do New York.

At the end of July, we began to bob and weave with Atlanta. On the West Coast in mid-August, I hit a stretch in which I pounded five home runs in six games, and Robin Ventura was right there with me, virtually matching long ball for long ball and RBI for RBI. Edgardo Alfonzo—Fonzi—wasn't far behind. That's how teams get hot.

After falling a few games behind the Braves again, we revisited the coast in September, starting in Los Angeles; starting with Kevin Brown, the pitcher the Dodgers had signed in the off-season for the money I'd been requesting. He was good that night. So was Hershiser, pitching as a Met against the team he won 135 games for. With one out in the sixth and the Dodgers up 1–0, Olerud reached on an error. The count on me went to two and two. I fouled off four pitches, mostly fastballs. Then Brown let one drift too far over the plate, and I dropped it into the left-field seats. The Los Angeles fans gave me a standing ovation. Hershiser held the Dodgers to two hits in eight innings, Armando Benitez finished them off, and the final was 3–1.

The next day, Bill Plaschke wrote in the Los Angeles Times,

> Thursday was poignant reflection of what has been evident around here since the day Dodger blue turned to black. The deal that Fox's Chase Carey cut behind everyone's back? The one that has made May 15 the most infamous date in club history? . . . Turns out, it was not a trade, it was a wound. Turns out, it was a cut so deep, 16 months later it is still there. . . .
>
> Come to find out, this suddenly unsteady organization needed Mike Piazza more than he needed it. Turns out, the complaining he did about his contract was just a whisper compared to the griping his former teammates have done since then. And today, I admit, I miss him. Despite his clubhouse aloofness, I miss his on-field stability. Even with his October disappearances, I miss his September presence. Part of me wanted to cheer him Thursday for taking another team toward the playoffs. Part of me wanted to boo him for leaving us behind.

Yet again, reports surfaced that the Dodgers had been attempting to get me back. The *Times* made it known that Kevin Malone, the Dodgers' general manager, had twice that year contacted Steve Phillips about trading for me. "The significance of the revelation," wrote Jason Reid, "is that Malone is trying to correct what many Dodger fans consider the worst mistake in franchise history." It was all very flattering, but otherwise of little consequence. I wasn't thinking about the Dodgers. I was thinking about the Braves.

We trailed them by only one game when we met in Atlanta in late September. I'd homered in the previous game, a victory over the Phillies, but was dealing with a sore and swollen left thumb, banged up two nights before *that* on a foul tip off the bat of Ron Gant. Since the X-rays were negative and the Braves were next, the thumb would just have to hurt. And I don't say that to sound valiant. That's just the way it is, for everybody, in a 162-game baseball season. But especially for catchers. And *most* especially for catchers in closely contested pennant races.

For all the hype surrounding the Subway Series, our chief rival was Atlanta. As a rule, the Braves worked us over pretty good. Hell, they owned us. At one point, I stated publicly that we always seemed to play tight against the Braves, as though they had a psychological advantage going in. The follow-up was a report that one Met said I should take a look at myself instead of trying to psychoanalyze the whole ball club. Over the years, in fact, there was a lot of stuff in the New York papers that the mysterious "one Met said." At any rate, my remark certainly didn't imply an insufficient respect for the Braves' incredible pitching. The fundamental problem, for us, was Maddux, Glavine, and Smoltz. Also Chipper Jones, the great third baseman.

This time around, it was more of the same. Smoltz handled us 2–1. Then Glavine took care of us 5–2. I hit my thirty-seventh homer that night, and got another the next day against Maddux, but Chipper Jones—the very guy we weren't supposed to let beat us—topped me with a three-run blast against Leiter, his forty-fifth of the season, and they did it again, 6–3. They got us nine times that year out of twelve, the same as the year before. The series sweep pretty much wrapped up another division title for the Braves, their fifth in a row and eighth in nine seasons.

When we hobbled out of Atlanta, we were no longer competing expressly with the Braves. It was now between us and the Reds for the wild card; and in spite of our beaten asses, we were looking good, still ahead by a couple games. The trouble was, the Atlanta series shoved us into a seven-game losing streak, which lasted until the Braves came to New York a few days later and we managed to win the middle game of three. But they went on to take the rubber match in eleven innings, after which Chipper Jones said something to the press about the good people at Shea being able to go home now and change into their Yankees jerseys. Atlanta's loose-cannon closer, John Rocker, chimed in that he hated the Mets, adding, "How many times do we have to beat them before their fans will shut up?"

We'd fallen two games behind Cincinnati by the time the Pirates arrived for the last series of the season. In the opener on Friday night, I was intentionally walked to load the bases in the bottom of the eleventh and Ventura delivered a two-out single for the win. On Saturday night, one of my heavy-metal heroes, Zakk Wylde of Black Label Society—I actually grunted a couple of backup words when "Stronger than Death" was recorded, and I'm the godfather of his son, Hendrix—ripped off a cool, controversial national anthem and presented me with an electric guitar. Then, in a 7–0 shutout by Rick Reed, I hit my fortieth home run. Ironically, the forty homers for the season went with 124 RBIs, numbers that happened to precisely match the totals of my last full year in Los Angeles.

The Saturday victory sent us into the regular season's final day in a wild-card tie with the Reds, who, thank you very much, lost the first two games of their series in Milwaukee. On that suspenseful Sunday, Hershiser turned in a clutch performance and I was at the plate in the bottom of the ninth, with one out and the bases loaded in a 1–1 game, when Brad Clontz relieved my old roommate, Greg Hansell. On his first pitch, Clontz fired up a wild one to hand us our ninety-sixth victory. But we didn't know what it meant because the Reds hadn't played yet. They were scheduled for a late-afternoon game in Milwaukee. So we all meandered up to the Stadium Club to have dinner and watch nervously, not knowing whether we were headed to Arizona for the first round of the playoffs or to Cincinnati for a sudden-death game.

The answer turned out to be Cincinnati, and I'd never seen it so wired. The crowd on Monday night was insane. But Al Leiter subdued it slowly, methodically, inning by inning, as he sliced through the likes of Barry Larkin, Sean Casey, Greg Vaughn, and Aaron Boone with a two-hit shutout. The final was 5–0, and it was, in effect, our fourth straight sudden-death victory; a loss in any of one of those games would have left us out of the playoffs.

Under the circumstances, it was maybe the best-pitched game I ever caught. Catching it was certainly the best thing I did that night—better, by far, than walking three times (and finishing the season at .303)—and also the most painful. After that foul tip from Ron Gant, my thumb had never healed. Leiter just pulverized it with that cutter of his. He made me sore and proud in roughly the same proportions.

• • •

With Leiter unavailable for the playoff opener in Arizona, we had to throw
Masato Yoshii up against the best pitcher in the National League that year.
Randy Johnson had led the league in ERA, complete games, and strikeouts,
which brought him his first of an amazing four straight NL Cy Young awards,
on top of the one he'd already earned in the American League. At six foot
ten, left-handed, side-wheeling, mullet-haired, with ferocious stuff and just
the right amount of wildness, Johnson scared the shit out of a lot of hitters.
He might have done the same to me if he'd been right-handed. I can't say
that I lit him up over the years, but I had my hits against him—mostly singles, except for one home run. Personality-wise, Randy was considered kind
of inscrutable and "out there," which only added to his mystique. That didn't
faze me, though, because we had something very much in common. Like me,
he was, and is, a hard-rock freak. On the occasions when we bumped into
each other, the conversation was more likely to be about Twisted Sister than
Sammy Sosa. Randy's also an amateur photographer, and goes from concert
to concert taking pictures. I mean, the man is seriously into it. I hooked him
up with my friend Eddie Trunk, the radio and TV personality and all-around
guru of heavy metal, and now the two of them talk a lot.

The matchup suggested that our game-one prospects were not especially
brilliant. They improved a bit, however, when Alfonzo went deep in the first
inning. Olerud did the same, with a runner on, in the third—no small feat
for a left-handed hitter against Randy Johnson. But Luis Gonzalez tied the
game, 4–4, with a two-run homer in the sixth, and the score hadn't changed
when we loaded the bases with one out in the top of the ninth. At that
point, the Diamondbacks' manager, Buck Showalter, took out Johnson—
who had eleven strikeouts, including me twice—in favor of reliever Bobby
Chouinard. The first batter Chouinard faced was Rickey Henderson, who
grounded into a force at home. That brought up Alfonzo, and I'll be damned
if Fonzi didn't hit it out. Benitez got the save, and afterward, speaking to
reporters, I said that we were now assured of going back to New York at least
even in the series at one to one and if anybody had offered us that three days
before we'd have been ecstatic. For my trouble, I was ripped by a columnist
for my lack of leadership skills.

I was on the right track, however. Game two was forgettable except for
the pain it inflicted upon my thumb. My thirty-three-ounce bat was feeling
like thirty-three rods of rebar.

On the off day before game three in New York, I showed the thumb to
Fred Hina. He dragged me to the doctor for a cortisone shot. A *big* cortisone

shot. That night, I woke up with my whole left hand throbbing. I'd had an allergic reaction that led to an infection. They put me on antibiotics and told me there was a slight chance that I'd lose the thumb.

The Mets didn't miss me much in the two games I sat out. Henderson and Olerud—two great ballplayers whose personalities couldn't have been more different—had big nights in the first of them, and we closed out the series the next day. Specifically, my replacement, Todd Pratt, closed it out with a walk-off home run against Matt Mantei—who threw *really* hard, by the way—in the bottom of the tenth.

With that, we'd earned ourselves the dubious privilege of playing the Braves in the National League Championship Series. But at least my thumb would have three days to get itself in working order, which it did.

Not that it mattered in game one. Maddux—who, unlike another great right-hander from our generation, was a credit to the game every time he took the mound—had no sympathy for me or us. Kevin Millwood then proceeded to beat us in game two, 4–3, when the Braves got to Kenny Rogers for four runs in the sixth on two-run homers from Brian Jordan and Eddie Perez. They brought in Smoltz to pitch the ninth, the first time he had ever relieved. He set us down in order and struck out Bobby Bonilla, who was pinch-hitting, to end the game.

Coming home to Shea, we got Glavine in game three. Leiter started for us but fell a run behind in the first inning on errors by him and me. He threw a ball wide of first base and I threw one away on a double steal. The inning ended when Bret Boone tagged up at third on a fly ball to center field and Melvin Mora gunned him out. At the plate, Boone led with his shoulder and knocked me backward, onto my head, which was all recorded from the tumbling view of my helmet cam. I got a mild concussion out of it. I also got two singles in that game, and Leiter pitched seven innings of three-hit ball, but we couldn't score against Glavine or Mike Remlinger. It was still 1–0 when Bobby Cox turned over the ninth inning to the man whom Shea Stadium had been impatiently waiting for. John Rocker took the mound to a downpour of boos and thundering chants of "Asshole! Asshole!"

It was his first appearance in New York since he had called out our fans in September. To the Mets crowd, Rocker was a more compelling target than Chipper Jones, who had actually fired the first shot. Naturally, the folks didn't take kindly to Chipper's remark, either, but he'd never been the villainous type in their eyes; just a good rival they could have some fun with. They called him Larry, which they got from me. The media had found out that I always used his real name when he came to bat: "Hey, Larry, how's it goin'?" I wasn't trying to be a jerk; I just couldn't call a grown man Chipper. The fans expanded that to a Three Stooges theme, but Larry took it well. In fact, I think he enjoyed it. When his third son was born, he actually named him Shea. Chipper's even-keeled temperament was part of what made him such a poised player, one who seemed to save his best for the big situations. He almost single-handedly beat us down the stretch that year. He earned your admiration.

Rocker was a different story. Working out of the bullpen, he was accessible to the fans in a way that Chipper wasn't, for one thing. Beyond that, he was much more detestable. As the series wore on, somebody apparently threw a bottle at him and somebody else dumped beer on his girlfriend. It kept building. Fans taunted him, flipped him the bird, held up nasty signs about him. In response, Rocker spat at them and fired a ball into the screen, then laughed when they ducked. Shagging balls before the game in the outfield, he'd make a motion to toss one to a group of fans, then turn and lob it back to the pitcher with an evil smile. Or he'd flip a ball toward fans standing by the rail as he walked off the field, but leave it a few feet short. He also bad-mouthed the crowd when talking to reporters. "I think the majority of the Mets' fans are not even human," he said. Rocker probably watched too much wrestling as a kid. Of course, I did, too, but I think he took it literally. Aside from the stupid things he said and did, though, I had to grudgingly give him credit. He had the kind of persona that I appreciated in a pitcher, that attitude of always coming at you. He put us on our heels. He'd flip the resin bag, take a breath, then come over the top blowing gas, throwing as hard as anybody I'd seen in a long time. For a while, Rocker was unhittable.

In game three, he spotted us an error to start the ninth, then put us away without a problem. We were twenty-seven outs from being swept.

Game four was all about Rick Reed and John Olerud, two players I thought very highly of. As a former scab, Reed had to win the respect of his teammates over time. I, for one, didn't care for his decision to cross the line, but I would never let that interfere with the integrity of a ball game. And there was no disputing that, on the mound, Reed was an impressive guy who won a lot of important games for us. He could hit any corner anytime; probably had the best control of anyone I ever caught. He walked nobody in the seven innings he pitched that night against the Braves.

Olerud, on the other hand, was a guy I respected from the moment I met him. When I'd first arrived in New York, John had counseled me on what it takes to succeed in the city, and he had the perfect makeup for it. I observed him with considerable interest and admired his unflappable approach to both hitting and the game in general. But that was *his* style, not mine. I was hoping like hell that he'd re-sign with us as a free agent after the season—he was a joy to hit behind—but he ultimately accepted less money to go back home to Seattle. In the meantime, it seemed as though Olerud was right in the middle of anything we did well as an offense. In game four, he drove in all of our runs, with a solo homer in the first and an enormous two-out, two-run, bouncing single in the bottom of the eighth to bring us from behind—to keep our season alive—and complete the scoring at 3–2. That one victimized Rocker, who, being the good sport and master grammarian that he was, described it to the press as "one of the more cheaper hits I've given up my entire life." The winning rally came half an inning after Gerald Williams cracked me on the knuckle with his backswing. Same hand as the hurting thumb. Even *beating* the Braves was painful.

The game five matchup was Maddux against Yoshii. Actually, Maddux, Terry Mulholland, Remlinger, Russ Springer, Rocker, and Kevin McGlinchy against Yoshii, Hershiser, Turk Wendell, Cook, Mahomes, Franco, Benitez, Rogers, and Octavio Dotel. Fifteen innings. I lasted thirteen. Olerud gave us a 2–0 lead with a home run in the first. The Braves tied it in the fourth on doubles from Boone and Chipper and a single by Brian Jordan. Somewhere in there, Ryan Klesko nailed me in the left forearm with a backswing. I don't know what it was with the Braves and backswings, but I was starting to feel like a piñata. It was still 2–2 in the top of the thirteenth when, with two outs, Keith Lockhart tried to score on a double to right by Chipper and was thrown out by Mora. Naturally, Lockhart pounded into the arm that Klesko had clubbed. I stayed in the game to bat against Rocker in the bottom of the inning and made it worse—it felt like I pulled something—swinging at the pitch that struck me out. Bobby informed me I was done for the day. With my hand tingling and my arm howling, I was in no condition to disagree.

Todd Pratt replaced me again and came to bat against Kevin McGlinchy in the bottom of the fifteenth with one out, the bases loaded, and the Braves leading by a run that Lockhart had tripled in. Pratt worked a walk to tie the game and bring up Robin Ventura. For a long time that year, Robin, in addition to being a good guy to hang around with, had ranked as a leading candidate for the MVP award, which Chipper Jones would win. (With thirty-two homers, 120 RBIs, and a .301 batting average, Robin finished seventh. I was next.) But what Ventura's 1999 season is best remembered for is the so-called grand-slam single he hit over the wall in right-center field to win game five of the league championship series. When the ball cleared the fence, Pratt was so ecstatic that he ran back and hoisted Robin off the ground between first and second base. Then the rest of us joined the mob. The ultimate ruling was that only Roger Cedeno, the runner on third, actually scored. It didn't matter. We were back in business.

There was a day off before the series resumed in Atlanta, and for twenty-four peaceful hours not a single Brave bruised me with a bat head or lowered shoulder. For that matter, the Atlanta hitters didn't exactly bash Leiter in game six; but they knocked him out in the first inning, nevertheless. Al hit the first guy and walked the second. Then, following the same old tired script, I made another throwing error on a double steal. Al hit Chipper, Jordan singled, Eddie Perez singled, it was 4–0, and just like that our best pitcher was out of the game. One more run scored after Pat Mahomes replaced Leiter. Millwood was the Braves' starter, and that's how it stood until the sixth, when Fonzi doubled, Olerud singled, I hit a sacrifice fly, Ventura doubled, and Darryl Hamilton singled. Suddenly it was 5–3. But in the bottom of the inning, the Braves tacked on two more. And made me very angry.

Turk Wendell hit Brian Jordan leading off, and Jordan was out for blood. He was on third with the bases loaded when Walt Weiss hit a ground ball to Olerud, who brought it home to me. There was no chance for a double play, so I stretched out like a first baseman to receive the throw. Jordan folded me up like a tea table—all but chopped my knees in half. I'd had enough. I snapped. Totally lost it. I screamed at Jordan, "Get your ass off the field! Keep walking, motherfucker!" The whole time, I was hoping desperately that he'd turn back toward me so I could do something stupid. Brian Jordan had played safety in the NFL and was a powerful dude who might have ripped my head off, but at that point, I didn't give a shit. Thankfully, he kept his cool, and I was still around in the seventh inning when Cox summoned Smoltz for another relief appearance.

This time, we jumped all over him. Double by Matty Franco. Double by Rickey Henderson. Single by Olerud to make it 7–5. And then me. I was squeezing my bat handle so hard that sap was coming out of the other end. Smoltz, in turn, was feeling challenged, and he responded by challenging *me*. With fastballs, that is. Bear in mind, Smoltz had enough stuff and control that he could throw a good breaking ball for a strike in any count. That had been verified for me when I caught him over the first two innings of the 1996 All-Star Game. I thought at the time, this guy's good. He was also one of the most intensely competitive pitchers I ever faced. As Olerud took his lead at first and I dug in representing the tying run, *that* was the reason for all the fastballs that Smoltz kept bringing and I kept fouling off. I knew he wasn't going to give in and send up a breaking ball, and that was fine with me. In fact, I loved it when pitchers threw down the gauntlet. It was a rush.

I've hit longer home runs than that one, but none that felt better, through and through. The game was tied.

In the top of the eighth, Melvin Mora put us ahead, 8–7, with an RBI single. In the bottom, the Braves brought in Otis Nixon, an old pal of mine from the Dodgers, to pinch-run for Eddie Perez against John Franco. As great as Franco was, and as close a friend as he was for a while there—like Olerud, he was a great help in guiding me through the challenges and pressures of New York—I have to say that I didn't enjoy catching him with a speedy runner on first. Johnny's best pitch was a kind of fading changeup, and I could never throw anybody out on that damn thing. In retrospect, I probably shouldn't have even tried to get Nixon. My throw ended up in center field, Nixon scooted to third, and Brian Hunter drove him in with a single to tie the game. I made the first out in the ninth against Rocker, and then Bobby put me out of my misery. He brought in Pratt to take over for me in a double switch.

Pratt had been uncanny in his reserve role, and once again, he came through, putting us ahead in the top of the tenth with a sacrifice fly that scored Benny Agbayani. In the bottom of the tenth, Ozzie Guillen singled in Andruw Jones to retie it. As Henderson and Bonilla played cards in the clubhouse, our memorable season ended in the eleventh, with Kenny Rogers on the mound. Gerald Williams led off with a double and Rogers intentionally walked both Chipper Jones and Brian Jordan to load the bases. Then he *un*intentionally walked Andruw Jones, and that was it.

I couldn't believe it when Atlanta got swept by the Yankees. It's often been said that the Braves underachieved by losing four out of five World Series and failing to get that far nine other times (after winning division championships) in their remarkable fifteen-year run (remember, there was no postseason in 1994). And that may be so, I suppose. But I prefer to remember them for all the games and titles they *did* win. The Braves were the worthiest opponent of my time.

That said, they could sure screw up a good summer. After they got us in game six, I was so disconsolate that I couldn't even fly back with the team. Instead, I rented a car, cranked up the music, and just started driving west through Georgia, Alabama, Mississippi, and Louisiana, checking out Civil War sites—loved Vicksburg—and fattening up at greasy spoons. I didn't tell anybody but Danny. I just needed to get the hell away.

My father, Vince, with his mom, Elizabeth, the daughter of Italian immigrants. Dad would take us to her house on Sunday afternoons—especially if the weather was nice—then he'd drop off my brothers and haul me out to a ball field for batting practice.

My mother, Veronica—everybody calls her Roni—was a nurse before she met my father. While Dad groomed me to hit a baseball, Mom took care of most everything else, seeing to it that I, like my brothers, was steeped in conservative Catholic values.

We got our season tickets at Veterans Stadium in 1976, and our seats were perfectly located along the third-base line, where I could study the movements of my hero, Mike Schmidt. He was my inspiration and role model. My brother Vince (left) and I had our picture taken with him that year on Fan Appreciation Day.

In 1977, the Dodgers clinched the National League pennant in Philadelphia. Tommy Lasorda arranged for Vince (left) and me to come down to the clubhouse for the postgame celebration. We became a part of it when Dusty Baker lifted us up to share the moment.

When you're ten years old—Vince was eleven (I was always bigger)—and your dad is a good friend of Tommy Lasorda, you get a Dodger uniform for Christmas.

In the basement of our house in Phoenixville, my father propped a mattress against the wall so I could hit and throw baseballs into it. He had plenty of gimmicks, and most of them worked.

When I was twelve, I was the Dodgers' batboy whenever they came to Veterans Stadium. My brothers Danny (left) and Vince got to hang around. I was beginning to realize the advantages that knowing Lasorda would provide me.

By the time I was sixteen, I was a serious student of the Ted Williams approach to hitting. I'd read his book countless times. So I felt like the luckiest kid on the planet when Williams, at the suggestion of local scout Eddie Liberatore, actually came out to our house in Phoenixville to watch me hit in the batting cage that my dad had built in the backyard. "I don't think I hit the ball as good as he does when I was sixteen," Williams said. "I'm not shittin' ya."

My brothers help me celebrate my birthday at our new home in Valley Forge. Front: Dan, me, and Tommy (who is officially Lasorda's godson). Back: Tony and Vince.

As a freshman at the University of Miami, I was known by my teammates as the best five o'clock hitter in the country. That meant I crushed the ball in batting practice, but games were a different story. After one year I transferred to Miami-Dade North, a community college.

After being called up to the Dodgers at the end of the 1992 season, I played for the Sun Cities Solar Sox in the inaugural year of the Arizona Fall League. It was there that I experienced my first big-league heartbreak.

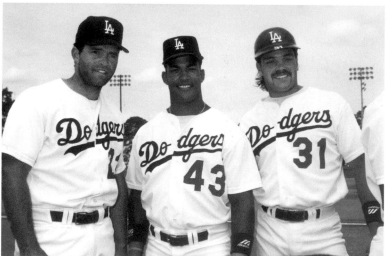

Eric Karros (left), my best friend in the game and the guy who showed me the ropes in Los Angeles, started a string of five straight Rookie of the Year awards for the Dodgers, from 1992 to 1996. I was second in line and Raul Mondesi (center) followed me. Then came Hideo Nomo and Todd Hollandsworth. (© Ken Davidoff/www.oldrockphoto.com)

After winning the Rookie of the Year award in
1993, I was honored at a restaurant in Philadelphia.
Curt Schilling and Bobby Bonilla spoke, and my
grandmother Mary Horenci, my mom's mom, took in
the festivities.

It's hard to imagine a pair
of brothers more devoted to
each other than Pedro (left)
and Ramon Martinez. Pedro
and I joined the Dodgers in
September 1992, and both
Martinezes were devastated
when the club traded him
after the 1993 season. I
caught Ramon's no-hitter in
1995, but he and I frequently
clashed, which meant that
Pedro and I had our problems
as well. (© Focus on Sport/
Getty Images)

I'm getting ready to catch Tom Candiotti. You can tell because I'm wearing my knuckleball mitt. Another clue is the look on my face, like I'm thinking hard about something, probably how I can get him to throw fastballs. (© Otto Greule/ Allsport/Getty Images)

For the record, Tommy Lasorda was not my godfather. But he was a godsend to me, collaborating with his friend my father to chart my course to the Dodgers, where he was my manager and biggest advocate. This scene is from August 1997, the day the Dodgers retired Tommy's jersey. Less than a year later, our relationship was complicated by my trade to the Florida Marlins. (© AP Photo/Mark J. Terrill)

My predecessor, Mike Scioscia, caught nearly 1,400 games for the Dodgers and was greatly respected by his teammates. Knowing that I was ticketed to take his job, Scioscia nevertheless helped me in any way he could. (© Rich Pilling/ MLB Photos via Getty Images)

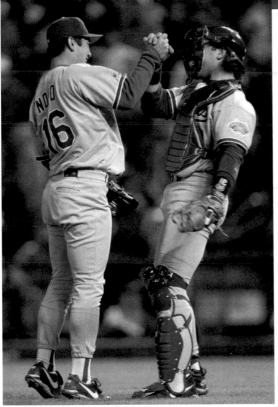

Catching Hideo Nomo's no-hitter in 1996 was one of the highlights of my career. In spite of a slippery mound at Coors Field, his forkball was unhittable that night. A game like that is a catcher's dream. My high regard for Nomo made it even sweeter. (© AP Photo/David Zalubowski)

At the ballpark in which I practically grew up—Veterans Stadium in Philadelphia—I caught the ceremonial first pitch of the 1996 All-Star Game from my boyhood idol, Mike Schmidt. Then I homered, doubled, and won the MVP trophy as we beat the American League, 6–0. Afterward, I told the media that the award was a tribute to my father, who was very much in his glory that night. (© Al Bello/Allsport/Getty Images)

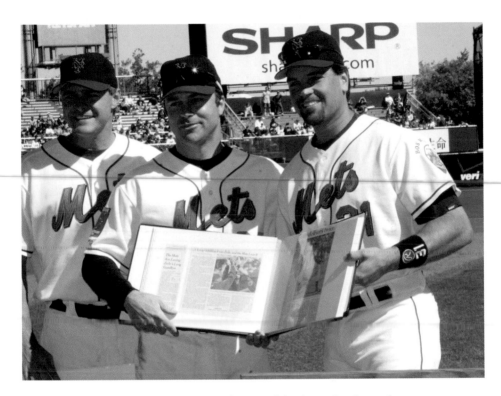

Al Leiter (left) came through with one of the best clutch pitching performances I ever caught when he shut out the Reds in our sudden-death game in Cincinnati in 1999, sending us into the playoffs. He also rose to the occasion in his showdowns with Roger Clemens and the Yankees. Todd Zeile (center) joined me in the gigantic trade from the Dodgers to the Marlins in 1998. We were reunited with the Mets in 2000, and again with the Mets in 2004. (© Barry Talesnick/Globe Photos/ZUMAPRESS.com/ Newscom.com)

When I came to bat against Roger Clemens in the second inning of a game at Yankee Stadium on July 8, 2000, I was seven for twelve against him in my career, including home runs in our three previous encounters, the most recent a grand slam. On an 0–1 count, Clemens hit me in the head with a fastball. I was very fortunate to come away with only a minor concussion. That's our trainer, Fred Hina, attending to me while our manager, Bobby Valentine (no. 2), looks on anxiously. Talking to reporters after the game, I shared my opinion that Clemens had purposely thrown at my head. (© Bernie Nunez/ REUTERS/Landov)

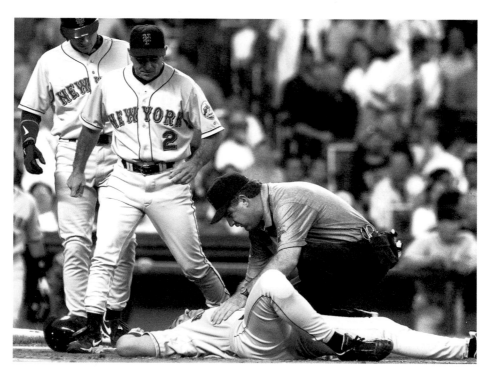

After Clemens beaned me, the next time we faced off was in that year's World Series, game two at Yankee Stadium. In the first inning, he jammed me with a two-strike fastball, and the bat blew into three pieces. I wasn't sure where the ball was (it was well foul, in the direction of the Yankees' dugout), so, with the fractured handle in my hand, I started toward first base. Meanwhile, the splintered barrel bounced Roger's way. He picked it up and fired it at my feet. I didn't even see it coming. Confused, I turned toward the mound, ready to throw a punch, and asked Roger what his problem was. He said he thought the bat was the ball. That wasn't what I was expecting to hear and it stopped me cold. The heavyweight fight that everybody seemed to be lusting for never happened. (Top left: © AP Photo/Mark Lennihan; top right: © Peter Morgan/REUTERS/ Landov; bottom left: © Matt Campbell/AFP/Getty Images; bottom right: © New York Daily News Archive via Getty Images)

STAR & STRIPES

DAILY NEWS
Sports
'S NO.1 SPORTS SECTION

Piazza, Mets sink Braves in emotional return home

Mike Piazza points skyward after eighth-inning homer rallies Mets past Braves, 3-2, on patriotic and dramatic night at Shea as baseball returns to city. Win pulls Mets within 4½ games of first-place Atlanta.   **Pages 62-64**

RIVERA FOR THE BIRDS
Orioles rally in ninth to top Yanks — McCarron, Pages 65-66

Ten days after 9/11, we played the first baseball game in New York City since the devastation at the Twin Towers. The Atlanta Braves led 2–1 in the eighth inning when, with Desi Relaford pinch-running at first base for Edgardo Alfonzo, I sent a fastball from Steve Karsay over the center-field fence. The whole stadium seemed to be rocking back and forth in a giant group hug as we held on to win, 3–2. It was the most emotion, and the most gratification, I've ever experienced on a playing field. That poignant night proved to me that baseball is far more than just a game. (© New York Daily News Archive via Getty Images)

Playing for Bobby Valentine was an adventure unto itself. There were not many dull moments. Bobby would tick me off on a regular basis and just as often leave me shaking my head—I had plenty of company in that respect—but I considered him an excellent manager nevertheless. I'll say this: he could make you smile. In a lot of ways, he reminded me of his mentor and mine, Tommy Lasorda. (© Doug Kanter/AFP/Getty Images)

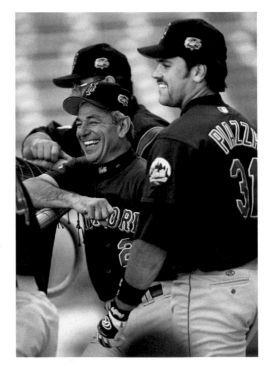

In 2004, six weeks after breaking Carlton Fisk's record for home runs by a catcher, I was humbled by a ceremony that brought the greatest living catchers to Shea Stadium—from left to right, Gary Carter, Johnny Bench, Fisk, Yogi Berra, and Pudge Rodriguez, who was playing against us that night for the Detroit Tigers. I considered the occasion an observance of the toughest position on the field. (© AP Photo/Bill Kostroun)

In January 2005, amid a whole lot of pink roses at St. Jude Catholic Church in Miami, I married the love of my life, Alicia Rickter.

I had the privilege of catching Tom Seaver's last pitch at the closing ceremony for Shea Stadium, after the final game of the 2008 season—my first season in retirement. Seaver remains the only member of the Hall of Fame who was inducted as a Met. I'd love to join him someday. (© George Napolitano/FilmMagic/ Getty Images)

Every summer, we take the girls (Nicoletta, in my arms, and Paulina) on a long vacation to Southern California to be near both Alicia's family and the beach—in this case, Santa Monica.

CHAPTER SEVENTEEN

A baseball team is a social circle. For at least seven months of the year, the players dress in the same rooms as each other, shower in the same showers, fly in the same planes, drink in the same bars, spit in the same dugouts, argue with the same umpires, complain about the same managers, get misquoted by the same writers, celebrate the same victories, and curse the same defeats. As it happened, our Mets clubs—the ones around the turn of the century, in particular—were uncommonly companionable. Groups of eight or ten of us would frequently sit around a table with glasses of wine and shoot the shit about the game, among other things. A carload or two would go out for karaoke, and I'd get it started with "Welcome to the Jungle." We'd rent out rooms to watch championship fights together; even Bobby would come.

I've found it wise, though, not to get too attached. With rare exceptions, baseball relationships are short-lived. Whether it's by trade, free agency, retirement, jealousy, disagreement, marriage, or no particular reason at all, we inevitably go our separate ways. Eric Karros remains my best friend in the game, but I rarely speak to him anymore; we live on opposite coasts. I enjoy the company of Al Leiter, but our paths seldom intersect. I see Johnny Franco on occasion, but it isn't the same.

My connection with Rickey Henderson lasted just over a year. The Mets released Rickey in May 2000, which meant that he helped us to the playoffs in his only full season with the ball club. He was instrumental in not only getting us there, but in how the playoff shares—the bonuses earned from MLB for each postseason series—were divided. The shares meeting is always an interesting exercise in human dynamics, sort of a microcosm of democracy. Rickey was the most generous guy I ever played with, and whenever the discussion came around to what we should give one of the fringe people—whether it was a minor leaguer who came up for a few days or the parking lot attendant—Rickey would shout out, "Full share!" We'd argue for

a while and he'd say, "Fuck that! You can change somebody's life!" I admired
Rickey's heart, but I usually came down somewhere in the middle.

Meanwhile, with Olerud gone, I'd lobbied hard for the Mets to sign my
old cohort, Todd Zeile, to play first base, which they did. As an example
of the fluid nature of baseball relationships . . . Zeile and I had been good
friends in Los Angeles and briefly in Florida. In his absence, in 1999, I'd
taken Robin Ventura under my wing. Robin, who had spent ten years with
the White Sox, was new to the Mets and funny as hell, a great storyteller.
Some of his best gags involved his old hitting coach, Walt Hriniak, who had
become a sort of baseball cult hero for his work with Wade Boggs. Robin
kept me laughing with Hriniak stories of "Boggsie," "green cathedrals," and
old-school stuff like telling opposing pitchers, as they walked by the batting
cage, that "we're getting ready for your ass." Not surprisingly, when Zeile
came to New York, he fell in with Robin and me. But Todd and Robin were
both married, and they had more in common with each other than they did
with me. I was the odd man out.

Generally, I enjoyed hanging around with married guys, because I
learned from them; but it always seemed to me that married players were
somehow a little less motivated—a little more satisfied, perhaps—than single guys. On the road, for instance, Todd and Robin might lie around by the
swimming pool until the early afternoon, something I'd never do and never
tell them *not* to do. In our case, another point of departure emerged when
several of us invested in a movie, *Dirty Deeds*, that Zeile was involved with
as a producer. It's not in my DNA to take my money lightly, and I didn't get
much of a kick out of losing it. I grumbled. Mostly I was angry at myself for
investing unwisely and ignoring the time-tested advice about doing business
with friends. It was a teaching moment. It also made me a little more savvy,
movie-wise, in a way that would later come in handy.

Ventura and I, however, remain linked by a dubious distinction. On
March 30, 2000, the two of us became the first players to go 0 for 5 in a
major-league game played outside North America.

We opened the century in Tokyo, playing exhibition games against the
Yomiuri Giants and Seibu Lions—whose star, Kaz Matsui, the Mets would
sign three years later, making him the first Japanese infielder to jump to the
major leagues—and two games that counted against the Cubs. Hideo Nomo
had given me a good name in Japan, and I enjoyed it there, but not excessively. I left that job to Matty Franco, a pinch hitter and utility guy. One
day, Matty assured me that, the night before, he and his gang had "brought
Tokyo to its knees."

For what it's worth, I can say that I hit a home run in the first major-league game played off the continent, though not before Shane Andrews of the Cubs. We lost that game and won the next one, when Ventura and I contributed our collective 0 for 10 in the middle of the order.

We played at that running-in-place pace for about the first month and a half, getting a lot of production out of Derek Bell, a funny man and veteran outfielder who had come over with Mike Hampton in a trade with Houston. Derek was a Florida guy who had his own style. His pants covered his shoes and he sported an oversize, old-school jersey. In the year he spent with the Mets, he lived on a boat he docked off the East Side. I might go so far as to say that Bell was our MVP for the first half of the season.

For me, however, it was a mixed bag. The good news was that I was hitting to all fields. The bad news was that I was *throwing* to all fields, too. A May game against Arizona was a prime example. I cracked a two-run homer to drive in the winning runs, and the Diamondbacks stole seven bases.

Mechanically, my throwing was all out of whack. I'd missed a few games with a right-elbow injury after Todd Helton of the Rockies crashed into me at home plate, and that surely didn't help the situation; but it was no excuse. For a catcher, getting run over at the plate simply comes with the territory.

That aspect of the game ultimately emerged as a point of controversy when Buster Posey, the outstanding young catcher of the Giants—who were the defending world champions at the time—got the worst of a collision with Scott Cousins of the Marlins in May 2011. The result was a gruesome injury to Posey's leg that ended his season more than four months early.

Cousins put his shoulder into Posey, knocking him backward, and there was an outcry from fans and critics who thought it was a dirty hit; but I didn't see it that way. There's a difference between a runner attempting to bowl over a catcher to knock the ball loose—which Cousins did—and one who is intent upon inflicting pain. I agree, absolutely, that an umpire should call a runner out if he thinks the guy is deliberately trying to hurt the catcher. I'd label it the "dirty slide rule" and base it on such things as whether the runner had some of the plate available to him and whether the catcher was actually in possession of the ball. It wouldn't bother me at all to see some kind of suspension attached to a dirty, dangerous play, because there's no place in the game for it. That said, one size doesn't fit all; every situation is a little bit different. I'd leave the call up to the umpire's discretion rather than implementing any kind of all-encompassing legislation. The commissioner's office has already neutered the sport too much in the area of retaliation. Enough's enough. Let the game play out.

The most egregious hit I ever took was the one in 1998 from Michael Tucker, which I thought was more out of line than the hard lick that Brian Jordan—another Brave—put on me in the 1999 playoffs. Until the Tucker play, the worst had been perpetrated by *another* Brave, Mike Kelly, in April 1994, when he came home in the tenth inning on a single to right by Jeff Blauser. I took the throw a couple of feet behind the plate, which made it easy for Kelly to score, but he came after me anyway with a late slide. I was able to get out of the way somewhat and avoid an injury, but to me, that's the kind of play that should carry repercussions. I hadn't put myself in a precarious or vulnerable circumstance.

In any scenario at the plate, a lot depends on variables, such as where the throw comes in. I thought that Posey's injury, as Johnny Bench said, was due mostly to him being inadvertently out of position. It was a short-hop throw and he got a little twisted up. His ankle was caught underneath him and couldn't withstand the impact. It was a horrible situation—but not Cousins's fault or the game's. I'm not being critical of Posey, either; he's a highly competitive athlete who was doing what he felt he had to do in the heat of a ball game. But, generally speaking, there are safeguards a catcher can observe on plays at the plate.

The biggest one is to prepare ahead of time. Know the runner, the fielder's arm, and the situation. If Rey Ordonez was making the throw, I could anticipate exactly where it would be coming in. Jody Reed, not so much. If it's the winning run in extra innings, yeah, you have to block the plate. But if it's the first run of the game in the top of the second, I'm going to give the runner a little bit of a lane to slide in—something I learned from Mike Scioscia, who was as tough as they came. In that situation, I owe it to my teammates to keep myself out of harm's way, if I can, because I know, and they know, that I can change the game later with my bat.

More than any other position, catching is rife with those kinds of complications. It's a grueling, tiring trade-off, a hazardous occupation that's inherently detrimental to hitting. But in an odd sort of way, my hitting also hurt my defense at times: It kept me in the lineup when otherwise I shouldn't or wouldn't have been.

When my throwing suffered in 2000, the talk started up about moving me to first base. That wasn't an option I embraced. Even though I'd lost confidence in my throwing, I'd gained it in my ability to handle a game. I liked being in charge and *needed* that feeling. My father urged me constantly to take ground balls at first base during infield practice, but it didn't work for me. In my mind, when I was no longer able to catch, I'd be a designated hitter. I just couldn't see me at first base, and neither could Bobby. Remember when I was in college and my dad took me to Port Charlotte, Florida, so I could work out for Bobby when he was managing the Rangers? Well, Bobby remembered it, too. He remembered watching me take ground balls at first base and thinking I had no chance of ever playing that position in the major leagues. "I always had that vision of Mike in Port Charlotte," he said.

And so, in early June, still catching and determined to do better, I was bonked again by a backswing. This time, it was on my dome, by Gary Sheffield, of all people. It actually cut my head open and bled—a minor concussion and some major fogginess. I was batting .372 at the time. I missed only one game, but a week later was down to .360 heading into a weekend series in the Bronx, with Roger Clemens starting the first game for the Yankees.

You could pretty much count on two things happening when Clemens pitched against the Mets. Al Leiter was going to beat him and I was going to take him deep. It had happened twice in 1999, and it was more of the same, in the extreme, on June 9, 2000.

There was no score in the third when I came up with the bases loaded and nobody out. Clemens had struck me out looking the first time around, but I was still figuring on laying off the split-fingered fastball and squaring-up a slider. And so it happened on a 1-0 count. I knew immediately that the ball was gone, and flipped my bat as it cleared the head of Bernie Williams and the 408-foot mark on the center-field fence—only the second grand slam Clemens had given up in his seventeen seasons.

I singled in the fourth but just missed the privilege of facing Clemens again in the sixth. Edgardo Alfonzo, the batter in front of me, chased him with a two-run homer to make it 7–2, on the way to a 12–2 final. The Yankee fans booed the hell out of Clemens as he ambled off the field. Of course, he was madder than they were.

Another month would go by before I felt the full effect of his rage.

The Yankee series put me into a groove that produced a twenty-one-game hitting streak and a fifteen-game RBI streak, which was only two off the all-time record. I did sit out a game in that stretch, though, after Preston Wilson of the Marlins banged me on the left elbow with *his* backswing.

On a Thursday night at the end of June, as the conclusion of a long home stand, we finally played the Braves for the first time that season, and the first time since John Rocker's infamous off-season quotes in *Sports Illustrated*, when he insulted New York, gays, blacks, women, foreigners, and—this part was nothing new, of course—Mets fans. (A little Rocker sampler, courtesy of *SI*: "Imagine having to take the [Number] 7 train to the ballpark, looking like you're [riding through] Beirut next to some kid with purple hair next to some queer with AIDS right next to some dude who just got out of jail for the fourth time right next to some 20-year-old mom with four kids. . . . The biggest thing I don't like about New York are the foreigners. I'm not a very big fan of foreigners. You can walk an entire block in Times Square and not hear anybody speaking English. Asians and Koreans and Vietnamese and Indians and Russians and Spanish people and everything up there. How the hell did they get in this country? . . . Nowhere else in the country do people spit at you, throw bottles at you, throw quarters at you, throw batteries at you and say, 'Hey, I did your mother last night—she's a whore.' I talked about what degenerates they were, and they proved me right.") There were seven hundred police officers on hand for the occasion, and a protective cover over the Atlanta bullpen. He received the traditional Rocker welcome when he entered the game in the eighth—"Ass-hole! Ass-hole!"—and chopped us down in order as the Braves won the opener of a four-game series, 6–4.

They jumped on us again the next night and were leading 8–1 in the eighth inning when, as if we refused to take it anymore—I wish baseball were that simple—we rose up against their bullpen. Unfortunately, Rocker was not involved, but we didn't mind roughing up Don Wengert, Kerry Ligtenberg, and Terry Mulholland. We took out a lot of pent-up frustration on those dudes—scored ten runs in the inning, nine of them with two outs, topped off by my three-run homer against Mulholland. Benitez closed out an 11–8 victory. For us, it was a rare taste of Atlanta blood, and worked up our appetite for more of it. Never mind that the Braves had Greg Maddux pitching the Saturday game.

As great as he was, Maddux wasn't the type of pitcher who gave a team, or a batter, a sense of foreboding. Nobody feared his fastball, which was what he threw most. On the other hand, not many guys *hit* his fastball, either. At least, not hard. He'd give you that feel-good 0-for-4, when you're always thinking that you *just missed* squaring one up. I had actually handled Maddux fairly well early in my career, before he figured me out. When he realized that I liked to take the first pitch, I found myself chronically behind in the count against him. That was his MO, anyway. He'd pour in strike one, then start varying the speed and location of his fastball, mixing in changeups. To me, the real test of a true pitcher is the ability, and the confidence, to take something off his pitches, as well as put a little extra something *on* them from time to time. Maddux was the master of that. For a while there, he was also the master of *me*.

Finally, Zeile suggested that, since Maddux was obviously a special case,

I set aside my usual approach and start going after the first pitch. With that, the game was on. As soon as he recognized that I had adjusted, which didn't take long, Maddux would throw ball one—just missing, of course—then nibble the corners with seemingly random velocities. We thought right along with each other, pitch for pitch, corner for corner. That's the swordfight within the game, the personal duel, the clash of skills and wits that makes baseball so damn much fun. When all was said and done, I'd gone to the plate eighty-one times against Maddux over the course of fourteen years, and hit .238, with four homers. The only pitcher I saw more of was Tom Glavine, which suited me just fine. As a general rule, I preferred batting against the best, most accomplished starting pitchers. We were both fully prepared for each other, and all too familiar. Typically, I had more trouble with the relief specialists, the one-trick ponies whose specific job it was to march into the game and get me out. They seemed to be readier than I was for the showdowns; more focused on them. You get only one chance against those guys.

If I'd had only one chance against Maddux on that particular Saturday, he'd have won the battle. I struck out in the first inning—struck out, in fact, on a wild pitch, which enabled Derek Bell to score. In the second, though, I solved him for a two-out, two-run homer, which capped off a six-run inning and got him out of the game. Leiter had no such trouble, and we rolled, 9–1.

Concerning Glavine, who pitched Sunday, I didn't need advice from Zeile or anyone else. For my career, I batted .343 against him in ninety plate appearances, with six home runs. (Jason Schmidt and Pedro Martinez were the only other pitchers off whom I hit that many.) When the umpires made Glavine throw the ball over the plate, I tended to like the results. But there were times against him when I took called strikes that, from where I stood, looked to be outside by the length of a football. Bear in mind, this was before MLB implemented the QuesTec system of charting pitch location, which was used to evaluate umpires. The umps were clearly generous with Maddux and Glavine, but I don't begrudge it. They had earned the benefit of the doubt. Anyway, I homered off Glavine in the final game of the set, but, hot as we'd been for two days, he beat us, as usual, 10–2.

We then made a quick trip to Florida, where my RBI streak ended in the first game, a 2-0 loss. For the second, on the Fourth of July, I was not in the lineup. As well as I was swinging the bat—my hitting streak was at twenty-one games—I was due for the day off. But in the ninth inning, when we trailed 9–8 with one out and one on against the Marlins' right-handed closer, Antonio Alfonseca, Bobby sent me up to pinch-hit for Joe McEwing, who was playing left field. I was a little surprised that he would jeopardize my streak in that manner, but it was bad form to say so and I'm sure Bobby was aware of that. Sometimes, I think, he just liked to remind us—especially *me*—that he was in control. But I also understood that, given the pressures of New York, he was certain to take some heat if he lost a one-run game without getting me to the plate. I grounded into a force-out.

We salvaged a win the next night, then flew right back home. There were four more games to play against the Yankees.

In the June series, we'd been rained out of the Sunday game at Yankee Stadium, which would be made up as part of an unusual day-night, two-venue doubleheader on Saturday, July 8. The first game was held at Shea, and the Yankees won it with Dwight Gooden pitching, 4–2. We then sat down for a team meal before most of the players boarded the bus for a motorcade across the bridge to Yankee Stadium, with police escorts and the whole shebang.

Since I lived in New Jersey, I wanted my car with me, so I drove over on my own. New York traffic is usually sufficient to take your mind off anything else, but for some reason, as I mulled over my game plan for Roger Clemens in the nightcap—unfortunately, our rotation wasn't set up for Leiter to oppose him this time—I couldn't shake the odd sensations in the atmosphere. To me, the entire day had a weird-energy, full-moon feel to it. The mood only thickened when, in the first inning, Clemens buzzed a pitch past the nose of our leadoff batter, Lenny Harris.

I was still picking up the peculiar vibe when I stepped in to lead off the second. In spite of my uneasiness, though, there was some comfort in the knowledge that, over the three years in which I'd faced Roger during interleague play, I was seven for twelve against him, with three home runs. And so, with a little sense of disdain—my way of saying, go ahead, show me what you've got, big boy—I took strike one right down the middle.

Somehow, like everything else from the time I got up that morning, it didn't feel right. I recall thinking, there's something strange going on here. Sometimes you just get an inexplicable premonition, and this was one of those times. It popped into my head to stay loose.

What I remember next is a two-seam fastball headed straight for my face. That vision is burned into my memory. Even if it weren't, it would have revisited me, year after year, during the Subway Series, when the stations and networks—mostly ESPN—replayed that infamous beanball to a point that, from my perspective, seemed sensationalized and just plain gross. I was repulsed by the overhyping. Of course, that probably had to do with the sickening feeling it brought back every time.

I truly believe that if I hadn't gotten my head down at the last instant, Clemens's two-seamer would have struck me in the eye and possibly killed me. Or led to a situation similar to that of Tony Conigliaro, who was hit in the cheekbone in 1967, missed a year and a half of baseball, and played only twenty-one games after the age of twenty-six, retiring early due to a permanent loss of vision. It was a deadly pitch that Roger hurled my way.

A four-seam fastball will come straight at you, and a hitter knows which way to move to get out of its path. It's predictable and consequently less dangerous than the type of pitch that bores in on a batter. A two-seamer is like a heat-seeking missile. Typically, it's a slightly less fast fastball that is kept low to produce a ground ball. That's the purpose of it. Sometimes, if a pitcher is trying to move a batter off the plate with a two-seamer, it'll shoot in like it's going to hit you in the back foot. But a *high* two-seamer just follows you. When I saw the ball come out of Clemens's hand—and like I said, I always saw it clearly when he was pitching—I was frozen until that very last moment, when I ducked just enough to get some protection from the front of my helmet.

I crumpled immediately, landing on my back, but I don't believe I ever lost consciousness. Fred Hina got out there right away, and Bobby with him, and when I looked up it felt like my face was two feet in front of the rest of my head. John Stearns, our bench coach, was screaming and cussing at Clemens, who stood there with his hands on his knees. I was a little shaky walking up the tunnel to the clubhouse. One of the Yankees' doctors was waiting there for me, to make sure there was no need for emergency measures.

Our half of the inning must have ended quickly—Clemens was so shaken up that he retired the next seven batters—because, before the doctor even took a look at me, he handed over the telephone and said that Roger wanted to talk to me. I grabbed it, threw it, and said, "Tell him to go fuck himself."

Roger Clemens had near-perfect control. I wouldn't have batted an eye if he had just brushed me off the plate—of course, that's what he said he was trying to do—and I wouldn't have thought twice about it even if he'd put the ball in my ribs. But to stick one in my forehead . . . that's another story altogether. Clemens had always come across to me as the playground bully, huffing and puffing and snorting and yelling at batters, doing whatever he could to intimidate them. Way back when Roger was named MVP in 1986, as the ace of the Red Sox, Hank Aaron expressed his opinion that pitchers shouldn't be eligible for the MVP award because they don't play every day. Clemens's response was "I wish he were still playing. I'd probably crack his head open to show him how valuable I was." I had every reason to believe that Clemens was throwing at my head, and I'll be damned if I was going to take his phone call before the doctor could even check me out.

A few minutes later, I was driven to the hospital, where X-rays showed just a minor concussion. So I went back to Yankee Stadium, and after the game, our PR director, Jay Horwitz, knowing that the media would swarm me in the clubhouse, suggested that we move to a separate room to accommodate them. That was fine with me, because I didn't want to answer the same question a couple of dozen times and I didn't want my teammates to be inconvenienced by the mob. Naturally, I was criticized for being a prima donna by holding my own press conference. In *The Yankee Years*, by Joe Torre and Tom Verducci, Clemens himself is quoted as saying (through Brian McNamee, the Yankees' assistant strength coach and Clemens's principal accuser in the steroids controversy), "Who gets hit and has a press conference?" (On the same page, again through McNamee, there is also a damning, very perplexing quote attributed to John Franco. Something about me being "a pussy." When asked about it for this book, Franco stated, "That's so far from the truth. I would never say that to Brian McNamee. I met him once at a St. John's baseball dinner. I never even talked to him about that. I would never say that about a teammate.")

At the so-called press conference, I stated my firm belief that Clemens had thrown at my head, and was criticized for that, too. A year later, Don Zimmer, who was coaching for the Yankees, took me to task in an interview with *Esquire*. He said, "Piazza made a little man out of himself. I don't care who knows it, I lost a little respect for Piazza." I suppose Zimmer was sticking up for some old-time baseball code that he lived by—he was once knocked out for two weeks by a hanging curveball and woke with four silver buttons in his skull, which was the impetus for pro players wearing batting helmets—but I can't respect a custom that tolerates a man throwing a baseball ninety-two miles an hour at another man's head . . . and doesn't tolerate an honest response to it. I might also point out that, in Zimmer's day, there were other ways to reply. Even in the American League, the pitcher had to bat.

Clemens pitched into the eighth inning that night and beat us, 4–2. Sunday, back at Shea, I watched as Mike Hampton combined with Armando Benitez to shut down the Evil Empire, 2–0.

The All-Star Game was two days later. I thought it best to sit it out.

On the first night after the all-star break, when I'd had four days to clear the mist between my ears, we drew the Red Sox and, wouldn't you know it, Pedro Martinez, the *other* hard-throwing, right-handed, superstar pitcher who had hit me after I'd been hitting him. This time, neither of us hit the other. I did single in the eighth off Rich Garces to drive in a run and put us up, 3–2, but Boston won the game on a two-run double by Brian Daubach with two outs in the bottom of the ninth.

There's always a little trepidation when you first come back from a beaning, and I found some relief in surviving Pedro. The next night, as the designated hitter, I tied the game in the fourth inning with a home run off Pete Schourek, and in the eighth, with Alfonzo on, put us ahead for good, 5–4, by driving a curveball from Derek Lowe off one of the giant Coke bottles on the light tower above the Green Monster. I went deep again against Garces in the ninth inning of the finale—I could get used to Fenway Park—but *Ramon* Martinez beat us to take the series. Boston was the beginning of a brutal eleven-game road trip that ended with two more losses in Atlanta. It was late July and we were six games behind the Braves.

August, for me, was a gauntlet. In Arizona, I sprained my medial collateral ligament when I turned abruptly to argue being called out at first. In Los Angeles, I slid into an outcropping of concrete trying to catch a foul pop fly, messing up my hip, and, going after another one, landed on my head in the box seats. At Shea against the Diamondbacks, our center fielder, Jay Payton, threw out Jay Bell at the plate, and in the process I took a forearm to the face. When I got up, the New York fans were chanting, "MVP! MVP!"

By then, I'd begun to enjoy the favor of the city. For one thing, we were suddenly stringing wins together and making a run at the Braves and the postseason. Along with that, I had gotten into the spirit of New York on the social level.

My informal tradition of in-season girlfriends was still going strong, and this time it was public. I'd met Darlene Bernaola when she was wearing an evening gown at a Playboy party in New York, not long after she and her twin, Carol, who were raised in Peru, had been featured in the January 2000 *Playboy* as the "Playmates of the Millennium." I still had an off-season place in Boynton Beach but was thinking of moving to South Beach (which I did in 2001), and I happened to know that Darlene lived in Miami. So, a couple of weeks later, I called to ask her about the area, using that as an excuse to buy her dinner. Next thing I knew, the season had started and she was practically living with me in New Jersey.

Dating Darlene was one of the more adventurous things I've done on the personal level. Up until then, I'd made an effort to keep my social life conservative and at least relatively private; but it's hard to be inconspicuous when you're dating the Playmate of the Millennium in New York City. (At various times, there had been rumors that I was seeing Jennifer Aniston and Cameron Diaz. I met Jennifer a time or two through her brother, when we worked together on a commercial. He told me she thought I was cute. But that was the extent of it. If I could take credit for dating her, I surely would. The closest I ever got to Cameron Diaz was knowing somebody who knew her.) What's more, the husband of Darlene's sister owned a club in town, and he liked to publicize our visits there to drum up business. Darlene was a hot item in the gossip pages.

I went into the relationship like a hopeless romantic, thinking, what a crazy story. We had each other's initials tattooed on our ankles. I gave her the baseball I hit off Clemens for the grand slam. But once the magic dust wore off, we found we had some serious philosophical differences. Complicating the whole thing was the pressure from my family. The relationship was a little too visible for my mom and dad's tastes, and just not traditional enough. By late summer, we were probably ready to break up, but I was leery of doing it then: I knew it would be in the papers and didn't need the distraction while the team was in the thick of a pennant race. It would have to wait until the season was over.

We pulled even with the Braves at the end of August. In September, true to form, they shook us off. I was dragging, paying the price for a long summer of lumps. The Braves led us by three games going into a late-season series in Atlanta—which meant we had a chance to catch up with them again—and proceeded to manhandle us the first two nights.

While we were still in good shape for the wildcard, those two losses didn't sit well with Bobby. The Braves had swept us in late September the previous two years, and he was sick of it. He wanted to do an intervention. So he called a meeting before the third game—which was a Wednesday night ESPN telecast—and screamed at us to get our heads out of our asses. Then, before it broke up, he said something to the effect of "Mike, I don't know if you're tired or if you don't give a fuck, but if you don't want to be in there, let me know."

Deep down, I knew what he was up to. Coming after me was a way to dramatize his message and give it some wow status. I figured he figured that if he tamed me, he'd have the whole team under his thumb. But I didn't give a shit what his strategy was. I wanted, *really* wanted, to kick his fucking ass, right on the spot. Instead, I headed straight to the laundry room looking for something to abuse. Dave Wallace, one of my old mentors with the Dodgers and Bob Apodaca's replacement as the Mets' pitching coach, eased in and tried to calm me down. He said, "What the fuck was that all about?" I couldn't answer. The whole thing felt like an ambush.

The next day, a reporter asked me, "Did Bobby say anything to you in that meeting yesterday?" I totally lied. And the whole time I was thinking, where could he have gotten that information? I don't claim to understand all the inner workings of the universe, but I felt I had a pretty good read on that one. My antenna was in the air, and it was picking up signals from the manager's office. There were plenty of instances like that, and it definitely affected the players' trust in Bobby.

> It's hard for anyone to understand how that dynamic works in a competitive media market like New York, but I can see how Mike and others had the impression that I talked too much to reporters. Sometimes it was probably reality. I might have said things I shouldn't have.
>
> —Bobby Valentine

At the same time, though, nobody—or at least, not many of us—thought he was a bad guy or a bad manager. The fact is, I *liked* Bobby. He was over-the-top sometimes, and probably took himself too seriously most of the time, but he could also be self-effacing in a way that would charm you. Once, we were challenging Scott Rolen with two-strike fastballs, because he was a very good breaking-ball hitter, and he was fighting them off, as he typically did. I looked over into the dugout and Bobby was giving me the sign for a curveball. I put down the curveball sign and Rolen stroked it out of the park. When I got back to the dugout, Bobby just shook his head and said, "Don't listen to me anymore." He could make you smile. The way I saw it, he had his quirks, but in the end he was just Bobby, the same as Tommy had just been Tommy. I was well trained for him.

We went ahead and beat the Braves on the night after the meeting and I homered in the eighth inning off Mike Remlinger, which Bobby probably thought was *his* doing. That was the game in which Chris Berman kept calling me Honest Abe because of the shape of my beard. The Dominican players—mainly, Armando Benitez—had brought in a Dominican barber to cut their hair, and I used the guy, too, because he was an artist. Unlike the Dodgers, the Mets had no policy restricting hair below the lower lip, which hadn't really stopped me anyway, so I let this guy go to work on me. He would spray some kind of clear shaving cream on my beard and then use a straight razor to carve in whatever crazy shape I wanted. Ballplayers are all

a little superstitious, and I was just looking for the right facial-hair combination. I hit a home run as soon as I went to the Lincoln look, so I kept it
for a while. I thought it looked pretty cool, actually. It also paid tribute to a
couple of my passions—home runs and American history.

The victory got us back on track. We won our last five games and eight
of the last nine to finish one behind the Braves and easily win the wildcard
spot. On a personal level, I felt as though I'd carried the team for significant
stretches—carried it, effectively, to the playoffs—but some of the writers
pointed out that, when the division title was on the line early in the month,
I went four straight games without a hit (we won three of those) and struggled through a two-for-twenty-seven slump.

So, with thirty-eight home runs, 113 RBIs, and a .324 average, I finished
third in the MVP voting behind Jeff Kent and Barry Bonds, teammates with
the Giants, who won three more games than we did. There were at least four
people who thought that, in spite of just 482 official at-bats (Bonds had only
480, but a lot more walks), I was actually the most valuable player in the
National League that year—three of the voters and yours truly.

The Giants happened to be our opponents in the NL division series, and I
was definitely *not* the MVP of that.

San Francisco, playing at home, won the first game, but we were in
control of the second until J. T. Snow hit a three-run, pinch-hit home run
off Benitez in the bottom of the ninth to send it into extra innings. In the
top of the tenth, Darryl Hamilton doubled and Jay Payton came through
with a two-out RBI single to give us back the lead, 5–4. Benitez returned
for the bottom of the tenth, and Armando Rios started it with a single. At
that point, Bobby called in Franco, who had just turned forty and didn't save
many games anymore but still had the stuff and brains to get anybody out. Of
course, Barry Bonds wasn't just anybody, and he came to the plate with two
outs and a runner still on first. The count ran to three and two, game and
possibly the series on the line. As the story goes, I called for a fastball at that
point, thinking that Bonds would be sitting on the changeup, and Franco
shook me off. Johnny wanted to throw his change, no matter what—he had
a good one that night, almost like a screwball—and since he'd saved more
than four hundred games over seventeen seasons, all because he knew what
the hell he was doing, I let the man throw the changeup. It was a classic.
Strike three, called. A lot of the papers alluded to Johnny shaking off the
fastball, and now and then he needles me about still wanting him to throw
it. The only thing is, I don't remember it that way. I remember calling for

the changeup because I knew that's what Franco would be determined to throw in that situation. The replays I've seen don't show him shaking me off. Either way, though, it was a great, gutsy pitch, by a great, gutsy pitcher.

The series then switched to Shea, and Benny Agbayani delivered a colossal home run in the bottom of the thirteenth to put us ahead, two games to one. In game four, I walked with two outs in the first and Ventura came through with a blast. That was more than Bobby Jones would need. He pitched a one-hitter in a 4–0 victory that set us up in the league championship series against the Cardinals. God bless them, they had beaten the Braves.

We started fast in St. Louis. In the first inning of the first game, against Darryl Kile, Timo Perez doubled to lead off, Alfonzo walked, I doubled in a run, and Ventura drove in another with a fly ball. My double—past Placido Polanco at third base, on the first pitch—was especially welcome, considering the funk I'd been in. At least our bench coach, John Stearns, thought so. When I was standing on second, Stearns, who was miked for television, suddenly went off, shouting, "The monster's out of the cage! The monster's out of the cage!" It became a mantra. Meat Loaf—a huge baseball fan—even recorded a song, "The Monster Is Loose!"

Mike Hampton took care of the rest, pretty much, with seven shutout innings, then turned it over to Leiter for game two. The Cardinals' starter was Rick Ankiel, a twenty-one-year-old, phenom lefty who'd been having serious problems with his control. He'd thrown five wild pitches in one inning against the Braves in their division series, an all-time record. As Timo Perez stepped in to lead off, Pat Mahomes came running down from the bullpen, yelling, "Hey, this is the motherfucker with the control problems, isn't it?" Then Ankiel fired his first pitch over Timo's helmet, sending him sprawling, and Mahomes goes, "God*damn!*"

Timo had just been called up for the first time in September and was not exactly a student of the game yet. He didn't know who anybody was, and got up all ticked off, assuming that Ankiel was throwing at him. He ended up taking strike three before the fun started. Alfonzo walked. Then, with me batting, Ankiel threw one in the general direction of the press box and Fonzi went to second. I fouled off a two-two fastball, and Ankiel finally walked me on another fastball to the screen that sent Fonzi to third. Zeile hit a fly ball to bring in Alfonzo, and Ankiel walked Robin on four pitches. Agbayani followed with a double and I scored all the way from second (yes, that's a joke). That was it for Ankiel. He would start only six more games in the major leagues before converting to the outfield.

I homered in the third against Britt Reames, but the Cardinals tied it, 3–3, in the fifth. Ultimately, the hero was again Jay Payton, who ripped a run-scoring, ninth-inning single to center field off Mike Timlin to put us up 6–5. When Benitez held them in the bottom of the inning, we had taken control of the series on the road.

At Shea, the Cardinals beat us in game three, but in the next one, after falling behind 2–0 in the top of the first, we jumped on Kile with back-to-back-to-back doubles by Alfonzo, me, and Ventura, and then another one from Agbayani. Altogether, we scored seven times in the first two innings. I homered in the fourth to put us up 8–3, on the way to a 10–6 victory that left us just one slim win from the Mets' first National League championship since 1986. In game five, we came out hitting, Hampton threw a three-hitter—he was the series MVP—and it was ours, by a score of 7–0.

The clubhouse celebration was positively euphoric. It was an incredible, spontaneous, dreamlike kind of happiness that I'd never before experienced.

We were in the World Series.

Against the Yankees.

CHAPTER EIGHTEEN

Give New York a big story and the city will inevitably make it bigger. The first World Series between the Yankees and Mets was not enough; not even with an irresistible, custom-made nostalgia factor—the flashback to the famous Subway World Series matchups of the 1940s and '50s, the Yankees against the New York Giants and especially the Brooklyn Dodgers.

In 2000, the boroughs were bloodthirsty. It would be the first time Clemens and I had faced off since he hit me in the head. They wanted a cage fight.

To the guys in our clubhouse, however, including me, the personal grudge match was, at best, number three in the pecking order of importance. Number two was taking out the Yankees and changing our image as second fiddles. Number one was winning a World Series, no matter who it came against.

Anyway, Clemens wasn't pitching until game two. In the meantime, we were loose enough, I suppose. The team chartered a couple of buses to the Bronx for game one, and John Franco rode shotgun in the police cruiser that led the way. Ventura—talk about keeping loose!—took batting practice without underwear. Then, about forty minutes before the game started, as I was putting on my road uniform, Bobby walked over and told me to come to his office because somebody in there wanted to say hello. I'll be damned if it wasn't Yogi Berra. What a treat. He made some small talk about the great rivalry between the Yankees and Brooklyn—their four World Series of the fifties occurred in a span of five years—and I didn't have much to offer in return. Since it was already October 21, I said, "We're getting started a little late, aren't we?" And Yogi said, "One year [1955], we played seven games and were done by October the fourth." When I walked out of there, I couldn't wait to get going: Saturday night at Yankee Stadium. Al Leiter versus Andy Pettitte. New York versus New York, for the championship of the world. There was no place in the universe I would rather have been.

That said, I'd have preferred not to be there beyond the ninth inning, under the circumstances. The game was scoreless in the top of the sixth when Timo Perez singled and was on first with two outs as Zeile lifted a long fly ball that bounced off the very top of the wall in left field. Thinking it was going to be a home run, as most of us did, Timo raised his arm in celebration and slowed up just enough to get thrown out on a relay from David Justice to Derek Jeter to Jorge Posada at the plate. We all make mental mistakes—especially as rookies—and I should point out that we might not have been in the World Series if it weren't for Timo; but the fact is, we'd had some momentum going for us, and there was a feeling that we lost it on that killer of a play.

Even so, Leiter had us ahead 3–2 when he left after seven innings. That's how it stood when a double by Kurt Abbott gave us runners on second and third with one out in the top of the ninth. A big hit would put us in great shape, but it would have to come against Mariano Rivera. He overmatched Perez and Alfonzo with that amazing cutter of his, and the damn Yankees tied the game in the bottom of the inning against Benitez, on a sacrifice fly by Chuck Knoblauch. Benitez fanned Jeter to send it into extra innings, but we could do nothing with Mariano or Mike Stanton. The Yankees beat us in the twelfth on Jose Vizcaino's bases-loaded single off Turk Wendell. We were now playing from behind.

On a cold, windy Sunday night, Mike Hampton—not I—was Clemens's opponent in game two. By the time I came up in the first inning, Timo and Fonzi had already struck out. The Rocket was on his game and obviously pumped up to maximum intensity.

In spite of all the flashbulbs popping and the feeding frenzy over Roger and me, the scenario was not as unsettling as that eerie night back in July. I sincerely believed that, with all the hype surrounding the showdown, Clemens wouldn't dare throw at me again. He'd taken a public beating for it the last time and since then had come under more scrutiny for buzzing Alex Rodriguez on consecutive pitches—he fired the ball up around A-Rod's neck—in the ALCS against Seattle. Rodriguez didn't have much to say about it afterward, but Lou Piniella, the Mariners' manager, did. And he wasn't the first manager to complain about Clemens. When Roger pitched for Toronto and hit Jeter and Scott Brosius, Joe Torre himself had been one of those calling him out. Now, with the microscope he was under and the stage he was on, I couldn't imagine him pulling any more of his macho bullshit. On the other hand, Roger was known for working himself into a competitive fever that led to some strange things.

I took strike one, as was my custom against just about everybody but

Greg Maddux. I also took strike two, on the outside corner, which wasn't the plan. Clemens was sharp, all right. I stepped out, blew on my hands, then watched ball one zip by, inside. Then he poured a fastball in on my fists. I tried to fend it off and my thin-handled bat blew apart in two places. About fifteen inches of it stayed in my grip, a fragment dropped in front of the plate like a bad bunt, and the splintered barrel bounced unevenly toward the mound. I didn't know where the ball was—for all I knew, it might have blooped over Tino Martinez's head beyond first base, which wouldn't be un-usual—so I took off running for a step or two, until I realized that I'd sliced the pitch toward the Yankees' dugout.

Right about then, the barrel came whizzing by in front of my feet.

What the hell?

Clemens had fielded it on the big hop and chucked it in my direction, jagged end and all, with plenty of velocity. Stunned, and with the bat handle still in my hand—I'm not sure if I even realized that—I turned toward the mound and walked that way with a purpose, yelling at Clemens, "What's your problem? What the fuck is your problem?"

He said he thought the bat was the *ball*.

Meanwhile, home plate umpire Charlie Reliford was arriving to inter-cept me, and Clemens, with his glove extended like he was asking for a new baseball, turned to him and hollered the same thing—that he thought he was picking up the *ball*. I asked Charlie what Roger was talking about, and all he would say was, "Let's go, let's go."

Both teams were out on the field by this time, and somebody was shout-ing at me to get the fuck back in the batter's box. I couldn't tell who it was. I was yelling back at a voice, pushing my way toward a closer, clearer con-frontation. The fans were howling. There was so much ambiguous energy buzzing around, I couldn't process it all.

My initial intention had been to get to Clemens and throw a punch at his face. It was a strategy that I'd actually mapped out ahead of time. When Robin Ventura had charged Nolan Ryan with his head down, as if to tackle him, that had only exposed Robin. I'd been working with a friend, John Bruno, who was a karate guy, with the express purpose of knowing what to do if Clemens ever threw at me again. I would approach with my fist pulled back. I figured he'd throw his glove out for protection. I'd parry the glove and then get after it.

But there were complications. The least of them was the realization that Clemens was a big guy and I stood a pretty fair chance of getting my ass kicked in front of Yankee Stadium and the world. That was a legitimate concern, but not a compelling one. A bigger factor was the World Series itself. It was the first inning of a critical game from which it would be patently stupid to get ejected. To indulge my anger and sense of revenge without regard for my team and teammates . . . that would simply have been bad baseball.

There was something else holding me back, as well. Leading up to this night, there had been so much public clamoring to see Clemens and me go mano-a-mano, such a loathsome display of bloodlust, that I wanted no part of it for that very reason. It had evolved into a gladiator mentality. It's my job to feed the mob? I have to run out and fight Roger Clemens because the fans *expect* me to? I had no interest in being the people's puppet. Never did. The whole atmosphere just sucked the steam out of me.

On top of all that, the situation occupied a gray zone in my personal rules of engagement. I had no predetermined response for somebody flinging the jagged end of a bat at my feet, but it fell under the general parameters of being thrown at. When that happens, you're seldom certain of the intent. You wait to see the pitcher's reaction. You yell at the guy and check his response. If he yells back, waves you to the mound, spreads his palms, glares at you the wrong way, tells you to get your ass to first base, or in any fashion attempts to intimidate you further, it's on. If he just rubs the ball and looks in the other direction, I was cool with that. Part of the game.

Clemens's reaction was of the latter variety, dragging the whole crazy scene even deeper into the murky realm of the bizarre. His hurl of the bat had looked blatantly, preposterously violent, and yet, there he stood, admitting his mistake and protesting his innocence. He wasn't looking for a fight. He wasn't staring at me and screaming, "Fuck you, Piazza!" He was addressing the umpire, trying to cool the situation down, pleading *confusion*—and in doing so, compounding the overwhelming sense of it. There was doubt. It all happened so fast. Maybe, with his adrenaline pumping, Roger just grabbed the bat instinctively and thought, get this shit out of here. Maybe, considering where the ball went, he didn't know I was running.

Images, questions, emotions, and raucous shouting all pounded me in a bewildering, paralyzing overload, trapping me in my spot, short of the mound. So did Reliford and the scrum of Mets and Yankees. There was no fight.

Once the field was cleared, the game resumed with no ejections, and on the next pitch I bounced out to second base. Immediately, Clemens dashed off to a room in the Yankee clubhouse to calm himself down. He did a good job of it. He was untouchable for the eight innings he pitched—no runs, two hits, nine strikeouts.

The Yankees had less trouble with Hampton and led 6–0 until we scored five in the ninth, two of them on my home run off the foul pole against Jeff Nelson—which I considered quite an accomplishment because that guy was murder on me. We even put up a couple of runs against Rivera, on a homer by Payton. But the only thing it got us was the hell out of Yankee Stadium.

After the game, Torre defended Clemens with a level of animation that he almost never showed and Clemens defended himself in a manner that illuminated nothing. The more I heard and later read, the angrier I got. If Roger thought the barrel was the ball, why was he throwing it at me—or toward the Yankees' batboy, as he insisted—instead of to first base? If he didn't know I was running, why did he register no surprise, or not apologize, when he saw that I *was*? But those thoughts occurred after the fact, in the sorting-out process that followed the fury—around the time the critics were assailing me for not rushing into a fight.

I suppose I should have expected as much from the media. It had been that way all year. Various writers had not only campaigned against me for MVP and harped on my failures in the playoff series against the Giants, but had conveniently neglected my contributions against the Cardinals. This was just another chance to pile on.

The charge was led by Wallace Matthews of the *New York Post*, who effectively called me a wimp in his column, then elaborated on the talk show circuit. "Piazza," he wrote, "did a pretty good impression of the old 'Hold me back, Charlie!' routine with home plate umpire Charlie Reliford. But that was as far as it went. From that moment on, the Mets were a beaten team, for the night, and possibly, for the rest of the World Series. . . . Piazza's move toward Clemens was half-hearted and in a way, kind of laughable. He is supposed to be one of the leaders of this team, and considering his anemia at the plate—he went 1-for-5 in the Mets' 4–3 Game 1 loss—he probably could have made no greater contribution to his team last night than to take a real run at Clemens and try to get him out of the game."

The next day, Todd Pratt got in Matthews's face and Wally acknowledged that he might have gone overboard in the swirl of the moment. That was swell, but how do you unring a bell?

Anyhow, Matthews had plenty of company. My teammate Darryl Hamilton questioned my pride. Even my pitcher, Mike Hampton, suggested that I should have gone after Clemens and it shouldn't have mattered if it was Mike Tyson. I guess Hampton figured he had proven his manhood by nipping David Justice in the elbow pad five innings later. He told the *Post*, "I think we should've fought, to be honest with you. But that's not my call. You can't make something happen if guys aren't going to defend themselves."

Because Mike [Hampton] was a football player, he'd sometimes be asked about certain things and, well, Mike wasn't always good at giving the right answer.

Taken in a vacuum, the incident would have required a different response. But the situation taken in the context of the first New York Met–New York Yankee Subway World Series, I think that was a much bigger moment than some people make it out to be. We were supposed to be putting forth our best foot.

The way it all transpired on the field, Mike was stunned. He took those couple steps and saw the bat and he was like dumbfounded, perplexed. He wasn't angry, because it didn't seem like it was an incident that came from anger. But because he had been hit in the head, because of the rivalry, people wanted these two titans to get into a wrestling match. The idea of having the two major stars of the competing teams in the greatest city in America out there fighting on the field . . . that would have been not only crazy but immature.

—Bobby Valentine

Belatedly, I did take a swipe, of sorts, at Clemens—through proper channels. I asked MLB for an investigation, describing him to the media as "unstable." I have no idea whether my request had anything to do with it, but Roger was fined fifty thousand dollars. Of course, that begs the question of why, if he was penalized so heavily, wasn't he thrown out of the game? I attribute it to the confusion of the moment. I think Reliford and the other umpires were as discombobulated and weirded out as I was.

To this day, I don't know beyond a doubt what Clemens was truly intending or thinking. He's never said anything different than he said that night. There remain questions only he can answer. But with the extra clarity that comes with time, perspective, and video, I'll go this far: there should have been a fight. It hadn't been possible in July, when I was lying on my back with my head ringing like school was out. In October, though, it was not only possible but—circumstances be damned—it was *in order*. Item one: Clemens threw a broken bat in my direction. Item two: I walked toward the mound and asked him what the fuck his problem was. Everything was in place, except that item three never happened. It should have been Roger saying something like, "Get your sorry ass back in the fucking box." Or saying *nothing*; just giving give me a look, a gesture, any small, subtle, actionable trace of defiance. If he does that, we're brawling. If he does that, the whole thing makes sense and continues down its natural path. I was right there. But I had my parameters for fighting on the field, and the World Series was sure as hell no time to set them aside. Before I could take a swing at him, it was imperative that Clemens note my objection and issue a proper invitation, a verbal or visible "go fuck yourself." Instead, he turned to the umpire and babbled on about *the ball*.

He screwed up the script. He sabotaged my payback. I won't repudiate my response, for all the reasons and mixed signals I've discussed; but looking back on it now, whether I kicked Roger's ass or he kicked mine, there should have been some closure.

Without a fight that night, revenge would be hard for me and the Mets to come by. Clemens wouldn't pitch in Shea Stadium—where he would not only have to face a hostile crowd but would have to *bat*—for two more years. And he wouldn't pitch again in the 2000 World Series.

Evidently, the Yankees thought that *Shea* was their turf, too. When the Series moved there, George Steinbrenner trucked a load of Yankee Stadium furniture into the visiting clubhouse. Maybe it was in response to July, when, after Clemens nailed me, Steve Phillips banned the Yankees from our weight room.

At any rate, it can be safely said that the two teams didn't like each other much. Except for Derek Jeter, of course. Nobody doesn't like Jeter. And I'm not being sarcastic. The guy's a pro, a gentleman, a tenacious competitor, and remarkably clutch. What most amazes me about him, though, is how long and well he's eluded major controversy as a single guy and the face of his ball club—the *Yankees*, no less—in New York City. I can appreciate how truly difficult that is. Jeter has been smart enough to keep his opinions to himself, for the most part, and let his ballplaying do the talking. The New York media loves a talker, of course, but the ramifications can complicate the lives and careers of those who have something to say. Jeter has always been able to maintain a kind of skillful ambiguity in his public positions. More power to him.

While I'm at it, I should also note my admiration for Jorge Posada. It's not unnatural or uncommon for Mets players to be a tad envious of all the attention and prestige heaped upon the Yankees, but guys like Jeter and Posada were certainly deserving of it. I could identify pretty closely with both of them—Jeter for his high profile and Posada for what he brought to the ballpark as a catcher. He was a tough out in that lineup and contributed plenty of intangibles behind the plate. As catchers go, I'd like to think that

New York was treated to a couple of pretty nice ones in those days. It wasn't center field in the fifties, with Willie, Mickey, and the Duke, but it wasn't too shabby, either.

Having won the previous two World Series, the Yankees, needless to say, were loaded with clutch, capable postseason players. That included their starter in game three, Orlando Hernandez. El Duque was 8–0 in the postseason, beating seven different teams. Nevertheless, I had faith in our guy, Rick Reed.

Ventura gave us a 1–0 lead with a homer in the second. Paul O'Neill put them up 2–1 with a triple in the fourth. Reed gave us six strong innings, and I led off the bottom of the sixth with a ground-rule double, then scored to tie the game on a double by Zeile. In the eighth, with El Duque still on the mound for the Yankees, Agbayani doubled in Zeile, went to third on an infield single by Payton, and scored on a sacrifice fly by Bubba Trammell. Benitez got the job done in the ninth, and we were off the mat.

That's when Jeter stepped up. He led off game four with a home run against Bobby Jones. He tripled to lead off the third and scored to make it 3–0. In the bottom of that inning, Perez singled and I hit a one-out homer against their starter, Denny Neagle, to get us back within a run, but it was still 3–2 when they called in Rivera, the ultimate World Series guy, for the last two innings. He did his thing. We were down to our elimination game.

But we had Leiter ready for game five, and I always felt good about it when Al was pitching under pressure. Of course, they felt the same way about Pettitte, who was making his nineteenth postseason start in six years—and wasn't half finished yet.

They scored first on a second-inning home run by Bernie Williams. We went ahead with a couple of cheap runs in the third. Jeter homered to tie it in the sixth. In the ninth, Leiter struck out Martinez and O'Neill but walked Posada and gave up a single to Brosius. And then, for all of the Yankees' handsomely paid, widely admired, big-game superstars, it was Luis Sojo who singled up the middle to bring in the lead run. Another came home on a throwing error by Payton to make it 4–2.

I stepped to the plate as the tying run in the bottom of the ninth, with two outs and Agbayani on—Rivera pitching, of course—but my fly ball to center field wasn't deep enough.

It was the story of the Series. I couldn't deliver a punch.

CHAPTER NINETEEN

We'd grown accustomed to winning. Over the three seasons beginning with 1998, the Mets had put up the best record in baseball short of the two teams we were chronically judged against, the Braves and Yankees. Notwithstanding our World Series disappointment, we were movin' on up. In that spirit, I sold my New Jersey house to a horse trainer and left for a penthouse condominium in Manhattan's Gramercy Park.

Meanwhile, Mike Hampton, after winning fifteen games and rubbing a few people the wrong way in his only season as a Met, sought his prosperity elsewhere, signing a free-agent contract with the Colorado Rockies that made him the highest-paid pitcher in the game. Our own free-agent signing, Kevin Appier, took his place in the rotation. We were positioned for more of the same in 2001.

At the end of May, however, we were somehow ten miserable games under .500, already trailing the Phillies by thirteen and Atlanta, which was having its own uncharacteristic troubles, by five. Inexplicably, we stunk. Zeile's production was down and Alfonzo's and Ventura's were way down.

My problems, once again, were primarily on the defensive end, throwing out base stealers. In June, Gary Carter, the Hall of Famer who was a minor-league catching instructor for the Mets, spoke out to the *New York Times* and suggested strongly that I consider switching positions. He referred to my percentage of throwing out runners as "horrible." I know that Gary was trying to be supportive in his own way, one of his points being that I could better preserve my knees, hands, and body if I moved out from behind the plate, presumably to first base. I appreciated the health benefits of what he was talking about—at the time, for instance, my back was acting up—but frankly, the whole thing stung me a bit, and it was getting old. From all directions, it was becoming an annual refrain that I just couldn't bring myself to hum along with. Catching had been my ticket into professional baseball in the first place, and on some fundamental level I equated my success with my position. I was reluctant and probably a little frightened to give it up. I felt that, if I began to dabble at first base, it wouldn't be long at all before I was over there full-time. To me, it seemed like more of a life change than just a position change; sort of like checking into a nursing home before the kids started college. I didn't care to entertain that notion until I absolutely had to. And the way I saw it, that moment had not arrived. I was still an all-star catcher.

Besides, I had a clever, one-step solution to all my problems. I dyed my hair blond. It was so intimidating that, in the tenth inning of a game in Houston, the Astros walked me intentionally with one out and nobody on base.

Roger Clemens avoided me, as well, when we played the Yankees that year. Joe Torre saw to it, even though Clemens's regular turn in the rotation came up when we played in June at Shea and again in July at Yankee Stadium, just before the All-Star Game. I guess Torre had seen enough of the circus. He said he was concerned that, if Roger hit me accidentally, nobody would believe it. (Incidentally . . . before the season, MLB had sent around a memorandum to umpires that confirmed their prerogative to eject a pitcher who they believed had deliberately thrown at a hitter's head. I'm not sure I would have supported that concept before my encounters with Clemens in 2000, but my perspective had effectively been revised.)

I did face Clemens at the All-Star Game in Seattle. He started for the American League, I batted sixth for the National, and my fly ball to right field on a three-two fastball completed his two perfect innings. That mundane little out was apparently so fascinating that it warranted twenty minutes of interviews after the game. I should note, though, that it wasn't the only topic of conversation. There was a more memorable moment that night, with indirect connections to me in two respects. It involved a broken bat and Tommy Lasorda.

Since we'd won the pennant the year before, Bobby Valentine was the National League manager. Although Lasorda had been Bobby's first minor-league manager, they'd never worked together in the same dugout; so Bobby invited him to Seattle in an honorary capacity. Tommy didn't disappoint. He delivered a classic, X-rated pep talk before the game: "Those mother-fuckers over there want to beat your fucking ass. . . ." MLB actually taped it and gave me a copy.

Unfortunately, the American League owned us in all-star games during that period. This time, I was catching my old teammate Chan Ho Park in the third inning when Cal Ripken Jr., in his last of twenty-one seasons and nineteen straight all-star games, opened the scoring with a home run. As poignant as that was, however, the night's enduring image came in the sixth inning, with the American League leading 2–1, Mike Stanton pitching to Vladimir Guerrero, and Tommy coaching third base. He was having a good time of it, chattering away in full glory, going through his whole repertoire and entertaining everyone within earshot, as Guerrero took a whack at a pitch in on his fists and fractured his bat at the handle. The fat part hurtled right at Tommy and caught him with a glancing blow to the left hip, sending him tumbling over on his back, feet in the air. He nearly completed a backward somersault, then rolled over on his side and popped right up. I was pretty scared—Tommy was seventy-three years old—but everybody else seemed to think it was hilarious. Bonds ran out to give him a chest protector. All right, *that* was funny. I thought it was less amusing, though, when they replayed the entire thing on the big scoreboard at Safeco Field. Maybe I just wasn't in a laughing mood, since we were on our way to losing our fifth straight All-Star Game.

For that matter, there was nothing humorous about the way the Mets' season was going, either. At the break, we were in fourth place and the Braves had finally found their groove to nearly catch the Phillies.

We continued to flounder, reaching our low point—fourteen games under .500—in Los Angeles on August 17. But we won the next two in Los Angeles, the first two back home against Colorado, and then, who can explain it? How can a team playing so badly all year start playing so well all of a sudden?

Over a stretch of twenty-one games, up to September 8, we won seventeen. The next day was a Sunday, and we had a chance to even our record for the first time since the fourth game of the season. Instead, we lost a slugfest in Florida. And on that down note we flew to Pittsburgh, where we'd have Monday off before starting a three-game series with the Pirates on Tuesday.

Danny came to Pittsburgh, and we met a few of the Mets at a bar to watch the Broncos beat the Giants on Monday Night Football. It was late, for me, when I got back to the Vista Hotel, so I turned off my cell phone and was sleeping hard on Tuesday morning when the room phone rang, which surprised me, because I'd checked in under an alias. When it wouldn't stop, I finally picked up.

It was Danny, shouting at me: "Turn on the TV!"

"What for?"

"They attacked the World Trade Center!"

"*What? Who* attacked the World Trade Center?"

"The terrorists! They hit us good! *Turn on the TV!*"

He didn't know yet what had actually happened. We stayed on the line and were both watching when the second plane flew head-on into one of the most famous landmarks in New York City. At that moment we realized, as most Americans did, that life in the world's greatest country had suddenly, tragically, changed.

We had no idea, however, that Al Qaeda terrorists had also hijacked a plane—United Airlines Flight 93, scheduled from Newark to San Francisco—that was crossing over our heads, eastbound toward Washington, D.C., after being turned around somewhere in Ohio; that four hijackers had taken over the cockpit; that the passengers, learning through phone calls that the World Trade Center and Pentagon had been struck by airplanes, were gathering to overpower the terrorists; that one of the heroes, Todd Beamer, would turn to the others and say, "Let's roll!" That Flight 93 would crash in a field about eighty miles southeast of us.

As the sickening day developed, there was an emotion inside me that overwhelmed the gloom. I felt rage. There were children on those planes. There were mothers and fathers in those buildings. It was peacetime. It was an unprovoked assault on a nation and system of values that mean everything to me. I was consumed.

I don't know if it even crossed my mind that we had a ball game that night. As it turned out, we didn't. The baseball schedule was suspended for the rest of the week. Our focus was getting back to New York; but of course, all flights were canceled. In the meantime, the Mets, afraid that Pittsburgh might be targeted, moved us to a motor inn outside the city.

The next day, we climbed into two buses for the ride back. Somebody put on a Jim Carrey movie—*Me, Myself & Irene*—thinking that maybe it would break the spell, but nobody was up to comedy. We switched to *The Cider House Rules*, but shut it off as soon as the New York skyline came into view, approaching midnight. We were still in New Jersey, on Interstate 78. After staring at pictures of the Twin Towers for two days, like everybody else, we knew generally what to expect; but even so, it was a shocking, chilling, numbing sight. All we saw was smoke and floodlights. I don't think there was a human sound on our bus. Nothing to say.

Jay Payton lived in the city and offered me a ride to my condo in Gramercy Park. We were stopped a couple of times at police checkpoints.

As we proceeded on slowly and gawked, the sound track was provided by the military aircraft buzzing overhead. We crossed into Manhattan over the Triborough Bridge, which, like all the others, was unlit. The stench was dreadful. This wasn't the America that I'd grown up in. We'd been invaded.

My condo was about eight or ten blocks from the cordoned-off area surrounding Ground Zero. I can't say that I was unafraid as we pulled up to it. The atmosphere was still too warlike to feel completely out of danger. As I shut the passenger door to Jay's car and stepped onto the sidewalk, there was, at least, some welcome familiarity in the sight of my building, intact. Everything else was disconcertingly different—the smoke, the smell, the constant wail of sirens. And most of all, the view. When I'd last stood in that spot, I'd been able to see the World Trade Center. In its place was the grisly spectacle of nothing at all, floodlit.

Over the rest of the week, police officers whom we knew from the ballpark picked up groups of Mets players every day and ushered us around the hospitals to visit firefighters, cops, and ordinary citizens who had been injured or suffered losses in the tragedy. I heard stories of people receiving calls from loved ones who were trapped inside the World Trade Center and knew they'd never make it out. An injured policeman, one of the last people out of the second tower, described to me, with a glazed look on his face, what it was like running down the stairs after the building had been hit, fully aware that it was going to collapse. I talked to a woman who had lost both of her sons.

My friend John Bruno came over to my apartment and we sat on the terrace sniffing death. I know that sounds melodramatic, but that's the only way I can describe the sensation of that first week or two in lower Manhattan. It smelled like death. I can still hear John saying in a matter-of-fact tone, as he gazed out at the scene, "They fucking got us."

The parking lot at Shea Stadium became a staging area for supplies, bottled water, you name it. The players and Bobby, too, helped load the vans and trucks headed to the city. Cots were set up in the tunnels for firefighters and workers who needed breaks. We invited them onto the field to take some swings with us. Our police buddies were in and out, and they drove several of us down to Ground Zero, where we walked through the security area just shaking hands with the cops and thanking them for risking their lives and saving other people's. Being at the scene of the catastrophe, breathing in that wretched odor and smoke, brought on a smothering sense of helplessness. The Mets called a meeting for the players and some front-office employees, just to talk things through. It was one of the few times we saw Fred Wilpon and Nelson Doubleday in the same room. They encouraged us to pitch in with the recovery, but didn't mandate it. In a players-only vote, we decided that everybody would donate a day's pay to the recovery effort.

On Monday, September 17, we were back in Pittsburgh, picking up the season where it left off. The Pittsburgh fans gave us a reception unlike any we'd ever experienced on the road. They were cheering for *New York*, and by extension, for America. In effect, the Mets—like the Yankees, no doubt— were representing the country. It was inspiring. Wearing the caps of the New York police and fire departments, we swept the Pirates.

After a day off, we were back at Shea to play the Braves. Friday's game would be New York's first professional sporting event since the city had been attacked.

Forty-one thousand people came to watch us play baseball on September 21, 2011. Can you imagine that? It was only ten days since dedicated terrorists had committed mass murder in Manhattan. The pall was a long, long way from being lifted. A crowded stadium was an obvious target. There were reports that a man had been found sitting in his car with ominously high-lighted maps of the area surrounding Shea and LaGuardia Airport.

And yet, they came. They came to say they weren't afraid. They came to support and celebrate New York City. That's what the Mets stood for, whether we wanted to or not, on the night of September 21. I don't know that I've ever felt so determined, so compelled, so *duty-bound* to win a base-ball game.

Nobody knew what to expect, except that the evening would involve police officers, firefighters, a twenty-one-gun salute, Mayor Rudy Giuliani, Diana Ross, Liza Minnelli, and unbridled emotions. Tears. I should have anticipated the tears. I was welling up as soon as I heard the first blast of bagpipes just before the game. Then forty-one thousand fans joined Marc Anthony in singing the national anthem. It was remarkable. When it was over, the stadium rocked with chants of "USA! USA! USA!" It gave me goose bumps. It *still* does.

Typically, high emotions are not of much benefit to a ballplayer. The game demands a cool head and an even keel. When strong feelings engulf you as they did that night, they have to be dealt with. I tried to reason with myself that it was still about catching the ball and swinging the bat. I also prayed. It's not unusual for me to pray, but it was unusual for me to pray about a baseball game. I said, Lord, please help me get through this night.

Bruce Chen was pitching for us, Jason Marquis—a New Yorker—for Atlanta. The game was scoreless until I dropped a throw in the fourth inning trying to tag Chipper Jones after a double by Ken Caminiti. I atoned, somewhat, in the bottom of the inning when I doubled, went to third on a single by Ventura, and scored on a fly ball from Tsuyoshi Shinjo.

It was still 1–1 when Diana Ross irrigated about eighty-two thousand eyes during the seventh-inning stretch, joining a local gospel choir for "God Bless America." Liza Minnelli followed with "New York, New York," legs kicking, arm in arm with cops and firefighters. We *had* to win that ball game.

As unique as the setting was, the situation, in baseball terms, was really not. Over the years, there had been countless times when we absolutely had to beat the Atlanta Braves. On those occasions, we almost never did. Believe me, we were well aware of that when Brian Jordan put them ahead again in the top of the eighth with a double against John Franco, who was New York through and through. I had one more shot.

It would come in the bottom of the inning. With one out and Steve Karsay pitching for the Braves—a Queens guy, Karsay, like Franco, was obviously pumped up—Fonzi worked a three-two walk. Karsay had also gone to three and two on Matt Lawton, so I figured there was a pretty good chance that he'd miss his spot and give me something to hit. And it would be a fastball, because he had a good one.

He was throwing pellets, and the first one was right there for me. I took it for a strike and didn't know why I did. As the ball slapped into Javy Lopez's mitt, I thought, *man*, that was the one. Then, ahead in the count, Karsay brought it. And I, by the grace of God, squared it up.

I caught that fastball with the full force of my emotional rush. When it cleared the fence just left of center and caromed off a distant TV camera, I thought the stadium would crumble into rubble. It was a moment for New Yorkers—the Americans on hand—to let it all out at last, whatever they felt. To scream, to cheer, to chant, to hug, to cry, to jump up and down in celebration of something happy again, something normal and familiar and fun again; of getting their lives back, at least in some small way. Franco said the hair was standing up on his arms.

Benitez set the Braves down in the ninth, and we'd done it, 3–2. Like I said, we *had* to.

I mean, are you kidding? Really. What an emotional time. It was hard to be normal in New York, when you saw those posters everywhere, all the reminders of the tragedy. Not only was it the first game back in New York after nine-eleven, but it's against your rival, the great Atlanta Braves, and who better to win the game than

our star, and the way he did it? Listening later to the Braves' comments—Chipper Jones, Bobby Cox—they all said that, if there was
one night they had to lose, that was the night.

—Al Leiter

At the time, it didn't hit me that the home run would become an iconic
event in the annals of New York sports. It was ultimately voted by fans as
one of the top three moments in Shea Stadium history, along with game
six of the 1986 World Series and game five of the 1969 Series. But as I was
circling the bases, and after Benitez did his job in the ninth, all I knew was
that it felt indescribably, overwhelmingly *good*.

I'd done something for the city—not enough, but *something*—and I'd
done it in my own particular way. I had channeled my anger and fought
back, just a little, with my weapon of choice. I savor that. I take professional
satisfaction in the fact that I was able to come through at a time when I
was needed, and personal satisfaction in the afterglow of that extraordinary
night. I never imagined that a home run—much less a *regular season* home
run, with no obvious ramifications in terms of the pennant—could resonate
so far beyond the boundaries of baseball. Even now, I never get tired of
people approaching me to say how much that home run meant to them. It
still stirs my emotions. It still makes me proud.

When I saw Karsay a few years later, we didn't talk about the 0–1 pitch
in the eighth inning of September 21, 2001. That's a touchy-feely thing for
ballplayers. But by the handshake, and by the smile, it was clear that there
was a common understanding. We knew what we shared.

In return for me not mentioning the home run, he was kind enough not
to bring up the rest of the season.

CHAPTER TWENTY

The energy of that extraordinary night carried us for nearly another week. We won the Atlanta series, then swept the Expos in Montreal. With that, we were 25–6 since bottoming out in Los Angeles in August. Somehow, we had closed to within three games of first place—of the Braves, that is, since they had passed the Phillies—with nine more to play.

The first three of those came, of course, in Atlanta. We lost the series opener but were looking good late in the second game. I'd cleared the bases with a double, and when Leiter completed the eighth inning, we led 5–1. Benitez started the ninth, but with two outs, two on, and the score now 5–4, he gave way to Franco. Johnny walked Marcus Giles to load the bases, and then Brian Jordan—that guy *killed* us—unloaded them with a grand slam.

We were effectively finished. The Braves had done it to us again. From that point, we petered out and finished six games behind.

Looking back, I believe that the passions of 9/11 ultimately drained us of the intensity we needed to stay in the race to the very end. The long haul of the baseball season makes it nearly impossible to sustain a high level of focus after an emotional stretch like the one we had in 2001. It's nearly impossible, as well, to sustain the high level of *success* that we experienced for more than a month. Unfortunately, we couldn't afford any letup. We had dug ourselves too deep a hole over the first three-quarters of the season.

I can't help but think that there was something else at work, too, as September wound down and the season extended into October. Being as absorbed as we were in the resonance of those times, a lot of us were dealing with unfamiliar, undermining doubts about the significance of what we did for a living. Suddenly, with fear in our stomachs and families suffering, baseball didn't seem so important. It had been important, certainly, on September 21; but after the crescendo of that mystical night, where was the relevance? I was rethinking my priorities, and I'm sure that some of my teammates were doing the same. A pennant can't be won without the players' hearts in pursuit of it, and ours, I confess, had strayed a bit. I'm convinced that the events of that year had a detrimental effect on our ball club. They took something out of us.

Of course, we were well-paid professionals and that's no excuse. The Yankees managed to represent New York all the way to the World Series, where they were upset by Arizona. The bottom line was, we underachieved. I might add that, in a normal year, the New York media would have skewered us for an 82–80 record, given the talent we possessed and the expectations that had built up around us; but, because of everything that happened in 2001, they didn't pile on, thank you.

Individually, I felt like I kept pace, for the most part. I batted at least .300—with no margin for error this time—for the ninth straight year, which was a record for catchers. For that matter, it was the ninth straight year I'd put up at least twenty home runs, which was also a record for catchers. I thought my thirty-six was a pretty nifty sum until I realized that Barry Bonds hit *more than twice that many.*

Seventy-three seemed, and still seems, like an absurd number of home runs. It was nearly 20 percent more than Roger Maris's record of sixty-one, which had stood until only four years before. Just as absurdly, Maris's mark had been exceeded six times in those four years, after being untouchable for thirty-seven. Prior to *that,* Babe Ruth's record of sixty homers had lasted for thirty-four years. Obviously, something about the game had changed dramatically in the 1990s.

The standard explanation is steroids. It seems an easy conclusion, starting with the fact that all three of the players who topped Maris's total—Bonds, Mark McGwire, and Sammy Sosa—have been linked to performance-enhancing drugs in varying degrees. There's no denying that, for a decade or more spanning the turn of the century, home run totals in general were out of whack in comparison to previous generations. It stands to reason that advances in medical science, including those in the areas of supplements and PEDs, may well have been a contributing factor.

But in order that the entire period and all the players in it are not colored carelessly by the same broad brush, it's helpful to start with a bigger picture of the times. Without condoning the use of illegal substances, I *am* compelled to evolve the discussion and defend my era. I find it regrettable that nearly every accomplished hitter from the 1990s and early 2000s has been subjected to scrutiny. In several instances, the mere raising of the steroids question—a single writer pondering, in print, whether a guy was aboveboard—has been damning enough to taint a player's image and slide him over to the user/cheater category, in terms of general perception. It's unjust. It shouldn't be *assumed* that every big hitter of the generation used steroids. I didn't. That's not to say, however, that the era didn't contribute to my power numbers and those of virtually everyone else who hit a lot of home runs in those years. It most certainly did.

For example, people tend to neglect the fact that, in the 1990s, baseball expanded twice, adding a total of four teams, an increase of more than 15 percent. That's 15 percent more pitchers, all of them either up from the minor leagues or hanging on beyond what would have been their time. Those guys made regular appearances in games that were over by the fourth or fifth inning, and hitters, as a rule, loved to lunch up on them, as we called it. The old expression was "riot at the bat rack," but ours referred specifically to feasting on pitchers who had no business being in the big leagues. Todd Zeile and I used to hash over who the best lunch-up hitters were. Some guys just had that knack. Others were on missions. For the Mets, Benny Agbayani was pretty remarkable in that respect; he'd just wear out middle relievers. But I don't think he could touch Sammy Sosa. Don't get me wrong; I certainly don't believe in giving away at-bats. But it'd be a 12–2 game in Chicago, we all just wanted to get our asses over to Gibsons for a steak, and Sammy Sosa's up there against our mop-up man *taking pitches*. As a catcher, especially, that sort of thing stood out to me, because, by the time a game got to 12–2, I'd be long gone, taking the opportunity to get a little rest. Bear in mind, also, that of those four expansion teams, three—the Rockies, Marlins, and Diamondbacks—were placed in the National League. All the guys who hit sixty or more home runs in that period did it in the National League. I'm just pointing that out.

While we're at it, what about the general strides made in nutrition during that time, and the increasing awareness of its value? And the vast improvements in conditioning? I recall, early in my Dodger days, a meeting in which Lou Johnson, a former outfielder, told us that he and the other players of his time never worked out with weights, for fear it would make them muscle-bound and slow down their bats. When Tony La Russa was managing the Oakland A's in the late 1980s and Mark McGwire and Jose Canseco were just becoming the Bash Brothers (this is according to what Tommy Lasorda told my dad that La Russa told him), he was leaving the ballpark one night, heard some noise coming from the weight room, peeked in, and was startled to see a bunch of players in there *lifting*, of all things. That had never happened before. But perceptions were changing. With salaries going wild as they were, and home runs being the big bargaining chip, guys were highly motivated to gear their games—their *bodies*—toward hitting the ball for distance, and willing to train year-round to that end.

At the same time, the more money the players made, the more it cost the teams when they were injured. An emphasis on conditioning in general and strength training in particular evolved quickly into a movement. When I started playing, baseball weight rooms weren't really adequate. They weren't outfitted with pull-downs and pulleys, etc. Living in Florida and then California, I had become acquainted with the cutting-edge equipment; so at spring training, instead of coming back to Dodgertown in the evenings to work out, I'd grab some rest and dinner and head over to the local World Gym in Vero Beach. But by the mid-nineties or so, ball clubs had modernized their weight rooms and hired staff to oversee them.

Unless you were an Otis Nixon or Brett Butler type, you *had* to make yourself stronger, just to keep up with the game. Everybody had heard that old yarn about becoming too muscular for baseball, but the reality was, you'd lift in the off-season, come back in the spring, take a few swings, and think, hey, wait a minute, the ball's jumping off my bat pretty nice. Strength was *good*, it turned out—especially if it came with good hitting mechanics. The prevailing attitude concerning muscle, in the space of my first few years as a pro, did a 180. All of a sudden, curls and presses were standard stuff in everybody's routine. I didn't know of a single player who wasn't in some kind of strength or conditioning program. It was like the California gold rush. PEDs played a part in the big power numbers of that period, no question, but they were an offshoot of weight training. The sea change came in the gym, not in the ass. I'll go to my grave screaming about that.

Meanwhile, for all the noise about the players being juiced, what about the ball itself? In the past, whenever home run totals were on the rise, controversies would break out about whether the baseball was being tinkered with. Why did that discussion suddenly vanish in the nineties?

I don't know the answer to that one, but—in the way of modifications to the equipment—I *do* know that guys were using lighter bats than they used to. Hitters could generate a lot more speed with the smaller bats, and also control them better. That led, in turn, to a feeling of empowerment and confidence at the plate; and don't underestimate the value of confidence. Guys became more aggressive. The padding we were permitted to wear on our arms and elbows added another dimension of confidence and aggressiveness. (For that matter, earflaps on batting helmets hadn't become mandatory until 1983.) Craig Biggio wasn't a power hitter, but he was the first guy I remember who batted with a protective sleeve, because he had been hit by so many pitches; the thing's displayed in the Hall of Fame. Of course, the most recognizable armor was that of Barry Bonds.

Not surprisingly, bigger swings led to more strikeouts, and suddenly that was okay. Even with two strikes, some hitters were still swinging as hard as they could. I'm a strong believer that the acceptance of strikeouts was a significant factor in the proliferation of home runs.

So, obviously, was the modern ballpark. One after another, playing fields became smaller and friendlier to hitters.

These were perfect conditions for a power surge. I'd like to add that it was also a fantastic and immensely fun time to be a big leaguer. The game had some fireworks. It had some offense. I'm a huge soccer fan, and if I want a 1–0 final—like baseball had so often in the sixties, for instance (Gibson versus Marichal)—I'll catch a game in the Italian Serie A league. Our generation fit somewhere between soccer and cricket, I guess, and I'm happy to have played in it. I'm proud of my era. It produced some of the greatest players in history—Ken Griffey Jr., Cal Ripken Jr., Alex Rodriguez, Tony Gwynn, Chipper Jones, Randy Johnson, Pedro Martinez, Maddux, Clemens, Bonds.

Now, in the case of Bonds, specifically . . .

I won't pass judgment, as the purists will—as if comparing statistics between generations isn't troublesome enough—on the validity of his records and numbers in the context of the BALCO steroids scandal. I'll just say this: Barry Bonds was the very best at the essence of hitting—waiting for his pitch and getting his bat head to the baseball. Not that he was a better all-around pure hitter than Albert Pujols. I can't go that far, because I don't think Pujols has any weakness at the plate. He's physically imposing, comes to bat with a very smart, intellectual approach, doesn't strike out a lot, and utilizes the whole field to hit for both average and power. It could change for Albert, because it often does for great hitters when they get older and start compensating, sacrificing hits for home runs. But in his first *ten* seasons, while never hitting fewer than thirty-two home runs or failing to drive in a hundred runs, Pujols never batted below .312. I admit to a little bias on his behalf, because he and I share Danny Lozano as an agent and I've come to respect him on a personal level. In terms of pure hitting, though, I don't know how you could praise Albert Pujols more than he has already been or deserves to be praised.

Bonds is, of course, a more complicated subject; but if you observe his

career in a vacuum and judge it for the way he played the game overall, the
same sorts of things can be said about him. The man was nearly impossible to
pitch to. There was simply nothing in his approach or swing that you could
exploit. He'd take a certain pitch and you'd think he didn't care for it, so
you'd give it to him again and he'd send it to the moon. (One windy day in
San Francisco, he hit a monster pop-up so high that I was reeling backward
trying to catch it and fell onto my funny bone. Naturally, he then proceeded
to blast a home run.) That was even in the first half of his career, before he
was walking two hundred times a year. When I was with the Dodgers, our
scout Jerry Stephenson once gave us his report on Bonds, and it consisted of
a *Peanuts* cartoon he'd cut out. As a batter came to the plate, Linus walked
up to Charlie Brown on the mound and said, "Charlie Brown, this is their
best hitter." And Charlie Brown said something to the effect of "Well, if you
stay here long enough, maybe he'll go away."

That was pretty much the strategy with Bonds. Personally, I didn't believe in intentionally walking him as often as a lot of teams did. I thought
it was actually counterproductive, because it magnified his stature and reflected a sense of awe. That's no way to compete. When I was calling the
game, I preferred to go at him and try to somehow put him on his heels,
unless the situation clearly precluded it.

I think Barry appreciated that. And I appreciated the things he could
do on a ball field. Barry Bonds was the most dominant player I ever played
against, and the most complete I've ever seen. If I could have swapped uniforms and been somebody else for a day or two, he's the guy I would have
wanted to be.

There's no upside to missing the playoffs, but in 2001 there was, at least, a
consolation—especially for those of us who lived in New York. It gave us
some extra time to spend with people who were personally affected by 9/11.

Bobby set the tone and the Mets organization pointed the way, to a large
extent. Among other things, they arranged a baseball clinic for Staten Island children who had lost family members in the attack. Also, some of the
team doctors showed us around at the hospitals where public safety workers
were being treated for their injuries. Gradually, my anger receded and the
sadness set in.

It was during one of the hospital visits that I learned about a firefighter
named Mike Carroll, who was one of a dozen from my neighborhood firehouse, Ladder 3, to lose his life. In addition to being a model fireman, Mike
had been a great shortstop for the firehouse softball team and a Mets fan

whose favorite player, for whatever odd reason, was a Sicilian-American catcher who didn't throw so well. For his funeral mass, held at St. Ignatius Loyola on Park Avenue, flowers were arranged on the pulpit in the shape of the NY on a Mets cap.

Through the graces of a mutual friend, I was put in touch with Carroll's family and had the honor of spending a day with his wife, Nancy; brother, Bill; and young son, Brendan, who was a pretty good kid for a Yankee fan. We met for lunch and went to an indoor batting cage, where I found out that Mike Carroll had instructed his son to position his hands, as he waited for the pitch, just like I positioned mine. Then we headed over to my condo, where Brendan and I played Madden video football. It was a special day, but I'm not sure whether the Carrolls realized that it meant as much to me as it did to them.

That winter, the New York chapter of the Baseball Writers of America honored Bobby for his work with the community after 9/11. At the same dinner, I was recognized with the "Good Guy" award for my cooperation with the media, if you can believe that. Here's the other ironic thing about it: when I was introduced, Roger Clemens made sure that he was the first guy to stand and applaud. I guess *he* wanted to be the good guy.

Anyway, I'd been scheduled as the last honoree of the evening, but somehow, at the urging of somebody, the order was switched around so that the festivities would end with Roger, who was receiving the Cy Young Award. Joe Torre also spoke, and the night turned out to be all about the Yankees, more or less. And Clemens. His mother was there, and he dedicated his award to her. My father was there, too, telling some obnoxious Yankee fans at the next table to shut up. A couple of them had been enjoying the free Yuengling and giving me a hard time, and my dad mentioned something about kicking their asses. Fortunately—considering that New York was supposed to be in a stick-together frame of mind and everything—the tables were packed in so tight, there wasn't room for that.

If nothing else, the attitude and general bullshit gave us an indication that New York was on its way back to being itself. At least as far as the trivial stuff. On the larger scale, of course, the country was still grieving, frightened, economically reeling, and very much at war. What we all fervently wished for, in 2002, was that life would return to normal.

I have to say, the Mets did their part. In 2002, we were Team Tabloid.

After the disappointment of our 2001 performance, the front office obviously wasn't going for continuity. Steve Phillips traded Zeile, Agbayani, Glendon Rusch, and Kevin Appier. Ventura left to sign a free-agent contract with the Yankees. On top of that, Franco would miss the season after Tommy John surgery. The only returning regulars would be me, Alfonzo, and our shortstop, Rey Ordonez. Only Leiter and Steve Trachsel were back in the starting rotation. But Phillips was working hard on the roster, and not being cheap about it. Coming our way were outfielder Roger Cedeno, who'd been with us in 1999; outfielder Jeromy Burnitz, who'd driven in a hundred runs for the Brewers the year before; Pedro Astacio, who'd been in the Dodgers' rotation when I was with them; Shawn Estes, another starting pitcher; and, through trades, two big-time, thirty-four-year-old veterans from the American League, Roberto Alomar and Mo Vaughn.

Alomar, known as a fantastic second baseman, had just put up a monster season in Cleveland. Vaughn, who had three years and $46 million remaining on a six-year contract he'd signed with the Angels, had been sidelined for 2001 with a biceps injury on top of his chronic knee and ankle troubles. He reported to Port St. Lucie at 275 pounds. Thus began our soap-opera season.

I had a prominent scene in the first week of Grapefruit games. It started rolling when I was smacked on the forearm as I raised it to block a fastball coming at my head from Eric Gagne of the Dodgers. The next inning, Brian Jordan, who'd been traded to the Dodgers by the Braves for Gary Sheffield, was brushed on the thigh by Mark Guthrie. Jordan—that guy again—got ticked off and accused Valentine of ordering Guthrie to hit him. Bobby more or less denied it, but also told the *L.A. Times,* "Good. Let everybody know we're going to protect our guys. No doubt, our pitchers know Mike is a very valuable part of our team. My guy got hit on the arm real hard, and he could have been hurt and sidelined for a while. Their guy got hit on the belt buckle."

Bobby was just fulfilling his obligation to discourage pitchers from fulfilling *their* obligations by throwing at me, the same way La Russa sometimes made a public stink when a pitch came in extra tight on Pujols. The underlying premise is that, in the tradition of protecting its own, it's not unusual for a team to make the point with a purpose pitch to the best player on the other side.

Sometimes that decision is made from the bench, but more often by the pitcher himself. The catcher rarely gets involved; or at least I didn't, unless I was asked for an opinion. For example, when Antonio Osuna clipped Barry Bonds in 1997, that was entirely Osuna's call—his reaction to Julian Tavarez throwing behind Eric Karros. Bonds was the only batter Osuna hit that year in more than sixty-one innings. He was happy to do it. I liked Barry, but it wasn't my position to interfere with the natural order of the game. When a catcher does that, people take note. I was told by Houston players that when Eric Yelding once crushed Jeff Reed of the Reds in a play at home plate, it was because Reed was observed giving the "flip" sign—the little signal, like flipping a coin, that tells a pitcher to get the ball inside and leave a mark. But I can say that, of all the times I was hit or thrown at, I never thought to blame the catcher.

At any rate, Bobby's warning didn't scare anybody off. In all, I was drilled four times that spring, which isn't right. The third time, I had to miss a couple games. By the fourth, I'd had it.

Coincidentally or not, we were playing the Dodgers again, in Vero Beach. Guillermo Mota, who'd just been traded to the Dodgers a few days before, was pitching in the seventh inning. The count was 3–0, and he nailed me in the small of the back. He'd been struggling with his control, and I might have given him the benefit of the doubt; but like I said, that always depended on the pitcher's reaction—or the pitcher's reaction to *my* reaction. Mota didn't appear to be in a conciliatory state of mind when I glared at him and asked, "What the fuck?" He answered with a stare and a gesture that reflected some belligerence, in my opinion.

Knowing that he'd be finished after that inning and had to walk past our bench on his way to the clubhouse, I took my time changing my shoes, waiting for an opportunity to chat. As I did, I happened to notice the other Dodgers slapping hands with him. It might have been a simple case of standard congratulations, but under the circumstances, it was one of those little things that made me go, hmmm.

By the time Mota strolled by our side, I was steaming. I threw my bag over my shoulder, strode up to him, and said, "You got a problem with me?"

He contended that he didn't mean to hit me. It wasn't convincing. I forget exactly what I said next, but as I said it I grabbed him by the collar of his jacket and pushed him away.

His subsequent comment, when talking to reporters, was "Why didn't he do that to Roger Clemens?" He also said that he'd remember what happened.

And I'd remember that he said it.

CHAPTER TWENTY-ONE

Bobby Valentine had some mysterious ways. On a Tuesday night in mid-April 2002, we beat the Braves for the second time in a row to hold our lead on first place and, more important, move three and a half games ahead of Atlanta. There was an afternoon game the next day, a circumstance in which it's fairly customary for the backup catcher to get the start. I figured that might be the case in this instance, considering that I'd been dealing with a bruised knee from when Chipper Jones rammed into me at home plate, a bump on the head from yet another guy—this time, Corey Patterson—conking me on his backswing, and a tight back, which had me taking muscle relaxers in the middle of ball games. It's kind of helpful to know ahead of time if you're going to get a day off, so before I left the park, I checked with Bobby. As I expected, Bobby said, "Oh yeah, yeah, you'll have tomorrow off."

There was no batting practice scheduled for Wednesday, so I showed up a little later than usual, dressed in a suit for the trip to Montreal after the game. I dropped off my suitcase with Charlie Samuels, our clubhouse manager, meandered over to the lineup card, and did a double take. My name was smack in the middle of it.

Naturally, the beat writers had already seen the lineup and taken note of my tardiness. They were watching me for a reaction, and I was hoping they couldn't read my thoughts. Al Leiter and I had talked about Bobby's occasional breaches of credibility, and this time he was making me look bad in full view of the media. It smelled like a setup, like the incident in 2000 when he reamed me out in front of the team. Bobby, I suspected, was messing with my head, embarrassing me for the purpose of proving who was in charge. He knew what he'd told me, he knew I'd come in late, and he knew how it would look if I were in the lineup.

We lost the game, 2–1, and I was held to one single. Afterward, Wallace

Matthews of the *New York Post* asked me about the mix-up. I laughed it off. It wasn't a big deal, but it *was* part of a bigger issue on the ball club.

Because of the huge shadow that the Yankees cast in the city, it seemed to me and other players that the Mets chronically catered to the press in the continual effort to get attention. In the process, they often exposed us—almost sacrificed us, in effect—to the jaws of the New York media monster. Our publicity director, Jay Horwitz, was a good guy who worked hard and loved the ball club, but I felt that he was more loyal to the writers and broadcasters than he was to the players. For example, I always had pretty good chemistry with Mike (Francesa) and the Mad Dog (Christopher Russo) on WFAN. They would rip me from time to time, but I could deal with that as long as it wasn't incessant or too personal. My problem, specifically, was with being asked to come on the show the day after they'd been tearing me to shreds. Jay would practically beg me to do it, and I'd be like "You can't reward them for that shit. You've got to make them hurt a little bit. You've got to say, 'Screw you guys. If you change your tune a little bit, maybe I'll come back on the show.'" They could respect that. They were big boys. I just felt that the Mets needed to look after their own a little bit. Their position seemed to be that players come and go but the newspapers and stations will always be around. The effect, for us, was a sense that we were constantly walking the plank with sharks circling below. That was certainly the feeling I came away with on that April 17.

Less than a week later, I was sidelined for five games with a strained hamstring. The last of those games happened to fall on a Sunday afternoon when they were giving away my bobblehead doll. That morning, while I was on the training table, trying to get myself ready to catch on Tuesday in Arizona, Bobby walked in and said, "You know, a lot of people are coming here to see you play."

I said, "Bobby, you want me to risk hurting myself more, and missing more games, so I can entertain the crowd on bobblehead day?"

No doubt, he was getting pressure from the front office. It was reminiscent of the time when I was nursing an injury before the first spring training game and Jeff Wilpon came around asking if I could at least pinch-hit because they were expecting a sellout. For the Mets, there was never a break in that perpetual struggle to please everybody. The fallout, for me, was major drama seemingly every time I was due for a day of rest.

That type of drama, though, I could anticipate. Nothing could have prepared me for the stuff that hit the fan on Monday, May 20.

• • •

It was a day off that we spent in Philadelphia, after flying in from San Diego. There was some convenience, I suppose, in being near my family when that kind of hell broke loose, but it wasn't really necessary. If I'd been holed up in my condo in New York City, with taxis honking and Guns N' Roses blasting in my headphones, I could have heard my father bellowing when he got the news.

The adventure began with an interview Bobby Valentine did for the June issue of a magazine called *Details*. Chris Isenberg, the young guy who put the interview together, had been a batboy for Bobby in Texas, and Bobby was trying to help the kid along. They talked about a variety of subjects, and then Isenberg asked whether baseball was ready for a gay player. Bobby offered up a straightforward, politically correct response.

The magazine itself wasn't out yet when a copy of the article reached Neal Travis, a gossip writer for the *New York Post*. His reaction was to publish an item based on Bobby's statement that, yes, baseball was "probably ready for an openly gay player." From that, somehow, Travis extrapolated that perhaps "Valentine is getting in first, before one of his big guns is outed."

And who might that be?

"There is a persistent rumor around town that one Mets star who spends a lot of time with pretty models in clubs is actually gay and has started to think about declaring his sexual orientation. The rumor even goes so far as to say that the player and a still-closeted local TV personality recently purchased a house together in a ritzy New York suburb."

The whole episode was such a strange, incredible phenomenon . . . I still don't get it. I don't know where the rumor came from—although I've heard many theories, including one that I suppose makes the most sense to me, involving a former teammate and his agent. (If I take that much further, I'll be like the *Post*. I'll stop at saying that the spurious gossip to which Travis referred might have started on Wall Street, passed through Long Island, and been the product of a coordinated campaign of misinformation.)

Anyway, as soon as Danny heard of the *Post* report, he phoned to say that he'd already received a call from Jay Horwitz of the Mets, informing him that the rumors were all over the airwaves and the club wanted to set up a conference call with those two (Danny and Horwitz), me, Steve Phillips, and Fred Wilpon.

When we got hooked up, Fred was supportive and very concerned, assuring me that all he cared about was my reputation and that the club would have my back. Knowing that there would be a lot of media waiting for me the next day at the Vet, somebody broached the idea of a press conference. I didn't want to do anything that formal. I respected and got along well with Dave Waldstein of the *Newark Star-Ledger*, so Danny suggested that we ask Dave to toss me a question about the rumors. We agreed, and Danny called Waldstein. We figured my comments would maybe show up in the notes sections of the papers and everybody would move on.

Tuesday evening, I made myself available outside our dugout during batting practice. The notebooks, cameras, microphones, and tape recorders came out, reporters leaned several-deep into a semicircle, and Waldstein asked me, flat out, if I was gay.

"I'm not gay," I said. "I'm heterosexual. I can't control what people think. I can say I'm heterosexual. I date women. That's pretty much it. I don't see a need to address it any further. I deny those rumors. I don't know how they got started. I don't know why. I don't know where. But obviously, these things do not apply to me at all.

"I can't control what people think. I can only say what I know and what the truth is, and that's that I'm heterosexual and I date women. That's it. End of story."

Yeah, I *wish* that had been the end of the story. Even the story about the story became a story. Wallace Matthews wrote a column critical of the article by Neal Travis, who was a colleague at the *New York Post*, and the *Post* refused to print it. The next morning, Matthews—who in effect was defending me against "scurrilous" (as he called it) journalism—successfully submitted the column to a national website, and prefaced it with harsh remarks about the *Post*. That afternoon, the *Post* released a statement saying that it had terminated him. (Matthews contended that he had quit.) I'd had my differences with Wally, but this time I had to tip my cap to him for his guts and principles.

Meanwhile, my dad wanted to sue everybody in sight. I think—no, I'm *sure*—the incident hurt him more than it hurt me. He was distraught. I was more dumbfounded than anything. And awakened.

The experience changed me almost immediately. I'd never strayed far from my Catholicism, but at that point I reaffirmed my faith. I became more inward and philosophical, lower-key. I realized that the life of the playboy sports star wasn't fulfilling me or even making me superficially happy. I was carrying on that way, in large part, because I felt like I should, and I felt like I should because everybody *else* seemed to think so. I'd allowed myself to be caught in a tangle of image and expectation. It had only made me excessively public and inherently vulnerable, an object of invasion, speculation, and innuendo.

What offended me most about the whole to-do was not the charge of being homosexual. It was the general insinuation that, if I *were* gay, I wouldn't want everybody knowing about it. That I'd perpetuate a lie in the interest of some personal agenda. I found it hugely insulting that people believed I'd go so far out of my way—living with Playmates, vacationing with actresses, showing up at nightclubs—to act out a lifestyle that would amount to a charade. If I was gay, I'd be gay all the way. I had plenty of faults and character flaws, but being fake was never one of them. I was proud of that.

I was proud, also, of the friends who came to my defense. A reporter from the *Post* got hold of Darlene Bernaola, and she told him, "Mike is definitely not gay. Our sex life was very, very healthy. Do you think a gay man would have my initials tattooed on his ankle?"

Vance Wilson, our backup catcher, was probably the most defiant guy on the ball club, saying that the rumors were an embarrassment to the New York media. Even opposing players offered support in their own ways. That Wednesday night, I singled and was standing at first base next to the Phillies' first baseman, Travis Lee, when some of the fans—good Philadelphia boys—yelled out, "Travis, don't get too close to his ass!" Travis said, "What the fuck is *wrong* with people?"

I couldn't answer that. And other than Neal Travis, I couldn't blame the situation on anybody in particular, at least not definitively. Certainly not Bobby. He had given an honest, seemingly innocuous answer that became embellished and distorted in the subsequent spinning. Then Travis repeated a rumor and fired the starting pistol. This all came at a time when blogs and online forums were just getting hot and a whole lot of silly stuff was going unchecked. The Internet was a cesspool of irresponsible rumormongering, and I was a convenient casualty. A common theme had me being spotted at gay bars in Manhattan's Chelsea district.

It didn't let up for a while. On one baseball website, the fashion was to post gay jokes under my name. They called it Piazza-posting. In the meantime, I received a call from a woman with Fox News in Los Angeles who said she wanted to sit down and let me tell my side of the story. My side of *what*? I didn't have a side of anything. There was no story. There was nothing to tell.

As I might have expected, David Letterman absolutely crushed me. It may have had something to do with the fact that I'd snubbed his show years before in order to take my trip to Hawaii with Debbe Dunning; but more likely, the material was just too easy for him. He got me more than once, and even held up the tabloid headline that screamed I'M NOT GAY next to a full-page picture of me. My brother Vince said I should go on the show and punch him in the face. I opted to laugh at the jokes.

Then there was the song called "Piazza, New York Catcher"—by a Scottish band, Belle and Sebastian—that made reference to the rumors ("Piazza, New York catcher, are you straight or are you gay?") and was actually on the sound track of the movie *Juno*. All in all, the saga had a phenomenal shelf life. Further adding to it was the ironic coincidence that there is a well-known activist named Michael S. Piazza, who was the leader of the world's largest gay-and-lesbian church and has authored several books on issues related to homosexuality. He lives in Dallas and, as far as I know, is not related to me.

At one point, it came out that the "local TV personality" to whom Travis had alluded was Sam Champion, a weatherman—he now does the weather for *Good Morning America*—whom I never met. There was also a subsequent report that I'd beaten him up over a lover's quarrel and gotten arrested. People were saying that the police covered it up. Wow. But that drivel *did* get around. When we played in Cleveland once, some hardworking heckler was having a great time shouting, "Sam Champion! Sam Champion!"

To this day, when there's an article circulated about a gay athlete, my name invariably appears. I read one recently about a gay *cricket* player, for Pete's sake; and there I was again. What bugs me about it is not the inference, but the way in which the media continues to sensationalize and exploit the situation for its own purposes. As a rule, I haven't been treated unfairly by reporters—especially those in the mainstream press, where I've come across an impressive amount of integrity and professionalism—but skepticism, it seems, is written into their job descriptions. Speculation makes the rounds. Sometimes, reality is strayed from and myth is manufactured. And with the lines increasingly blurring between genuine news media and the modern alternatives—the likes of bloggers, message boards, fan pages, gossip media, shock media, and social media—the trend is taking us further removed from accountability.

I should point out that the gay community itself hasn't really stoked the rumors or gotten involved in any perpetuating way. For that matter, I can think of only one occasion when I felt I was being checked out by another man. It was a year or two later, when I was buying a CD in Union Square. A guy came up to me in a manner that was unusually friendly. He definitely had the gay-dar up, as they call it. But all he said was "I thought you handled that situation very well." I appreciated that.

My favorite remark, though, came from a website named iSteve.com. It said: "What's with the NYC media calling obviously straight baseball stars gay? Piazza is a metalhead whose obsession is playing heavy metal tunes on his electric guitar. Trust me, a guy whose favorite band is AC/DC isn't AC/DC himself."

Not much more than a week after the gay flap, *Sports Illustrated* published Tom Verducci's special report on steroids in baseball, in which Ken Caminiti became the first big-time player to publicly admit using them and estimated that half of all major leaguers did. Naturally, the New York press jumped all over it, buzzing around our clubhouse with questions. My response was "Whatever happened to baseball? It's not baseball anymore."

That may have been a dismissive remark, but it reflected how I was feeling right about then. The reckless reporting of the gay rumor had sensitized me to the media's exploitation of athletes and public figures, and the *SI* story struck me as possibly another instance of it. Ultimately, Verducci's investigation would be hailed as a significant turning point in the recognition and correction of the steroids problem in baseball, and in that respect it served its purpose; but when it came out, I was frankly more concerned about its effect on Caminiti.

Beyond that, I simply wanted all the noise to stop so I could get back to just playing the game. At age thirty-three, with my skills declining after catching an average of 136 games in the six full years since the strike (not counting 1995, which was abbreviated), baseball was hard enough without extracurricular distractions every week. It was so hard, in fact, that I went more than two months without throwing out a base stealer. The Marlins got seven against me one night.

But I wasn't the only one on the ball club feeling the pressures of age and New York. Our new headliners—Vaughn, Alomar, and Burnitz—were all scuffling. Mo could never get as healthy as he wanted to and struck me as a little disengaged, for whatever reason. Roberto seemed uncomfortable with all the trappings of the city. Burnitz wasn't the same hitter he'd been for five years running in Milwaukee.

All the while, Nelson Doubleday and Fred Wilpon, who simply couldn't coexist, were still haggling over their negotiated divorce, which would involve Wilpon buying out Doubleday. To a degree, I thought their creative tension had been a helpful thing—Doubleday was the aggressive, free-spending owner and Wilpon kept him in check as the more conservative party—but by this time it had deteriorated to the point of dysfunction, which trickled down to field level. Somehow, we hung in with the Braves and everybody until the end of May, but couldn't put together all the pieces that Phillips had assembled over the winter. Steve had brought in proven run producers, and it was hard to blame him for that, but the ball club had a contrived look and feel to it. On a good team, players make each other better. We didn't fit that description. Over the first couple weeks of June, we fell seven and a half games behind. We needed something to galvanize us. We needed some collective focus.

Roger Clemens was usually good for that. He would actually be pitching in Shea Stadium on June 15, the middle game of our weekend series with the Yankees—his first time facing us since the hurling of the splintered bat. But even that wasn't the pure, uncluttered baseball that I was starving for. The shows and papers were full of retaliation speculation. There was also a bonus subplot concerning Clemens, who was being investigated by baseball for plunking Barry Bonds after saying he would introduce himself to Bonds's elbow guard just to make things sporting. Bobby was in his element expounding on all of it. Shawn Estes was pitching for us.

When Clemens came to bat, Estes threw his first pitch at Roger's rear end and somehow missed it. In his own way, though, Shawn *did* eventually get him. He dinged Clemens with a home run in the fifth inning. The next inning, I nailed him, too, with a leadoff shot. Roger was gone a couple of batters later, having bruised his foot running out a double. Meanwhile, Estes pitched seven innings of shutout ball as we pounded the Yankees, 8–0. In spite of Shawn's great game, however, Rob Dibble criticized him on ESPN for not continuing to throw at Clemens until he actually hit him. Bobby, of course, fired back at Dibble. Another day, another sideshow.

A week later, the Braves were in town. It was a series we badly needed to take. You'd think everybody in the organization would be zoned in on that challenge, but before the second game—we'd lost the first—Doubleday announced at the batting cage that he would be suing Wilpon over the appraisal that set the price for the sale of the club. (Doubleday's suit never happened, but two weeks later, Wilpon actually sued *him* to force him to sell at the established price.) Then, during the national anthem, Alomar and Roger Cedeno had to be separated in the dugout.

Nobody—possibly including Alomar and Cedeno—was ever quite sure what they were fighting over. First off, as players, they were diametrically different. Roberto was the intellectual, analytical type, stealing signs, breaking down pitchers, and picking up on all the little things. I think he'd tried to develop some synergy with Cedeno on the bases, and it wasn't working. Roger was more of a raw-talent guy. He was an amazing physical specimen, but not the most intuitive or graceful player. The two of them just weren't a match. To make it worse, they were probably both feeling a little testy. For really the first time in his career, Roberto wasn't playing like a star, and the Mets crowds were riding Cedeno something awful. Even coming from Philadelphia, I've never heard fans open up on a player with such relish and contempt. For whatever reason—mostly, I guess, because he struggled in the outfield—Roger Cedeno was the people's whipping boy, and it hurt him. Hell, it hurt *me*.

Around that time, also, some of the players had been ribbing Roberto about the photo on his rookie baseball card fourteen years before, which was reprinted in the Mets' yearbook. When he'd heard enough, he shouted back and knocked some dominoes off a table in the clubhouse. The next day, Cedeno cut out the picture and taped it onto Alomar's locker. They had some words by the lockers, then a few more in the dugout, and then, by the rockets' red glare, Mo Vaughn had to step between them, which was a good thing for Roberto. With his shirt off, Roger Cedeno was shredded wheat, packed with natural muscle like no other ballplayer I've ever seen. Later that year, David Weathers did something or other with one of Roger's suits for a practical joke, the problem being that Roger had a bad game that night and wasn't in a joking mood when he came into the clubhouse afterward. David Weathers is a big man, but Cedeno picked him up practically with one arm and put him against the locker. I said to Weathers, "Let me tell you something, dude. You're lucky you still have a head." Anyway, the little skirmish with Alomar didn't amount to much; wasn't a big deal, really. Except in New York. Valentine was absolutely right when he told Joel Sherman of the *Post*, "It's a constant struggle to get everybody into a baseball mode."

In that respect, baseball itself was setting a poor example. The commissioner's office is forever talking about the integrity of the game, but what about the integrity of the *All-Star* Game?

It was held that year in Milwaukee, and I happened to drive in the first run with a ground ball in the second inning. We scored three more in the third, two of them on a home run by Bonds off Roy Halladay, at which point it looked as though we beleaguered National Leaguers would break our five-game losing streak. But the American League rallied in the seventh and eighth to tie the game, 7–7, and that's where it stood after eleven innings, when the commissioner, Bud Selig, called it off because both teams were out of pitchers. Which was ridiculous. We had used up ten and the American League nine. You mean to tell me that a pitching staff of nine or ten can't make it through *one game*?

Obviously, the All-Star Game is a different animal than all the rest, because pitchers work only an inning or two to save their arms and allow somebody else to make an appearance; but it wasn't always that way. Not that long ago, starting pitchers would routinely throw three innings and the next two or three guys would go two or three more. The teams played to win. It had never been the most fiercely competitive day or night of the season, but there used to be some intensity and pride involved. Ask Ray Fosse, whose shoulder was separated by Pete Rose on the last play of the 1970 game. By the twenty-first century, however, because of the television spectacle and the movement to protect highly paid pitchers, among other things, the All-Star Game had become commercialized and distorted to the detriment of pure baseball. It had devolved into a much less serious, less meaningful event, and suffered significantly for that. The 2002 debacle was the tipping point. When the out-of-pitchers decision was ridiculed in the media—for once, I agreed with most of the writers and commentators— Selig answered by awarding home-field advantage in the World Series to the league that won the All-Star Game, starting in 2003. I thought that was silly, too, because nothing is proven by a single game in which the starting players are 1) elected and 2) then removed just on general principle. If the World Series schedule were determined by the winner of the overall inter-league competition for that year, I could go along. As it stands, the home-field advantage merely adds to the all-star farce.

Back in real time, the Mets of 2002 just couldn't seem to get our act to-gether. We were actually a few games above .500 at the end of July, but August began with five straight losses. My left wrist was constantly sore and I didn't know why. It was just a nagging kind of year. I took some anti-inflammatories, kept swinging, and on a winning night in Milwaukee—the one that stopped the five-game skid—managed to homer off Ben Sheets to tie Johnny Bench for second place all-time among catchers, trailing Carlton Fisk.

That caused me to take stock, for the first time, of what kind of company I was keeping. I mean, Johnny Bench! For my critics, however, the moment had a different effect: it seemed only to serve as a reminder of how much better Bench was defensively. (Amid all of that, Bobby was kind enough to point out that my catcher's ERA—that is, the earned run average compiled by pitchers while I was catching them—was among the best in the league, which wasn't unusual.) I suppose that losing tends to taint everything associ-ated with it. And that month, we lost *a lot*.

A few days after we snapped the five-game slump, we began a free fall of twelve straight defeats. Then came another five. Incredible as it sounds, we never won a home game in the month of August. Zero and thirteen for Shea Stadium. Altogether, we lost fifteen straight in our own park, a National League record. Bobby was quoted saying that certain veteran players—he meant Leiter and Alfonzo, who were definitely *not* the problems on our ball club—were distracted by the new contracts they'd have to negotiate after the season. Whatever was at the core of our misery, at least we made Doubleday feel better about unloading his half of the franchise, whatever the price. By the time the sale went down, we were in last place, a humiliating twenty-three games behind the Braves.

In early September, Keith Hernandez, the great first baseman who was a color analyst for our games on Madison Square Garden Network, tore us apart in an article on the MSG website. He wrote, "The club has no heart; the Mets quit a long time ago. Bobby Valentine could've chewed this team out in June when this stuff started creeping in. He was quoted as saying, 'We brought veteran players in here who I felt were professionals, and I can be more hands off and they can police themselves. Obviously, I was wrong.'" I took the "heart" reference as a personal affront and lashed back at Hernandez, calling him a voice from the grave. I also compared his remarks to farts in the wind, which goes to show how composed and dignified I remained through all of it. It was a tough time to be a Met. To his credit, Hernandez came into our clubhouse and apologized to the team. That was nice, but it was *still* a tough time to be a Met.

We actually won seven in a row right about then. Prosperity, however, was not for us. In late September, *Newsday* came out with a story charging that seven Mets had used marijuana during the season. One of the players implicated was a young relief pitcher, Grant Roberts, who was pictured smoking a bong back in 1998, when he was in the minor leagues. Roberts was devastated. Apparently, a scorned former girlfriend of his, a baseball groupie, was trying to extort money from him and had released the photo when he wouldn't comply. There was also a report about players smoking pot in a limousine. I have to say, we were an easy target for the press and public both. At Shea, one fan held up a miniature Mr. Met toking on a joint, along with a sign that said, "2002 Mets. Up In Smoke." Others called it the season that went to pot, which sounded about right to me.

Of course, the marijuana rumpus was another occasion for the media to descend upon our clubhouse—when you lose in New York, they're like dogs after scraps—and Bobby, as usual, didn't disappoint them. "I guarantee you no one was in uniform and smoking marijuana, unless they were running around with a whole lot of Visine in their eyes," he said. "I grew up in the sixties. I think I could tell by looking in a guy's eyes if he was smoking dope." Then he launched into an animated, hilarious pantomime depicting a player trying to hit a baseball while he's high. He was staggering around, like he was spaced-out, flailing at something invisible. Bobby might have been feeling the pressure at that point. He also told reporters that he had been concerned about players using marijuana during spring training and had spoken to Grant Roberts about it, a statement he retracted the next day.

None of it helped Bobby's cause. It was no secret that Phillips had wanted him gone for a long time. Fred Wilpon was the guy in Valentine's corner, and the one, no doubt, who got him through the season. Toward the end of the year, when stories were circulating about players being unhappy with Bobby—and some certainly were—Fred called a meeting in the clubhouse and went apeshit on us. He was very emotional, telling us that, "If you don't want to be here . . ." Then his voice cracked and he said something like "you can just . . . go swimming!" Nothing gets a ball club going like the prospect of chlorinated water.

But there was no mistaking Fred's message. He assured us that Bobby would still be the manager at the end of the season, and the following season, as well. When Wilpon endorsed him that way, Bobby, who had been sitting at a locker off to the side, turned around theatrically and smiled at all of us with a very discernible smugness, like the cat who swallowed the canary.

Bobby took a lot of flak for our fucked-up season, but the failures were far from his alone. The high-priced veterans, in particular, came up short, and I include myself in that group. My power numbers were okay—I had thirty-three homers and ninety-eight RBIs (Vaughn was second on the club with twenty-six and seventy-two)—and I won my tenth straight Silver Slugger award as the best hitter at my position; but like everybody else, I got caught in the trap of being on a bad team.

When a season goes to shit the way ours did, the cohesion breaks down and players tend to fend for themselves. It's only natural, in a way, because winning, in the big picture, is no longer an option. The drill becomes every man trying to show it wasn't his fault. The 2002 season was the first time I'd felt that way. There was a point in the year—in *August*, specifically—when I said to myself that all bets were off and just went to hacking. My deal was, what's the point of giving myself up to move a guy over? Nobody else was driving in runs, anyway. Might as well get mine. Like I said earlier, I embraced a certain level of selfishness on the field, because it's closely related to doing the most you can do for your team; but in that ridiculous season, I, like most of the Mets, took it to another level.

If there's a defense for my attitude—and I'm not saying there is—it has to do with being the so-called star. In that respect, my situation wasn't much different than it had been in Los Angeles: I knew damn well that if I didn't have the numbers to prove otherwise, I—this time, along with Bobby—would bear the brunt of the blame for our performance. The pressure I felt was concentrated mainly on hitting home runs, and I let that dictate my response, which was to screw everything else and swing for the fences. The trouble was, that doesn't really work. It especially didn't do anything for my batting average. I'd entered the season with the highest career average of any active player (Tony Gwynn had retired), but, at .280, I failed to reach .300 for the first time since my September call-up ten years before.

Part of the reason for the drop-off was that I was being pitched much differently than I had been earlier in my career. Because pitchers didn't want me to extend my arms, they were pounding me on the inside part of the plate. I actually made a pretty good adjustment and developed a shorter swing, which enabled me to pull more home runs to straight left field than I ever had; but as a rule, pull hitters are not high-average hitters.

I had always placed a premium on base hits, whatever the length. Whether it was coincidence or not, for nine straight years I'd finished with at least a .300 average and my team had finished with at least a .500 record. The first time I fell under, so did the ball club.

The day after the season mercifully ended, I was called into the principal's office. It was odd, because I had no particular rapport with Fred Wilpon or the front-office personnel in general. They never asked me how to run the ball club and I never offered any advice. Leiter and Franco were at ease talking about big-picture stuff—Johnny and Wilpon had a natural connection because they'd attended the same high school in Brooklyn (although obviously not at the same time)—but I was more of a see-the-ball-hit-the-ball kind of guy. Plus, after my experience in Los Angeles, I was inclined to keep management at a distance.

The invitation upstairs left me puzzled and wary. I got the idea that Fred had summoned me, but I couldn't be certain. He was accompanied at the meeting by his son, Jeff; Steve Phillips; and Phillips's assistant, Jim Duquette.

The topic, it turned out, was Bobby.

Right off the bat, Fred said, just as he had in the clubhouse, that Bobby would be the manager again in 2003. I sensed that he was fishing for a reaction. It was already out there that the likes of Leiter and Franco had issues with Bobby—his handling of the marijuana story was a prime example—and my distinct impression was that the guys in the room wanted me to join the chorus. That way, as I figured it, they could fire him and more or less pin it on the players, which was the organization's standard MO.

I wasn't taking the bait. I said, "I don't have a problem with Bobby if I play hard and do my job." And that was that. End of meeting.

About ten minutes later, my father called. He told me that Bobby had phoned him and said, "Mike saved my job."

The next day, the Mets fired Bobby Valentine.

Not surprisingly, the media suggested that Leiter and Franco had something to do with it. I disagree with that, and so do Al and Johnny. In the words of Franco, who to this day, in spite of all the idiosyncrasies that came along with the package, considers Bobby the best manager he ever played for, "That was so far from the truth. If we'd had that kind of power . . ."

Leiter saw the situation pretty much as I did. "[There was] a way in which the organization was trying to disperse blame," he said. "Whether it was firing a manager or justification of a bad record, somebody had to get blamed and nobody in the highest seats wanted to blame themselves. It was a case of trying to defuse and divert the obvious. It was a franchise struggling, not going in the right direction, not really knowing what the plan is."

For his part, Bobby didn't hold Al or Johnny or any of the players directly responsible. He did allow, however, that "the hardest thing for a manager to do is understand and manage aging stars. The hardest thing for an aging player to do is understand his place in the world."

The club, true to form, didn't try very hard to let anybody off the hook for what had happened. Wilpon delivered the company line at the press conference, saying, "We put very good players in place who didn't play very well. It's best to jump-start and get a manager to motivate these players and get the best out of the veterans and the young players. I believe these guys are as good as we all thought they were." Fred's belief cost him about $2.7 million, for the last year of Bobby's contract.

For me, meanwhile, as screwy as the baseball season had been, the year as a whole didn't turn out so badly. In the fall, I met a very intriguing woman named Alicia Rickter.

CHAPTER TWENTY-TWO

My first year in New York, I became friends with a hockey player for the New Jersey Devils, a defenseman with a sizzling slapshot named Sheldon Souray. He was traded to Montreal just before our World Series season, and in August 2002 married Angelica Bridges, an actress who played on *Baywatch* and was ranked by *Maxim* as one of the fifty sexiest women in the world. Sheldon and I didn't keep in touch too much after he left town, but at some point he mentioned a friend of Angelica's from California—also a *Baywatch* actress, and a former Playmate, to boot—whom he wanted to set me up with. Sounded pretty good to me.

Alicia, as it turned out, remembered me from some old commercials but had barely heard of baseball, which was fine. We got acquainted with a few phone calls, and she asked me what position I played. When I told her I was a catcher, she said, "Is that the one behind the batter?" She was better informed in other areas, and sharp and funny besides, and when I picked her up on a Sunday night in October for our first date—she rented half of Sheldon and Angelica's house in Hollywood Hills, since they were in Canada so much—I saw that she was also the most beautiful woman I'd ever gone out with.

We had dinner at the Ivy and talked about God and fashion, among other things. She liked my religious side but not my wardrobe. I was wearing jeans and what she described as a "dorky, baggy turtleneck sweater." My daytime style was surfer shorts, and she didn't care for those, either—a little young for me, I suspect. Needless to say, I was no longer consulting my California clothes guy. When Alicia moved in, the first thing she did was clean out my closet and take me shopping.

In retrospect, it was a blessing that I met Alicia when I did and not sooner, when there was no room in my sights for anything but the game. Nine-eleven had changed me not only socially and spiritually; it had also marked a dividing point in my playing career. It spent me for the rest of 2001 and the aftershock lingered into that miserable 2002 season, the one that made it clear my star was no longer on the rise. Life after baseball was approaching faster than I'd realized a year or two before.

Looking ahead to it, I bought into a Honda dealership in Langhorne, Pennsylvania, a suburb of Philadelphia: Mike Piazza Honda, "where you always catch a good deal." My dad more or less brokered the sale, finding me a partner who was a friend of his. Mets fans would drive down from New York or over from New Jersey to buy cars there. I also had an interest in the family partnership, Piazza Auto Group. Baseball still dominated my life, but it no longer consumed it totally.

The upshot was that, for the first time, I could handle the concept of a relationship with a future. And suddenly, I had a pretty good idea of what that future looked like.

It would have to wait, though, until I got back from the old country. Before I started seeing Alicia, I'd been contacted by MLB about a goodwill tour that involved visits to baseball academies in London, Berlin, and Rome. Except for a family trip when I was a kid, I'd never been to Europe. So Danny Lozano and I stocked up on cigars, scoped out the World War II sites we wanted to see, and decided to make a vacation of it. Alicia sent me off by saying, "Now don't fall in love with any European girls."

The last stop on the itinerary was Rome, where I also met with the higher-ups of the Italian baseball federation about coaching and putting on a promotion for their Olympic team. The promotion was a clinic for kids, which included a hitting exhibition. I knocked some balls out of the park and there were some Italian variations on *ooh* and *ah*.

Then, while I was doing my thing for the national team, the Italian sports council surprised me by arranging a visit with the granddaddy of higher-ups. I was going to meet the pope. First, though, the Vatican had to conduct an investigation on me to find out who my priest was and make sure that I'd been baptized and confirmed; basically, that I qualified as a Catholic in good standing.

The visit was an incredible honor. The papal audience takes place in a large auditorium in the Vatican, and there were maybe five thousand people in attendance the day I was there, including a bunch of bishops and cardinals speaking different languages. Of those received by the pope, only four or five were laypeople.

Pope John Paul II was obviously not in good health at the time, but it was thrilling, nevertheless, when they wheeled him out. I almost missed it.

I was sitting right up front, with an Italian usher next to me. When I heard the cheering I turned around to see, thinking that the pope would be coming down the middle aisle, which he usually does when he's healthy. But the usher fellow, speaking English through his thick Italian accent, goes, "Eh, no. No pope-a that-a way. There. *There* is-a the pope-a."

When the pope is situated, a Spanish cardinal stands up and says, "We have a group from Chile, we have a group from Venezuela, we have a group from Mexico . . ." The groups all stand and cheer and sing hymns. Then a German cardinal gets up and says, "We have a group of pilgrims here from Stuttgart, we have a group of pilgrims from Frankfurt . . ." And they stand up and cheer and sing. And then a cardinal from England and a cardinal from Australia, and then an American cardinal. There was a group from Iowa that sang a hymn. It's like a pep rally, more or less, and extremely cool. They do it every Wednesday. Even if you're not Catholic but a Christian, you should go, because you will see and feel that this is the epicenter of Christianity.

After the group portion, the individuals who have been invited—there were about fifty to seventy-five the day I was there—go up one at a time to meet the pope. I was carrying a Mets jersey with me, Piazza 31. There was a guy I'd been talking to from Chicago, so I asked him, "What do you think, should I give him this jersey?"

He goes, "Yeah, man. That's your hammer, dude. That's your craft. Be proud of it."

When my turn came, I went up nervously and tried to talk, but I didn't really say anything. I just knelt, and John Paul put his hands on my head. I was kind of embarrassed, not sure what to do.

I held out the jersey. The cardinal next to him, who was like his aide, accepted it. I gave it in the spirit of "This is my offering. This is what I do. This is who I am."

So the cardinal bends down and whispers to the pope, "Holy father, this is Mike Piazza. He's a baseball player."

And the pope, speaking English with an inflection that, to me, sounded as much Italian as Polish, said, "God-da bless-a Mike Piazza, the baseball-a player."

I heard his voice in my ear, with his two hands still on my head. I really can't say if he knew who I was, but I'd like to believe that he did. I truly felt a connection. I felt very warm. I felt very special.

I had my rosary with me, and later gave it to my grandmother. When she died, it was buried with her.

• • •

As if to prove that I wasn't *really* a grown-up yet—to, you know, ease the transition and assure myself that love and religion hadn't taken all the punk out of me—I felt it necessary to make a drunken ass of myself at an Axl Rose concert.

He had put together a new version of Guns N' Roses and gone on tour after being underground for several years. In early December 2002, they closed out the tour at Madison Square Garden. I went to the concert with my buddy Eddie Trunk, the host of *That Metal Show* on VH1 Classic. Axl's manager gave us VIP tickets, so we hung out in the hospitality tent while Axl was busy being a couple hours late. I started throwing back vodkas until I was inebriated, and then threw back a few more. I rarely drink like that, but this was a special occasion; this was Guns N' Roses, back from the dead.

The manager gave us great seats for the show, about ten rows from the stage, and I should have shown my appreciation. Instead, I stood on a chair the whole time, pumping my fist and going through the whole angry drunk routine. Eventually, my assisted rage focused on Axl's shirt. He had a tradition in which he would wear the team jerseys of whatever town he was playing in. He'd play a few songs in one jersey, then take a break and come back sporting another one. In New York, he wore a Rangers shirt, then a Knicks shirt, and then a Yankees shirt. Never a Mets shirt. That kind of lit my fuse. All of a sudden I yelled out, in my rambling, bad-drunk voice, "Yo, Axl, what the fuck? I'm here at the show, man. There ain't no Yankees at the show. I'm a real fan, and you can't even put on a Mets shirt?" It must have been my latent issues coming out. Or something.

We went to the meet-and-greet afterward, and Eddie's telling me, "Axl never comes to these things." And then, boom: Axl Rose is standing right in front of us.

Of course, I'm obliterated. I go, "Hey, yo, Axl! What the fuck, man? Like, you know, you think you could've mixed in a Mets jersey?"

Axl was like "Dude, I'm really sorry. I didn't even buy them. I send my guy out to get some and he's a Yankee fan, and you know . . ."

The whole thing was embarrassing, but a hell of a lot of fun.

It did not successfully cleanse me of my built-up anger, however. There was still the matter of Guillermo Mota, the Dodgers reliever who had said the previous spring that he wouldn't forget our little encounter in Vero Beach. For that matter, he couldn't have forgotten it if he'd wanted to, because during the winter Pedro Martinez had criticized him for not fighting me when I grabbed him by the collar.

I hadn't faced Mota during the 2002 regular season, so when we played a Grapefruit League night game against the Dodgers during the second week of March 2003, in Port St. Lucie, I thought about approaching him during batting practice with the let-bygones-be-bygones spiel. Something like "Hey, you know, man, I've had a chance to think about it, and maybe I got carried away." I decided against it.

I decided in favor of batting against him, though, when he entered the game in relief. Our new manager, Art Howe, asked me about it and I said, well, I'm gonna have to do it sometime.

The first pitch buzzed in tight, around my belt. Shit. With that, my spirit of conciliation evaporated. I thought, if this guy hits me now I'm going to fucking murder him.

And he did. In the top and back of the shoulder, which is way too high. If I hadn't known it was coming, it might have gotten me even higher.

I flipped off my helmet, glanced over at the Dodgers' bench—not sure why I did that—pulled back my fist, and went after him. When I got to the mound, Mota threw his glove at me and backpedaled. As the glove bounced off my forearm, I was ready to launch at him—I was doing everything just like I'd wanted to—but the catcher, David Ross, grabbed my arm from behind. Three guys wrapped me up, and Mota was about to come in and take a cheap shot as I was being held. At that point, Jeromy Burnitz made a strong move at him, which persuaded Mota to keep hauling ass backward toward second base. When Burnitz was intercepted, Joe McEwing took over the charge. Ty Wigginton was involved, too. Together, they chased Mota all the way into the Dodgers' dugout.

It was one of the better brawls you'll witness on a baseball field. It was also some of the fastest backward-running you'll see anywhere. The fight ended with the cowardly pitcher safely ensconced in the dugout, yelling; three or four players—including Brian Jordan, who probably could have managed the job by himself—still holding me; and my eyes smoking as I glared at Mota and made a lewd gesture that referred to him as a female body part. Not a shining moment in my career. I'm just thankful I never got to Mota, because I honestly think I could have strangled him. Back in our dugout afterward, I was still screaming across the field at him, this time being vulgar in Spanish.

After a period of not cooling off, I went into our clubhouse, removed my spikes, slipped on my running shoes, got in my car, and drove around the stadium to the Dodgers' clubhouse. When I walked in, the guys in there went silent. I half shouted, "Where the fuck is Mota? Where *is* that motherfucker?" I caught a glimpse of an infielder named Jolbert Cabrera standing on a scale in the training room and thought it was Mota. I was about to punch him when I realized I had the wrong guy. Cabrera gave me a pretty strange look. Then one of the trainers, Stan Johnson—I knew him from my time in the minor leagues with the Dodgers—said, "He's gone, dude. Get out of here before you get in trouble."

The Dodgers' manager, Jim Tracy, had told Brian Jordan to whisk Mota off the premises and drive him back to Vero Beach. Jordan must have been their de facto security guard. I heard later that he'd been getting ready to leave the dugout when I'd come to bat, and Tracy asked him to wait a minute until this hitter was finished. (Howe even speculated that Tracy had set the whole thing up by letting Mota pitch a second inning of relief. In fact, Mota had *batted* between his innings and hit a three-run homer off Benitez.) Anyway, I knew that Jordan had a white Range Rover, so I ran out to the parking lot to look for it. I was too late. My next play was to try to catch them. If they stopped at a light, I was going to break the window and pull Mota out of the car. If that didn't work, I'd try to chase them down on the freeway. One way or another, Mota was going to get hurt and I was going to end up in jail. I got in my car, raced out of the parking lot, saw no Range Rover, and finally realized how incredibly stupid I sounded to myself.

Mota and I were both fined and suspended for five games. It aggravated me that he'd now gotten in two good licks (not counting the glove he threw at me), we received the same punishment (although my sentence was later reduced to four games, starting with the second game of the regular season), and I still hadn't touched him (except for holding him by the shirt collar). I've often thought about how I might have done a better job of landing a punch. I got to the mound pretty quickly, so obviously the direct route wasn't foolproof. If I'd attempted a feint by starting to first base instead and then breaking off to the left, Ross and the umpire would have escorted me down the line, so I wouldn't have had a clear path to Mota. I've decided that the best strategy might have been to assume my place on first, take my leadoff, then, as he went into his stretch, sprint over and nail him. The only problem with that would have been that he'd still have the baseball, which I'm pretty sure he would have fired at me from close range. If he didn't throw the ball at me, he could tag me out, but who cares? It was just an exhibition game.

The last word on the incident—until now, I guess—came a few days later from my old pal Pedro Martinez, who was quoted in *Sports Illustrated* saying, "Maybe he had to show off his testosterone. But this may be more embarrassing than the one before. Why do you go after skinny Guillermo

Mota in spring training and do nothing to Roger Clemens in the World Series?" I thought he sort of answered his own question there. And for the record, Clemens is listed as six foot four, 205 pounds, Mota at six five, 235.

But I didn't bring that up when the New York press asked me about Pedro's remarks. I just wondered aloud what his thoughts might be on the Kennedy assassination, as long as he was offering theories on events he knew practically nothing about.

For the 2003 season, the Braves lost Tom Glavine and we gained him. After all the moves of 2002, our roster was still shifting. Glavine was a welcome addition, but the best was Cliff Floyd, an outfielder who hit well and got along with everybody. Mo Vaughn was back and the Mets still owed him $32 million for the next two years, so there wasn't much talk in spring training about moving me to first base. In fact, Art Howe—who could hardly have been more different from Bobby Valentine—made it clear, right off the bat, that I was still the catcher and there was no particular need for me to be taking ground balls, in spite of the fact that our backup, Vance Wilson, was the best in the league at throwing out base stealers. Howe was probably aware that I needed sixteen more homers to catch Carlton Fisk, who had the career record for catchers. Art was a good man.

It was cold, as usual, to start the season, and I was feeling some soreness in my groin to go along with a bone bruise on my knee that I sustained in spring training. Thankfully, we were back in Miami on the second week. Alicia, who was my fiancée by that time, came down and went to the games with my dad.

One night, the dudes sitting in front of them, obviously showing off for their dates, were going on and on about me being gay. According to Alicia, the girls were saying stuff like "Ooh, I'll take a Piazza with fries," and the guys were telling them, no, no, his girlfriend's a beard (a bogus romantic interest intended to deceive people about your actual sexual orientation). One of them said the reason I couldn't throw so well was that my wrist was too limp. Naturally, my dad was seething and started mumbling things like, "If you think he's so gay, why don't you give him ten minutes with your girlfriend?" But Alicia was the one who actually confronted the guys. She tapped one of them on the shoulder and said, "What you're saying is bullshit. This is Mike's father, I'm his fiancée, and we'd appreciate it if you'd shut up." Needless to say, my dad was impressed.

After we left Florida, Father Time persisted in hounding me, making a nuisance of himself. The knee cost me a game after it locked up while I was catching. In St. Louis, I ripped my elbow on some Plexiglas when I slid for a foul ball at the backstop. (I complained to the players association about that one.) In Pittsburgh, I jammed my foot trying to beat out a grounder. My groin was so sore that the trainers began compression-wrapping it. On a routine physical, doctors found and removed a benign mole—they called it "precancerous"—on my lower abdomen and put in six sutures, which caused me to miss three starts. My shoulder was growling because I'd landed on it diving to first base. I had a hip flexor. My wrists bothered me.

My throwing, which had shown significant improvement, suffered more than anything else. Taking note of that and putting it together with the fact that I was closing in on Fisk, my critics arrived at a typical conclusion: I was clinging to the catcher position for the sole purpose of breaking the home run record. Even Todd Zeile, now playing for the Yankees, threw that out there.

The charges carried with them an implication that I was an imposter behind the plate. I disagreed, of course, but was most offended by the suggestion that I would willfully hold back the ball club in the interest of a personal agenda. A player can't be insulted much more harshly than that.

My deficiencies against base stealers were well documented, and I don't disavow them, but I strongly suspect that the reputation itself was part of the problem. I'm not saying this to challenge the integrity of the umpires—it's a human thing—but I had the definite sense that we weren't going to get the call at second base unless the ball was there waiting for the runner on a perfect peg. On bang-bang plays, I never received the benefit of the doubt. Many times, I felt that if Pudge Rodriguez or Yadier Molina had made the very same throw in the very same scenario, the guy would have been rung up.

Meanwhile, the rest of my catching credentials were roundly neglected. It didn't seem to count for much that I'd caught two no-hitters and, while calling nearly every single pitch that I received over my career (except for the occasional pitchout ordered from the bench), my catcher's ERA was 3.81, more than half a run better than the league average. In my eleven full years, the league ERA had never fallen below 4.49. If you look at it that way—and I don't mean to take credit away from all the very good pitchers I caught—my bottom line, defensively, was considerably better than average. I thought Craig Wright said it kindly, thank you, in his article in the *Hardball Times Baseball Annual*:

> It is pure speculation on my part, but I honestly believe [that Piazza's] obviously below-average throwing arm actually helped his development as a catcher. I've seen more than a few catchers with

good throwing arms who put too much focus on the aspect of defense they are good at—stopping the running game. In steal situations they'll tend to call a good pitch to throw on rather than a good pitch to get the batter out, and some will let the finer nuances of catching slide because they are already perceived as being good catchers simply because they throw well. Piazza knew he didn't throw well and would always be limited in his ability to contain the running game. I believe that drove him to learn the skills of catching that have nothing to do with arm strength. And it paid off. He knew what he was doing back there. Pitchers liked working with him; they were successful, and Piazza was a part of it. . . . Piazza was the #1 catcher for eleven pitching staffs and 10 of the 11 finished in the top five in ERA.

It is reasonable to estimate that in the career sample of matched plate appearances of Mike Piazza [comparing the statistics of pitchers when they threw to him with their numbers when they teamed with other catchers], that through his work with the pitchers in stopping the hitters, that he prevented 344 base runners and helped pick up 265 more outs. And if we assume quite reasonably that his influence was approximately at that level for all the plate appearances that Piazza was behind the plate in his career, it becomes 758 base runners and 584 outs for his career. That's a lot of defensive value, and those positives are far, far more valuable than the negative of what was surrendered to the opposition's running game by his weak arm.

In early 2012, speaking to the same theme, a new study presented in *Baseball Prospectus* rated the top catchers since 1948 in the telling category of preventing runs. The author, Max Marchi, ranked me third over that sixty-four-year period (actually tied with Javy Lopez, who appeared in fewer games), behind Tony Pena and my predecessor with the Dodgers, Mike Scioscia. I was credited with a defensive contribution of 205 runs prevented, fourteen more than Fisk. "The first thing that will probably strike you," wrote Marchi, "is Mike Piazza's ranking. Piazza has always been considered a poor defensive catcher because of his inability to throw out basestealers. However, he fared well at avoiding passed balls and wild pitches (as Tom Tango showed in *With or Without You* in *The Hardball Times Annual 2008*) and now emerges as one of the best ever at handling the pitching staff."

The case against my catching received a boost when Tom Glavine was quoted by anonymous sources as saying that he didn't want to pitch to me. He denied it vehemently, but that doesn't always work in New York—especially when there's circumstantial evidence to the contrary.

It was no secret that the two of us weren't always tuned in to the same station. As an example: Shea had been one of the first stadiums equipped with the QuesTec system for critiquing ball-and-strike calls, and Glavine thought the umpires were squeezing him out of fear that they'd grade poorly if they didn't. After facing him for so many years when he was with the Braves, we all knew damn well that he made his living on the corners—or, rather, just off them. So I guess I wasn't too tolerant of his point of view. On one occasion, when he was complaining about the calls, I said, "Dude, so you gotta throw the ball over the plate!" I'm sure he wished he was still working with Javy Lopez. As it turned out, Glavine was 3–9 at Shea that year and 6–5 everywhere else; so you can see where he was coming from.

At any rate, I certainly respected his professionalism, and for the most part we managed to get along well enough, I thought. He's Catholic, and we often went to church together on the road. Frankly, I was a little surprised when Glavine later took a backhanded swipe at me in his book *Home of the Brave*, implying that he'd grown up with a lot less privilege than I had. I thought I'd gotten past all that.

Mo Vaughn's career ended suddenly on the second day of May—bone spurs in his arthritic knee. When it did, I figured that I might start seeing some action at first base.

I didn't figure, however, that the Mets would tell the press about it before they told me. Steve Phillips mentioned it in a media scrum on the field before a ball game, and Howe alluded to it in a television interview that was widely publicized. I felt a little idiotic, and not a bit pleased, when reporters asked me about the new arrangement, assuming I knew.

When I finally talked to Howe, he assured me that they'd break me in gradually, after I'd had a chance to work out at first for a while. In the meantime, Jason Phillips, a rookie who had come up as a catcher, took on most of the duties there. That was a relief, at least.

But it didn't pacify me; and once again, playing angry brought out my best at the plate. Two days after the awkward announcement, in an afternoon game following a night game—Mo Vaughn bobblehead day—I hit a two-run, tenth-inning, walk-off homer to beat the Padres. That got me going on a six-game tear in which I was eleven for twenty-three, as hot as I'd been in some time.

On the rare occasions when I would get on a roll like that, I'd step into the batter's box, turn to the pitcher, and actually feel in my *hands* that I was going to hit the ball hard. Most hitters would tell you roughly the same thing. It's almost like a spiritual experience, a Zen thing. There's a sort of music to it. The year before, there was a similar stretch when I was feeling it, and every time I settled into my stance, Led Zeppelin's song "No Quarter" would be playing in my head. Bartolo Colon might be cutting his slider loose, the stadium could be howling, and all I'd hear was Robert Plant: *They ask no quarter. The dogs of doom are howling more!* At times like that, you're so calm, relaxed, and confident that there's not a shred of fear, doubt, or negativity in your system. Other times, you stand up there and it's like, oh man, how am I going to do this? You've got to somehow scratch and scramble just to get back to the basics. It's all based on confidence, and confidence is based, in large part, on prior results, which is why streaks happen. Sometimes a hitter can even detect a *lack* of confidence in a pitcher, and feed on that. It's a short step from confidence to intimidation. When a hitter knows he has intimidated a pitcher, the battle is largely won.

In mid-May 2003, I had arrived at that point. Over a three-game series in Colorado, I went seven for eleven with three home runs, which left me only nine behind Fisk. The next day, I picked up two more hits in San Francisco. My batting average was suddenly up to .336, and the way I was seeing the ball, I was pretty confident that, if I could hold it together physically, I was going to put up one of my best seasons. I was still aching all over, but that can be disregarded when you're raking like I was—especially when your team is on the ropes; we were already a dozen games behind the Braves.

On the second day of the Giants series, May 16, I took my first practice session at first base. Then, top of the first inning, I came to the plate against Jason Schmidt, feeling indomitable, and promptly fell behind in the count. At one and two, I was guessing a slider away—a strikeout pitch—but instead, the ball came directly at my neck. I jumped back to get out of its path and suddenly it felt like somebody was holding a blowtorch to my right groin. It was a crazy, overwhelming jolt of pain. I hopped on my left leg a time or two, went down hard, and actually couldn't breathe for a few moments.

The injury is called an avulsion. It might as well be called a gunshot. There are four abductors attached to your groin, and when one of those pulls away, you won't be dunking, dancing, walking your dog, or swinging a baseball bat anytime soon. I'm guessing that the stitches—the ones put in when I had a mole removed from my abdomen—had something to do with what happened, because the area was still tender. It's entirely possible that my weight training contributed, as well, which is part of the reason why it was discouraged for so long in baseball. At any rate, the strain was a grade 3, the worst kind. I couldn't even undress; they had to cut off my uniform pants. I left Pacific Bell Park in a wheelchair. When I went in the next day for an MRI, my leg was purple all the way down to my knee.

What hurt most, though, was the fact that I'd been crushing the ball. To be so hot and get stopped so cold . . . it made me feel beaten. I'd never planned to succumb to the line of thought that catchers start to break down after a certain age; but there I was.

The team arranged for me to rehab with Lisa Kearns from SportFit in Coral Gables, Florida. It was nearly a month before I could even exercise. I more or less knew what to expect, because the same thing had happened to my dad a few years before when we were playing golf. He took a swing and just crumpled to the ground. I thought he'd tripped, and I started to laugh until I realized what kind of pain he was in. But my dad could still sell cars with a groin strain. All I could do was train carefully and watch news reports about the war in Iraq. My days were devoted to the underwater treadmill and the BBC.

Even when I got back to New York, I was as far from catching as the Mets were from catching the Braves. Alicia was there with me, and one night, when we were walking to dinner, I had to make it up some stairs. I guess I didn't look so good doing it, because a guy watching me shook his head and said, "Man, your shit is fucked up." It was a depressing period, exacerbated by the knowledge that when I returned—and even that wasn't certain—it would be to a last-place team.

The Mets were playing badly enough to get Steve Phillips fired as general manager (replaced by Jim Duquette). Still, it was hard to blame the GM for the depletion of our high-priced starting lineup. On top of Vaughn and me, injuries had also claimed Alomar and Burnitz, who was having an excellent year. It was grim. All of a sudden, the prospect of playing baseball just wasn't as compelling as it had always been. At the same time, though, I was determined to get back on the field in 2003, even if it was just for a week or month. I never wanted to end a season on the disabled list.

To my mounting discouragement, the calendar kept turning. When I was still hobbled after the all-star break, I sat down next to Cliff Floyd, all pitiful, and said, "Dude, I got nothin' right now." Cliff—what a great teammate—told me, "Don't stress, man. Don't mess yourself up. Get your shit right and come back when you're ready."

Finally, on August 13, after I had grumbled through seventy-six games of misery and restlessness, Howe penciled me into the three-hole against the Giants, ironically, at Shea Stadium. A rookie pitcher named Jerome Williams was working for San Francisco, and it was the first time I'd ever played with our rookie shortstop, Jose Reyes, whose speed and talent were downright astonishing. Reyes had come up in June and won a few games almost single-handedly. One night, when he was beating some team or another with his bat, his legs, his glove, everything, David Weathers and I looked at each other and I said something like, "Who *is* this guy?"

Against Jerome Williams, Reyes led off the bottom of the third with a bunt single and then stole second. I was the next batter and somehow caught one well enough to get it out of the park. I finished the night with five RBIs. It felt *good*.

Unfortunately, I couldn't keep it going. After the adrenaline rush of getting back on the field, it didn't take long to realize that I just wasn't myself, psychologically. I'd lost that feeling of invincibility. My personal myths had been shattered. The doubts had taken root. I was no longer able to clear my mind of the questions and fears that can hold an athlete back, and inevitably do.

For obvious reasons, my groin injury had postponed the first-base experiment. I'd been restored to my customary position, but with the self-awareness, this time, that I couldn't catch 140 games a year anymore and probably never should have. A catcher needs some days off. In my years with the Dodgers, Joe Ferguson used to remind Tommy now and then that I was due for a blow, but Tommy would just tell him that November will come around soon enough. And I was with him all the way—I didn't *want* him to sit me down. It was a point of pride. Or stubbornness. With Bobby and the Mets, the program was pretty much the same.

Without a doubt, though, the innings had taken their toll. Three months on the disabled list had brought it all home. The irony is that, if I hadn't hit so well for those first ten years, I likely would have stayed longer at the top of my game because I'd have been afforded more rest. That said, I'm not willing to return any of the extra hits or home runs that came from being in the lineup every day. And I surely wouldn't have wanted to take any longer to catch Carlton Fisk.

When we went to Atlanta near the end of August, I drew within four of the record by reaching Shane Reynolds and Greg Maddux on consecutive nights. (Fisk's record was 351, and I actually had 358 homers altogether, but eleven of mine had come as a DH or pinch-hitter.) The second of those was the eleventh and last home run I would hit that year.

September was a tough month to endure. We finished a wretched twenty-nine games under .500 and 34½ behind the Braves. As the season wound down, I swung the bat so horribly that my average dropped all the way to .286.

True to New York, however—true to the Mets—the last week would not pass quietly. We were about to lose our final home game, against the Pirates, when Howe made a ninth-inning double switch that seemed to stop the trains and rattle the windows in the Empire State Building. Vance Wilson came in to catch and I took over at first base.

I actually made all three putouts in the inning, on a line drive from Carlos Rivera—a bullet, of course, the very first batter—and throws from Pedro Feliciano in front of the mound and Ty Wigginton at third. It doesn't sound like much, but from where I stood, it was all pretty damn scary. And pretty damn lucky, because none of the plays required any range, which I knew I didn't have.

Of course, those three insignificant outs only escalated the speculation about whether I'd switch to first base full-time in 2004. The corollaries included untrue reports that I'd continue to resist the move—mostly, I just doubted that I'd be very good as an infielder—and public discussion over whether I should be traded for a *real* first baseman. There were even rumors that I'd *asked* to be traded. That was bogus; but I wouldn't have minded at all if somehow, from somewhere, a proven first baseman had been found and brought over. In my mind, that would have been the ticket not only for my purposes but for the ball club's, as well. When no move was made along those lines, it felt as though, rather than going properly about the business of building the team, the Mets were taking the easy way out, putting the onus on me. The message seemed to be that, with the money I was making, I had to be the answer, no matter what the problem was.

To tell the truth, the whole deal was kind of frightening. I could handle pressure in the batter's box—I was accustomed to that—but wasn't so sure about fielding it at first base.

Nevertheless, I had no intention of filing for divorce. As unimpressed as I was with the way the organization had been run for the past couple of years, I felt a strong connection to the Mets. By the end of 2003, I'd actually played more games in their uniform than I had as a Dodger.

In November, Major League Baseball announced that between 5 and 7 percent of the players who had been tested for steroids that season were found to have used them. The Major League Baseball Players Association had agreed to the survey on the grounds that it was anonymous, with the consequence that if at least 5 percent of the tests turned up positive, we'd be randomly checked over the next two years, with punishments established for offenders identified by those results.

There would be no sanctions based on the 2003 findings, and since names were not to be released, either, some guys had regarded the season as sort of a free spin. And yet, the season stats didn't reflect any significant up-tick in power. It was actually the first year since 1995 that nobody in either league had hit fifty home runs.

In the end, the survey proved to be not quite as anonymous as everybody had been assured it would. The union neglected to destroy the list of guys who had tested positive, and a grand jury subpoenaed it for the BALCO investigation the following spring.

When that occurred, Dan Lozano said to me, "Mike, this list might be coming out. You'll probably be hearing from the media." He was right, of course. I wasn't involved, but that made no difference. Whenever there was news on the steroids front, various reporters were eager to link me to it.

The same thing happened three years later, when the *New York Daily News* broke the story about Kirk Radomski pleading guilty to distributing performance-enhancing drugs to major-league players between 1995 and 2005. Radomski, who was a principal source for the Mitchell Report—baseball's investigation into the PED issue, released in 2007—had been an assistant in the Mets clubhouse from 1985 to 1995, which meant that he'd been gone for nearly three years when I arrived in New York. I guess there was some confusion over the timing, because just before the news got out, Gene Orza, the chief operating officer of the MLB Players Association, called to alert me that I might be asked about Radomski. Orza was good about keeping players apprised of what was going on and sending out a heads-up when it was in order. I was playing in Oakland that year, and Gene caught me early in the day as I was walking the streets of San Francisco, just off Union Square.

I didn't know Radomski, but I knew I wasn't on any list of steroids users that might appear in the Mitchell Report or anywhere else. So I took the opportunity to say, "Gene, I want to clear my name. I want for writers to be able to call you and ask you if I'm on a list."

Orza was sympathetic, but he told me, "I can't do that, Mike. If I do that, the writers will put every single player on the spot and say, 'Hey, can I call the union and ask if you're on the list?'"

Sure enough, the next day a reporter from the *Daily News* showed up in Oakland to ask me about Radomski. I had nothing.

Ultimately, my skeptics were undeterred by the fact that I wasn't implicated in either the 2003 tests (the government eventually limited its BALCO subpoena to ten players, and theirs were the only names that went public) or the Mitchell Report, which was released in 2007. A certain baseball blogger came out with the curious observation that the acne on my back had mysteriously disappeared between 2002 and 2004, citing that as compelling evidence that I'd used and then stopped using steroids. What he wrote, specifically—actually calling it an online column as opposed to a blog, I should point out—was "Then all of a sudden the acne was gone. Piazza's back was clear and clean. There was not a speck of acne on it. His back looked as smooth as a baby's bottom. What a remarkable development. It was a medical miracle."

I frankly don't know if my acne receded or not around that time; or if it did, how much or why. But I know bullshit when I see it.

CHAPTER TWENTY-THREE

At my age and level of wear and tear, facing a very possible switch in position—the plan, as it stood, was to give it a try and go from there—I needed a different kind of off-season training regimen. I needed now to address mobility and flexibility; to back off a bit on the strengthening of my body, which I'd undertaken from the time I was barely a teenager, and concentrate on its preservation.

I didn't junk the weight training but I supplemented it with more-athletic workouts, including a lot of the fashionable core stuff. At the time, my rehab trainer, Lisa Kearns, was working with Ty Law, a defensive back for the New England Patriots, and I'd meet them at a track for agility and speed drills. I have to say, it was sobering; actually, scary, in a sense. I admire and defend the skill of baseball players, but I was knocked for a loop by the realization of how much of a nonathlete I was compared to someone who really *is* an athlete, in the traditional sense. Ty Law was a physical specimen, and I doubt that, among football players at his level, he was an exception in that respect. Up close, the combination of size and speed simply blew me away. I developed a sudden and profound appreciation for the athletic demands on a professional football player. Those guys have to block, tackle, throw, catch, fake, juke, accelerate, change direction, think quickly, and, with it all, endure, to boot. Hitting a baseball is a special talent, and chances are that most football players wouldn't be able to do it against major-league pitchers; but at the same time, I don't know that there are a lot of baseball players who are pure, classic, world-class athletes.

Later in the winter, a few weeks before reporting to spring training, I flew with Alicia to California, where she introduced me to a lanky, uncombed, unshaven guy she knew named Andy Bourell, a sort of personal trainer and nutritionist for some of her friends. Andy was well schooled in the methods he preached, and by practicing them had lost a lot of weight at one point.

Alicia suggested that some of the stuff he advocated, such as sophisticated stretching and dietary habits—less beer and red meat, in my case—could help get me through the season, and I couldn't disagree. So I hooked up with Andy and liked it.

The first time he saw me, he noticed a problem with my right calf and the arches of my feet when I went into my catcher's crouch. In his opinion, my groin injury had developed from a strain of the tendons on my right side and could have been prevented with more stretching. He went to work correcting my posture through yoga. In a short time, I felt so much better that I brought Andy to Florida when I reported to spring training with the pitchers and catchers. He was there for a couple of weeks, staying at my house and preparing me uncooked dinners involving, among other things, spinach, mushrooms, alfalfa sprouts, garlic, and sunflower seeds. We'd stretch and do some yoga poses. I called him my yogi. He'd also accompany me to the ballpark, wearing an old wool cap and carrying a bag of apples and seeds along with a drink he concocted from apple cider vinegar, grade-B maple syrup, flaxseed oil—sugars and carbs—and cayenne pepper, which is good for circulation. Naturally, my yogi became a big story in New York. Eventually, though, the Mets asked Andy not to come into the clubhouse anymore, because MLB had restricted the access for what they called personal assistants.

For all the flexibility work I'd put in, I was still venturing into new territory at first base, subjecting myself to unfamiliar strains, twists, and twitches of the body. I'd been in shin guards for sixteen years, and even though I'd played first base in high school and college and occasionally even in the minor leagues, it wasn't like riding a bike. At the age of nineteen, without much of an identity defensively, I'd been able to reinvent myself as a catcher. Starting over at thirty-five, after nearly fourteen hundred big-league ball games in a squatting position, was a different deal altogether. I labored. I also tweaked my left thigh and missed valuable practice time.

It appeared, though, that first base would be at least a second home to me in 2004. I was okay with that. Scared as hell, but okay. Pretty sure that it was happening too damn fast, but okay. As much as I still considered myself a catcher and still believed that was what I *should* be, I'd come to grips with the fact that life as I knew it was changing in a lot of ways.

I'd have preferred, though, that the whole world didn't watch me bumble through the transition. I knew my hands were good enough to handle first base; I was mainly worried about the footwork and finesse. At one of the first spring-training workouts, the Mets covered the chain-link fence of the practice field with a dark privacy screen so I could fumble and stumble in privacy. When Jeff Wilpon saw it, he ordered it taken down immediately. Whatever.

One way to deflect attention from the position issue was to hit the ball like I used to. I was pleasantly surprised how well the new off-season regimen had gotten me into hitting shape. The very first day of camp, I blasted so many balls out of the park that Art Howe declared me back. He was well aware—and so was I, believe me—that, at the end of 2003, I hadn't homered in my last eighty-eight at-bats, the longest, most troubling dry spell of my career. That suddenly seemed like a long time ago. In a Grapefruit game against the Expos in Viera, Florida, I crushed two home runs and really *felt* like I was back. I lingered a while in the clubhouse trying to burn those swings into my brain. I knew that if I could stay in that groove, it would take the pressure off my defense, wherever I played.

Incidentally, I wasn't the only one on the club changing positions that spring. For reasons I've never figured out, the Mets decided to move Jose Reyes from shortstop, where he'd been spectacular as a rookie, to second base, so that Kaz Matsui—the first Japanese infielder ever signed by a major-league team—could move in at short. We also had a new center fielder, Mike Cameron, and closer, Braden Looper. Both of them were terrific teammates. I'd always hated hitting off Looper—he owned me—but I loved the guy.

Braden wasn't a natural closer, however, so I figured I'd help him out a little. I felt it was my duty and obligation to find him an appropriate coming-in-from-the-bullpen song that wasn't "Enter Sandman," which was the choice of Mariano Rivera and, to my extreme annoyance, just about everybody else who even *thought* he was a closer. I was highly motivated to come up with something different for Looper. I ended up picking a tune called "Lightning Strikes," from the only Aerosmith album that Joe Perry, the guitarist, wasn't a part of. Unfortunately, it didn't really cut it.

Cameron, meanwhile, was batting behind me, and I was *catching,* when we opened the season in Atlanta. Matsui, who hadn't hit well in the spring, led off and went three for three with a home run. I homered, also, and we won, 7–2, behind Glavine.

Our old teammate Mike Hampton started against us in the second game and I reached him for a two-run homer in the first inning. We took a 6–0 lead, but the Braves scored eleven runs in the third. Damn. My second home run of the game, to straightaway center in the seventh inning—it was measured at 456 feet, the second-longest ever recorded at Turner Field—tied me with Joe DiMaggio for fifty-eighth place on the all-time list and left me one short of Fisk's record for catchers. In the bottom of the inning, I made my first appearance of the season at first base and handled a ground ball off the bat of Adam LaRoche. I then doubled in the eighth to complete a five-for-five night, which didn't count for much in an ugly 18–10 defeat.

My maiden voyage as a starting first baseman occurred in San Juan, Puerto Rico, in the Sunday afternoon finale of a three-game series we played there against the Expos. It went well enough—I took care of a foul pop-up, a throw in the dirt, and three ground balls, without incident—except for a little collision at first base that I got the worst of. Peter Bergeron, Montreal's speedy leadoff guy, had bunted to Glavine, who didn't have a good grip on the ball when he tossed it to me. Just as Bergeron crossed the bag, I reached for the throw and took an elbow to the back of the head. It left me a little dingy. I also hyperextended my elbow, which caused me to miss our home opener the next day. Swell. I'd made my peace with the move to first base, in part, because it was supposed to spare my body the beating it took behind the plate. So much for that theory. Mask, please!

Two days later, I was back at first. The good news was that, on a cold and nasty night, hardly anybody came to watch. The bad news was everything else. To get us started right away on the act of losing, I made my first error as a first baseman on the first play of the game, a hard grounder down the line by Dewayne Wise that I whiffed at. It was looking like I might not be such a horrible catcher after all.

Glavine, for one, must have gotten his fill of me at first base pretty quickly, because he complimented my game-calling when he beat the Dodgers in Los Angeles on April 28 (the night after I appeared on *Jimmy Kimmel Live* and Kimmel had me fire a BB gun at Roger Clemens bobbleheads). Of course, he might have been influenced by my home run in the sixth inning off my old friend Hideo Nomo, which put us ahead and made Tommy the winning pitcher. The homer came after I'd gone sixty-three at-bats without one, and gave me 351 as a catcher. I was tied with Fisk.

I was still tied with Fisk when the Giants came to Shea during the first week of May. In my head, and also in my conversations with reporters, I tried to downplay or even marginalize the record. For one thing, I knew it wasn't DiMaggio's hitting streak or Aaron passing Ruth. For another, it's not cool to preoccupy yourself with personal accomplishments in a team sport. And lastly, I was fed up with the way the record had been twisted into a symbol of my resistance toward playing first base. All things considered, I was happy to be the secondary story to the arrival in town of Barry Bonds, who happened to be tearing up the league at the time. A couple of weeks before, he'd hit eight home runs in eight days. He was in the high 600s now, with a bead on Ruth's and Aaron's career totals.

I was happy, also, on Wednesday night, May 5, to get the count to three and one in the first inning against Jerome Williams, the guy I had touched up the year before in my first game back after the groin injury. This may sound trite, but it's true: As he released the next pitch, a strange feeling of peace came over me. It was like time stood still—one of those rare occasions when the game actually slowed down. I distinctly recall how clearly I saw the ball leaving Williams's hand, and saying to myself, this is going to be a home run to right field.

It was a little sinker that caught too much of the plate. I took a rip and it landed in one of my favorite spots, off the bottom of the scoreboard in right-center, just over the Mets' bullpen. I ran the bases to the accompaniment of the theme song from *Chariots of Fire* and video highlights of my career as a Met. As much as I had tried to soft-pedal the record, I decided right then, under the influence of bliss, to simply own it. To celebrate. In the best tradition of Bonds—who sat out the game with a sinus infection—I tapped my chest and pointed to the heavens when I stepped on home plate.

Meanwhile, my mind was dancing. *I'm the greatest home-run-hitting catcher in baseball history.* That incredible thought was crowded in with fly-by memories of all the skepticism and cynicism that had followed me into the sport and hung around; of those who had doubted, dismissed, discouraged, resented, or out-and-out rooted against me. In a surge of inspiration, I found myself surprisingly *grateful* for all of that. Suddenly, I *got* it: that nothing worthwhile comes easy; and if it did, a person couldn't possibly appreciate it as much as I was appreciating that very moment.

I flashed through the scenes along the way: my backyard batting cage, practically begging to be signed, the tarantulas in the Dominican Republic, chasing balls to the backstop, sitting on the bench in Vero Beach, the negotiations, the trade, the Marlins, the booing, the World Series, the game after 9/11, the face of my dad . . . Then I ducked into the dugout, hugged my teammates, and jumped back out to acknowledge the crowd.

When I returned inside, I said to Art Howe, "Get me to first base. I'm tired of catching."

Just so you know: I was joking.

An hour later, I was wondering if I really *had* set the record. It rained so hard, the game was delayed after the fifth inning, with the score tied 2–2. If we couldn't resume, the stats would be wiped out and the whole thing replayed. It was a substantial delay, but we finished. And we scored six times in the eighth to make it all good.

Afterward, Fisk graced me with a thoughtful phone call and issued a statement that made my day. "When someone broke my home run mark," he said, "I was hoping it would be Mike."

I was too, actually. I told the reporters, "I'm blessed. I've lived a dream. Everything from here on in is icing."

The next night, we completed the sweep of the Giants. I was back catching, Bonds was back in left field, and in the eleventh inning he leaped in vain to catch a ball I hit over his head and the fence to win the game, 2–1, after great pitching from Leiter, Looper, Mike Stanton, and David Weathers. They walked Bonds twice, and it worked. Jim Brower pitched to me, with two outs, and it *didn't* work.

In a strictly baseball kind of way—in its spontaneity and timeliness—that home run might have been more satisfying and emotional than the one the night before. When you're celebrating purely for the *team*, there's no need to pull your punch. There's no self-consciousness holding you back. I raised both fists into the air as I circled the bases. At that instant, the game was good.

A week later, after discussing it with me, which I appreciated, Howe announced that I'd be catching only a couple of games a week for the rest of the season and playing first base on most of the other days. Jason Phillips and Vance Wilson would take over the majority of the catching. I'd be sharing first with Todd Zeile, whom we had signed as a free agent. It was our fourth shift as teammates—Dodgers, Marlins, Mets, and now the Mets again—and, for Todd, would be the last of sixteen seasons in the major leagues. I needed three more years to get to sixteen. It made me wonder.

For the time being, though, I was feeling frisky. At Houston in mid-May, we got a rare shot at Clemens, who was 7–0 after signing with the Astros as a free agent. He was zoned in, giving up only two hits in seven innings, neither of them to me. But in the ninth, with two outs, two strikes, Eric Valent on second base and Octavio Dotel pitching, I homered into the Houston bullpen to tie the game, 2–2, and deprive Clemens of his victory. The Astros' manager, Jimy Williams, had come to the mound to suggest to Dotel that he walk me, but Dotel disagreed. Jason Phillips finished off the comeback in the thirteenth with his first homer of the season. Afterward, the writers tried to get me to say that there was some personal gratification in pulling the rug out from under Roger that way. I ducked the question by telling them, "I just do my thing." Suffice it to say, it was a hell of a day.

For that matter, it was a hell of a month or so. In June, Fisk, Johnny Bench, Gary Carter, and Yogi Berra—a Catchers Hall of Fame—came to Shea Stadium to honor me for the home run record. I'd had my differences with the Mets, but that night they stepped up big.

What I thought was going to be a low-key affair took on a life of its own. We happened to be playing the Detroit Tigers, which pulled in two more esteemed members of the catching fraternity—Lance Parrish, a nineteen-year veteran with fifteen seasons of double-figure home runs, in addition to being the guy the Dodgers brought to camp in 1993 just in case I didn't make it; and Pudge Rodriguez, the best defensive catcher of my era. Also, Doc Mainieri, my old coach at Miami-Dade Community College, was nice enough to come. Mainieri had been one of the first to endorse my move to catcher, more or less. (He did that by promising me I could catch if I played for his son, Paul, the next year at St. Thomas University. It might not sound like a whole lot, but solid encouragement had been hard for me to come by in those days.)

The presence of all the famous catchers turned the event into a testimonial for the position, which, thankfully, deflected the attention from me, to some extent, and spared me some serious discomfort. In no way did I care to be exalted above the likes of Johnny Bench.

My opinion is that, as the complete catcher, Johnny will always be alone on the island. It's difficult to compare the two of us because I was just a different animal. I feel that I was a complete *hitter*—power and average—who could also catch. (Bench compared my bat speed to Bonds's and George Foster's.) Obviously, I wasn't the greatest defensive catcher in the game, but, in spite of all the hullabaloo, I wasn't the worst, either. While I had some terrible times throwing out base stealers, my career average of 23 percent was not all *that* far off the major-league average, which was 31. Given that I normally gave up a hundred or so stolen bases a season, that comes out to roughly eight extra bases a year that were attributable to my arm, about one every three weeks. My fielding percentage was almost dead-on the average. More important, I prided myself on receiving pitches in a way that would encourage the umpires to call them strikes—not "framing" them, per se, but letting the ball close the glove, keeping my body still and my mitt quiet so that the ump got a good, long look and didn't think I was trying to manipulate him. Recent studies have shown that a helpful receiver can get his pitchers a couple hundred extra strike calls over the course of a season, and save his team as many as thirty or forty runs. I'd like to think that my efforts in that respect had something to do with the damn good catcher's ERA that I maintained over my career, which, for my money, is the most significant measure of a catcher's defense. Putting it all together, I can state with confidence that my body of work in the tools of ignorance lands me somewhere around the middle of the pack, at the very least. The fact is, I've seen a lot of backup catchers who have stuck around the big leagues playing worse defense than I did.

That said, I was never in Bench's realm as a receiver, and few have been. I've seen the films. I've seen his athleticism. I've seen his hands. Hell, I've *shaken* his hand. Nobody compared to Johnny Bench defensively. But as a hitter . . .

I have to be careful here, for two reasons. One, because the last thing I want to do is crack on my teammates. And two, the second-to-last thing I want to do is diminish Johnny Bench in any capacity. I repeat, he is the greatest all-around catcher who ever played the game, without a doubt. I'm compelled, though, on my own behalf, to point out that Bench had Pete Rose, Joe Morgan, George Foster, and Tony Perez on his side. He batted in a Hall of Fame lineup. Unquestionably, I benefited quite a bit from the other run producers on my teams—Karros, of course, plus Raul Mondesi and Todd Zeile with the Dodgers and John Olerud, Robin Ventura, Edgardo Alfonzo, and later David Wright with the Mets—but up until the time I broke Fisk's record, I was rarely in a lineup I wasn't counted on to carry. There aren't many other catchers you can say that about, if any. There aren't any who won five Triple Crowns for their teams (Dodgers in 1993, 1994, and 1997, Mets in 2000—although Alfonzo and I had the same batting average—and 2001). Over my first ten years, I led my teams in batting average seven times (with one tie), RBIs eight times, and home runs all ten (with one tie). Those are just the facts. In the book *Baseball's All-Time Best Sluggers*, author Michael J. Schell, using a complicated formula that includes adjustments for eras and ballparks, ranked me as the top-hitting catcher of all time by a considerable margin, with Joe Torre second. Bench was fourth, Fisk ninth, Berra eleventh, and Carter twelfth. For what it's worth, I was rated the sixty-third best hitter overall. My adjusted batting average was thirteenth. I'm going to take a flier and assume that the twelve ahead of me were also a wee bit fleeter afoot.

Schell's appraisal was seconded by Craig Wright. "With Mike Piazza we can say with certainty that he is—without question—the greatest offensive catcher in the history of the major leagues," Wright wrote in the *Hardball Times Baseball Annual*.

There is no one else who is even remotely close. Piazza's raw numbers are so impressive that it is easy to overlook that every single season of his career his home field was one that favored the pitcher. Particularly during his years in LA, he was performing in the toughest park in the league for hitters, especially in hitting for batting average. Yet one could just throw out the park factors, and his offensive numbers remain mind-boggling for a catcher.

[The] combination of high average and power made Piazza truly unique among catchers . . . Piazza's career slugging percentage as a catcher (.560) is over 50 points higher than any other catcher in history. . . . And remember, not a one of these numbers has been park adjusted. None of these other great offensive catchers played with home fields as tough as Piazza's. . . . Most important of all, he was an absolute monster in his ability to shrug off the pain and fatigue of catching and knock the snot out of the ball.

As awkward as it felt to have Bench, Berra, Fisk, and Carter at the ballpark just for *me*, what a fantastic thing it was for my father. What a night.

Thankfully, I caught that game, made a couple plays, had a couple hits, and we won, 3–2, on a walk-off homer by Mike Cameron.

I was now the starting first baseman for the Mets, but the starting catcher for the National League all-star team. And Roger Clemens was the starting pitcher. You can imagine how the press tore into that story line.

The game was at Minute Maid Park in Houston, where Clemens had gone to high school and was now pitching. It was my tenth all-star selection in eleven years—I'd missed out in 2003 because of my groin injury—and my ninth start. The one I *didn't* start, or even play in, was the 2000 game, which came three days after Clemens hit me in the head. Four years later, that drama apparently hadn't played out yet; at least, not in the eyes of the media.

There were no man hugs or fruit baskets exchanged between Roger and me, but we did meet privately in the training room the day before the game. The other players were getting too many questions about us, so at one point Clemens put his arm on me—photo op!—and said something like, "When are we gonna go over some things?"

I said, "Yeah, let's talk after the workout."

It was an amicable conversation, but not quite what I was looking for. I didn't really expect an apology—Roger didn't earn his reputation by being *nice*—but it would have gone a long way. For me, it would have provided some closure, at last. The bat-throwing episode still ate at me, and in the broader, career context, it does to this day; mostly because it stole my World Series. I had earned and relished the privilege of playing in the first Subway World Series since 1956 and intensely hoped to make my mark on it. Instead, my place in Series lore was ordained by a dramatic role in an idiotic incident that was none of my doing. I felt cheated.

Short of an apology, I wasn't seeking even an explanation from Clemens, because, face it, for what he did that night, there *was* none. But I thought maybe he'd at least admit to being a little reckless with the beanball that started the whole soap opera. I'd have accepted that. As it turned out, I don't think we accomplished much.

We were on different pages even in the bullpen warming up before the introductions. Roger threw me a couple of pitches, and as I squatted, waiting for more, he stopped, toweled himself off, and rested for a while. I finally walked back to the dugout and somebody else took over.

When the game started, with 26 percent more people watching in New York than the year before—nationally, on the other hand, the ratings were down 7 percent—flashbulbs went off and so did the American League. Ichiro Suzuki started it with a double. Pudge Rodriguez followed with a triple. Manny Ramirez homered. Alfonso Soriano homered. Under normal circumstances, I'd have been out to the mound a time or two during the rally, but Roger and I were all talked out. By the time the top of the first was over, it was 6–0.

Afterward, some writers actually asked me if I'd tipped off the American League batters. I wasn't out for revenge against Clemens, but if I *had* been, I'd have gotten far more satisfaction out of catching three no-hit innings from him. That way, he'd have had to tell the media that I'd been solid back there. It would have been a much better story, and a much better night, if we'd worked well together, shut them down, and won the game.

When the season resumed at Shea, Howe had me catching, for a change, and we beat the Phillies in eleven innings, on an RBI single by Ty Wigginton, to pull within a game of them and the Braves. But I was in the throes of a pretty serious power failure, and hearing the boos to prove it. The slump was aggravated by the fact that I could barely run.

Back on Memorial Day, in Philadelphia, after sprinting over from first base to try to catch a pop foul, I'd banged my left knee sliding into the fence in front of the dugout. It hadn't seemed like a big deal—I wasn't feeling much pain around that time—but two months later it was still swollen and getting crankier. My acceleration wasn't there. The knee would give out when I climbed stairs. The pain could be controlled by cortisone shots and anti-inflammatories, but even then it felt like there was a golf ball inside. I played through it, then missed a few days after spraining my wrist while manning first base. It happened against the Marlins when Juan Pierre bunted and the throw arrived on the home plate side of the bag. As I reached for it, my hand crashed against Pierre's shoulder and bent backward.

By that time, my slump had spread to the rest of the lineup. David Wright came up from the minors, took over third base, and showed the stuff of a star, but it didn't help. Meanwhile, at my request, the organization signed Lasorda's *real* godson, my youngest brother, Tommy, a catcher and hardworking guy who had experienced some knee problems and been released by the Dodgers from their minor-league system after playing, or *not* playing, behind Russell Martin. It was a nice gesture, and I was glad for Tommy, but that didn't help us, either.

At the end of July, we were eight games out and still sinking. In early August, playing in Milwaukee, I barely made a double out of a ball I hit to the wall. It worried me.

In fact, I was feeling fragile all the way around in those days; diminished. Unless Al Leiter was pitching—Al understood that there were things he could do on the mound to neutralize the running game—I rarely caught. It was understandable, of course, given my difficulties behind the plate, which were intensifying at a troubling pace. Not only was my mobility compromised, but the criticism of my throwing clanged so loudly in my head that I developed a mental block about it—not as bad as Steve Sax, when he couldn't make the throw from second to first, but bad enough. I was insecure and leery of cutting loose. Ironically, I didn't have that trouble when I played first base. Runners would actually take off on pickoff plays, thinking that I couldn't throw the ball over to second. I'd wonder what the hell they were doing and just gun them down easy as could be. I mean, c'mon, it's only ninety feet. It happened three or four times.

Otherwise, though, first base and I were not getting along so well, either. Selena Roberts wrote in the *New York Times* that "the first-base experiment has failed with a transition that has been awkward and inglorious for Piazza. . . . The move has only exposed Piazza to ridicule."

Truthfully, it exposed me to more than ridicule. It was the first time I'd ever been frightened on a baseball field. A major leaguer is not supposed to admit something like this, but I was terrified of a ball being hit in my direction. It felt as though every time a pitch was sent on its way, all the eyes on the planet turned to me. I didn't mind that when I had a bat in my hands; I had prepared for it my entire life and welcomed the chance to do what I did when it meant the most. But I hadn't prepared for playing first base—at least, not nearly enough—and was rattled by the knowledge that I would be roundly judged after any play that came my way. I felt like I was sitting at a piano on the stage of Carnegie Hall with sheets of Chopin in front of me. Wearing mittens. The whole scenario made me so nervous that, between innings, especially if I'd just hit, I'd run back to the clubhouse and *eat*. They had great food back there, so I'd just whip up a sandwich or grab some little something. I actually gained weight, up to 236, the heaviest I'd ever been. All because I was stressed over playing first base.

Naturally, the extra weight put more burden on my knee, which wasn't up to the task. Finally, after an 0-for-4 night in a loss at St. Louis on August 6, I sat down with Art Howe to talk. I felt as though I was at a crossroads—if not career-wise, at least New York–wise. I was a bad first baseman, the Mets didn't want me to catch, and the whole situation was beating me up. My spirit was broken, my confidence sapped. In short, I was a mess. I told Art that I'd certainly play if he needed me to, but it was painfully obvious that I wasn't helping the club at the moment.

He and I agreed that a couple days off were in order, and so was an MRI. The diagnosis was white fluid on the knee. It was chronically sprained. The risk, if I continued to play, was tearing an ACL.

I had another chat with Art, and he said he was just going to put me on the DL. Jeff Wilpon was in on that conversation, as well, and told me, supportively, "Go take a few days off. Take three or four days, get yourself together, then we'll send you down to Port St. Lucie, get you in rehab. . . ."

It was a good plan, but I had an idea how to make it better. Without wasting any more time, I hurried to Kennedy Airport, got on a JetBlue flight to Long Beach, California, where Alicia was staying, and proposed to her.

My intention was to take her to dinner and hide the ring underneath her pillow after we got back. But when she picked me up at the airport and we checked into a place in Laguna Beach, I thought, hey, wouldn't it be nice to go to dinner as an engaged couple?

So I got down on my knee in the hotel room and asked her to marry me. Normally, Alicia would have some kind of irreverent, smart-aleck reply for whatever I said or asked. This time, she just said yes. We set the date for January. Just like that, the low point of my career had morphed into the high point of my life.

I stayed in California for a few days before heading to Florida for rehab. The Mets held steady for a couple weeks; then came the crash.

When I returned to the lineup on August 30, feeling stronger and re-freshed, we had lost seven of the last eight. I homered my first night back, but beyond that provided no relief whatsoever. Altogether, we dropped eleven straight to make it a miserable sixteen defeats in seventeen tries.

Within a couple weeks, I was thoroughly embarrassed, deeply perplexed, and more discouraged than I'd been before I went on the DL. I thought I'd gotten better. I also thought I was better prepared, psychologically, for first base. But my performance there only reinforced the obvious, operative truth about my change of positions: it was *wrong*.

Maybe if the transition had been more deliberate and people had been conditioned to the fact that I wasn't *really* a first baseman yet—if there had been a learning curve, maybe a year or so of dabbling over there before mov-ing in as a starter—it might have worked better. Maybe, even, if I'd had a full spring training at first base, following some special instruction in the offseason . . .

Or maybe the Mets simply shouldn't have forced the issue. Wouldn't my defensive difficulties have been moderated a bit if I'd just cut back on the catching to, say, four games a week, DH'd in the American League parks, played first base here and there—maybe against certain left-handers—and been available off the bench the other days?

Unfortunately, there were business complications. I was making too much money for that. My contract was back-loaded, which meant that I was actually pulling in more salary at this point—about $16 million—than I had in the initial years of it, when I'd been in my prime. At those rates, the Mets wanted to get as many games out of me as they could. What's more, if they'd sat me down a couple times a week, the city would certainly have pitched a fit.

Case in point: I'd been given a day off in the middle of July for the afternoon wrap-up of a series against the Phillies. We'd won the game, but nevertheless, a *New York Post* writer, Steve Serby, tore me apart the next day. He wrote, "It served as a reminder why Derek Jeter, who refused to sit at Shea less than 24 hours after landing face-first in the seats diving for a Trot Nixon foul pop, remains the Captain of New York Baseball. As a franchise player, Piazza didn't have to take the manager's decision sitting down in the most important July 18 game the Mets have played in four years. The Mets need Iron Mike, not Tirin' Mike."

The story just struck me as weird. A few years back, I'd become friendly with Serby when he wrote a lifestyle piece on me during the Subway Series. Then, shortly after 9/11, he tracked me down one day on the street, near my condo, which made me uncomfortable. He told me about an article he wanted to do with me; but under those circumstances, I wasn't interested. I could be wrong, of course—it's always a tricky thing to assign motives—but when Serby wrote the cheap shot in 2004, I had the sense that it was his payback for me not cooperating with him in 2001.

Of course, when the public reads a point of view in a newspaper, it's not privy to the personal background that might be involved. The public didn't know, for instance, that Mike Lupica, the *Daily News* columnist, was upset with me; or that I'd called out a *New York Times* reporter for lounging on one of the players' couches in the clubhouse—breach of protocol—and he hadn't forgotten it. In this case, the only thing the public could derive from the story was what Serby wrote: that I obviously wasn't a tough-minded team guy like Derek Jeter, because I hadn't challenged the manager's decision to give me a midsummer afternoon of rest and recuperation. One game. Imagine if I'd been getting days off all year, on pace for sixty or more.

But here's the thing: knowing what the fallout would be, the Mets wouldn't have put themselves in that situation. To a fairly significant extent, the press was able to push the ball club around in that respect. The Mets, time and again, predicated their moves on what they perceived would be the reaction of the media, and in turn the city. That's ultimately what happened in 2004, I believe. When the clamor built up about moving me to first base, and continued, the team responded by moving me to first base, whether I was ready or not.

From the Mets' perspective, look at it this way: If I took well to the position, stayed healthy all year, and hit forty homers, they'd have come out ahead. If I *didn't*—if it turned out the way it actually turned out—that would make it easier for them to part ways with me after my contract expired at the end of 2005; a *hell* of a lot easier. It would make me look obsolete and in the way. Besides, by 2005 or at least 2006, they would almost surely have a new face of the franchise: David Wright, most likely. Not only was he a terrific and appealing young player, but New York fans tend to be more tolerant of guys who come up through the organization. David Wright was the man-in-waiting. Jose Reyes fit the bill, as well.

At the end of the season, my take on the first-base quandary hadn't really changed from the way I'd seen it at the end of the season *before*: the most sensible solution would have been for the Mets to acquire a legitimate first baseman and simply have me share the catching duties with Jason Phillips, if they were looking to break in a young guy, or Vance Wilson, whom I really admired as a receiver. I respected the payroll considerations, but to put me at first on a regular basis, unready and unequipped, was simply not in the best competitive interest of the ball club. It reflected the seat-of-the-pants approach to roster construction—the lack of vision, essentially—that doomed our team in those days, from the moment Nelson Doubleday sold his interest to the Wilpons.

We finished 2004 at twenty games under .500, which, sadly, was exactly our average in the three full seasons following 2001. Maybe it's just my personal regard for Art Howe, but the whole debacle didn't seem like the manager's fault. He took the fall nonetheless, when he was fired as soon as the season ended—actually *before* it ended, although, gentleman that he is, he agreed to finish it out. Jim Duquette, who had served as general manager for a little over a year since replacing Steve Phillips in 2003, was canned, as well. Willie Randolph, best known as a Yankee, would take over for Howe. The new GM would be Omar Minaya, whose first order of business seemed to be trading me.

I really don't know how the talks initiated, or if they actually *did*, for that matter; but for a couple of hot weeks in November, stories flew around about the Mets and Dodgers considering a swap of me and Shawn Green, a veteran, left-handed-hitting outfielder who could also handle first base. It made sense, actually. Both of us would be playing out the last years of our contracts, making almost identical money. The Mets needed a first baseman and the Dodgers needed a catcher. The Dodgers missed me and the Mets probably wouldn't. If the prospect of returning to my old team didn't thrill me, the thought of returning to my old *position* certainly did. Meanwhile, other rumors had me going to the Angels.

I knew my time in New York was winding down, and the concept of leaving a year ahead of schedule didn't seem all that disagreeable. On the other hand, I'd bought a condo in TriBeCa—half of a penthouse, across the hall from Jon Stewart of *The Daily Show*, which gave the floor a nice political balance. I was looking forward to living there with my bride.

CHAPTER TWENTY-FOUR

Donald Trump's wedding to Melania Knauss took place in Palm Beach a week before ours, which was in Miami, so a lot of the paparazzi stayed over. His guests included Oprah Winfrey, Muhammad Ali, Clint Eastwood, Luciano Pavarotti, Usher, Elton John, Billy Joel, Arnold Schwarzenegger, Shaquille O'Neal, Joe Torre, Derek Jeter, and a couple princes. We had none of those folks. And yet Hugh Hefner—who wasn't there, either—said of ours that it was one of the best-looking wedding parties in history.

Needless to say, Alicia gets most of the credit for that, and not just for being incredibly beautiful herself, especially in her white satin gown. My only contribution along those lines was my brother and best man, Tony, who's a good-looking guy. Hers included bridesmaids who were Playmates and *Baywatch* types, such as Brande Roderick, Lisa Dergan—who married Scott Podsednik, the outfielder—and Angelica Bridges, the wife of my friend Sheldon Souray. Alicia also made her mark on the church, St. Jude (because it's Melkite, an ancient Byzantine branch of Catholicism that originated in the Middle East, we needed special permission and class instruction to get married there), which has an impressive amount of stained glass that she embellished with pillars of candles and arches of pink roses. Of the hundred or so people who attended the service, the vast majority sat on her side, which made me realize that, after sixteen years in professional baseball, I didn't have too many close friends to show for it. Franco and Leiter came. Lasorda didn't. I did supply the priest and the Cuban dude named Arturo, I think, who rolled cigars at the reception.

The priest, Ignatius Catanello, was an auxiliary bishop from the Brooklyn diocese and a serious Mets fan. He conducted some of our Sunday masses at Shea Stadium, which I really enjoyed, and we'd hit it off. I was able to talk to Bishop Iggy about everything—Alicia, faith, sex, slumps, first base, life changes, theology, history, whatever. He became a strong influence and helped me see things in a more spiritual light. It meant a lot to us that he agreed to come to Miami to officiate our ceremony, which was just about perfect. We had a guy shoot the whole thing on Super 8 motion-picture film, and it's like a piece of art. I've watched the video so many times that Alicia thinks it's weird.

After the wedding, everyone went to the house of our friends J. R. and Loren Ridinger to take pictures, then boarded a couple of yachts—one of which belonged to Pudge Rodriguez, who lived on the water—to ride over to the reception at the mansion on Fisher Island, a gorgeous place (the island had the highest per capita income in the United States) that was once owned by the Vanderbilts. We'd met J.R. and Loren a few years before when I mentioned to a friend that I wanted to go to a Dolphins game (when the Eagles were in town) and the guy hooked me up with J.R., who had a suite at the stadium. He and Loren own Market America, a large online shopping network.

Loren and Alicia made three different test runs on the yachts and timed them to ensure that we all arrived on the island at just the right moment, when it was not too dark but dusky enough that the candles would stand out. Somehow—you can only get to Fisher by boat—the paparazzi were already there. Loren had them escorted out, because it wasn't the time or place. There really weren't that many celebrities, anyway. Some of the newspaper stories said that Shaq came and Billy Ray Cyrus sang at the wedding, but it wasn't true. It was a great time, though. We had a DJ playing Moroccan music. All the guests were given their own golf carts so they could ride around the grounds and dodge the peacocks. Of course, most of the guys hung out around the pool, where the cigar roller was set up. That was before it was hip. We were pioneers. Arturo rolled me a big cigar in the shape of a baseball bat. I still have it in my humidor.

The next day, the *New York Post* ran a picture of Alicia and me on the front page, coming out of the church and looking up as our friends tossed flower petals at us. The headline was "Mr. and Mrs. Met." Just below, there was a little streamer that said, "Iraq Votes." Even after seven years in New York, the city still amazed me sometimes. I thought, man, are we really that big a story? I suppose it was flattering. And I was at the stage of my career when flattery felt kind of nice.

To me, the symbolism of the wedding reached beyond even love and commitment. It was the start of a new chapter. For such a long time, I'd been dead set against getting married, for fear that it would compromise my single-mindedness; but things were different now. The rest of my life was upon me. While my mission in baseball wasn't yet complete, it was clearly approaching that point. I was an aging catcher who couldn't play any other position and my contract was up at the end of the season. To be honest, I wasn't sure that I'd still be in uniform after 2005. I was less confident and more injury-prone than ever before. By default, I guess, I was still "the man" on the Mets, but that would last only until somebody else stepped up. Bottom line: my place in the game, as I'd known it, was no longer secure.

Inevitably, that reality fostered a feeling of *in*security, which, for an athlete, feeds on itself. As my stature dwindled, I'd wake up thinking, What are they gonna write about me today? When I was young and invincible, I could blow right through all that clutter; I trusted that, within a day or two, I'd bust three hits and a long home run and everything would be good again. I raked, we won; it was simple. Now neither was happening very often. I'd become sensitive. Vulnerable. I needed somebody to hold my hand and assure me it was okay; to listen to me rant and tell me to shut up and get a grip; to *be there*. Alicia had a way of making me feel better.

I'd first realized it early in the 2004 season, after she'd moved in with me at my Gramercy Park place. It was a cold, rainy night at Shea, we had a small crowd to start with and by late in the game most of it was gone. I looked up at my box and saw this little head up there, sticking out the window. It just made me smile to myself. I can't say for certain whether that was the instant I knew I'd marry Alicia—I'd had a pretty good idea right from the start—but it was one of those that reduced the world to her and me. That was a way better world than the one I'd been struggling through.

There was also this: The week of the wedding, the *Daily News* conducted a poll on baseball's hottest wife. In a close vote over Anna Benson— the former stripper whose husband, Kris, was a starting pitcher who had just signed with us as a free agent—Alicia won.

In other news, I didn't get traded.

Benson wasn't the only starter we'd brought in for 2005. Except for Glavine, our whole rotation turned over.

Al Leiter, my best friend on the ball club, was gone after a great seven-year stretch. Steve Trachsel sustained a herniated disk in spring training and would miss most of the season. In their stead, we were counting on, among others, Victor Zambrano, who had been acquired through a trade with Tampa Bay at the 2004 deadline. (To get Zambrano, the Mets had given up Scott Kazmir, which didn't make sense to many people, including me. There was a rumor that Kazmir, a twenty-year-old lefty who threw about ninety-five miles an hour, had been dealt because he'd been disrespectful to Leiter in spring training. It was one of those ludicrous stories that always seemed to pop up when the Mets were in a public-relations pickle. What actually happened was that Al and Johnny Franco were riding bikes in the weight room at spring training, listening to a CD of old Motown stuff, most likely, and Kazmir, who I think was in his first big-league camp, strolled in after a throwing session, walked over to the CD player, and stuck in Eminem or some such. Leiter looked at Franco, kind of raised his eyebrows, and said, "Do you believe that?" Franco replied with something like "When you were coming up, would you have done that to Guidry and Righetti?" Then Al turned to Kazmir and said, "Hey, Scotty, we're listening to some music here, man," and Kazmir said, "Okay, all right, I see how it works around here." He changed the CD back, and that was it. No more problems, no hard feelings, nothing. Until the media started questioning the trade of a phenom left-hander.) We'd also picked up Kazuhisa Ishii from the Dodgers in a swap for Jason Phillips. And then there was the coup de grâce: Pedro Martinez.

I admired Pedro's competitiveness and didn't actually dislike him. Ironically, he and my father became pretty good friends. If I ran into Pedro today, I'd probably give him a hug. Nevertheless, our differences ran deep and were a matter of record. At various times in our personal history—which was tied to my chilly relationship with his brother Ramon, in spite of catching his no-hitter in 1995—he had hit me in the hand, questioned my manhood, and referred to me publicly as "Fucking Piazza." So this wasn't going to be easy, seeing as how, once again, I was a catcher and only a catcher.

Thanks to Willie Randolph and Omar Minaya for that, incidentally. It turned out Omar didn't have to deal me away to solve the first-base problem. With Willie's blessing, he put me back where I belonged and traded for Doug Mientkiewicz, going for the maximum upgrade around the bag. It was what the Mets should have done the year before.

As far as Pedro was concerned, I was resolved not to let the team be affected by our little feud. I'd mellowed a little bit, I guess, and had come to realize that, for the most part, you don't achieve the level of success that Pedro ultimately did—especially in a foreign country—without being a motherfucker; without having the fire and fury inside you. The fact is, I couldn't relate to players who *didn't* have that, the ones who were just kicking the can down the road. And sometimes, in cases like Pedro's, I locked horns with the guys who *did*, because we were snorting bulls in the same pen. That's probably why I never had many friends in the game. For whatever reason or reasons—immaturity, selfishness, trying too hard, or some other of my numerous character flaws—I wasn't always the best teammate.

Apparently Pedro was feeling the same spirit of conciliation. At his first press conference in New York, he stated that "whatever happens before when we were not teammates or whatever—whatever words were said—have to be forgotten the first moment I became a teammate. He's now my family."

Détente had its reward on Opening Day in Cincinnati, when Pedro struck out twelve Reds in six innings, although we lost in the bottom of the ninth, 7–6, on back-to-back home runs off Braden Looper by Adam Dunn and Joe Randa. Our working relationship remained good enough, and Pedro settled in nicely as our ace; had a hell of a year, in fact. I can't say, however, that he and I ever became confidants, or even buddies.

Our relationship was part of a bigger scheme of things, and a very strange dynamic. Going back to my days with the Dodgers, there was a bizarre sort of energy between me and the Spanish-speaking pitchers, in particular—Pedro, Ramon, and Ismael Valdez. Fraternization is widespread in the big leagues, especially between Latin American players, and honestly, I felt as though there was some kind of weird Hispanic conspiracy against me, almost like a secret brotherhood, a Latin mafia type of thing that had it in for me. I know it sounds paranoid—a dramatic way of describing what could just be a combination of coincidence, the nature of the game, and a few friends comparing notes—but there's a litany of circumstantial evidence for something on that order, winding through my experiences in the low minor leagues, the comments from Ramon and Valdez in Los Angeles, the verbal assaults from Pedro, and getting hit with pitches from Pedro, Guillermo Mota—twice—and, later in 2005, Julian Tavarez. And that's just the conspicuous stuff. The real sense of it comes simply from the vibes you pick up.

That said, I suspect the Latin players were picking up vibes from *me*, as well. It was a clash of styles. I'm not anti-Latin by any means. For Pete's sake, I had the initials of a Peruvian woman tattooed on my ankle. There were plenty of Latin players whom I liked, respected, and got along with just fine. Generally speaking, those were the guys who felt blessed and lucky to have the opportunity to play Major League Baseball in the United States and make a lot of money at it, just like I felt blessed and lucky. It's a privilege. I admire the Spanish-speaking players who honor that privilege by learning the language of the nation where the dream comes true.

When I played in the Dominican Republic and Mexico, I picked up some Spanish so that I could order my meals, talk to taxi drivers, and communicate better with my teammates. I'm currently taking Italian lessons so that I can converse with the guys I coach for the Italian national team and do a few interviews with the Italian media. It's a matter of respect. Except for Toronto, which is an English-speaking city, Major League Baseball is played in the United States. For some Latin players, there seems to be a mentality that since they come from a less advantaged socioeconomic background, it exempts them from having to adapt to our culture. That's misguided, in my opinion. I strongly disagreed, for instance, with Ozzie Guillen's complaints that organizations typically provide translators for Asian players but not Do-minicans, Puerto Ricans, Venezuelans, or Mexicans. The fact is, a Japanese or Korean player would be totally isolated without an interpreter. A Latin player is far more likely to find himself in the company of teammates and even coaches who speak his language. In a sense, the Latin guys have inter-preters all around them.

I can't speak for every club, but in my experience with the Dodgers, in particular, no category of player was more catered-to than the Latin Ameri-can. To start with, the organization ran an academy in the Dominican Re-public with English teachers and three square meals a day. From what I've seen on the larger scale, major-league teams go to great lengths to prepare their Spanish-speaking players for successful careers in the United States. And they should. I certainly don't dispute that Latin players are entitled to the same dreams and opportunities I had, but I'm sorry: when they arrive on U.S. soil, the onus isn't on the American players to learn Spanish, although that certainly helps; it's on the Latin players to learn *English*. Speaking En-glish permits them to better serve the ball clubs they play on, just like learn-ing the signs or staying in shape in the off-season. It also provides benefits from the personal standpoint, connecting them to the public and making them more marketable. It's in everybody's best interests.

No doubt, my views on the subject—in general, on the privilege of being a big leaguer—came through, one way or another, to the Latin play-ers, and their attitude toward me, at least to some degree, was a response.

There were some mixed messages coming from Mike, in a way. He had this Southern California flip-flop thing, this GQ guy with his kick-back disposition, a father who adores him and was there all the time; but there was also this stern, play-the-game-right, don't-be-a-hotdog, run-the-ball-out attitude. Not one time did I ever see Mike just jog to first base on a ground ball, even a ground ball to the second baseman. Here he is catching a hundred and forty games a year, trying to leg out infield singles. Often, on ground balls to the shortstop, he wouldn't run past the bag but just bang his foot down on the bag trying to beat it out. The trainer would cringe. It always seemed amazing that he didn't blow out an Achilles or something.

That's just how he approached the game, and sometimes the Dominican [style] would bother Mike. When guys were fucking around, his thing was, cut it out, let a sleeping dog lie. He'd say that all the time. Don't make other players want to kick your ass.

—Al Leiter

We hung in the race for the first few months of the season, and I have to say that Pedro Martinez had more to do with it than I did. In the back of Randolph's mind, he probably wished he didn't have to play me as much as my salary more or less dictated. Around mid-April, I did muscle up for one of my longest home runs—a shot off Vicente Padilla at Citizens Bank Park in Philadelphia that landed up by Bull's BBQ (Greg Luzinski's place) in the left-center-field pavilion—but my stats stunk and my throwing hadn't gotten much better, in spite of the fact that I had hired Steve Yeager to work with my catching mechanics.

That was my dad's idea. I learned a lot from Yeager, but my body was simply deteriorating at that point. I did think, however, that I did a nice job with the pitching staff, Pedro included, although Ramon Castro got several of the starts when Pedro pitched.

In June, I actually got ejected arguing balls and strikes on Pedro's behalf. Well, that's stretching it, I guess; but it started out that way. Eric Cooper was the umpire on a Sunday afternoon when we played the Angels at Shea, and I thought he squeezed Pedro on the first two pitches of the ball game. So Cooper and I had a chippy little dialogue going on (some of my teammates, in fact, were calling me Chip in those days), and when I came to bat he rang me up on a three-two pitch. I had a thing or two to say about it, and kept riding him when I got to the dugout, at which point he tossed me. In a rage, I bolted out of the dugout toward Cooper and might have earned myself a hefty suspension if Mientkiewicz hadn't intercepted me in the on-deck circle.

Mientkiewicz, in fact, kept me in check on a regular basis with his interventions. When I was slumping and moping—so out of sorts at the plate that I was chasing bad pitches, which I didn't ordinarily do—he told me that I'd probably be leading the league in home runs if I played in a normal ballpark, which was a lie but a helpful one. Cliff Floyd was another guy with a talent for being able to make a friend feel and sometimes play better. That's what a good teammate is all about.

Floyd also had a huge power season going, which made him an even *better* teammate. Together, he and David Wright, who came into his own as a big-time player that year, more than compensated for the drop-off in my hitting. We had also added Carlos Beltran, a switch-hitting center fielder who strengthened the middle of our lineup when he moved into the three-hole. For the first time in a few years, we weren't bad. I only wish I could have said the same about myself.

I did, however, make my twelfth all-star team, joining Beltran at Comerica Park in Detroit. I started the game for the eleventh time and was hoping to catch Clemens again, to improve upon our misadventure of the year before. But when he entered the game to pitch the fifth inning, I left in favor of Paul Lo Duca, who, like me back in the day, had been traded from the Dodgers to the Marlins.

A couple of days before the all-star break, Randolph had nudged me from the cleanup spot back to fifth in the batting order. Floyd moved up. I understood. Then, less than a week *after* the break, Wright moved up, deservedly, to the five-hole, and I found myself batting sixth. In early August, I sank to seventh.

It was a blow to the ego, but nothing I was compelled to complain about—I didn't want to be just another guy who couldn't face the fact that he wasn't what he used to be—and nothing that I didn't see coming. All signs pointed to the fact that the Mets were phasing me out. It was a reality I chose not to fight.

Then, for three weeks starting in mid-August, I wasn't in the lineup at all. A bone in my wrist was fractured by a foul tip off the bat of Freddy Sanchez of the Pirates. By that time, although we still had a winning record, we'd fallen into last place in our loaded division. When I came off the disabled list on September 10, we had dropped under .500, twelve games behind the Braves.

That night we played in St. Louis, and in my first at-bat I gave us a 1–0 lead with a solo home run off Jeff Suppan. But we trailed, 4–1, when I led off the eighth against Julian Tavarez, a tall, slender right-hander from the Dominican Republic. He humped up and nailed me in the right earflap.

I left the game with a concussion, but something happened in the bottom of the inning that hurt worse. Randolph and Sandy Alomar, a former big-league infielder from Puerto Rico who was one of our coaches, got hooked up in a heavy discussion over who we were going to throw at in retaliation. Randolph's original thought was to wait for Albert Pujols, who was due up fourth against Aaron Heilman, but Sandy said something like "No, you can't hit Albert. He's a *much* better player than Mike is right now."

That jolted me on two levels. One, it sounded like a little more of the Latin conspiracy that I was increasingly convinced of. And two, it was a big-time reality check. Make that a kick in the nuts. A couple of years before, I'd have been an even exchange for Pujols. I like Albert a lot, and I didn't want to see him hurt, but he knew he was the one who was supposed to get drilled in that situation. Instead, we hit *David Eckstein*. Don't get me wrong, Eckstein was a tough dude and I admired the way he played; but he stood five foot six and muscled up for a home run about every other month or so. All of a sudden, the payback for me is *David Eckstein*? That was a big, fat humble pie in the face.

It also let me know exactly what the Mets thought of me at that point, confirming, for all practical purposes, that they had no intention of re-signing me and I'd be out of there in a few weeks. But not before I had a few choice words for Sandy Alomar. I confronted him on the spot.

That, however, didn't settle the matter of Tavarez. After the game, I stormed over to the Cardinals' clubhouse to find him. Tony La Russa spotted me first and took me back to his office. He apologized, and one of the St. Louis owners did the same, which I appreciated; but I still wanted to see Tavarez. It didn't happen. Plan B was to fight him the next day before the game. I waited through batting practice to catch him coming off the field, but he eluded me by walking out through the center-field gate. That was my last shot at him for the season.

The following spring, I was training in Florida with the Italian national team before the World Baseball Classic and riding with Frank Catalanotto of the Blue Jays, telling Frank how badly I wanted to beat the shit out of Julian Tavarez, when we pulled up to the Ritz-Carlton and there he was. Frank said, "Here's your chance."

I walked up and Tavarez goes, "What's up, my friend Mike Piazza?" He had a phone to his ear.

"Get off the phone," I said. "I want to talk to you. Let's take a walk."

I was waiting for him to say, "Fuck you," but he started yammering and yabba-dabba-dooing and asked me why I didn't charge Roger Clemens. Mota, Pedro, Tavarez—they all said the same thing. I'm not sure why I didn't punch him right then and there.

Out of all the guys who hit me, I felt that Julian was the one whose ass I definitely should have kicked. But I guess I've mellowed since then. Away from the game, my anger has subsided somewhat. When I saw Tavarez on the occasion of the Marlins' last game at Sun Life Stadium, we exchanged greetings and he even introduced me to his family. Seemed like nice people.

As the Mets' support of me slackened, the fans' actually picked up. It was a significantly different dynamic than I'd endured in Los Angeles, when the organization had effectively alienated me from its constituency. At Shea, the customers gave me a standing ovation every time I hit a home run.

I was moved—not only by the gestures but by the evolution of my relationship with New York. That first year, the Mets' crowds had booed me unreasonably. Seven years later, here they were *cheering* me unreasonably. I think—I hope—that, through all the weirdness and drama, they appreciated my role in reestablishing the Mets as a credible, capable franchise. It's something I was proud of.

The loudest home run cheer may have been the one for my nineteenth and last of 2005, a 450-footer in the opener of our four-game, season-ending series against the Rockies, which everyone pretty much understood would mark my farewell as a Met. Appropriately, David Wright hit two that night, and Glavine threw a two-hit shutout that I thoroughly enjoyed catching. The victory, 11–0, assured us of at least a .500 season.

By the time Sunday came around—the final game of the year—I thought I was ready for it. The warmth of the fans hadn't budged my feeling that it was time to move on, and I was fairly certain it hadn't changed the organization's position, either. In my mind, in fact, the good karma served as reassurance that this, indeed, should be my so-long to Shea. I went to the stadium mass that morning in a melancholy mood.

The sermon was about the victims of 9/11. It got me. Combusting with my frame of mind, it rekindled all the emotions of that time, from the horror of the event to the high of the home run. It reminded me, also, of how that ternble day in 2001 had clearly divided my eight seasons with the Mets. We'd been on the rise before it and the decline thereafter; and the same applied to me. As I listened, the scenes and tribulations of those years came swirling back in my memory—that first day at Shea, with thousands of people walking up for tickets; the sleepless nights that year; the tough decision whether to stay in New York; seeing your breath in April home games; Bobby V; the Subway Series; Clemens; the smoke over the city; the rumors; the injuries; first frigging base . . . Finally, I had to get up and move to the back of the room, off by myself.

Ordinarily, when there's a lot running through a ballplayer's mind, the field itself is a refuge. But on the way to it this time, walking through the

tunnel, I had to stop and collect myself. The weight of the day was pushing on my head, and along with it, there was something else—something even heavier—that I found uncomfortable. It was the first time I'd ever sensed that a particular ball game was largely about *me*.

To start, I'd always felt a certain amount of uneasiness about being a star, especially in New York. I wasn't drawn to the spotlight the way Reggie Jackson was, for instance, or Joe Namath. If anything, I shied away from the attentions of the media. The more they pried, the more I shied. Usually I could get away from all that by losing myself in the competitiveness of a baseball game, but the outcome of this game wouldn't make a hell of a lot of difference. If we lost, the Marlins could tie us for third place in the division. The Rockies would finish last in theirs, either way. Other than my every move, there was little else for 47,718 pairs of eyeballs to focus on.

I might have convinced myself that the whole ballpark wasn't *really* watching me if half the people there hadn't been wearing the number 31. But I was flattered by that, and also by the observation of Sheldon Souray, the hockey player who had introduced me to Alicia. He said the cool thing about my jersey was that anybody could wear it, from a teeny-bopper to a punk rocker to a young professional to a pipefitter to a grandparent. There certainly seemed to be all types at Shea that day. To indulge them, and me, Randolph turned back the clock and wrote me into the cleanup spot.

Victor Zambrano was pitching for us—and pitching and pitching and pitching. He walked only three, but it seemed like a dozen. In less than six innings, his pitch count approached 120. The Rockies were swinging at first pitches—they wanted to get the hell out of there and go home—but Zambrano insisted on running up the count anyway. Colorado, meanwhile, was pitching a sinkerballer, Aaron Cook, and he kept grounding me out to the shortstop. Three times, I grounded out to short and the crowd cheered as though I'd smoked the ball off the scoreboard, where, from time to time, the Mets were putting up video highlights of some of my better swings and moments.

Then, during the seventh-inning stretch, they showed my feature video, which, to their credit, was very cool, set to "The Great Divide" by Scott Stapp from Creed. I happened to look over into the Rockies' dugout, and they were standing and applauding—a nice gesture. When the video was finished, the fans brought me out for three curtain calls. I gotta tell you, it was touching. To be taken in as a true, appreciated Met, after all the ups and downs and controversies . . . Not knowing quite what to do, I bowed and blew kisses.

I was still 0 for 3 when I reported to my position behind the plate in the top of the eighth and Mike DiFelice trotted out to replace me. Randolph was

allowing me to receive one final ovation as I left the field. It was a loaded moment. I could see people crying in the crowd. At the same time, my dad and brothers were up in our box going, "No! Give him one more at-bat! He may go deep!"

Willie was criticized for removing me prematurely, because I would have come up to hit in the bottom of the eighth, but I had no complaint. There was no dramatic stroke in me at that point; no stirring send-off about to happen. There just wasn't. Jay Horwitz, the Mets' PR guy, had said to me that he'd never seen a player who could rise to the occasion in a big-time situation the way I could, and I cherished that remark, but, to me, this wasn't that kind of situation. We were losing badly in a game that scarcely mattered. Besides, I was emotionally spent and Aaron Cook was still firing up that damn sinkerball. As they say, it was all over but the shouting. And I was okay with that. I actually thought there was a metaphor in the fact that I hadn't been able to deliver that one crowning memory. My tank was empty. I had some more baseball left in me—of that, I was pretty sure—but no more New York.

The city had made me older faster, in this respect: While it's true that, as the years pile up, it gets harder for your body to recover, it's even harder for your *spirit* to keep bouncing back. Passion is what New York uses up in a player, like no other town. Mentally exhausted, generally jaded, and physically torn apart, I had none in reserve. Not as a Met, anyhow. The emotion of my final game at Shea was a reaffirmation not only of that but also of the wrenching judgment I'd made seven years before, when I decided, against the testimony of all that had happened and the advice of people I respected, to sign and stay. It was the right call.

This time around, there would be no call to make. I needed a change of scenery and the Mets were clearly headed in another direction. Omar Minaya was ready to put his own stamp on the ball club, rebuilding around Wright, Reyes, and Beltran. Our equipment manager, Charlie Samuels, always looking out for me, asked Jeff Wilpon what he thought it would take to get me signed, and Jeff told him it was simply time to move on. I totally agreed.

In that spirit, I made it clear to Danny Lozano that we would put no pressure on the Mets to re-up with me. We knew that, if we told the press I wanted to stay in whatever capacity and would play for whatever they wanted to pay me, it would become a talking point and put the club on the spot. I didn't want to go there. I didn't want to leave New York the way I'd left Los Angeles.

I was just fine, even pleased, with the way it had ended in the eighth inning on October 2—with the fans on their feet. Thank you, New York.

CHAPTER TWENTY-FIVE

That Christmas, my first as a married man, was also my first in seventeen years without an employer. Frankly, I hadn't anticipated that.

As a free agent with a .311 lifetime batting average and 397 home runs, I'd been expecting to hear from a handful of American League teams in search of a designated hitter. But now the off-season was winding down, and only the Phillies and Padres had shown the slightest interest. (The Mets, incidentally, continuing their tradition of good-hitting Italian catchers from the Northeast who had been with the Dodgers and Marlins, had picked up Paul Lo Duca to replace me.) It was discouraging to the point that it forced me to consider retirement. Reluctantly.

Without too much difficulty, though, I was able to willfully put that thought aside on the grounds that, 1) I didn't like the idea of going out on two bad years in a row—I needed to prove I was better than that—and 2) I was eager to see how I could do if I were away from the madness of New York. The second factor got me thinking harder about San Diego, which was about as far away as anywhere. At the same time, though, there was some appeal to the notion of playing for the team I grew up watching. That was clearly what my father wanted me to do. He'd been in the ear of Hank King, who was the Phillies' advance scout and a friend of his, about them signing me, going so far as to tell King what he figured they could have me for.

Shortly after the holidays, Charlie Manuel and Pat Gillick, the manager and general manager of the Phillies, flew down to Miami for lunch with me and Danny Lozano. We hunkered over a table at the Mandarin Oriental and they set about flattering me, which was definitely a good strategy. But they also told me the truth, which included the fact that their starting catcher was still Mike Lieberthal, who was due to make $7.5 million that year.

I didn't understand every last thing about the machinations of baseball, but I understood that $7.5 million players don't sit the bench. Besides that,

I didn't *want* to make Lieberthal sit, even if I could have. He was a career Phillie, a local fixture, in the last year of his contract. Of course, I might have felt differently about the whole thing if I'd known that Lieberthal would get hurt a few times in 2006 and catch only about sixty games. The way it stood, though, Manuel's plan was to have me catch here and there, DH in the interleague games, and put in a little work at first base. As he laid it out, I imagined myself sitting around for two weeks and then pinch-hitting against Billy Wagner—who, ironically, had signed with the Mets—in the bottom of the ninth. As cool as I thought it would be to play eighty-one games in front of my friends and family (being a Phillie would also have given me a chance to work on my relationship with Phoenixville, which, frankly, has never been quite what I'd like it to be), and as much as I wanted to please my dad, and as grateful as I was for the organization's interest in me, and as enticing as it sounded to swing the bat in Citizens Bank Park for six months, that was a big thanks-but-no-thanks.

San Diego it was. If we could work it out.

The Padres—in the person of the general manager, Kevin Towers—put a million and a quarter on the table, along with the starting catcher position, which was more important. Tommy Lasorda suggested I take it, which helped ease my father's disappointment that I'd turned down the Phillies. Apparently my dad wasn't *too* upset about the way things were going, because, before we'd announced a deal with the Padres, he let it out that I was signing. That was a little awkward for Danny, who was still trying to squeeze a few more dollars out of Kevin Towers, but my dad enjoys his visits with the media. He'd been talking to a San Diego radio guy named Bill Werndl, whom he knew from back home—Philly Billy, as he was called, had been trying to enlist me as a lobbyist for Pete Rose to get into the Hall of Fame—and got a little ahead of himself. I blew up at him, which wasn't unusual, and we had a little bit of a rift for a while. It was nothing serious—mostly just me venting about being a married man of thirty-seven, the leading home run hitter among all catchers in the history of the game, and still feeling like a daddy's boy at times. Of course, if my father hadn't been the way he was, I wouldn't have grown up with freakish forearms, a backyard batting cage, and a batboy gig for the Dodgers, etc. I wouldn't have been drafted, most likely. I probably wouldn't have eaten noodles at the Mandarin Oriental with Pat Gillick and Charlie Manuel, either. I realized all of that. I was still mad at him. That was just our methodology.

A couple of weeks after becoming a Padre, I reported with the pitchers and other catchers to their spring-training camp in Peoria, Arizona, but stayed only a few days before I left to join the Italian team in Florida for the inaugural World Baseball Classic. I was eligible because my grandfather, Rosario Piazza, had been born in Sicily; but my connection to the old country seemed to have been magnified by my visit to the pope. I was referred to in the press as baseball's ambassador to the Vatican.

Playing for Italy was an honor I took very seriously. It was something that my Italian-blooded predecessors—great players like Joe DiMaggio, Yogi Berra, Roy Campanella, Ernie Lombardi, Joe Torre (those last four were all catchers, by the way), Tony Lazzeri, Phil Rizzuto, Rocky Colavito, Carl Furillo, Ron Santo, and Tony Conigliaro—hadn't been afforded the privilege of doing. Over the course of a century, Italian-Americans had gained enormous stature in the game, and if I could bring some of that cachet back to the homeland of my ancestors, it made me immensely proud. Our first baseman, Claudio Liverziana, told reporters, "The first time we saw him, for us, baseball-wise, it was, God is among us."

Remarks like that, I realized, were vastly overstated, and I took them for what they were worth; but please understand something: As baseball players, most of us know that what we do is not the most important thing in the world. And most of us, one way or another, would like somehow to make our work mean a little more than two runs in the sixth and a victory over the Astros now and then. We desire to benefit people and good causes, if we can. I love baseball, and if I'm able to help grow it in a country I also love, it's a contribution I can cherish.

In that spirit, it irks me that teams and critics complain about the WBC diverting players away from spring training. For one thing, it's not like the guys are off sailing or snowboarding. They're playing competitive, meaningful, good-for-the-game *baseball*. As for wearing themselves out—there really aren't enough games involved to do that; not nearly as many as in the Latin American winter leagues or spring training itself. I really don't have any tolerance for those complaints.

Our Italian team lasted three games in the historic WBC tournament of 2006, mercy-ruling Australia, 10–0, in the first, in which I caught and doubled, and losing the next two to Venezuela and the Dominican Republic, when I was the DH. (I guess our coaches had heard about my arm.) Wearing number 31 on a blue and gray uniform that made me feel like I was back with the Dodgers, I mustered just one hit in eleven at-bats. Thus ended my career as an international player.

I told the Italian officials, though, that I'd be happy thereafter to help coach, conduct clinics, eat truffles, or whatever.

• • •

The Padres' manager, Bruce Bochy, had been a catcher. That must be why he understood the game, and me, so well.

It was a nice situation. I loved the feel of the ball club, and also the city. I'm not sure that San Diego would have been the best place for me when I was young and over-the-top in my intensity, but in 2006 I'd been around the league fourteen times already—*aging* was the operative word—and was letting my hair down. Literally. (*Sports Illustrated* called it a "scruffy mop.")

Alicia and I rented a nice apartment a few blocks from the beach, she enrolled in some classes to get started on her master's degree in psychology, and I batted fourth in a pretty good lineup that included Adrian Gonzalez, Brian Giles, and my former Mets teammate Mike Cameron. I homered off Jason Schmidt in my first at-bat as a Padre, caught a strong performance from Jake Peavy, and we took care of the Giants to start the season properly.

That, however, was about all that went right over the first month. Approaching the end of April, we were seven games under .500 and, although I'd hit my four hundredth home run (off Jose Valverde of Arizona), I was batting a dismal .210. It was a midlife crisis.

I called Danny from San Francisco and said, "I'm done!"

Then I called Alicia and said, "I'm done!"

Danny said, "Give it a few more weeks. You've always hit well in May."

Alicia said, "Mike, it's just April. You need to think about this."

For a player's wife, it's torture to see them struggling or getting booed when they come to the plate. You feel helpless. You wish you could pick up a bat and hit the ball for them. It was probably even harder in our case, because Mike was so intense and emotional about baseball. There were times when he would come home and actually throw temper tantrums because he wasn't hitting well or whatever. I'm talking about full-blown tantrums, with all the f-words and throwing things and everything else. Or he'd just be in a horrible mood and wouldn't say anything. I'd tell him, "Mike, you're losing touch with reality. You have to get a grip." I had to say that for his own well-being, and also because I was going to have to deal with being married to this person.

I'd become accustomed to the temper tantrums and the over-reacting, but that time, I actually believed he might quit. This one was for real. He called when I was buying produce at the grocery store and said that he was retiring because he respected the game too much to go on playing the way he was. He said the game was trying to tell him something. I understood about the respect for the game, but it just didn't feel right. Not for him. Mike's a finisher. I told him to calm down and finish his contract.

We all rallied around him, urged him to just get through it. Then I got on a plane and flew to Chicago to meet him there. And all of a sudden he started playing well.

—Alicia Piazza

So, boom, I go into Chicago and go four for five in the first game and in the second I hit a three-run, two-out, ninth-inning, game-winning homer off Ryan Dempster. Just like that, we're on a winning streak, I'm jacking up my average and it was like, okay, I'll hold off on that quitting thing, no big deal here. That was pretty interesting. We ended up winning fourteen out of fifteen and taking over first place. It was nice, incidentally, to play in a division that the Braves weren't part of.

The moral support made a big difference, but I also tinkered with my stance. I crouched a little more and kept my weight back to make myself quicker to the ball. It was a fairly dramatic change. Tom Robson, my old hitting coach with the Mets, had once said that my posture was the most important factor in my swing, and it was based on the strength in my legs. A hitter's torque, which results in bat speed, begins with his legs. Robson timed my swing at fourteen-hundredths of a second from the time it began until contact with the ball. The only player who ever equaled that, by his watch, was Paul Molitor. But with age and injuries, I'd lost some of the quickness that had enabled me to fight off inside pitches. Consequently, pitchers had taken to pounding me in on my fists. I'd been overcompensating, in a way, by gearing myself to pull the ball more regularly than I had in my prime, thereby sacrificing some of my natural power to right field. Now, by revamping my setup to get into the hitting zone earlier, I wouldn't have to make that concession.

The modification in my stance was a more conspicuous change than most I'd made over the years, but in essence it was just another step in the process. There was nothing new to me about the practice of making adjustments. It's a critical part of hitting. Major-league pitchers are good enough that they won't allow a hitter to succeed by doing the same thing the same way all the time. They figure something out, then it's the batter's turn. It was nice to know that I still had enough left to take my turn in that ritual. I also—and this is vital—still had my twenty-ten eyesight and my depth perception, which the Mets' doctors described as stunning. Even Alicia, who's chronically hard to impress, was in awe of my eyes. She'd buy shoes or something and try to hide the receipt in the bottom of the shopping bag, but I'd peek in and say, "You spent six hundred dollars for those?" My vision was something else I had in common with Ted Williams, who was said to be able to read the label of a 78 RPM record while it was spinning on the turntable.

Once I got back on track in Chicago, I was able to relax. For the next three months—half the season—I batted .330. It helped that I was hitting in front of Adrian Gonzalez, who was fast becoming a star. It also helped that Bochy stuck with me in spite of my throwing issues. He had a good system of spotting and spelling me—the three-headed monster, they called it. I'd catch for seven innings, get my three or four at-bats, and then he'd bring in Rob Bowen for defense if we were ahead. A couple of times a week, he'd give me the day off and Josh Bard would start.

The only downside, from my perspective, was that I seldom had the opportunity to catch Trevor Hoffman, our great closer and the all-time leader in saves. Of course, Trevor himself might have preferred it that way, because after a while I got a little tired of hearing about his fabulous changeup. The changeup was a tremendously effective pitch for him, obviously, but I thought that his two-seamer, cutter, and slider were pretty good, too, and shouldn't be neglected. I put that opinion into practice one night when I happened to catch him in the ninth inning of a scoreless game against the Rockies. Trevor wasn't sticking his changeup where he wanted it and gave up a single to Matt Holliday, followed by a double to Brad Hawpe, to start the inning. I went out to the mound and said, "Here's the deal, dude. We're not gonna throw one more fucking changeup."

He said, "What?"

I said, "Just do what I say, okay?"

"Well, if you're feeling it . . ."

I wanted to get out of the jam with his other stuff because I was sick of the changeup, and besides, I knew that the Rockies would be sitting on it. Trevor was cool enough to understand that I'd said what I said in a light tone but with serious intent, and I appreciated the fact that he had enough trust in me to play along. He proceeded to strike out Troy Tulowitzki, Chris Iannetta, and Yorvit Torrealba without a single changeup and we won the game in the eleventh on a two-out, pinch-hit home run by Paul McAnulty, the only pinch home run he ever hit.

I really enjoyed playing for Boach. He has a great feel for the game and could invariably tell if I was getting tired or being nagged by something I didn't want to talk about. Boach was the kind of manager I'd run through a wall for. He just got me; understood the psychology part of it. And truthfully, being a catcher might have had something to do with that, because working with pitchers can be very much an exercise in psychology. It's not merely a matter of coddling. Sometimes it's about being straight with people; blunt, if necessary. And nobody was blunter than Bochy.

For example, we were playing at Arizona one night in May and El Duque (Orlando Hernandez) was pitching for the Diamondbacks. Boach looked at me and said, "You know what you're hitting against this guy?" Some pitchers, I just knew when I stepped into the box that I was going to crush them. I could feel it as I gripped the bat. Other guys, it was like, oh man, I've got to put on a good act here. I can't explain it. Why do you like pepperoni on your pizza and I like anchovies? It's just the way it is. I couldn't do a thing with El Duque.

I said, "Uh, no, not exactly, but I can assure you it's pretty bad."

Bochy said, "It's fucking horseshit. One for thirteen. You're not playing tonight."

"All right, Boach."

"Be ready in the eighth inning to pinch-hit if I need you."

"All right, Boach."

Sometimes, that kind of plain talking can be a form of respect, a token of appreciation that you can handle the truth. It also allows for better communication. Bochy knew that I didn't take offense where none was intended, and it freed him up to speak his mind.

There was also the time when we were battling the Dodgers for first place, the game was tied in the bottom of the sixth, they had runners on first and second with nobody out, Alan Embree, a tough lefty, was pitching for us, and Cla Meredith, a righthander who threw from down under, was getting ready in the bullpen. Bochy marched out to the mound and said, "All right, no bullshit here. Make the easy play and be sure you get the out, then I'll bring in the submariner."

The next guy bunted the ball to Embree's glove side, and I'm out there yelling, "three, three, three!" We had plenty of time to get the lead runner at third, except that Russell Branyan, our third baseman, had taken a couple of steps in for the bunt and got tangled up going back to the bag. Everybody was safe. So Boach comes back out to make his pitching change, turns to me, and goes, "What the fuck did I tell you?" There wasn't much I could say.

After Meredith took over, Rafael Furcal grounded the ball to Josh Barfield at second, and I had to stretch and scoop the throw out of the dirt to get the force at home for the first out. Kenny Lofton, one of the fastest runners in the game, was the next hitter. He bounced the ball right back to Meredith, and we got a home-to-first double play to end the inning.

I was feeling pretty good about it. When we got to the dugout I said, "I think you owe me an apology, Boach."

He said, "Go fuck yourself."

(Unfortunately, that was the night when the Dodgers hit four consecutive home runs to tie us in the ninth, and then, after Josh Bard had put us ahead with an RBI single, Nomar Garciaparra beat us with a two-run shot in the tenth.)

By spotting me sensibly and simply working with me, Bochy got some pretty good mileage out of my rusted old chassis. I worked with him, too. Once, when we had a day game after a night game—a situation in which I usually received a rest—there was a left-hander going for the other team, and Bochy says, "You think you can suck it up and play?"

"Absolutely, Boach. Whatever you need." We had an understanding. It clicked.

I'll tell you what else clicked for me. San Diego. One newspaper. A beach. Pleasant fans. If I struck out with a runner on second, nobody booed. If I went one for nineteen, nobody shouted, "Retire!" If I made a bad throw, nobody screamed, "Play first base!" Nobody ripped me on the radio. Nobody questioned my toughness, sexual orientation, or moral rectitude. A courteous constituency can actually be a good or bad thing for a player, depending on his wiring and history; but for me, coming off a litany of challenging times in New York City, it was just what the doctor ordered.

I had more fun in San Diego than a thirty-seven-year-old man ought to be allowed. For one thing, I hadn't imagined how much music I'd find there. I went three or four times with various teammates to see Metal Skool. They let me play some drums, and on one occasion Jake Peavy, Clay Hensley, and I joined them on stage to sing "Sweet Home Alabama," which was the only country song they knew. It had to be country for Peavy to sing it.

As for me, I'll sing anything. Metallica once handed me the mike for "Enter Sandman," which, like I said, I was sick of hearing when Mariano Rivera was strolling in from the bullpen—it meant that the Yankees were about to win—but didn't mind so much in street clothes. Skid Row let me sing, too, which was like a dream come true. I have to say, the bands have been great to me over the years. They don't take themselves too seriously, and neither do I. When it comes to music, I'm totally uninhibited, because, hell, it's just *fun*. I don't care how bad I sound. Danny Lozano and I were at a karaoke club in New York one night and I told him to get up there and do a song and he kept saying he couldn't. I don't get that. I was like, "Dude, so you stink—who cares? That's part of the fun!" When I get hold of the mike, I'll hang around for three or four songs and people will be going, "All right, enough, enough! Get off the stage!"

I guess baseball loosened me up for that sort of thing. You can't succeed as a ballplayer, or an athlete of any kind, if you're unwilling to put yourself on the line. I was blessed to be fairly free of the fear of failure—except for when it came to playing first base. In San Diego, fortunately, I didn't have to do that.

There was only one significant downside to being with the Padres, and it wasn't their fault. Petco Park is a canyon. It's considered the most "pitcher-friendly" stadium in the big leagues, which makes it a bitch for hitters. I still wonder what numbers I might have put up in four hundred at-bats at Citizens Bank Park. We played three games there that year, around the Fourth of July, and I enjoyed it to the extent of six hits. Meanwhile, Lieberthal was into his eighth week on the disabled list.

We were a couple of games up in first place, with everyone else bunched closely together, when we arrived in New York in early August. The Mets and their fans were hospitable only to an extent.

Before the first game, the scoreboard guys played another video of me, to the tune of the Beatles song "In My Life," which was nice but a little schmaltzy, and the fans did a singsongy "Mike Pee-OTS-a" cheer when I got to the on-deck circle for the first time, which was also nice and not too schmaltzy. Then the Mets swiped four bases on me and beat us, 3–2. The next night, I threw out Endy Chavez trying to steal second in the second inning and he immediately jumped all over the umpire, as though there was no conceivable way the call could be right. His body language said, "What the *hell*? Are you *kidding* me?" I'm thinking, come on, I can't throw anybody out? Get the fuck off the field. The crowd seemed kind of taken aback that I could still do that, on the order of, why'd we get rid of him?

Pedro Martinez was pitching for the Mets. They were up 4–0 when I took him out to right-center in the fourth inning. The fans gave me a standing ovation and kept it up until I went out for a curtain call. Somebody told me it was the first time a visiting player had ever gotten a standing ovation after hitting a home run at Shea Stadium. Somebody else told me it was reminiscent of when Tom Seaver returned for the first time in 1977, after being traded to the Reds, and beat the Mets with a complete game. Frankly,

I don't know which was more satisfying—the incredible reception or hitting a home run against Pedro.

In the sixth, we were still down 4–1 when I got him again. This time, the crowd response was more along the lines of polite applause, like, oh, wow, great . . . all right now. The Mets were trying to nail down a division title themselves. When Pedro walked Giles and Cameron with one out in the eighth, Randolph brought in Aaron Heilman to pitch to me. I had the distinct feeling that if I homered again, which would give us the lead, my welcome would be worn out in no uncertain terms. Heilman threw me a changeup on the first pitch and I drove it deep enough to Beltran in center field that both runners were able to tag up and advance. Unfortunately, that was as close as we got to winning a game in New York. The Mets completed the sweep the next day and suddenly we found ourselves trailing the Dodgers, tied with Arizona.

We dropped as many as four games behind in early September, then put together a couple of nice little winning streaks. The club and I both finished strong—the season hadn't beaten me down bodily or emotionally, like the past several had—and, by taking our last four series, we wound up in a dead heat with the Dodgers. Since we'd beaten them head-to-head over the course of the season, we were declared division champions. Our reward was drawing St. Louis in the first round of the playoffs.

We belonged where we were, but at the same time I knew we'd have to be at our very best, and catch some breaks, to win or even make it to the World Series. A similar thing could have been said for the Cardinals, who'd won only eighty-three games during the regular season, five fewer than we had. In retrospect, it was evident, four innings into the series, which team had destiny going for it.

Game one was scoreless, Peavy versus Chris Carpenter, when Pujols came to bat with a man on base. He skied a pop-up over my left shoulder, back toward the screen, and when I got there I grabbed the mesh, not realizing it wasn't tight. It gave, I lurched, my toe stubbed against the concrete, and the ball fell out of my mitt. Naturally, Pujols proceeded to hit a home run.

After the inning, Peavy let me have it. He did that a lot, actually, and I didn't mind, because he wasn't trying to embarrass me. He was just a supercompetitive, straight-up guy, not unlike Bochy in that respect. He said, "Why didn't you catch that fucking pop-up?"

I said, "Why'd you hang that three-two fucking cutter?" We got along. But we couldn't beat Carpenter, who was rolling.

Bochy sat me down for the second game, which wasn't the reason we got shut out or Pujols picked up three more hits. Chris Young had it working and

we won game three when the series switched to St. Louis, but the next day
Carpenter wrapped it up for the Cardinals. They had found it. Next thing
we knew, they were beating the Mets—who had eliminated the Dodgers in
the post-Piazza playoff round—to take the pennant, and then the Tigers in
the World Series. Damn.

The Padres held an $8 million option on me for 2007, but, in spite of the
way everything had worked out—I'd finished at .283 with twenty-two homers
and sixty-eight RBIs, while the three-headed monster had collectively produced more home runs than any catching combination in all of baseball—I
was under no illusions that they'd exercise it. I'd be thirty-eight and unlikely
to catch another ninety-nine games, like I had in 2006. For that matter, I
didn't expect to be back in San Diego at a reduced rate, either. Lozano and I
were looking for a contract in the neighborhood of two to three million, and
we knew that Kevin Towers wouldn't be able to get that past Sandy Alderson,
the Padres' CEO. Sandy was looking for fresh faces, to the extent that he let
Bochy get away to the Giants even though Boach had just won the division
with a team that wasn't particularly loaded. Bochy's replacement was Bud
Black, a former pitcher who wasn't especially keen to keep me.

Once again, I turned my attention toward the American League. This
time, gainfully.

The Oakland A's had just won ninety-three games, and Billy Beane
was casting around for a veteran to replace the bat and presence of Frank
Thomas, who'd given them thirty-nine home runs as the designated hitter
before leaving for Toronto as a free agent. Smart guy that he is, Beane understood that I'd put together decent numbers in the toughest hitters' park in
baseball and produced very well away from it. Refreshed by the West Coast,
I'd posted my best slugging percentage since 2002. I'd remained relatively
healthy. I didn't seem to mind a small market or daunting field dimensions.
And defensively, I shaped up as a hell of a DH. (The A's already had a fine,
durable catcher in Jason Kendall.)

Beane proposed a two-year contract for around $15 million. Honestly,
though, I didn't know if I had two years left in me. I wasn't altogether certain
that I'd enjoy the American League, either. Or Oakland, as far as that goes.

Danny thought I was being ridiculous. He said, "Mike, take the money. You
can always ask for a trade or retire if you want. But that's guaranteed money."

I told him, "Nah, I just want a one-year deal."

I left six and a half million bucks on the table. But eight and a half for
a season of DH'ing?

Dude.

CHAPTER TWENTY-SIX

Our first child, Nicoletta, was born on February 3, 2007. Otherwise, out of habit and stubbornness and against the advice of the A's, I'd have probably reported to spring training with the pitchers and catchers.

When I finally got there with everybody else for the first time in my career, I had with me five catcher's mitts, three of them brand-new and still wrapped in plastic. I understood the DH part of my arrangement with Oakland, but a large portion of my constitution as a baseball player involved working with pitchers. I felt I had a lot to contribute along those lines, whether I actually caught ball games or not. I mentioned to our rookie manager, Bob Geren, that I'd be happy to do bullpen sessions in the spring if he needed an extra set of hands. He said hell no. He had his orders from Billy Beane. At one point—nervous, I guess, that I'd catch a foul tip on the toe or finger, or maybe get hit in the head with a backswing for the umpteenth time—they actually took my gear away from me.

I have to admit, it kept me focused and ready to hit. Traditionally, I was not a quick starter with the bat, but I swung it well in Phoenix. I was feeling strong. That was officially confirmed when a Japanese television crew staged a strength test across the major-league camps, using a grab-and-grip contraption with a meter connected to it. They tested Pujols, Ryan Howard, Roy Halladay—practically everybody, as far as I know—and nobody could match my number. The A's had signed me for power, and it was nice to know that I could still muscle up as well as anyone. The new gig was going to be interesting.

It certainly began that way. We opened on the road at Seattle and Anaheim, with me hitting cleanup between Milton Bradley and Eric Chavez. Seattle was rough—what the hell do you do on the bench with no pitcher to study and the rest of the guys on the field?—but in the first game against the Angels, I came up in the ninth inning with two outs and two hits under my belt, facing the ace reliever, Frankie Rodriguez, who the next year would set the major-league record with sixty-two saves. On a one-one pitch, it felt like old times. I sent the ball just to the right of center, like I used to, and it traveled about as high and far as it often had, landing well back in the bleachers. Huston Street set them down in the ninth for the win.

It was a four-game series, and I scorched it for ten hits. Frankly, it surprised me a bit. For most of my career I had emphasized base hits and been unwilling to give them up for more home runs, but I'd finally accepted the fact that my average would have to suffer in the interest of power, which, given my lack of speed, I couldn't do without. For whatever reason, though, it didn't go down that way in April 2007. The homer against K-Rod was the only one I would hit that month, in spite of playing nearly every day. I'd certainly have understood if Geren had dropped me out of the four-hole, but he evidently shared my confidence that the power would show up in May, as usual. There was no reason why it wouldn't; the DH role was going easy on me.

In fact, I wouldn't have felt thirty-eight at all if the music in the clubhouse weren't hurting my ears the way it did. When it comes to music, I feel I'm as open-minded as anybody out there, but we had a young roster and, well, *man*. I like rap just fine—hell, I was wearing gold chains back when Olivia Newton-John was getting physical—if it's classic rap, or even the new stuff when there's a strong rhythm to it. As a thrash-metal guy from way back, I feel like I can handle some rough language and graphic lyrics; but some of the more contemporary rap is so blatantly hard-core that even an old Slayer and Anthrax man like me has a tough time dealing with it. I guess it's a matter of age and tradition both. You have to understand, I came up with the Dodgers when the stadium music consisted exclusively of Nancy Bea Hefley at the organ. When that was cut back to modernize the atmosphere—to make the ballpark sound like every other ballpark—they turned to entrance music, with each player picking a theme song. With the Mets, I recall Tony Tarasco coming to the plate to an X-rated, in-your-face rap number that had the whole stadium sounding like a bad-ass clubhouse. Can't say I cared for that.

But at least the young pups on the A's could appreciate my familiarity with music (if not my considerable skill on the air drums). Huston Street, who was only twenty-three, enlisted my help in picking his closer anthem, even though I'd whiffed on behalf of Braden Looper. It was still my mission to wean the bullpens of the world off "Enter Sandman" or even "Hells Bells." For Street, I suggested "Man in the Box," by Alice in Chains, but he wasn't buying it. Eventually we compromised on "Hate Me Now," by Nas, which, for me, was a damn big compromise. Judging by the season he had, it worked for him.

I don't think the guys were quite as tolerant of my humor, though. Before one game, I advised them, "Everybody be alert out there. We need more lerts." They just looked at me with blank stares. I felt like a *dad* in that clubhouse. I was the stodgy old conservative, although, politically at least, Street lined up on the same side. Naturally, that made him a smart guy in my book. He even discussed art with me. On the sly—I didn't want to get fined for thinking like a catcher—I talked a little pitching strategy with Huston and whoever wanted to sit in.

Anyhow, it was all good. Until the second day of May, at Fenway Park.

I was at second base in the sixth inning, with two outs and a runner also at first, when Bobby Crosby rolled a grounder to Mike Lowell at third. Lowell backhanded the ball in front of the bag and was intending to just take a couple of steps back and stomp on it. But I'd gotten a good jump for a change and was closer than he'd expected. His only play was to lunge and tag me. I swerved, fell, and Lowell fell on top of me, crushing my right shoulder. It was a grade-three acromioclavicular (AC) joint separation. Designated hitting had failed to keep me off the DL.

The next day, Beane traded with San Diego for Jack Cust, an outfielder who had been around for a while but played in only seventy games for four different teams. Billy saw something in him that others hadn't—mostly, a combination of power and the willingness to take a walk—and almost immediately Cust became our DH. He did well. He, in fact, became practically the quintessential Billy Beane (in other words, Moneyball) player.

In light of that, the A's were in no hurry to bring me off the disabled list. By the middle of June, when we were eight games over .500, I felt I was ready to go; but they kept putting off my activation. When I pleaded my case, Beane told me that there was no room for another DH—and he wanted me to start *catching*.

I couldn't do that. After what they'd said in spring training about me catching, I was stunned that they'd ask; but that wasn't the point. While my shoulder was healed enough to swing the bat, there was simply no way I could throw the ball to second or third base. I said as much to Billy, but it didn't make any difference.

When we played a weekend series at Shea in late June, Geren let me bring out the lineup card—to a nice standing ovation—but that was all. Then, on July 16, Beane traded Jason Kendall to the Cubs. One of the players the A's received in return was Rob Bowen, who'd been part of our three-headed monster in San Diego. They also brought up Kurt Suzuki, a rookie catcher. Another three-man rotation seemed to make sense, except for the little complication that *I couldn't throw.*

So the A's simply kept me on the disabled list. Beane had made up his mind that I'd stay in rehab until I was ready to catch. When I kept trying to throw and couldn't, I went in for an MRI that revealed two old tears of the rotator cuff that had been aggravated by the AC joint injury. I suggested to Billy that he send me down to the minors for a week or so to get my swing together, and after that he could activate me, trade me, or release me outright. Instead, in an abrupt change of direction—I guess he had finally accepted the fact that I couldn't come back as a catcher—he went ahead and took me off the DL right then. I'd been on it for eleven weeks, which was about five too many, in my opinion. In the meantime, we had slipped to five games under .500 and eleven out of first place.

It was a weird scenario all the way around, so weird that it made me wonder. Had Beane been trying to get me back behind the plate in order to showcase me for a trade? Had he kept me on the DL, and pressed the point about catching, to try to get me to quit? Was there a money angle here? I had no tangible evidence of that, but the very possibility gave rise to a pertinent question. If Billy Beane is the general manager of the ball club and also a partial owner (with Lew Wolff), isn't that a conflict of interest? Billy is one of the sharpest general managers in the business, no question; but theoretically, the GM is the guy who's supposed to fight tooth and nail to convince the owner to go out and spend that last dollar to get that last guy who's going to make the ball club better. He's the one counted on to represent the baseball side. If the GM is *also* an owner, however, then he's involved with the bottom line, and he's coming at the whole thing from a different perspective. In that arrangement, it seems like there might be a balance problem between the yin and the yang.

Meanwhile, in *this* arrangement, as I saw it, there was a balance problem between player and management. I'd done the A's a favor—had saved them close to $7 million—by signing for one year instead of two. But they were doing me no favor in return. Not that I expected them to, or had one coming; I'm just pointing out the way it was. Fans, typically, are quick to pounce on players for swinging the hammer at contract time, but they don't see the other side. They don't understand that a ball club looks after its own interest—sometimes with a vengeance—and it's up to the player to look after his. I certainly don't mean to portray myself as a victim, because I made a hell of a lot of money in the game. For that matter, I was making a hell of a lot of money that very year. I'd simply like for the public to better appreciate the players' position in these situations. I got hurt by playing hard for the Oakland A's. After that, Billy Beane was just trying to put out the cigarette. It's a tough business.

At any rate, on my second day back, July 21, DH'ing against the Orioles, with Cust playing right field and batting in front of me in the three-hole, I started on an eight-game hitting streak that included fifteen hits altogether and my first home run since April 5. Then we flew down to Anaheim, where I picked up six hits and two homers and drove in six runs in the three-game series . . . and an ignorant Angels fan made a big mistake.

The dude hit me in the helmet with a water bottle.

I wasn't in the most agreeable mood to start with. It was an afternoon game, the series finale, and I'd homered in the fifth inning against John Lackey to put us ahead 3–2, although the lead hadn't lasted. It felt great to rake again, but it also underscored the frustration of missing eleven weeks— nearly half of them unnecessarily—at this late stage of my career. From where I stood, an important opportunity, for both me and the ball club, had been senselessly squandered. It was a lost season, and very possibly my *last*. I was feeling cheated.

Then, in the ninth inning, as we were trying to rally from three runs down, I was standing in the on-deck circle studying Frankie Rodriguez when there was a loud, unnerving pop and my head began to ring. At first, I couldn't be sure what it was. It scared the shit out of me. When I realized that somebody had actually beaned me with a bottle of Dasani, about three-quarters full, the fear turned to fury. If you've watched any of the videos of the time I went after Guillermo Mota and seen the wicked expression on my face when I was being held back from getting at him, you know the look I had when I turned to the crowd and yelled, "Who the fuck did that?"

Immediately, four people pointed to the same guy. So I made it five and charged up to the wall, screaming, "You're a chickenshit! You're a piece of shit! Get your fucking ass down here!"

It wasn't my finest moment. Bottle rage, I guess. But an act like that is so malicious, so hateful, so asinine and out of line that it just sends a bolt of anger up your spine and out your mouth. The guy only made it worse when he gave me some obscene and cocky body language—the very signals that would tell me to rush a pitcher. Fortunately, I couldn't get over the wall. If I had, I'm pretty sure I would have done something I'd have regretted. In the meantime, the sucker just turned and walked up the steps. I yelled, "Grab that guy!" He almost made it to the tunnel before security got to him.

When the game resumed, I singled to center, but we fell short by a run. Afterward, a lieutenant from the Anaheim police department came down to the clubhouse to tell me that they had the fellow.

I said, "I'm pressing charges."

He's like, "*What?*"

"Yeah, I'm pressing charges for assault."

The cop's expression said, oh geez, here we go. But he took me to the security office to identify the guy, who was standing there with two others.

"Yeah, that's him," I said. "And I'm pressing charges."

A couple of days later, I got a follow-up call from the district attorney's office. My guess is that they expected me to drop the complaint, since it would require another trip back to Anaheim to testify, but I told them to just give me a few days' notice and I'd be there. My response might have been a bit extreme, but things had piled up and I'd had enough. I was going to make this guy pay for all the shit—the insults, rumors, baseballs, whatever—that people had been throwing at me for twenty years. Plus, by that time I'd heard he was going to be a *teacher*. I sure as hell didn't want a jerk like that teaching *my* children.

As it turned out, there was no trial. When he heard I was willing to testify, the bottle chucker pled guilty and was sentenced to thirty days in prison.

My pleasant season in San Diego had spoiled me, I suppose. In Oakland, the drama was back. And reminiscent of New York, the media was in the middle of it.

A beat writer for the *San Francisco Chronicle*, Susan Slusser, asked me, ostensibly off the record, about some minor mistake that Bob Geren had made—so minor that I don't even recall what it was. I explained it as his fault, more or less, but instead of leaving my comment out of the paper, as I'd expected, she ran it as an anonymous quote. I don't know if Geren figured out from the context that the quote came from me—it definitely *sounded* like me—or if Slusser told him or what, but he was obviously bothered by the remark. He called a meeting the next day and, in front of the team, asked me how a situation like that should be handled.

I flashed back to when Tommy Lasorda would call similar meetings, hold up the newspaper, and tell us, in a way that only Tommy could, that if we didn't have the guts to say something to somebody's face, we shouldn't be saying it in the paper. So I replied, "Well, you have a meeting and tell everybody, 'If you're not man enough to say it to my face, then you shouldn't be saying it in the paper.'" I didn't happen to mention that *I* was the player quoted. So I'm mentioning it now, Bob. I apologize for not coming forward at the time. I can't adequately explain why I didn't, except to say that I'd reached the point, I think, at which I actually didn't care enough anymore to take an ethical stand and do what I knew was right. I was falling out of touch with my professional principles. I'd never been a fan of clubhouse lawyering, or party to it. In New York, I'd always detested the stories in which "one Met said." Now *I* was that guy, that one Athletic. I didn't care for what I saw myself evolving into. I should have been more accountable.

The whole thing had started out as a trivial incident, but, to me, ballooned into a symbol of a season gone bad. At my age, I didn't have time for that. I was disappointed by all the little annoyances that 2007 had brought with it—I thought I'd outdistanced those days—and, more to the point, by my own breaches of discretion. I was well aware, for instance, that when teams are down and out of it, the press likes to fan the brushfires into full-fledged controversies. Normally I played pretty good defense against that sort of thing. But this time around, I'd only aggravated the situation, which told me, in turn, that my guard was down; I was no longer on top of my game. I wondered if it was a sign that I was ready to move on to another team or profession.

At the trade deadline, I was hitting around .300, leading the club in that respect—of course, I hadn't come to the plate very many times—and still batting cleanup; but, in spite of rumors, I wasn't dealt anywhere. Once again, I was stuck playing out the string for a struggling team that was looking toward a future that didn't include me. This time, though, I hadn't seen it coming. Given the youth of the A's and the success they'd experienced the year before, I'd sincerely hoped that the 2007 season would get me another crack at a World Series title, the pursuit of which still drove me. But the playoffs weren't happening for us, and they weren't happening in a big way. It was a lousy situation that affected my appetite for the game. For my whole professional career, and long before it even started, I'd been a circling shark on a relentless mission to satisfy some deep-down hunger. Now I didn't have the stomach to play that way anymore, and I couldn't play any *other* way, either.

That said, I was grateful for the opportunity—and yes, the money—that Oakland had given me, and for the chance to share my experience with the younger players. I thoroughly enjoyed that part of it, working, for instance, with Kurt Suzuki on things like blocking the plate and with Huston Street on even more urgent matters, like his taste in music.

Our last road trip of the season ended with two games in Boston. I loved hitting in Fenway Park, but didn't play in the opener. In fact, I'd started only once in nearly two weeks and hadn't had a solitary hit in all that time. Hoping I'd be in the lineup and knowing it might be his last chance to see me in a major-league uniform—we'd finish up with three in Oakland—my brother Vince came to the second game.

> It was the fifth inning, and he hadn't done much. The Red Sox had a left-hander pitching, Jon Lester. I'm sitting there thinking, "Please, God, just let him get a home run." I hadn't been to church in a long time, but I said to myself, if he gets a home run here, I'm going back to church. And no sooner did I complete the thought than, crack, home run to left field. I freaked out. But I held up my end of the bargain. I started going to church.
>
> —Vince Piazza Jr.

The Red Sox took it to us both games, and afterward Vince asked me, "Are they that good or are you guys that bad?"

I said, "They're that good."

That was the year they swept the Rockies in the World Series. Meanwhile, we finished in third place in our division, ten games under .500. But we did beat the Angels, 3–2, in the final game of the season, on a rally that started when I singled to right, off Chris Bootcheck, leading off the ninth inning. Shannon Stewart pinch-ran for me and scored the game-winner on a hit by Suzuki.

My little single, which left my batting average at .275 for the year and .308 for my career, was hit number 2,127 over my sixteen seasons. I had no idea whether there would be another one, but I hoped there would.

Danny made some calls after the season. There were only eight teams that I was interested in playing for at the age of thirty-nine, and he contacted all of them. Two or three replied. None offered right away.

So I waited. I hadn't had any closure in Oakland, I hadn't won a World Series, and I definitely didn't feel like major-league pitching had overtaken me. All those factors impelled me toward one more season of baseball. I questioned only two things: my intensity and my market.

Admittedly, my competitive edge hadn't stayed sharp in my lost season with the A's, but that could be attributed to the circumstances. At least, that's what I told myself. Ideally, a player should never allow any kind of issue or distraction to affect his levels of focus and drive, and I wasn't proud that I had; but realistically, that's a hard standard to live up to. I was willing to believe that my loss of passion was nothing that a better situation wouldn't take care of. The bigger issue was finding the situation, or having it find *me*. In the meantime, I worked out, searched my soul, and got to know the sweetest baby in America.

In mid-February, I also played in the annual Tico Torres—the drummer for Bon Jovi—charity golf tournament at PGA National in Palm Beach. My partner was Gary Carter. We talked a little about catching and a lot about his two knee replacements. It was something to bear in mind when I kicked around the idea of undertaking a seventeenth season, very possibly as a catcher again. In fact, I couldn't get it *out* of my mind. At this stage of the game, with a family started and no pressing financial concerns, did I really want to run the risk of another injury, or of exacerbating any of the problems I was already dealing with?

The way things were looking, though, it would probably be a moot point. Late in the process, I heard a little something about the Royals, a little something about the Reds, but nothing happened. As always, there was a Dodgers rumor. Tommy told me he was going to talk to Ned Colletti, the general manager, about bringing me to Los Angeles as the backup catcher to Russell Martin. My dad said that Tommy was also talking to Kim Ng, the assistant GM. It was, at best, a lot of talking.

Ultimately, the word from Tommy was that yeah, they *were* going make me an offer but decided instead to sign Gary Bennett. I thought, isn't that typical? Even to the end, ten years after they'd traded me, the Dodgers were still jerking me around. If they'd brought in Pudge Rodriguez, sure, I could understand that. But Gary Bennett? No offense to Bennett, but he'd been with seven teams in seven years; not exactly a priority signing. He ended up contributing four hits to the Dodgers in 2008.

All the while, Danny had been telling teams that I'd come to spring training and we could take it from there. The idea of playing at home appealed to me, so he went to the Marlins and laid out a scenario by which I'd report to their camp, try out—I was pretty confident that I'd be their starting catcher by May—and sign for whatever they wanted to pay me, even if it was just the major-league minimum. They didn't even go for *that*. I was beginning to get the message. Spring training came and went.

The lack of interest was humbling—a blow to my pride, I guess you could say—but not nearly as depressing as I might have expected. I was loving my extra time with Alicia and Nicoletta, who was now a year old. I was also catching up on my reading, riding my bike around South Beach, outfitting our home theater, expanding my musical interests—nothing like a little Dvorak to chase down Dangerous Toys—and checking in on my Honda dealership in Philadelphia.

After the season started, there was some chatter about the Mets signing me for one day and letting me retire in their uniform, except that it wasn't coming from the Mets themselves. I was interested, but I wasn't about to call them and ask. In addition, I hadn't yet resigned myself to the notion of not playing anymore. It wasn't inconceivable that, at some point—after an injury, somebody not cutting it, whatever—a team would take another look at its roster and figure it could use a bat like mine at a bargain rate.

I wasn't entirely sure how I might respond to a situation like that, especially if the team had little chance of making the postseason . . . until I went to the papal mass in Washington on April 17. Stan Kasten, the president of the Washington Nationals, was there, which was interesting, because he'd studied at a rabbinical college and remained active in the Jewish community. Maybe he somehow knew I'd be attending. Maybe he was just interested in theology. At any rate, he approached after the mass and asked me, "Are you in shape?"

Before I answered, it suddenly, finally, emphatically occurred to me how I felt, deep down, about coming back for one final season. I suspected there might be an opening here if I said, "Yeah, sure, Stan, I'm in shape. Give me a call. I'll go down to Triple-A for a few weeks and play and see how it goes, and if it goes well, we can talk some more." But I didn't say that.

I said, "Nah."

Baseball, I realized right then, was out of my system.

There was some tangible relief in that thought—a sense of liberation in the fresh understanding that I could leave it all behind and get on with my new life—but some melancholy, as well. I lamented the lessening of my enthusiasm for the sport, and felt that I'd somehow enabled it; that I hadn't guarded my heart as I might have.

On the other hand, I had hit the hell out of the ball. The game and I had gotten everything we could get out of my body and soul.

I let it all sink in for a while, hashed it out with Alicia, had a talk with my dad, and then told Danny it was time. My preference was to just ride off into the sunset without a word; no fuss or fanfare and certainly no press conference. Danny persuaded me that there had to be *some* kind of announcement, just for the sake of closure, so we put together a press release and sent it out on May 20, by email.

The statement said: "After 19 wonderful years, I have come to the decision to officially retire from Major League Baseball. At this point in my career and after discussing my options with my wife, family and agent, I felt it is time to start a new chapter in my life. It has been an amazing journey and everything I have, I owe to God, for without His help, none of this would be possible. He blessed me with the ability to play the greatest game in the world and it has been a dream come true."

I went on to write, with genuine feeling, about the two decades since I'd been a sixty-second-round draft choice, and thanked, by name, my owners, general managers, managers, clubhouse managers, teammates, agent, wife, kids, mom and dad, and, not by name, the fans.

"I can't recall a time in my career when I didn't feel embraced by all of you. Los Angeles, San Diego, Oakland, and Miami—whether it was at home or on the road, you were all so supportive over the years. But I have to say that my time with the Mets wouldn't have been the same without the greatest fans in the world. One of the hardest moments of my career was walking off the field at Shea Stadium and saying goodbye. My relationship with you made my time in New York the happiest of my career, and for that, I will always be grateful.

"So today, I walk away with no regrets. I knew this day was coming and over the last two years I started to make my peace with it. For 19 years, I gave it my all and left everything on the field. God bless and thanks for a wonderful ride."

That was it. I got a few calls, but didn't take them. I didn't want to talk about it. Sometimes, things are self-explanatory. One letter came—a nice one from my general manager with the Marlins, Dave Dombrowski, who by then was the president of the Detroit Tigers.

As I saw it, and still do, the end was almost symbolic. I went out as inconspicuously as I'd come in, even though I hadn't envisioned it quite that way, either time.

EPILOGUE

Election to the Hall of Fame would, for me, validate everything.

I'm not being presumptuous here. I know better. I know that I wasn't the most popular player with the media, I know that my defense will be an issue for some voters, and I know, most of all, that there are plenty of people who simply don't buy my story, who still have a tough time with the concept of a sixty-second-round draft choice—a slow-footed suburban kid picked only as a favor for a friend of his father—legitimately doing what I did in my career. But I also know that I held my own at the most demanding position on the field and established records while I was at it. I know that, as a hitter, I set my goals high, striving every year for a .300 average, thirty homers, and a hundred RBIs, and accomplished that feat twice as many times (six altogether, with a few near-misses) as any other catcher in baseball history (my old mentor Roy Campanella did it on three occasions and nobody else has managed it more than once). I know that only nine other players have hit more than four hundred home runs with at least a .300 lifetime batting average without ever striking out a hundred times in a season, and their names are Babe Ruth, Lou Gehrig, Mel Ott, Ted Williams, Stan Musial, Hank Aaron, Chipper Jones, Vladimir Guerrero, and Albert Pujols.

So, yeah, without being presumptuous, I think about the Hall of Fame. I picture myself in it, in the company of Mike Schmidt, Ted Williams, Roy Campanella, Sandy Koufax, Johnny Bench, Jackie Robinson, Yogi Berra, Gary Carter, Carlton Fisk, Rickey Henderson. Tom Seaver, and Tommy Lasorda. I savor the sweetness of that prospect. That legacy.

I'd be less than truthful if I didn't admit that my legacy is something I ponder quite a bit. Mostly, it bewilders me. I honestly don't know why it is, exactly, that, from start to finish, I've been the object of so much controversy, resentment, skepticism, scrutiny, criticism, rumor, and doubt. I've thought about it quite a bit. Maybe it's because my dad was rich. Maybe it's because Tommy Lasorda looked after me. Maybe it's because, off the field, I didn't make much news on my own account and the press figured it had to latch on to anything that resembled it. Maybe it's because I was a jerk from time to time. Whatever the reason, I suppose I might be a little oversensitive about it all, except that I feel I'm defending more than just my reputation. I'm standing up for what I consider to be—deeply *wish* to be—a fundamentally and triumphantly American story.

I set out to write this book with the ambition that it would make its mark as inspirational. It would be a true fairy tale of sorts, the chronicles of a kid who loved and lived for baseball, who dedicated his childhood to getting better at it, and still, in the eyes of others—in the view of nearly everyone but himself and his father—just wasn't good enough to make a career of it; yet, in the face of continuing doubt and even the denial of opportunity, kept believing, striving, learning, kept *hitting*, until he was a big leaguer, a Rookie of the Year, an all-star, the best-hitting catcher in the history of the game. That's the magic-carpet ride I *feel* I've been on, a sort of real-life Horatio Alger underdog adventure. Apparently, though, that kind of story is not for everybody. At least, my particular variation of it seems not to be. Whether it's out of suspicion, envy, bad information, personal agendas, or insights I'm not privy to, some people find fault and fire away. They'll sit you on the bench, throw at your head, withhold their votes, magnify your weaker moments, or make up stories about your lifestyle. They'll associate you with illegal substances.

I've addressed the subject of steroids more than I wanted to or was comfortable doing. I was reluctant to cast aspersions on others players or lend credibility to my accusers. (I didn't intend to use foul language, either, but, as you know, shit happens. I apologize to anyone whom I may have offended in the interest of being real.) Ultimately, though, I knew I *had* to discuss it, not just on my own behalf, but on my generation's, as well. I felt it was important to paint the big picture that nobody seems interested in looking at; to supply some of the context that has been so roundly neglected. Besides that, if I didn't provide my personal take on PEDs, others would continue to do it for me without knowledge of the facts. The bogus accusations are still out there, fifteen years after they first arose. That offends me.

I'm not, however, out for sympathy, and I know damn well that I wouldn't get any if I were. And I shouldn't. I haven't been shortchanged. I've had a great life. I was raised with the unanimous support of a fantastic family. I've made a pile of money playing the game I love. I married the woman of my dreams. I live in paradise, with a boat in my backyard. Woe is far from me. I'd simply like to reiterate that it hasn't all been as storybookish and fair-weathered as it might have looked from afar; certainly not as much as I'd once expected it to be, with all the idealism of a smitten kid starting out. Some of that, of course, is my own doing, a consequence of the playing face I put on in the minor leagues for the sake of self-defense.

I feel, in fact, that what I've done best in my career is ball up my fists and beat back the challenges. I played with a chip on my shoulder, and admittedly—unapologetically—I'm writing with one, too. More than five years since my final single started a ninth-inning, game-winning rally, more than seven since my twelfth All-Star Game, more than eight since I broke the home run record for catchers, I still feel the need for validation. Someday, I can only hope, election to the Hall of Fame will take care of that.

In the same spirit, my fervent desire for this memoir is that the reading public will approve my story. If that happens, and *only* if, then maybe the book can serve the intended purpose and prove to be, above all, inspirational.

In September 2011, the Seattle Mariners called up a six-foot-four, 230-pound third baseman named Alex Liddi, who had participated in MLB's first European academy and played for the Italian team in the World Baseball Classic. From the town of San Remo, situated on the Mediterranean near the French border, Liddi was the first player born and raised in Italy to make it to the major leagues.

It was a milestone I'd looked forward to seeing, and hopefully it won't prove to be an anomaly. I'm pretty confident that others will follow. A team from Italy made it to the Little League World Series in 2008, and the national team has traditionally done well in the European Cup, although the last few tournaments have been dominated by the Netherlands. International competition, however, doesn't require that players be native to the country they represent, and the Netherlands has loaded up with guys of Dutch descent from Curacao. By contrast, Italy carries a relatively high percentage of natives on its roster; maybe half, or a little more. That said, the catcher Juan Pablo Angrisano is from Argentina, and he's got a gun. I watch him and think, man, if I had an arm like that I'd still be playing.

A few years back, a right-hander named Alex Maestri was signed by the Cubs and became the first pitcher from Italy ever to make it to the minor leagues. Then the Reds signed a lefty named Luca Panerati at the age of eighteen. It's progress. In 2005, there were no Italian-born *players* in the minors; by 2010, there were six. One of the obstacles for Italian prospects is that they don't get the opportunity to play as much organized baseball as Americans or Dominicans or South Americans. There's an eight-team Italian professional league that has been around since 1948, but they only schedule games for three or four days a week, fifty-four in all. When league officials told me that they'd like to arrange a working agreement with MLB, I had to advise them that major-league organizations are not going to send players over there to be idle half the time.

My role with the national team is to consult with the coaches and directors, do some promotional work, instruct the hitters here and there, then put on my number thirty-one jersey and help out at the big tournaments. The Italian lessons I take in Miami have been good for my rapport with the players, and so, in a different way, has the little bit of Sicilian dialect that my dad taught me; they get some nice laughs at my expense. But even with the bad accent, I feel as though I've connected with the old country. These days, I can hop on a plane and fly to Rome as easily as Philadelphia. Italy seems hardly foreign anymore. As I write this, in fact, I'm close to receiving my Italian citizenship, which will be a very emotional moment.

The whole experience has also gotten me *thinking* more about Italy and history. In large part, my fascination with the country in general and Rome in particular comes from the saturating sense of Christian tradition. After returning from one of my trips, I found myself pondering the great general and Roman emperor Constantine, who institutionalized Christianity in Rome and spread it across the Roman Empire. He's a controversial figure in the respect that there's some debate as to whether he was sincerely Christian or just used religion to unify his empire. Constantine wasn't considered Christian as he prepared to lead his army into the great battle for Rome in the year 312. However, on the eve of the attack, while poised at the edge of the city, he saw in a vision that the battle would be won if his soldiers fought it with the symbol of the cross on their shields. The victory occurred just as Constantine had dreamt it, and marked his conversion to Christianity, which, in the view of some scholars, led to the founding of the Catholic Church. Anyway, Constantine kept bouncing around in my head to the extent that I prayed about this subject, searching for what my thoughts all meant and where I should take them. Before long, I was meeting with David Franzoni, a screenwriter (*Amistad, Jumpin' Jack Flash*) who has lived in Rome and wrote and coproduced *Gladiator*. Our eventual agreement was that I would commission him to write a movie script about Constantine. I guess that makes me a producer of some sort. It doesn't make me Hollywood, though, and I don't want it to. I'm in it to get the story told.

I'm proud to be Roman Catholic. My Christian faith is fundamental and precious to me—the cornerstone of my life. I think it was a gift, not unlike my ability to hit a baseball. But I'm not a theologian. I'm just a former ballplayer who wishes to join the fight against the decline of religion in our society. According to the Catholic faith, I became a missionary when I was baptized, and my particular role in that regard—at least, how I perceive it—is to promote a healthy discussion and help people become historically informed. The fact is, you can't separate religion and history. When Christopher Columbus arrived in America, he planted a cross and said a prayer with a Franciscan priest at his side. Our country was founded on Judeo-Christian principles. I don't wish to preach, but think how much simpler things would be if, instead of complicated laws and ordinances, we all followed the Ten Commandments. You want to buy my house? Let me show you the leaky pipe and the crack in the foundation. You willing to take that on? Is your word good? Okay, then, why do we need an inspection? Why do we need a title search? Why do we need lawyers? I give you the keys, you give me the money, and we shake hands.

Those are the sorts of thoughts to which I've been able to devote myself since I stopped playing baseball. I'm a board member of Catholic Athletes for Christ. At one point, I was seriously contemplating becoming a deacon, if I could, but came to realize that it required a level of commitment I hadn't yet achieved; that my timetable and God's, as usual, were totally different. In the meantime, I share my devotion in ways that I can. I give faith-based speeches at men's conferences and the like, and was honored to do a radio interview with Cardinal Timothy Dolan, the archbishop of New York. On occasions like that, I testify in all sincerity that faith is what pulled me through a lot of adverse, daunting, humbling situations in my baseball career. I didn't always stick close to my spirituality—I strayed from it much more than I should have—and yet, it stuck *with me* unfailingly. I had a little talent and a lot of determination, but the fact was, I had no business doing what I did in baseball. My career, frankly, was a miracle. In retrospect, I can see that clearly.

So I try to be mindful of the blessings I've received and, in turn, to do right by the Lord and a family that now includes two daughters—Paulina was born in 2009—who get my mornings going. They're my link between sleep (often preceded by a glass of wine and a good cigar) and Starbucks.

As for the rest of the day, it would appear that, besides this book, I've become fairly predictable. My interests and hobbies fall pretty close to the tree, by and large: I'm Italian by blood and an Italophile as a result. I've been Catholic since my mother saw to it. My attraction to history—and, for that matter, my sense of patriotism, to some extent—is probably related to the fact that my family lives at Valley Forge. (I mean, I collect *muskets*.) We're in the automobile business; I'm a fan of Formula One racing. After being the object of more media coverage than I was ever comfortable with, I'm now an avid newshound instead (most of it "fair and balanced," of course). I played golf at Phoenixville High School and still knock it around, the only differ- ence being that now I get to do it in tournaments like Michael Jordan's in the Bahamas, where my partner was Mario Lemieux—I admire the hell out of that guy—and we were paired with Wayne Gretzky and Jordan himself. (We finished third, in spite of me thinking the whole time, How cool is this? I mean, what am I, a snot-nosed kid from Phoenixville, Pennsylvania, doing in *this* group? I played with Mario again a couple of years later when the Jordan tournament was in Las Vegas, and that time we finished second, tied with Gretzky and Drew Brees.) My obsession with European soccer is not quite as easy to account for, although it's been well fed by my visits to Italy. Mostly, I think, it's a case of addiction. Soccer is the biggest reason I carry a smartphone; I need my updates on Palermo, the team in the pink jerseys. (And by the way, I have one of those. The last time I was over there, I met a team official and swapped one of my Mets jerseys for a Palermo shirt with my name on it.)

The last game at Shea Stadium was held on September 28, 2008, against the Marlins. It was grim—the Mets' sixth defeat in their final nine games, during which time they fell out of first place (losing the division to the Phillies, who won thirteen of their last sixteen) and also squandered the wildcard (by one game to the Brewers, who won six of their last seven). I hate to say it, but it was typical Mets.

The closing ceremony was held after the game, which was a real mood killer. Other than *that*, it was a cool event. The festivities started Friday with a tribute to the greatest moments in Shea history. Number one was clinch- ing the 1986 World Series, number three was clinching the 1969 World Series, and I slipped in between at number two, the home run to beat the Braves in the first game after 9/11.

On Sunday, they laid out red carpets for the former players' entrances into the stadium. Tom Seaver and I were the last two to walk in. He came from left field and then I came from right, with my dad at my side. The fans were screaming my name, and of course my dad got emotional, which of course made *me* emotional. But I wouldn't have had it any other way. I felt strongly about giving back to my father, because, indisputably, he had been a tremendous inspiration in my career. He was a major reason why I was there. Honestly, I sometimes felt as though I played more for my dad than I did for myself. But I didn't mind. I *wanted* to do it for him.

The script had Seaver throwing the last pitch and me catching it. He was sixty-three years old, so I asked him if he wanted me to move up in front of the plate. "No, no, no," he said. Naturally, he bounced the ball to me. Ace defensive catcher that I was, I was able to snag it, even while nearly ripping my black dress slacks.

The whole affair felt good, and it spoke to why, if I *do* make it to the Hall of Fame—I'll be eligible for induction in 2013, along with Barry Bonds, Roger Clemens, Sammy Sosa, Craig Biggio, and Curt Schilling—I hope to go in as a Met. Technically, it's not the player's call; the Hall of Fame itself makes that decision. But players can let their preferences be known, and mine is pretty strong. Maybe I'm hypersensitive in this respect, but I appreciate appreciation. Over the years, the Mets have shown me theirs. I seldom felt that the Dodgers did.

In terms of pure baseball, the case for either team is not much different from that for the other. I hit more home runs (220-177) and drove in more runs (655-563) with the Mets, but had a higher batting average (.331-.296) with the Dodgers. I was Rookie of the Year with the Dodgers, but played more games (972-726) with the Mets. I went to the World Series with the Mets, but most of my best seasons (four of my top five finishes in the MVP voting) came with the Dodgers. Overall, largely because I suffered more injuries in New York and passed my prime there, I was probably a better player in Los Angeles, but the margin is not overwhelming. More important, performance is not entirely the point.

When I retired, Tommy Lasorda told *USA Today,* "I would hope he would go into the Hall of Fame as a Dodger. We're the one who gave him an opportunity." He's certainly right about that. Nobody else did, and the organization never let me forget it. It was a good deal for the Dodgers—a *great* deal—and yet, every time we negotiated a contract, they made me feel that I owed them. The last time, they turned the fans against me. Then they traded me. Ultimately, it was the Mets who gave me an opportunity. They also gave me the market-value contract that the Dodgers wouldn't. If there's a single person in my career with whom I feel most closely associated, yes, it's definitely Tommy. If there's a *team,* however, it's the Mets.

In a hard-to-explain, total-picture sort of way—probably because of all that happened in those times, or maybe just because I'm an easterner—my years in New York represent real life to me. To that extent, the chief connection I felt was actually more with the fans and the city than the franchise itself, especially when my days as a Met were winding down. Two things, I believe, bonded me to Mets fans. The first was choosing to sign with the ball club after I was relentlessly booed in 1998. The main reason the people had given me a hard time in the first place was that they didn't believe I was committed to the organization. When they found out I *was*, it changed everything. The second factor was 9/11. It was a shared and profound experience, the kind that people can only get through together. Everyone suffered, and grew closer for it. That was still evident at the ten-year anniversary in 2011, held at Citi Field.

The anniversary was especially poignant. I caught the first pitch from Johnny Franco, with the infield ringed by first responders, representatives of Tuesday's Children (an organization dedicated to helping people affected by 9/11), and former teammates. It was a gratifying example of how, even after I'd left New York, Mets fans embraced me as one of their own. It didn't turn out that way in Los Angeles.

It's unfortunate that my relationship with the Dodgers had to end like it did. I wish I could look back on my first team and feel about it the way Carlton Fisk felt about his. He chose to go into the Hall of Fame wearing a Boston cap, even after the Red Sox cast him off. When his contract expired, they never even made an offer to keep him. Fisk eventually played longer with the White Sox, and had some of his better years in Chicago—I, for one, identify him more with the White Sox than the Red Sox—but when he retired, his heart was still with the franchise that brought him to the big leagues. Of course, my circumstances were a little different. Carlton turned thirty, played in the World Series, and went to most of his all-star games before changing colors. I did all of that with my third organization. Also, having grown up in New England, his feeling for Boston is obviously a little different, by nature, than mine is for Los Angeles. Even so, I can't say that I fully understand his decision. I don't have that inside me.

I'd rather pull a Catfish Hunter. On his Hall of Fame plaque, the hat is blank, generic. To me, that's gutsy. That's integrity. If the Hall came to me and said, "We want you to go in as a Dodger," I'd say, "Well, then I'll go in as nothing." I just wouldn't feel comfortable with LA stamped on my head for all of eternity.

Nah, if I'm fortunate enough to go to Cooperstown, it needs to be with New York of the National League. Seaver could use some company, anyhow.

• • •

Before Omar Minaya was fired as general manager of the Mets, he offered me an unspecified, whatever-you-want-to-do kind of job with the organization, which is sometimes code for "roving minor-league instructor," though not necessarily. It was a nice gesture, but I didn't *know* what I wanted to do, or even if I wanted to do it in baseball. I was enjoying other things for a change. I wasn't ready.

A year or two later, when I was working with the Italian team in Florida and the Wilpons were being hammered for their ties to Bernie Madoff, the Mets asked me if I'd talk to the press and make a nice remark or two about their owners. I was happy to do that, but, as is so often the case with New York media, the subject turned. I was asked if I had any interest in buying into the ball club myself or had made any inquiries along those lines. I said that I'd discussed it only vaguely, through conversations with people who weren't really involved. Around the same time, Dan Lozano had actually reached out to Frank McCourt about me becoming a party in the ownership of the Dodgers—yes, the Dodgers—but McCourt was preoccupied with his public spectacle of a divorce and its implications for the franchise. At any rate, I'm still not sure if I'm ready to get back into baseball—or whether I ever will be, for that matter. I have a lifelong tendency to move on.

Since I left Phoenixville, for instance, I haven't really kept up with it. When I visit home, several times a year, it's to Valley Forge, which is nearby but not the same. The fact is, I don't have much of a relationship anymore with the place where I grew up. For the most part, that's on me. I've never been one to try to organize a legacy for myself on the way out, or after the fact. In the case of Phoenixville, there were also some family situations that factored in. My brother Tony quit the high school baseball team. My brother Tommy moved down to Florida, close to me, for his senior year. My dad felt that local organizations expected him to subsidize their projects. And so on. Through it all, feelings have been hurt. In 2008, I was inducted into the inaugural class of the Chester County Sports Hall of Fame, along with Andre Thornton, former football coach Dick Vermeil, and former Mets pitcher Jon Matlack, among others; but that wasn't a Phoenixville thing. Understanding the disconnect between me and my hometown, and hopeful of repairing it, Doc Kennedy, my old high school coach, arranged a little ceremony last spring in which my number 13 was retired and hung on the fence of the baseball field. A bunch of former teammates, including Mike Fuga and Joe Pizzica, were on hand, and Doc's number was retired at the same time. A couple thousand people showed up. It felt good. Afterward, I joined Vince,

my mom and dad, and most of the old Phantoms for pizza and beer at the Polish Club.

On the broader scale, I fully realize that I've alienated plenty of people over the years. Especially in New York, where I felt an enormous amount of pressure to earn my salary, silence my critics, and carry the Mets to the play-offs, I simply wasn't the guy who was going to come to your bake sale. Alicia thought I became a different person every time I set foot in the city—edgy, more intense. But I can't blame it all on New York. I've been a brat on a fairly regular basis.

Looking back, I wish I'd been able to loosen up a little. I wish I'd had more fun playing the game. Al Leiter used to ask me, "When are you going to *enjoy* this shit?" I never really did. That's the principal regret I have about my career. Poetically, I guess, that happens to be Mike Schmidt's main re-gret, as well. He said it straight-out in an interview with Tim McCarver. Funny how that works.

In the clarity that comes with retirement, I understand that, as a player, I was too moody, too brooding, too consumed, too unlikable. I wasn't really *interested* in being likable. I somehow felt that, if I tried to be everybody's best friend, my guard would be down. It would betray weakness. My persona was: to hell with all this other shit; I'm here to play ball. It was an attitude that drove me. I wanted to be the Mike Schmidt that I watched from my box seat on the third-base line. I wanted to be the Ted Williams that I read so much about and met in my backyard. I wanted to be as cool as Joe DiMag-gio, who, you might say, was beloved in spite of himself. Those were the guys whose style appealed to me and set a standard. Aloof, a little surly, all busi-ness. Reluctant stars. Or so it seemed.

It worked for me, but not without contradictions. For much of my ca-reer, I suppressed my spiritual side. I also made myself less approachable than I intended to. Only after the fact—the exercise of writing this book has helped, I think—have I come to terms with my desire and need to touch people. I aspire, now, not only to inspire but to be somebody you'd like to hang out and have a beer with.

I was that guy, at least to a partial extent, when I lived with Eric Karros in Manhattan Beach. Eric had it right when he said we were "just a couple of jackoff ballplayers" in those days. It was a great time in my life, and it felt like it would never end. Then came the contract negotiations. Like my summer at Vero Beach eight years before, they educated and permanently changed me.

Americans are kind of funny about athletes and contracts. We're all for

the spirit and principles of capitalism and everyone's opportunity to make of themselves what they will . . . but only up to a point. For some odd reason, this seems to apply more to baseball than practically any other occupation or pastime. A ballplayer exceeds the general public's comfort level—tests its good graces—when he makes *too* much money, whatever that number is. In Los Angeles, in particular, I felt like the poster boy for that phenomenon.

Before I battled the Dodgers over dollars and terms, I was regarded, publicly, as relatively charmed and not too bad a dude, an L.A. kind of guy. By the time they traded me, though, I had, by negotiating unsentimentally—from what I perceived as a position of strength—depleted my popularity and polarized the fan base.

Even now, though, I can't apologize for driving a hard bargain, for wanting to cash in that great big chip on my shoulder. I couldn't suddenly lose the attitude just because it was contract time. That attitude was indispensable to what I'd become. It was my functioning baseball ego. If I'd considered myself lucky to be there, I wouldn't have been there.

Through stubborn pride and grim single-mindedness, I was able, ultimately, to accomplish more in baseball than anyone ever thought I would; and I would find it gratifying if *that* were remembered as my contribution to the game and the culture; if the tough crowd that we've become could still find a place in its heart to be inspired by an old-fashioned, American-style success story.

From where I sit, that's what mine amounts to.

ACKNOWLEDGMENTS

Countless people warrant thanks for their generous help in putting this work together. The authors wish to especially recognize the following: Vince and Roni Piazza; Vince Piazza Jr.; Danny, Tony, and Tommy Piazza; Alicia Piazza; Tom Lasorda; Dan Lozano; Doc Kennedy; Brad Kohler; Joe Pizzica; Blaine Huey; Eric Karros; Greg Hansell; Mark Cresse; Al Leiter; John Franco; Fred Claire; Bobby Valentine; Martie Wheeler; Clark Wheeler; Allison Hemphill; David Black; Jonathan Karp; Johanna Li; and Bob Bender.

APPENDIX

BATTING STATISTICS

YEAR	TEAM	GAMES	AT BATS	RUNS	HITS	2B	3B	HR	RBI	BB	SO	BA	OBP	SLG	OPS
1992	LAD	21	69	5	16	3	0	1	7	4	12	.232	.284	.319	.603
1993	LAD	149	547	81	174	24	2	35	112	46	86	.318	.370	.561	.932
1994	LAD	107	405	64	129	18	0	24	92	33	65	.319	.370	.541	.910
1995	LAD	112	434	82	150	17	0	32	93	39	80	.346	.400	.606	1.006
1996	LAD	148	547	87	184	16	0	36	105	81	93	.336	.422	.563	.985
1997	LAD	152	556	104	201	32	1	40	124	69	77	.362	.431	.638	1.070
1998	TOT	151	561	88	184	38	1	32	111	58	80	.328	.390	.570	.96C
1998	LAD	37	149	20	42	5	0	9	30	11	27	.282	.329	.497	.826
1998	FLA	5	18	1	5	0	1	0	5	0	0	.278	.263	.389	.652
1998	NYM	109	394	67	137	33	0	23	76	47	53	.348	.417	.607	1.024
1999	NYM	141	534	100	162	25	0	40	124	51	70	.303	.361	.575	.936
2000	NYM	136	482	90	156	26	0	38	113	58	69	.324	.398	.614	1.012
2001	NYM	141	503	81	151	29	0	36	94	67	87	.300	.384	.573	.957
2002	NYM	135	478	69	134	23	2	33	98	57	82	.280	.359	.544	.903
2003	NYM	68	234	37	67	13	0	11	34	35	40	.286	.377	.483	.860
2004	NYM	129	455	47	121	21	0	20	54	68	78	.266	.362	.444	.806
2005	NYM	113	398	41	100	23	0	19	62	41	67	.251	.326	.452	.778
2006	SDP	126	399	39	113	19	1	22	68	34	66	.283	.342	.501	.843
2007	OAK	83	309	33	85	17	1	8	44	18	61	.275	.313	.414	.727
16 Yrs		1912	6911	1048	2127	344	8	427	1335	759	1113	.308	.377	.545	.922

BIBLIOGRAPHY

Claire, Fred, with Steve Springer. *My 30 Years in Dodger Blue*. Champaign, IL: Sports Publishing L.L.C., 2004.

The Hardball Times writers. *The Hardball Times Baseball Annual 2009*. Chicago: ACTA Publications, 2008.

James, Brant. *Mike Piazza*. Philadelphia: Chelsea House, 1997.

New York Daily News. *Piazza*. Champaign, IL: Sports Publishing L.L.C., 2002.

Noble, Marty. *Mike and the Mets*. Champaign, IL: Sports Publishing, Inc., 1999.

Pearlman, Jeff. *The Rocket That Fell to Earth*. New York: HarperCollins, 2009.

Plaschke, Bill, with Tommy Lasorda. *I Live for This*. New York: Houghton Mifflin, 2007.

Schell, Michael J. *Baseball's All-Time Best Sluggers*. Princeton, NJ: Princeton University Press, 2005.

Williams, Ted, with John Underwood. *The Science of Hitting*. New York: Simon & Schuster, 1971.

The authors would also like to credit the following publications and sites:

Baseball Prospectus; baseball-reference.com; *Deadspin*; *Gentlemen's Quarterly* (April 1999); *Los Angeles Times*; mlb.com; *New York Daily News*; *New York Post*; *New York Times*; *Newsday*; *Oakland Tribune*; observer.com; *Philadelphia Inquirer*; *Phoenixville Evening Phoenix*; *Playboy* (June 2003); *Sacramento Bee*; *San Francisco Chronicle*; *Sporting News*; *Sports Illustrated*; *Wall Street Journal*.

INDEX

Aaron, Hank, 225, 291, 292, 337
Abbott, Kurt, 234
Abboud, Joseph, 115
AC/DC (band), 29, 204, 264
Acee, Kevin, 166
Acta, Manny, 57
Adande, J. A., 194
Aerosmith, 290
Affleck, Ben, 32
Agbayani, Benny, 201, 205, 216, 231,
    240, 251, 255
Alderson, Sandy, 325
Alex (Best Dressed by Alex), 115
Alfonseca, Antonio, 223
Alfonzo, Edgardo "Fonzi," 227, 231,
    247
  and contracts, 268
  as hitter, 208, 211, 215, 221, 232, 295
  and Mets, 205, 241, 256
  and World Series, 234
Alice in Chains (band), 327
Allen, Marcus, 119
All-Star Games:
  (1993), 118, 119
  (1994), 129
  (1995), 144–45
  (1996), 215
  (1997), 226
  (2000), 296
  (2001), 242–43
  (2002), 266–67

  (2004), 296–97
  (2005), 310
  in Japan, 153
Alomar, Roberto, 256, 264, 265–66,
    283
Alomar, Sandy, 310–11
Alpine, New Jersey, house in, 199
Al Qaeda, 244
Alston, Walter, 143, 146
Alvarez, Joe, 64, 66, 67, 68, 69, 70–71,
    78
Amalfitano, Joey, 135, 163
Amelung, Ed, 20
Anderson, Pamela, 114, 132
André the Giant (wrestler), 26
Andrews, Shane, 219
androstenedione, 204
Angrisano, Juan Pablo, 339
Aniston, Jennifer, 228
Ankiel, Rick, 231
Anthony, Eric, 94
Anthony, Marc, 246
Anthrax (band), 204
Apodaca, Bob, 187, 205, 228
Appier, Kevin, 241
Arizona Fall League, 96–97, 98
Arocha, Rene, 103
Arturo (cigar man), 303, 304
Ashby, Alan, 94
Ashley, Billy, 72, 90, 94, 131, 134, 144,
    147

Astacio, Pedro, 94, 95, 96, 101, 136, 151, 162, 256
Atlanta Braves, 192–93, 209–10, 214–16, 220, 222, 228, 247–49
Atlas, Tony, 26
AutoZone commercial, 202
Avila, Al, 48, 56
Avila, Ralph, 48, 56, 57, 255

Baar, Bryan, 86, 87
Babe Ruth league, 17–18, 19
Backlund, Bob, 26
Bad Company (band), 204
Bagwell, Jeff, 166, 175, 198
Baker, Dusty, 3
Bamberger, Michael, 176
Bane, Eddie, 181
Banks, Ernie, 116
Banyacskay, Joe, 27
Barbuscia, Lisa, 161
Bard, Josh, 320, 322
Barfield, Josh, 321
Barkley, Charles, 132
Barrios, Manuel, 177, 181
baseball:
    arbitration in, 155, 174
    ballpark size, 253
    changes in game, 250–53
    collective bargaining agreements, 154
    "dirty slide rule," 193, 219–20
    equipment modifications in, 252–53
    expansion draft in, 171
    expansion teams in, 251
    Hall of Fame, 316, 337, 339, 343–44
    increase in strikeouts, 253
    interleague play, 161–62
    international competition, 339
    Latin American winter leagues, 317
    and nutrition, 251
    player incomes, 252
    player-management balance, 329–30

    players' strike (1994–95), 127, 129–31, 132, 133, 137, 139, 213
    players' theme songs in, 327–28
    playoff shares in, 217
    power surge in, 253
    QuesTec system, 223
    revenue sharing, 154
    and September 11 attacks, 244–48, 249, 312, 342, 344
    social relationships in, 217–18
    steroids and drug issues, 156–59, 168, 203–4, 226, 250–51, 252, 253, 264, 268–69, 285–87, 338
    and weight training, 251–52
    World Baseball Classic, 317, 339
Baseball Prospectus, 280
Baseball's All-Time Best Sluggers (Schell), 295
Baseball Writers of America, 255
Baylor, Don, 111, 162
Baywatch (TV), 131–32
Beamer, Todd, 244
Beane, Billy, 325, 326, 328–30
Beatles, 323
Bechler, Steve, 158
Beck, Rod, 121, 163
Bedrosian, Steve, 100
Bell, Derek, 219, 223
Bell, Jay, 227
Belle, Albert, 154
Belle and Sebastian (band), 263
Beltran, Carlos, 310, 314
Bench, Johnny, 75, 112, 158, 220
    and Hall of Fame, 337
    record tied by Mike, 267
    and Shea event honoring Mike, 1, 2, 294, 296
    as top-ranking catcher, 1, 295
Bene, Bill, 53, 63
Benes, Andy, 194
Benitez, Armando, 199, 229
    vs. Atlanta, 214, 247, 248, 249

as pitcher, 211, 222, 226, 230, 232,
   234, 240, 247, 248, 249, 277
and World Series, 234, 240
Bennett, Gary, 334
Benson, Anna, 305
Benson, Kris, 305
Berg, Dave, 184
Bergeron, Peter, 291
Berkow, Ira, 190
Berman, Chris, 129, 229
Bernaola, Carol, 227
Bernaola, Darlene, 227–28, 262
Berra, Yogi, 1, 233, 294, 295, 296, 317,
   337
Bettis, Jerome "Bus," 131
Beyers, Tom, 60, 63, 67, 72, 75, 77
Bichette, Dante, 141
Biggio, Craig, 198, 253, 343
Black, Bud, 94, 325
Black Label Society (band), 210
Black Sabbath (band), 29
Blades, Bennie, 43
Blades, Brian, 43
Bland, Mike, 27
Blaney, Charlie, 56, 66, 67, 68, 69,
   78–79
Blauser, Jeff, 220
Blob, The (movie), 25
Bochy, Bruce, 152, 318, 320–22, 324,
   325
Bodet, Gib, 52, 53
Boggs, John, 98
Boggs, Wade, 218
Bold and the Beautiful, The (TV), 132
Bonds, Barry, 169, 243, 293
   and All-Star Game, 144, 153, 266
   at bat, 230, 256, 265
   and Hall of Fame, 343
   as hitter, 104, 140, 163, 250,
      253–54, 291–92, 294
   and MVP, 120, 230
   and protective armor, 253, 265
   socializing, 118–19

Bonds, Sun, 118–19
Bonilla, Bobby, 177, 181, 206, 212, 216
Bon Jovi, 30, 334
Boone, Aaron, 210
Boone, Bob, 81
Boone, Bret, 98–99, 212, 214
Bootcheck, Chris, 333
Boros, Steve, 60
Boston (band), 29, 204
Boston Red Sox, 333
Bosworth, Brian "The Boz," 43
Bourell, Andy, 288–89
Bournigal, Rafael, 90, 98
Bowa, Larry, 13
Bowen, Rob, 320, 328
Bowen, Ryan, 112
Boynton Beach, Florida, 35, 184
Bradley, Milton, 326
Bradshaw, Terry, 202
Brantley, Jeff, 140, 153
Branyan, Russell, 321
Bratton, Melvin, 43
Braun, Eddie, 115, 132, 175
Brees, Drew, 342
Bridges, Angelica, 272, 303
Brock, Greg, 20
Brogna, Rico, 200
Brooklyn Dodgers, 233
Brosius, Scott, 234, 240
Brosnan, Jason, 79
Brower, Jim, 293
Brown, Jerome, 43
Brown, Kevin, 181, 182, 208
Bruno, John, 190, 235, 245
Buhler, Bill, 113
BulletBoys (band), 175
Burba, Dave, 121
Burkett, John, 120, 121
Burnitz, Jeromy, 96, 97, 256, 264, 276,
   283
Busch, Mike, 137–38, 139
Butler, Brett, 137–38, 140, 142, 162,
   169–70, 173, 252

Cabrera, Jolbert, 276–77

California, Mike's enjoyment of, 114–16, 124

California League, 74, 77, 79, 85, 86

Calogero (hermit), 5–6

Cameron, Mike, 290, 296, 318, 324

Caminiti, Ken, 146, 150, 151–52, 156, 158, 247, 264

Campanella, Roy, 2, 54, 100–101, 109, 123, 317, 337

Candelaria, John, 74, 94

Candiotti, Tom, 101, 108, 110, 116, 135, 136, 142, 148

Cano, Raul, 79, 80

Canseco, Jose, 18, 120, 251

Carey, Chase, 178, 182, 208

Carpenter, Chris, 324–25

Carroll, Donnie, 60

Carroll, Mike, 254–55

Carter, Gary, 75, 241, 295, 334
    and All-Star Game, 118
    and Hall of Fame, 337
    and Shea event honoring Mike, 1, 294, 296

Casey, Sean, 210

Castillo, Frank, 164

Castro, Ramon, 309

Catalanotto, Frank, 311

Catanello, Bishop Ignatius, 303–4

Catholic Athletes for Christ, 341

Catholic Church, 67, 116, 195–96, 261, 273–74, 303, 335, 340–41

Cedeno, Roger, 205, 215, 256, 265–66

Chamberlain, Wilt, 105

Champion, Sam, 263

Chariots of Fire (movie), 292

Chavez, Endy, 323

Chavez, Eric, 326

Chen, Bruce, 246

Cher, 132

Chester County Sports Hall of Fame (Pennsylvania), 345–46

Chouinard, Bobby, 211

Christina (crush), 96–97

Claire, Fred, 139, 146, 149, 162
    and contracts, 99, 125, 126, 154, 166, 171
    as Dodgers' general manager, 77, 84, 85, 86, 88–89, 99, 121, 135, 151
    fired, 181
    Mike traded to Marlins, 175–76, 177, 178, 181
    My 30 Years in Dodger Blue, 181

Claritin commercials, 202

Clark, Jerald, 91

Classic Sports Network, 175

Clemens, Roger, 253, 255, 291, 311
    and All-Star Game, 242, 296–97, 310
    and free agency, 293
    and Hall of Fame, 343
    Mike at bat against, 221, 224–26, 234–35, 265
    as pitcher, 206, 207, 221, 226, 236, 293, 296
    throwing at batters, 224–26, 234, 235, 236, 237, 238, 242, 265, 296–97
    and World Series, 233, 234–39, 257, 297
    and Yankees, 206, 207, 221

Clontz, Brad, 210

Cohen, Brian, 98, 117

Colavito, Rocky, 317

Colletti, Ned, 334

Collins, Jocko, 35

Collins, Terry, 86

Colon, Bartolo, 282

Columbus, Christopher, 341

Conigliaro, Tony, 225, 317

Constantine (Holy Roman Emperor), 340

Cook, Aaron, 313, 314

Cook, Dennis, 94, 187, 214

Cooper, Eric, 309

Cooper, Michael, 26

Counsell, Craig, 184
Cousins, Scott, 219, 220
Cox, Bobby, 118, 152, 212, 215, 248
creatine, 203, 204
Creed (band), 313
Cresse, Brad, 41–42
Cresse, Mark, 20, 41, 49, 52, 61, 62, 84, 101, 119, 181
Crews, Tim, 90
Criss, Peter, 29
Crosby, Bobby, 328
Cust, Jack, 328, 330

Daley, Ken, 92
Damon, Matt, 32
Dangerous Toys (band), 76
Darwin, Bobby, 52, 53
Daubach, Brian, 227
Daulton, Darren, 118, 119, 130
Davis, Eric, 26, 102–3, 104, 109
Dawson, Andre, 12
Dean, James, 120
Delahoya, Javier, 74
DeLeon, Jose, 83
DeLury, Bill, 90
Dempsey, Rick, 58
Dempster, Ryan, 319
Depeche Mode, 76
Dergan, Lisa, 303
DeShields, Delino, 58, 135, 138, 162
Deye, Marc, 27
Diaz, Cameron, 228
Dibble, Rob, 265
Dickey, Bill, 165
Dickinson, Bones, 176, 182
Didier, Mel, 75
DiFelice, Mike, 313
DiMaggio, Joe, 21, 290, 291, 317, 346
Dio (band), 30
Dirty Deeds (movie), 218
Divac, Vlade, 98
Doctor J, 26
Dodger Stadium, 135, 140

Dodgertown, see Vero Beach
Dolan, Cardinal Timothy, 341
Dombrowski, Dave, 176, 179, 185, 336
Dominican Republic, 56–58, 148, 292, 307, 308
Dotel, Octavio, 214, 293
Doubleday, Nelson, 185, 187, 197, 245, 264, 265, 268, 302
Dr. Dre, 105
Drysdale, Don, 54
Dufresne, Chris, 182
Dunn, Adam, 307
Dunning, Debbe, 117–18, 195, 262
Duquette, Jim, 270, 283, 302
Dye, Jermaine, 152, 153
Dykstra, Lenny, 130
Dymetadrine, 158

Ebel, Dino, 181
Eckersley, Dennis, 47, 163
Eckstein, David, 311
Eisenreich, Jim, 177, 181
Elia, Lee, 70
Elway, John, 168
Embree, Alan, 321
ephedra, 158
ESPN, 120, 127, 224
Estes, Shawn, 256, 265
Estrada, Frank "Paquin," 80, 81–82

Fabio, 132, 176
Fan Appreciation Day, 120
Feliciano, Pedro, 285
Ferguson, Joe, 47, 49, 57, 59, 61, 78, 100, 109, 206, 284
Fernandez, Chico, 57
Fernandez, Sam, 125–26, 154, 166–68, 171, 173–74, 180
Finley, Steve, 151
Fish Tacos (band), 175
Fisk, Carlton:
    and Hall of Fame, 337, 344
    records targeted/tied by Mike, 2,

Fisk, Carlton (*continued*):
    267, 278, 279, 282, 284, 291–93,
    295
  and Shea event honoring Mike, 1,
    294, 296
Fletcher, Darrin, 128
Florida Marlins, 183–85
  Mike traded to, 175–82, 183–84, 208
Florida State League, 64, 70–71
Floyd, Cliff, 183, 278, 283, 309–10
Floyd, D. J., 55
Fonville, Chad, 140
Food and Drug Administration (FDA),
    157, 203
Ford-Bey, Abdul, 15–16
Fosse, Ray, 267
Foster, George, 294, 295
Fox Group, 166–68, 171, 176, 181,
    182, 208
Fox Television, 178
Francesa, Mike, 185, 259
Franco, John, 2, 153, 233, 256
  vs. Atlanta, 192, 193, 214, 216, 247,
    249
  and front office, 270–71
  and media, 226, 271, 306
  and Mike's trade to Mets, 186, 188
  as pitcher, 192, 193, 216, 230–31,
    249, 344
  socializing, 217, 303
Franco, Matt, 207, 215, 218
Franzoni, David, 340
Fraser, Ron, 40, 42, 46
Fuga, Mike, 34, 345
Furcal, Rafael, 321
Furillo, Carl, 317

Gagne, Eric, 256
Gainer, Jay, 75, 77
Galarraga, Andres, 110–11, 136, 153
Ganino, Eric, 55
Gant, Ron, 209, 210
Garber, Bill, 8

Garber-Piazza Auto Sales, 9
Garces, Rich, 227
Garciaparra, Nomar, 322
Gardner, Mark, 129
Garvey, Steve, 121
Gehrig, Lou, 337
Geren, Bob, 326, 327, 328, 331–32
Gibson, Kirk, 47, 55, 58, 165
Gibson, Paul, 84
Gilbert, Dennis, 99, 125, 126
Giles, Brian, 318, 324
Giles, Marcus, 249
Gilkey, Bernard, 193
Gillick, Pat, 315, 316
Giuliani, Rudy, 246
Glavine, Tom, 103
  as Braves pitcher, 142, 144, 153,
    209, 212, 223
  Home of the Brave, 281
  as Mets pitcher, 280–81, 290, 291,
    305, 312
  signing with Mets, 278
Godri, Joe, 33
Goetz, Geoff, 186
Gold's Gym, 124
Gonzalez, Adrian, 318, 320
Gonzalez, Juan, 153
Gonzalez, Larry, 63
Gonzalez, Luis, 211
Gonzalez, Pete, 46, 64–65, 67, 69
Gooden, Dwight, 224
Good Will Hunting (movie), 32
Gordon, Tom, 207
Gott, Jim, 107, 109, 110, 147
Grace, Mark, 90, 119
Grapefruit League, 83–84, 290
Graziano, Bob, 168, 171, 178–79, 180
"Great Divide, The" (Stapp), 313
Grebeck, Craig, 206
Green, Shawn, 181, 302
Gregg, Eric, 137
Gretzky, Wayne, 171, 342
Griffey, Ken Jr., 155, 169, 253

Griffin, Marc, 53–54
Grissom, Marquis, 181
Gross, Kevin, 94, 101, 107, 121
Gross, Kip, 90
Guerrero, Pedro, 121
Guerrero, Vladimir, 80, 243, 337
Guidry, Ron, 306
Guillen, Ozzie, 216, 308
Guns N' Roses, 275
Gunze commercial, 136
Guthrie, Mark, 136, 256
Gwynn, Chris, 139, 151
Gwynn, Tony, 128, 135, 253, 270
    as hitter, 138–39, 150, 151, 165, 169
    on steroids/drugs issue, 156

Hall, Derrick, 175
Halladay, Roy, 266, 326
Hall of Fame, 316, 337, 339, 343–44
Hamilton, Darryl, 215, 230, 237
Hampton, Mike, 237–38
    and Clemens, 234
    and free agency, 241
    as pitcher, 226, 231, 234, 236, 290
    traded to Mets, 219
Hansell, Greg, 74–77
    and Arizona Fall League, 96
    hospitable family of, 98, 102
    as pitcher, 74, 75, 77, 210
    as roommate, 74, 75–77, 86–87, 97, 101
Hansell, Margo, 74–75, 86
Hansen, Dave, 90
Happening, The (movie), 24
Hardball Times Baseball Annual, 84–85, 88–89, 279–80, 295–96
Harkey, Mike, 90
Harnisch, Pete, 95, 135
Harris, Lenny, 58, 79, 91, 224
Hart, Anita, 131–32
Hartsock, Jeff, 55, 59
Harvey, Doug, 95–96
Hatcher, Mickey, 181

Hawpe, Brad, 320
Hayes, Charlie, 111
Hefley, Nancy Bea, 327
Hefner, Hugh, 303
Heiden, Eric, 23
Heilman, Aaron, 311, 324
Helton, Todd, 219
Hemond, Roland, 48
Henderson, Rickey, 199, 205, 211, 212, 215, 216, 217–18, 337
Henry, John, 178
Hensley, Clay, 322
Hermoso, Rafael, 203
Hernandez, Angel, 192, 193
Hernandez, Bobby, 44–45
Hernandez, Carlos, 89, 101, 121
Hernandez, Keith, 48, 268
Hernandez, Livan, 183, 184
Hernandez, Orlando "El Duque," 240, 321
Hernandez, Xavier, 143, 144
Hershiser, Orel, 115, 214
    as pitcher, 91, 101, 165, 207–8, 210
    and team spirit, 108, 110, 111
Herzog, Whitey, 170
Highsmith, Alonzo, 43
Hill, Glenallen, 130
Hill, Jim, 100, 101
Hill, Ken, 106
Hina, Fred, 203, 205, 211, 225
Hoffman, Trevor, 135, 151, 202, 320
Hogan, Hulk, 202
Hollandsworth, Todd, 142, 151
Holliday, Matt, 320
Hollins, Dave, 130
Holmes, Darren, 164
Home Improvement (TV), 117
Hooton, Burt, 59, 62, 63–64, 83
Horenci, Grandma, 24–25
Horenci, Grandpa, 24
Horenci, Joe (uncle), 29–30
Horner, Bob, 12
Horwitz, Jay, 186, 226, 259, 260, 314

Househusbands of Hollywood (TV), 90

Howard, Frank, 113, 121

Howard, Ryan, 326

Howard, Thomas, 129

Howe, Art, 292
    fired, 302
    as manager, 276, 278, 281, 284, 285,
        290, 299, 302
    and Mike as catcher, 278, 293, 297
    and Mota, 276, 277

Howitt, Dann, 88

Hriniak, Walt, 218

Huckaby, Ken, 61

Hudson, Maryann, 113, 123, 147

Huey, Blaine, 12

Huizenga, Wayne, 178, 185

human growth hormone (HGH),
    203–4

Hundley, Todd, 181, 185, 188–89, 191,
    194, 199, 200

Hunter, Brian, 216

Hunter, Catfish, 344

Iannetta, Chris, 320

Indocine, 158, 203

"In My Life" (Beatles), 323

Instructional League, 53, 54–55, 72

Iron Maiden, 29, 30

Irvin, Michael, 43

Isenberg, Chris, 260

Ishii, Kazuhisa, 306

iSteve.com, 263–64

Italy:
    Mike's citizenship in, 340
    national baseball team, 307–8, 311,
        317, 340, 345
    players' heritage of, 317, 339–40
    soccer in, 342
    and World Baseball Classic, 317,
        339

Jackson, Mike, 121

Jackson, Reggie, 159, 313

James, Dion, 59

Jeffries, Kim, 31

Jeter, Derek, 207, 234, 239, 240, 300,
    301

John Paul II, Pope, 273–74, 317

Johnson, Brian, 163

Johnson, Charles, 177, 179–80, 181

Johnson, Jimmy, 127

Johnson, Lou, 251

Johnson, Randy, 211, 253

Johnson, Stan, 277

Johnstone, John, 70

Jones, Andruw, 152, 216

Jones, Bobby, 71, 231, 240

Jones, Chipper, 212–13, 253, 258
    and Atlanta, 209, 214, 215, 216,
        247, 248
    as hitter, 209, 214, 337
    and media, 210
    and MVP, 210, 214

Jones, Dave "Robot," 15–16

Jones, Doug, 96

Jordan, Brian:
    and Atlanta, 214, 215, 216, 220
    and Dodgers, 256, 276–77
    hit by pitches, 215, 256
    as hitter, 184, 212, 214, 216, 247,
        249

Jordan, Michael, 342

Judas Priest, 30

Juden, Jeff, 188

JUGS machine, 11

Justice, David, 152, 234, 237

Kalas, Brad, 16

Kalas, Harry, 16

Karros, Eric, 102, 113–14, 127–29, 137,
    152, 168
    and contracts, 126, 154–55, 167, 171
    and Dodgers, 90, 111, 123, 136,
        147, 151, 153, 180, 182, 295
    and friendship, 55, 74, 101, 104–8,
        115, 117, 121–22, 182, 217, 346

as hitter, 139, 140–41, 149, 162, 163, 295
and labor strike, 130, 131, 133, 139
and Manhattan Beach condo, 104–6, 346
and Mike's trade to Marlins, 177, 180
and MVP, 162
and pitchers, 111, 127–28, 256
Rookie of the Year, 104, 121, 125, 142, 153
Karsay, Steve, 247, 248
Kasten, Stan, 335
Kauffman, Bruce, 93
Kawano, Nobe, 19
Kazmir, Scott, 305–6
Kearns, Lisa, 283, 288
Keegan, Tom, 169
Kelley, Brad, 42, 46
Kelly, Mike, 220
Kendall, Jason, 325, 328
Kennedy, John "Doc," 33, 36, 37, 345
Kennedy, Kevin, 54–55, 60, 61
Kent, Jeff, 230
Kerrane, Kevin, *Dollar Sign on the Muscle*, 48
Kile, Darryl, 231, 232
Kimmel, Jimmy, 291
Kimmel, Sidney, 196
Kiner, Ralph, 31
King, Hank, 315
Kirby, Wayne, 151
Kiss (band), 30
Klesko, Ryan, 147, 214
Knauss, Melania, 303
Knoblauch, Chuck, 234
Kohler, Brad, 36, 38
Komatsu company, 136
Koufax, Sandy, 54, 337
Krell, 132
Kruk, John, 119
Kuhlmann, Fred, 91, 93
Kung Fu Theater (TV), 113

Lackey, John, 330
LaMacchia, Al, 65
Langston, Mark, 102
Larkin, Barry, 139, 141, 210
LaRoche, Adam, 291
La Russa, Tony, 251, 256, 311
Lasorda, Tommy, 35, 207, 298, 331
and All-Star Game, 242–43
commercials by, 83
connections of, 41, 45, 46–47, 48, 51
and Dodgers, 20, 52–53, 58, 60–61, 143–44, 146, 153, 168, 181
early years of, 6–7
and Grapefruit League, 83–84
and Hall of Fame, 337
health problems of, 144
and Mike's attitude, 113, 229
and Mike's career, 21, 41, 47, 49–50, 51, 52–53, 55–56, 61, 65, 68–69, 77, 84, 85–86, 89, 90, 91, 100, 103, 109–10, 127, 145, 177, 178, 180, 187, 194, 197, 284, 316, 334, 338, 343
and Mike's childhood, 3–4, 6, 18
as Mike's goombah, 40, 147, 169–70, 174, 180
and Mike's injuries, 103, 135, 138
and Mike's teen years, 33, 36
and the opposition, 119
retirement of, 144, 147, 153, 180
and Vince, 8–9, 10, 40, 44, 50, 68, 146
Latin American winter leagues, 317
LaValliere, Mike, 89
Law, Ty, 288
Lawton, Matt, 247
Lazzeri, Tony, 317
Leary, Tim, 130
Led Zeppelin, 29, 282
Lee, Bruce, 113
Lee, Travis, 262
Legion ball, 45

Leiter, Al:
    and contracts, 199, 268
    and friendship, 187, 190, 217, 303,
        305
    and Mets, 186, 187, 199, 211, 233,
        248, 256, 270, 305–6
    and Mike's attitude, 112–13, 190,
        309, 346
    as pitcher, 187–88, 206, 207, 209,
        210, 212, 215, 221, 223, 231,
        233, 234, 240, 249, 293, 298
    and Valentine, 258, 268, 270–71
    and World Series, 233, 234, 240
Leiter, Mark, 138, 175
Lemieux, Mario, 342
Lester, Jon, 333
Letterman, David, 118, 262
Leyland, Jim, 183, 185
Liberatore, Eddie, 21–22, 35, 46, 48–50
Liddi, Alex, 339
Lieberthal, Mike, 315–16, 323
Ligtenberg, Kerry, 222
Lima, Jose, 194
Little League baseball, 11–12, 15–17
Liverziana, Claudio, 317
Lockhart, Keith, 214
Lo Duca, Paul, 310, 315
Lofton, Kenny, 322
Lombardi, Ernie, 138, 317
Looper, Braden, 2, 290, 293, 307, 327
Lopez, Javy, 153, 247, 280, 281
Los Angeles, Mike's enjoyment of,
        114–16
Los Angeles Dodgers:
    Catcher Olympics, 61–62
    and contracts, 125–27, 143, 146–47,
        154–55, 173–75
    in Dominican Republic, 56–58
    and Fox, 166–68, 171, 176, 181,
        182, 208
    global roster of, 136, 160–61
    and leadership, 159–61, 164–65
    and loyalty, 126, 152, 170

Mike as batboy for, 19–20, 41, 59,
        136, 316
    Mike drafted by, 49–50, 51–53, 72
    Mike traded by, 175–82, 183–84,
        208
    pitchers vs. hitters in, 147–49, 160
    sale of, 153–54, 155, 166–68, 171,
        182
    soul of, 143, 179
    team chemistry, 160, 169
    and Triple Crown, 295
    in Vero Beach, see Vero Beach
Los Angeles Raiders, 105
Lott, Billy, 72, 74
Lowe, Derek, 227
Lowell, Mike, 328
Lozano, Dan, 77, 97–98, 101, 117, 216,
        253
    and contracts, 99, 125–26, 127,
        155, 166–68, 171, 174, 195–96,
        197–99, 316, 325, 333, 334
    and endorsement deals, 136
    and European trip, 273
    and karaoke, 322–23
    and media rumors, 260–61, 286
    and Mike's retirement, 314, 315,
        335, 345
    and trade to Marlins, 176, 177, 179
    and trade to Mets, 185, 186, 189, 195
Ludy, Dick, 36
Lund, Ed, 75, 78
Lupica, Mike, 301
Lurie, Bob, 92
Luzinski, Greg, 13, 38, 309
Luzinski, Ryan, 125, 126
Lynch, Dave, 81
Lyons, Ed, 84

Madden, Bill, 187
Maddux, Greg, 109, 253
    and Braves, 209, 214
    as pitcher, 136, 141, 153, 209, 212,
        214, 222–23, 235, 284

Madoff, Bernie, 345
Madonna, 132
Maestri, Alex, 339
Magnante, Mike, 175
Mahomes, Pat, 206, 214, 215, 231
Mainieri, Demie "Doc," 45, 46, 48, 66,
    294
Mainieri, Paul, 46, 48, 294
Major League Baseball Players Associa-
    tion, 285–86
Malone, Kevin, 181, 209
Manhattan Beach, condo in, 104–7,
    115, 131, 134, 182, 196, 346
Mantei, Matt, 212
Mantle, Mickey, 240
Manuel, Charlie, 313, 316
Manwaring, Kirt, 123
Marabell, Scott, 66
Marchi, Max, 280
Maris, Roger, 159, 250
Marosek, Vic, 15
Marquis, Jason, 246
Married with Children (TV), 132
Marsh, Randy, 206
Marshall, Mike, 20, 22
Martin, Russell, 298, 334
Martinez, Pedro, 57–58, 253
    and Dodgers, 58, 74, 149, 307
    fire and fury of, 306–7
    and hit batters, 191–92, 227, 306,
        307
    income of, 171, 198
    and media, 192, 275, 277–78, 307
    and Mets, 306, 309, 323–24
    as pitcher, 57, 74, 111, 149, 223,
        227, 309, 323–24
    and Ramon, 58, 149
Martinez, Ramon, 57, 98, 136
    and Dodgers, 111, 149, 151, 307
    and hit batters, 110–11
    and media, 147, 179
    and Pedro, 58, 149
    as pitcher, 101, 109, 110–11, 129,

    134, 137, 139, 147, 151, 152,
        162, 164, 227, 306
Martinez, Tino, 235
Matlack, Jon, 345
Matsui, Kaz, 218, 290
Matthews, Wallace, 237, 259–60,
    261
Mauer, Joe, 165
Mays, Willie, 240
McAnulty, Paul, 320
McCarver, Tim, 14, 162, 346
McCourt, Frank, 182, 345
McCourt, Jamie, 182
McDowell, Jack, 155
McDowell, Roger, 94, 109, 117
McElroy, Chuck, 194
McEnroe, John, 202
McEwing, Joe, 223, 276
McGlinchy, Kevin, 214
McGraw, Tug, 186
McGriff, Fred, 112, 153
McGwire, Mark, 130, 251
    and batting records, 156, 159, 250
    and contracts, 162–63
    and drugs/steroids issue, 156, 157,
        158–59, 204, 250
    as hitter, 156, 158–59, 163, 183,
        184, 250
    nonprofit foundation of, 162
McKernan, Pat, 86, 88
McKnight, Bob, 115
McNamara, Julianne, 177
McNamee, Brian, 226
McPeak, Holly, 131
McQueen, Steve, 25
McRae, Brian, 204
Meat Loaf, 231
Mendoza, Ramiro, 207
Mercker, Kent, 184
Meredith, Cla, 321, 322
Mesones, Monica, 198
Messina, Gene, 5
Metallica, 29, 76, 322

Metal Skool, 322
Mexicali Aguilas (Eagles), 79–82
Mexican Winter League, 79–82, 307
Miami, University of, 42–44
Miami-Dade North, 45–48
Miami Hurricanes, 40
Mientkiewicz, Doug, 306, 309
Mike Piazza Honda, 273, 335, 342
Miller, Lemmie, 20
Millwood, Kevin, 212, 215
Minaya, Omar, 302, 306, 314, 345
Minnelli, Liza, 246, 247
Minor, Ryan, 185
Mitchell Report, 286–87
Mizuno bats, 120
Molina, Yadier, 279
Molitor, Paul, 319
Mondesi, Raul, 115, 143, 152, 161
    and contract, 167
    and Dodgers, 74, 129, 162, 295
    and drugs/steroids issue, 158
    as hitter, 162, 163, 164, 295
    as Rookie of the Year, 129, 142
Monster Pak, 157, 203
Montalvo, Rafael, 133
Moody Blues, 26
Mora, Melvin, 212, 214, 216
Morales, Jose, 20
Morgan, Joe, 112, 129, 166, 295
Morrissey, Jim, 76
Morrow, Chris, 60
Mota, Guillermo, 257, 275–78, 307,
    311, 330
Mota, Manny, 19
Mulholland, Terry, 214, 222
Mulligan, Blackjack, 26
Mungo, Van Lingle, 3
Murdoch, Rupert, 166, 173
Murphy, Bob, 31
Murphy, Dale, 58
Murray, Eddie, 58, 162, 163
Murray, Jim, 140, 148, 179
Musial, Stan, 337

Nagy, Charles, 145
Namath, Joe, 313
Nas (rapper), 328
National Labor Relations Board
    (NLRB), 130–31
Nattle, Butch, 17
Nattle, John John, 31
Nattle, Tony, 31, 37
Natural, The (movie), 17
Neagle, Denny, 152, 240
Nelms, Jim, 9
Nelson, Jeff, 237
Nelson, Lindsey, 31
Newhan, Ross, 109, 160, 162
News Corporation, 166, 182
Newson, Warren ("the Deacon"), 79
New York:
    as exhausting venue, 314, 322
    socializing in, 227–28
New York Giants (former), 233
New York Mets, 185–99, 200–216,
    241–48, 249–50, 255–71, 283,
    305–7, 309–14
    endgame with Piazza, 300–302,
        310–14, 344
    and fans, 202, 205, 210, 212–13,
        227, 246, 248, 297, 301, 312,
        314, 323–24, 336, 344
    final game at Shea (2008), 342–43
    and Hall of Fame, 343
    and media, 201–3, 204, 209, 211,
        229, 230, 237, 239, 250, 259,
        260–64, 268–70, 271, 281,
        286–87, 296, 300–301, 302, 305,
        306, 307, 313, 345
    QuesTec system, 281
    sale of, 264, 265, 268, 302
    and September 11 attacks, 244–48,
        249, 254, 255, 342, 344
    and Subway Series, 207–8, 209, 224,
        300
    team chemistry, 217–18, 269, 271,
        307–8

as Team Tabloid, 255–57, 265
and Triple Crown, 295
and World Series, 232, 233–40, 297,
   342, 343
New York Yankees, 206–7, 259
Subway World Series (former), 233
and World Series, 232, 233–40, 250
Ng, Kim, 334
Nicklaus, Jack, 133
Niemann, Randy, 205
Nightengale, Bob, 133, 145, 156–57,
   159
Nixon, Otis, 162, 216, 252
Nixon, Trot, 300
Nokes, Matt, 120
Nomo, Hideo "the Tornado," 177, 218
and Dodgers, 133–34, 140, 153
and friendship, 133, 143
as pitcher, 135–36, 142, 148, 150,
   151, 153, 160, 165, 291
as Rookie of the Year, 133, 142
Nomura, Don, 136

Oakland, media in, 331–32
Oakland A's, 325, 326–30, 332–33
Offerman, Jose, 135
Oh, Sadaharu, 73
Oingo Boingo, 76
Ojeda, Bob, 91, 94
Olerud, John, 188, 208, 218
and friendship, 213–14, 216
as hitter, 202, 206, 211, 215
and Mets, 205, 212, 213–14, 215,
   295
Oliver, Darren, 194
O'Malley, Peter, 68, 83
and Dodgers, 63, 133, 143, 147,
   161, 166–68
and Dodgers sale, 153–54, 166–68,
   182
and Giants sale, 92
and Mike's contract, 167, 170, 171
O'Malley, Walter, 143

O'Neill, Paul, 240
Ordonez, Rey, 220, 256
Ortiz, Hector, 63
Orza, Gene, 286
Osteen, Claude, 59
Osuna, Antonio, 163, 256
O'Toole, Teri, 134, 176, 191
Ott, Mel, 337

Padilla, Vicente, 309
Palmer, Jim, 136
Panerati, Luca, 339
Park, Chan Ho, 148
and Dodgers, 125, 133, 136, 160–61
as hitter, 143
as pitcher, 143, 151, 160, 163, 165,
   175, 243
Parker, Dave, 12
Parks, Derek, 96
Parrish, Lance, 101, 294
Patterson, Corey, 258
Payton, Jay, 227, 230, 232, 237, 240,
   244
Peavy, Jake, 318, 322, 324
Pena, Alejandro, 20
Pena, Tony, 280
Pendleton, Terry, 152
Pentagon, September 11 attack on,
   244
Penthouse, 195–96
Perez, Carlos, 181, 194
Perez, Eddie, 212, 215, 216
Perez, Timo, 231, 234, 240
Perez, Tony, 295
Perry, Joe, 290
Peters, Rex, 77
Pettitte, Andy, 233, 240
Pfeiffer, Michelle, 105
Phillips, Jason, 281, 293, 301, 306
Phillips, Steve:
and Clemens, 239
and contracts, 197
and Dodgers, 209

Phillips, Steve (*continued*)
    and Mets, 185, 187, 188, 189, 197,
        205, 255, 256, 260, 265, 283, 302
    and Mike at first base, 281
    and Valentine, 269, 270
Philo, Alan, 28
Phoenixville, Pennsylvania, 23–24, 25,
    316, 345
Phoenixville High School, 33–39, 124
Piazza, Alicia (Mike's wife), *see* Rickter,
    Alicia
Piazza, Danny (brother), 5, 6, 18, 23,
    25, 41
Piazza, Mike:
    and age, 241, 264, 273, 278–79,
        283, 284, 288, 293, 298–99, 305,
        309, 310–11, 314, 318, 319, 325,
        332
    and agents, 77, 97–98; *see also*
        Lozano, Dan
    agility and speed drills, 288
    attitude of, 42, 51, 65–67, 69, 71,
        73, 87, 102, 109–10, 112–14,
        120, 127, 141, 147–48, 151–52,
        165–66, 169–70, 174, 179, 184,
        190–91, 193, 224, 228–29, 248,
        269–70, 275–78, 281, 292, 304,
        306, 307–9, 311–13, 314, 318,
        330, 332, 334, 339, 346, 347
    and auto dealership, 273, 335, 342
    awards and honors to, 123, 127,
        145, 152, 255, 269, 345–46
    and baseball draft, 35–39, 48–50,
        51, 53, 72, 174
    and baserunning, 129
    batting statistics of, 349
    birth of, 6, 9
    as catcher, 47, 48–49, 53, 55, 59–60,
        61, 63, 78, 278–81, 291, 293,
        294–96, 306, 328
    catcher's ERA of, 267, 279, 280,
        294–95
    childhood of, 3–4, 6, 18, 23–24, 25

and the Church, 67, 116, 195–96,
    261, 273–74, 303, 335, 340–41
and clubhouse leadership, 159–61,
    162, 165, 169, 211, 237, 295,
    305, 312
in commercials, 6, 11, 120, 136, 202
conspiracies against, 307–8, 311
and contracts, 54, 124–27, 143,
    146–47, 154–55, 166–72,
    173–75, 180, 189, 191, 194, 195,
    197–99, 208, 300, 301, 305, 343,
    346–47
diet of, 157
and distractions, 138, 172, 190, 228,
    246, 249–50, 264, 265, 268, 291,
    304, 334
as Dodgers batboy, 19–20, 41, 59,
    136, 316
drafted by Dodgers, 49–50, 51–53, 72
endgame with the Mets, 300–302,
    310–14, 344
eyesight of, 319–20
facial hair of, 120, 229–30
and fame, 75, 115, 270, 313
family background of, 5–6, 24–25
and fans, 104, 109, 110, 115–17,
    121–22, 145, 170, 173, 175, 178,
    179, 186, 188, 189–90, 193, 194,
    202, 205, 208, 209, 297, 301,
    312, 314, 322, 323–24, 329–31,
    344
and fear, 298–99, 323
at first base, 64, 75, 77, 220–21,
    241–42, 281, 285, 289–90, 291,
    293, 296, 298–99, 300, 301–2,
    323
and free agency, 155, 166–67, 170,
    175, 180–81, 185, 189, 191, 193,
    315
and gay rumors in media, 260–64
and golf, 27–28, 132–33, 334, 342
and Hall of Fame, 316, 337, 339,
    343–44

and hand grippers, 14–15, 76–77, 326

in *Hardball Times*, 84–85, 88–89, 279–80, 295–96

and his parents, *see* Piazza, Veronica; Piazza, Vince

income of, 99, 285, 300, 309, 329

injuries to, 102–3, 134–35, 138, 140, 142, 146–47, 150, 192–93, 204–5, 209, 210–12, 214, 215, 219–20, 221, 224–26, 227, 238, 256, 258, 259, 267, 278–79, 282–83, 284, 289, 291, 296, 297–98, 299, 305, 307, 310, 319, 328–30, 343

loss of virginity, 67–68

and music, 28–30, 76, 204, 211, 322–23, 327–28

and MVP, 135, 140–41, 145, 146, 150, 151–52, 162, 163, 165–66, 169, 174, 230, 237, 343

and pitchers, 111–12, 127–28, 147–50, 222–23, 256, 267, 270, 280, 282, 294

records set or tied by, 1, 2, 120, 121, 125, 165, 250, 267, 278, 279, 282, 284, 291–93, 294–96

reputation of, 101–2, 116, 279

and retirement, 314, 315–16, 318–19, 334–36, 343, 345–46

in right field, 80

Rookie of the Year, 123, 142, 343

as slugger, 19, 21, 33, 38, 41, 48, 52, 70, 77, 82, 90, 101, 103–4, 111, 120, 121, 140, 149–50, 152–53, 156, 164, 166, 170, 194–95, 208, 210, 216, 227, 231, 232, 247–48, 269, 270, 281–82, 290–91, 293, 294, 295–96, 312, 318, 319, 325, 327, 333, 337, 349

and social life, 30, 107–8, 114–19, 217, 227–28, 278

and steroids rumors, 156–59, 203–4, 251, 338

teen years of, 20–23, 25–28, 33–39, 41–48

and throwing, 148, 159, 219–20, 241, 264, 279–80, 294, 298, 320, 329

traded to Marlins, 175–82, 183–84, 208

traded to Mets, 186–88, 195

wedding of, 303–5

weight training, 44–45, 56, 73, 124, 131, 157, 288

in World Series, 232, 233–40, 297, 343

as wrestling fan, 25–26

Piazza, Nicoletta (Mike/Alicia's daughter), 326, 334

Piazza, Paulina (Mike/Alicia's daughter), 341

Piazza, Rosario "Russell" (grandfather), 4–5, 6, 317

Piazza, Tommy (brother), 40, 298, 345

Piazza, Tony (brother), 124, 303, 345

Piazza, Veronica "Roni" Horenci (mother), 9, 25, 27, 30, 37

influence of, 61, 67, 116, 196

and Mike's career, 145

and Mike's social life, 118, 228

scrapbooks of, 18

Piazza, Vince (brother), 41, 262, 333, 345

birth of, 9

childhood of, 3, 4, 12, 18, 26

Piazza, Vince (father):

and agents, 98

and auto dealerships, 8–10, 273

and baseball, 12, 255, 306

bid to buy the Giants, 88, 91–94, 161

connections of, 21–22, 46–48, 345

discipline from, 25–26

early years of, 6–10, 159

family background of, 5–6

and final game at Shea, 342–43

Piazza, Vince (father) (*continued*)
  and his father, 5, 6, 7
  and injuries, 283
  and Lasorda, 8–9, 10, 40, 44, 50,
    68, 146
  and Marlins, 184–85
  marriage of, 9
  and media, 316
  and Mike's career, 40, 46–48, 51,
    55, 63–65, 77–78, 81, 86, 90,
    117, 145, 168, 196–97, 199, 261,
    296, 308, 315, 316, 335, 337,
    338, 343
  and Mike's childhood, 3, 23–24, 25
  and Mike's social life, 30, 117, 118,
    228, 278
  and Mike's teen years, 28, 33, 37,
    38, 39, 41
  and Mike's training, 7, 11–12, 14,
    15, 17–18, 28, 31, 41, 42, 44, 76,
    157, 174, 220, 309, 316
  work of, 4
Piazza Auto Group, 273, 342
Piazza Management, 10
Pierre, Juan, 298
Piniella, Lou, 205, 234
Pizzica, Joe, 20, 31–32, 35, 37, 123, 345
Plant, Robert, 282
Plaschke, Bill, 169, 182, 208
Podres, Johnny, 59
Podsednik, Scott, 303
Poffo, Randy, 41
Polanco, Placido, 231
Polignano, Marc, 124
Polonia, Luis, 152
Poole, Jim, 55
Portugal, Mark, 175
Posada, Jorge, 185, 207, 234, 239, 240
Posada, Leo, 57, 68
Posey, Buster, 219, 220
Pratt, Todd, 204, 212, 214, 216, 237
Prince, Tom, 160
Puhl, Terry, 94

Pujols, Albert, 253, 256, 310–11, 324,
    326, 337
Putski, Ivan, 26

Radinsky, Scott, 163
Radomski, Kirk, 286
Rakoczy, Gregg, 43
Ramirez, Manny, 297
Randa, Joe, 307
Randolph, Willie, 302, 306, 309, 310,
    313–14, 324
Ratt (band), 30
Reames, Britt, 232
Reece, Gabrielle, 131
Reed, Jeff, 257
Reed, Jody, 111, 126, 220
Reed, Rick, 137, 210, 213, 240
Reed, Steve, 94
Reid, Jason, 172, 174, 209
Reinsdorf, Jerry, 93
Reliford, Charlie, 235, 236, 237, 238
Remlinger, Mike, 212, 214, 229
Retton, Mary Lou, 32
Reyes, Jose, 284, 290, 301, 314
Reynolds, Shane, 284
Rhoden, Rick, 205
Rickey, Branch, 59, 179
Rickter, Alicia, 271, 272, 273, 278,
    288–89, 313, 334
  and comfort, 305
  and Mike's career, 318–20, 335, 346
  Mike's proposal to, 299
  wedding of Mike and, 303–5
Ridinger, J. R. and Loren, 304
Righetti, Dave, 121, 306
Rios, Armando, 230
Ripken, Cal Jr., 130, 153, 243, 253
Rivera, Carlos, 285
Rivera, Mariano, 207, 234, 237, 240,
    290, 322
Rizzuto, Phil, 31, 317
Roberts, Grant, 268, 269
Roberts, Kari, 29

Roberts, Selena, 298
Roberts, Tony, 29
Robinson, Brooks, 136
Robinson, Frank, 54
Robinson, Jackie, 101, 337
Robson, Tom, 205, 319
Rocker, John, 210, 212, 213, 214, 216, 221–22
Roderick, Brande, 303
Rodriguez, Alex "A-Rod," 153, 234, 253
Rodriguez, Frankie "K-Rod," 327, 330
Rodriguez, Ivan "Pudge," 1, 153, 155, 167, 279, 294, 297, 304, 334
Roenicke, Ron, 181
Rogers, Kenny, 212, 214, 216
Rolen, Scott, 136, 229
Rome, Jim, 174, 176
Rookie of the Year, 123, 142, 343
Rose, Axl, 275
Rose, Pete, 267, 295, 316
Roseboro, Johnny, 54, 57, 61, 72, 78, 100, 108, 109
Ross, David, 276, 277
Ross, Diana, 246, 247
Royster, Jerry, 87
Runge, Paul, 112
Rusch, Glendon, 255
Russell, Bill, 200
    and Albuquerque, 87, 146
    and Dodgers, 20, 145–47, 151, 160, 181
    and Lasorda, 144, 146
    and Mike's trade to Marlins, 175, 177
    and MVP, 162, 169
Russo, Christopher "Mad Dog," 185, 259
Ruth, Babe, 140, 250, 291, 292, 337
Ryan, Mike, 168
Ryan, Nolan, 235

Samuel, Juan, 42
Samuels, Charlie, 258, 314

Sanchez, Freddy, 310
Sandberg, Ryne, 90
San Diego Padres, 316, 318–25
San Francisco Giants, Vince's bid to buy, 88, 91–94, 161
Santo, Ron, 317
Savage, Randy "Macho Man" (Poffo), 41
Sax, Steve, 20, 298
Schell, Michael J., 295
Schilling, Curt, 343
Schmidt, Jason, 223, 282, 318
Schmidt, Mike, 3, 12–14, 16, 18, 21, 66, 136, 145, 337, 346
Schourek, Pete, 139–40, 227
Scioscia, Mike, 58, 99, 162
    and Campanella, 100, 109
    as catcher, 94–95, 101, 220, 280
    and Dodgers, 86, 89, 95, 102, 181
    training and rehab with, 134, 148, 159
Scott, Byron, 98
Scott, Dave, 42
Scott, Mike, 94
Screnar, Pat, 134–35
Scully, Vin, 102, 151, 169, 170, 173
Seaver, Tom, 323, 337, 342–43, 344
Selig, Bud, 266–67
September 11 attacks, 243–48, 249, 254, 255, 312, 342, 344
Serby, Steve, 300–301
Shaw, Jeff, 181
Sheary, Kevin, 43
Sheets, Ben, 267
Sheffield, Gary, 153, 176, 177, 181, 182, 221, 256
Shepherd, Keith, 111
Sherman, Joel, 202, 266
Shinjo, Tsuyoshi, 247
Showalter, Buck, 211
Skid Row (band), 322
Skippack Skippers, 40–41, 45, 48, 50
Slayer (band), 29, 30

Slusser, Susan, 331
Smiley, Brett, 37
Smiley, Don, 185
Smiley, John, 38
Smith, Dwight, 90
Smith, Emmitt, 127, 202
Smith, Ozzie, 108
Smith, Pete, 103
Smith, Randy, 156
Smith, Reggie, 60, 67, 72, 73–74, 134, 181
Smiths (band), 76
Smoltz, John, 152, 153, 209, 212, 215
Snider, Duke, 121, 240
Snow, J. T., 230
Snuka, Jimmy "Superfly," 26
Snyder, Cory, 110, 111
Sojo, Luis, 240
Soriano, Alfonso, 297
Sosa, Sammy, 153, 211, 250, 251, 343
Sotomayor, Sonia, 130–31
Souray, Sheldon, 272, 303, 313
SportsChannel Florida, 178
Sports Illustrated, 179, 264
Springer, Russ, 214
Stanton, Mike, 234, 243, 293
Stapp, Scott, 313
Stearns, John, 13, 225, 231
Steinbrenner, George, 130, 239
Stephenson, Jerry, 254
Stern, Howard, 195, 196
Steve Miller Band, 29
Stewart, Jon, 302
Stewart, Shannon, 206, 333
Stottlemyre, Todd, 184
Strasser, Charlie, 157–58, 175
Strawberry, Darryl, 20, 102, 104, 136
Street, Huston, 327, 328, 332
Strom, Brent, 59
Suppan, Jeff, 175, 310
Sutherland, Gary, 181

Suzuki, Ichiro, 297
Suzuki, Kurt, 329, 332, 333
Swift, Billy, 121

Tango, Tom, 280
Tarasco, Tony, 327
Tatum, Jim, 79
Taubensee, Eddie, 96
Tavarez, Julian, 256, 307, 310–12
Teed, Dick, 53
Telemaco, Amaury, 184
Ten Commandments, 341
Testaverde, Vinny, 43
Texas League, 86–87
Texas Rangers, 47, 200
Thomas, Frank, 125, 325
Thompson, Rob, 34
Thompson, Tim, 35, 84
Thornton, Andre, 37, 345
Timlin, Mike, 232
Tipton, Gordon, 78
Tirendi, Vince, 92
Titanic (movie), 182
Tomlin, Randy, 90
Topps, 6
Torrealba, Yorvit, 320
Torre, Joe, 31, 226, 234, 237, 242, 255, 295, 317
Torres, Salomon, 121
Torres, Tico, 334
Towers, Kevin, 316, 325
Trachsel, Steve, 256, 305
Tracy, Jim, 277
Trammell, Bubba, 240
Travis, Neal, 260–63
Traxler, Brian, 55, 102
Treadwell, Jody, 78
Triple-A ball, 87–89
Trump, Donald, 303
Trunk, Eddie, 275
Tucker, Michael, 192–93, 220
Tuesday's Children, 344
Tulowitzki, Troy, 320

Twisted Sister, 29, 30, 211
Tyson, Mike, 31, 199, 237

United Airlines Flight 93, 244
University of Southern California,
    98–99
Usher (singer), 201

Valdez, Ismael, 136, 145, 147, 150, 151,
    153, 307
Valent, Eric, 293
Valentine, Bobby, 217, 233, 278
    and All-Star Game, 242
    on batters hit by pitchers, 225, 238,
        256, 257, 265
    and Lasorda, 47, 187, 194, 242
    and media, 188, 193, 200–201, 229,
        260, 262, 266, 268–69, 271
    and Mets, 187, 205–6, 228–29, 230,
        258–59, 269–71
    and Mike's injuries, 214, 225, 238,
        258
    and Mike's playing, 216, 221,
        223–24, 267, 284
    and September 11 attacks, 245, 254,
        255
    and Texas Rangers, 47, 200
    and umpires' calls, 193, 206
Valverde, Jose, 318
Van Halen (band), 204
Van Halen, Eddie, 132
Vaughn, Greg, 210
Vaughn, Mo, 256, 264, 266, 269, 281,
    283
Velazquez, Guillermo "Memo," 79–80
Ventura, Jesse "the Body," 26
Ventura, Robin, 115, 235
    and free agency, 255–56
    as hitter, 208, 210, 214, 215, 231,
        232, 240, 247, 295
    in Japan, 218–19
    and Mets, 199, 205, 218, 241, 295
    and World Series, 233, 240

Veras, Dario, 151
Verducci, Tom, 158, 163, 168, 226,
    264
Vermeil, Dick, 345
Vero Beach, Dodgertown in, 58–62,
    64–67, 70, 72, 78–79, 112, 127,
    174
Vioxx, 157, 158, 203
Vizcaino, Jose, 234
Voltaren, 158, 203

Wade, Ben, 50, 51, 52–53
Wagner, Billy, 194–95, 316
Wahlberg, Mark, 168
Wakamatsu, Don, 101
Waldstein, Dave, 261
Walker, Larry, 162, 163, 165, 166, 169
Wallace, Dave, 59, 60, 65, 150, 160,
    228
Wallach, Tim, 111, 139, 153
Washington, George, 41
Weathers, David, 266, 284, 293
Weber, Joe, 18, 37
Weider, Joe, 45, 157
Weiss, Walt, 192, 215
Welch, Bob, 20
Wells, David, 140, 201
Wendell, Turk, 214, 215, 234
Wengert, Bill, 59
Wengert, Don, 222
Werndl, Bill, 316
West, Joe, 91
Wheeler, Chris, 200
White, Bill, 31
White, Devon, 175, 184
Wigginton, Ty, 276, 285, 297
Wildwood, New Jersey, 30–32
Williams, Bernie, 206, 221, 240
Williams, Gerald, 192, 214, 216
Williams, Jerome, 284, 292
Williams, Jimy, 293
Williams, Matt, 121
Williams, Mike, 149

Williams, Ted:
  and Hall of Fame, 337
  as hitter, 85, 104, 138, 140
  honored at Fenway, 207
  influence of, 11–12, 14, 33, 63, 73,
    320, 346
  Museum & Hitters Hall of Fame,
    152, 195
  The Science of Hitting, 21, 22
  visit to Mike's house, 21–22, 48
Wilpon, Fred:
  and media, 185, 187, 260, 271,
    345
  and Mets, 185, 187, 197, 264
  and Mets sale, 264, 265, 302
  Mike signed by Mets, 185, 187,
    197–98
  and September 11 attacks, 245
  and Valentine, 269, 270, 271
Wilpon, Jeff, 2, 259, 270, 299, 302,
  314, 345
Wilson, Preston, 186, 221
Wilson, Vance, 262, 278, 285, 293,
  301
Wise, Dewayne, 291
Wismer, Mike, 66
Wladika, Vince, 169
Wolff, Lew, 329
World Baseball Classic, 317, 339
World Series:
  historic moments in, 248
  home-field advantage in, 267
  Mets in, 232, 233–40, 297, 342, 343

World Trade Center, September 11
    attacks on, 243–46
Worrell, Todd, 144
Worthy, James, 98
Wright, Craig, 84–85, 88–89, 279–80,
  295
Wright, David, 295, 298, 301, 310,
  312, 314
Wrigley Field, 90
Wylde, Zakk, 210

Yankee Stadium, 205
Yarnall, Ed, 186
Yeager, Steve, 4, 101, 109, 173, 309
Yelding, Eric, 257
Yesterday and Today (band), 204
Yoshii, Masato, 211, 214
Young, Chris, 324
Young, Eric, 70, 83, 90, 145, 162, 163,
  169

Zambrano, Victor, 305, 313
Zaun, Gregg, 192
Zebra (band), 204
Zeile, Todd, 2, 163, 169, 184
  and free agency, 162, 293
  as hitter, 162, 175, 231, 234, 240,
    295
  and Mets, 218, 241, 255, 293
  on pitchers and batters, 222–23, 251
  trade to Marlins, 175, 176, 177, 179
  and Yankees, 279
Zimmer, Don, 226